Lecture Notes in Computer Science 10506

Commenced Publication in 1973
Founding and Former Series Editors:
Gerhard Goos, Juris Hartmanis, and Jan van Leeuwen

Editorial Board

More information about this series at http://www.springer.com/series/7407

Matthew Hague · Igor Potapov (Eds.)

Reachability Problems

11th International Workshop, RP 2017
London, UK, September 7–9, 2017
Proceedings

 Springer

Editors
Matthew Hague
Royal Holloway University of London
London
UK

Igor Potapov
University of Liverpool
Liverpool
UK

ISSN 0302-9743   ISSN 1611-3349 (electronic)
Lecture Notes in Computer Science
ISBN 978-3-319-67088-1   ISBN 978-3-319-67089-8 (eBook)
DOI 10.1007/978-3-319-67089-8

Library of Congress Control Number: 2017951439

LNCS Sublibrary: SL1 – Theoretical Computer Science and General Issues

Printed on acid-free paper

This Springer imprint is published by Springer Nature
The registered company is Springer International Publishing AG
The registered company address is: Gewerbestrasse 11, 6330 Cham, Switzerland

Preface

This volume contains the papers presented at the 11th International Workshop on Reachability Problems (RP), held on September 7–9, 2017, at Royal Holloway, University of London, UK. Previous workshops in the series were located at: Aalborg University (2016), the University of Warsaw (2015), the University of Oxford (2014), Uppsala University (2013), the University of Bordeaux (2012), the University of Genoa (2011), Masaryk University Brno (2010), École Polytechnique (2009), the University of Liverpool (2008), and Turku University (2007).

The aim of the conference is to bring together scholars from diverse fields with a shared interest in reachability problems, and to promote the exploration of new approaches for the modelling and analysis of computational processes by combining mathematical, algorithmic, and computational techniques. Topics of interest include (but are not limited to): reachability for infinite state systems; rewriting systems; reachability analysis in counter/timed/cellular/communicating automata; Petri nets; computational aspects of semigroups, groups, and rings; reachability in dynamical and hybrid systems; frontiers between decidable and undecidable reachability problems; complexity and decidability aspects; predictability in iterative maps, and new computational paradigms.

The invited speakers at the 2017 workshop were:

- Hana Chockler, King's College London
- Laurent Doyen, LSV-ENS Cachan
- Raphaël Jungers, Université catholique de Louvain
- Andreas Podelski, University of Freiburg

The workshop received 17 submissions. Each submission was reviewed by three Program Committee (PC) members. The members of the PC and the list of external reviewers can be found on the next two pages. The PC is grateful for the high quality work produced by these external reviewers. Based on these reviews, the PC decided to accept 12 papers, in addition to the four invited talks. Overall this volume contains 12 contributed papers and one paper by an invited speaker. The workshop also provided the opportunity to researchers to give informal presentations, prepared shortly before the event, informing the participants about current research and work in progress.

It is a pleasure to thank the team behind the EasyChair system and the Lecture Notes in Computer Science team at Springer, who together made the production of this volume possible in time for the workshop. Finally, we thank all the authors for their high-quality contributions, and the participants for making RP 2017 a success.

September 2017

Igor Potapov
Matthew Hague

Organization

Program Committee

C. Aiswarya	Chennai Mathematical Institute, India
Paul Bell	Liverpool John Moores University, UK
Patricia Bouyer-Decitre	LSV, CNRS & ENS Cachan, Université Paris Saclay, France
Laura Bozzelli	Technical University of Madrid (UPM), Spain
Giorgio Delzanno	DIBRIS, Università di Genova, Italy
Matthew Hague	Royal Holloway, University of London, UK
Piotrek Hofman	University of Warsaw, Poland
Salvatore La Torre	Università degli studi di Salerno, Italy
Peter Lammich	TU Munich, Germany
Martin Lange	University of Kassel, Germany
Ranko Lazic	University of Warwick, UK
Ondrej Lengal	Brno University of Technology, Czech Republic
Jerome Leroux	CNRS, France
Rupak Majumdar	MPI-SWS, Germany
Igor Potapov	The University of Liverpool, UK
Ahmed Rezine	Linköping University, Sweden
Tachio Terauchi	Japan Advanced Institute of Science and Technology, Japan
Hsu-Chun Yen	National Taiwan University, Taiwan

Additional Reviewers

Haddad, Serge
Kreiker, Joerg
Prianychnykova, Olena
Sorrentino, Loredana

Abstracts of Invited Talks

Trace Abstraction

Andreas Podelski

University of Freiburg, Germany

Abstract. Trace abstraction refers to a new approach to program verification algorithms. Instead of trying to construct a proof for the input program directly, we first construct auxiliary programs from proofs. We construct each auxiliary program (which can be of general form) from the proof for a program in a specific form, namely a program in the form of a trace (i.e., a sequence of statements). A trace is a program (where the statements have a semantics). At the same time, a trace is a word over a finite alphabet (where the semantics of statements is ignored). As a word, a sequence of statements can be read by an automaton. Just as we ask whether there exists an accepting run of a given automaton on a sequence of letters, we can ask whether there exists a correctness proof for a sequence of statements, a correctness proof that can be assembled from a given finite set of Hoare triples. We iteratively construct auxiliary programs from proofs for traces. The iteration stops when the constructed programs together cover all possible behaviors of the input program. A crucial step here is the covering check. This step is based on algorithms for automata (inclusion test, minimization, ...). The approach applies to a range of verification problems, for sequential programs with (possibly recursive) procedures and concurrent programs with possibly unboundedly many threads, and even to real-time programs.

How Do We Know That Our System Is Correct?

Hana Chockler

King's College London, UK

Abstract. A negative answer from the model-checking procedure is accompanied by a counterexample – a trace demonstrating what went wrong. On the other hand, when the answer from the model-checker is positive, usually no further information is given. The issue of "suspecting the positive answer" first arose in industry, where positive answers from model-checkers often concealed serious bugs in hardware designs. In this talk, I discuss some reasons why the positive answer from the model-checker may require further investigation and briefly and in broad terms describe algorithms for such investigations, called *sanity checks*.

The talk also (briefly) introduces the theory of causality and counterfactual reasoning and its applications to model-checking, mostly in the context of the subject of this talk, including some recent complexity results and applications of structure-based causality.

The talk then attempts to define the main goal of the sanity checks, explanations, and related algorithms, or at least provide some food for thought regarding the question of the mail goal.

I conclude the talk with outlining some promising future directions.

The talk is based on many papers written by many people, and is not limited to my own research. It is reasonably self-contained.

Path-Complete Lyapunov Techniques: Stability, Safety, and Beyond

Raphaël M. Jungers

ICTEAM Institute, Université catholique de Louvain
raphael.jungers@uclouvain.be

Path-complete Lyapunov Techniques[1] are a family of methods that combine Automata-Theoretic tools with algebraic formulas in order to derive ad hoc criteria for the control of complex systems. These criteria are typically solved with Convex Optimization solvers. They initially appeared in the framework of switched systems, which are dynamical systems for which the state dynamics varies between different operating modes. They take the form

$$x(t+1) = f_{\sigma(t)}(x(t)) \tag{1}$$

where the state $x(t)$ evolves in $\mathbb{R}^n$. The *mode* $\sigma(t)$ of the system at time t takes its value in a set $\{1, \ldots, M\}$ for some integer M, and each mode of the system is described by a continuous map $f_i(x) : \mathbb{R}^n \to \mathbb{R}^n$.

When the functions f_i are linear functions, we say that the system is a *linear switched system*. The *stability problem* is reputedly very hard, even in the restricted case of linear functions (see e.g. [14, Sect. 2.2]). In this case, one can easily obtain a sufficient condition for stability, through the existence of a *common quadratic* Lyapunov function (see e.g. [18, Sect. II-A]). However, such a Lyapunov function may not exist, even when the system is asymptotically stable (see e.g. [17, 18]). Less conservative parameterizations of candidate Lyapunov functions have been proposed, at the cost of greater computational effort (e.g. for linear switching systems, [19] uses sum-of-squares polynomials, [12] uses max-of-quadratics Lyapunov functions, and [4] uses polytopic Lyapunov functions). *Multiple Lyapunov functions* (see [7, 13, 21]) arise as an alternative to common Lyapunov functions. In the case of linear systems, the multiple *quadratic* Lyapunov functions such as those introduced in [6, 8, 9, 16] hold special interest as checking for their existence boils down to solving a set of LMIs. The general framework of *Path-Complete* Lyapunov functions was recently introduced in [1, 15] in this context, for analyzing and unifying these approaches.

In this talk, we first present these criteria guaranteeing that the system (1) is stable under *arbitrary switching*, i.e. where the function $\sigma(\cdot)$ is not constrained, and one is

R.J. is supported by the Communauté française de Belgique - Actions de Recherche Concertées, and by the Belgian Programme on Interuniversity Attraction Poles initiated by the Belgian Federal Science Policy Office. He is a Fulbright Fellow and a FNRS Fellow, currently visiting the Dept. of Electrical Engineering at UCLA.

[1] Path-complete techniques are implemented in the JSR toolbox [22].

interested in the worst-case stability. We then show how this very natural idea can be leveraged for much more general purposes: we present recent works were the same idea has been applied to more general systems than the ones described above [20], or for proving different properties than stability [10].

These techniques give rise to many natural questions: First, they essentially provide algebraic criteria, that is, equations and inequations, that can be solved numerically in order to (hopefully) conclude stability, if a solution is found. But what do they mean in terms of control systems? Do they have a geometric interpretation in the state space? Second, among the different criteria in this framework, which one should an engineer pick in practice? Do these criteria compare with each other (in terms of conservativeness)? How to algorithmically choose the good criterion, when one is given a particular problem? While recent progress has been done to provide a geometric interpretation of these criteria [3], several problems remain open, like the one of comparing two given path-complete criteria [2].

Finally, we draw connections with other recent works in Control and Computer Science, which bear similarities with path-complete techniques, in safety analysis of computer programs [5], or in connection with tropical Kraus maps [11].

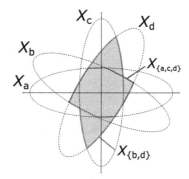

Fig. 1. Graphical illustration of the level set of a path-complete Lyapunov function. We will show in the talk that these level sets can always be expressed as unions of intersections of Ellipsoids.

References

1. Ahmadi, A.A., Jungers, R.M., Parrilo, P.A., Roozbehani, M.: Joint spectral radius and path-complete graph lyapunov functions. SIAM J. Control Optim. **52**(1), 687–717 (2014)
2. Angeli, D., Athanasopoulos, N., Jungers, R.M., Philippe, M.: A linear program to compare path-complete lyapunov functions (2017, submitted)
3. Angeli, D., Athanasopoulos, N., Jungers, R.M., Philippe, M.: Path-complete graphs and common lyapunov functions. In: Proceedings of the 20th International Conference on Hybrid Systems: Computation and Control, pp. 81–90. ACM (2017)
4. Athanasopoulos, N., Lazar, M.: Alternative stability conditions for switched discrete time linear systems. In: IFAC World Congress, pp. 6007–6012 (2014)
5. Balakrishnan, G., Sankaranarayanan, S., Ivančić, F., Gupta, A.: Refining the control structure of loops using static analysis. In: Proceedings of the Seventh ACM International Conference on Embedded Software, pp. 49–58. ACM (2009)

6. Bliman, P.-A., Ferrari-Trecate, G.: Stability analysis of discrete-time switched systems through lyapunov functions with nonminimal state. In: Proceedings of IFAC Conference on the Analysis and Design of Hybrid Systems, pp. 325–330 (2003)
7. Branicky, M.S.: Multiple lyapunov functions and other analysis tools for switched and hybrid systems. IEEE Trans. Autom. Control **43**(4), 475–482 (1998)
8. Daafouz, J., Riedinger, P., Iung, C.: Stability analysis and control synthesis for switched systems: a switched lyapunov function approach. IEEE Trans. Autom. Control **47**(11), 1883–1887 (2002)
9. Essick, R., Lee, J.-W., Dullerud, G.E.: Control of linear switched systems with receding horizon modal information. IEEE Trans. Autom. Control **59**(9), 2340–2352 (2014)
10. Forni, F., Jungers, R.M., Sepulchre, R.: Path-complete positivity of switching systems (2016). arXiv preprint, arXiv:1611.02603
11. Gaubert, S., Stott, N.: Tropical kraus maps for optimal control of switched systems (2017). arXiv preprint, arXiv:1706.04471
12. Goebel, R., Hu, T., Teel, A.R.: Dual matrix inequalities in stability and performance analysis of linear differential/difference inclusions. In: Current Trends in Nonlinear Systems and Control, pp. 103–122. Springer (2006)
13. Johansson, M., Rantzer, A., et al.: Computation of piecewise quadratic lyapunov functions for hybrid systems. IEEE Trans. Autom. Control **43**(4), 555–559 (1998)
14. Jungers, R.: The joint spectral radius. Lect. Notes Control Inf. Sci. **385** (2009)
15. Jungers, R.M., Ahmadi, A.A., Parrilo, P.A., Roozbehani, M.: A characterization of lyapunov inequalities for stability of switched systems. IEEE Trans. Autom. Control **62**(6), 3062–3067 (2017)
16. Lee, J.-W., Dullerud, G.E.: Uniform stabilization of discrete-time switched and markovian jump linear systems. Automatica **42**(2), 205–218 (2006)
17. Liberzon, D., Morse, A.S.: Basic problems in stability and design of switched systems. IEEE Control Syst. Mag. **19**(5), 59–70 (1999)
18. Lin, H., Antsaklis, P.J.: Stability and stabilizability of switched linear systems: a survey of recent results. IEEE Trans. Autom. Control **54**(2), 308–322 (2009)
19. Parrilo, P.A., Jadbabaie, A.: Approximation of the joint spectral radius using sum of squares. Linear Algebra Appl. **428**(10), 2385–2402 (2008)
20. Philippe, M., Essick, R., Dullerud, G.E., Jungers, R.M.: Stability of discrete-time switching systems with constrained switching sequences. Automatica **72**, 242–250 (2016)
21. Shorten, R., Wirth, F., Mason, O., Wulff, K., King, C.: Stability criteria for switched and hybrid systems. SIAM Rev. **49**(4), 545–592 (2007)
22. Vankeerberghen, G., Hendrickx, J., Jungers, R.M.: JSR: a toolbox to compute the joint spectral radius. In: Proceedings of the 17th International Conference on Hybrid Systems: Computation and Control, pp. 151–156. ACM (2014)

The Multiple Dimensions
of Mean-Payoff Games

Laurent Doyen

LSV, ENS Paris-Saclay & CNRS

Abstract. We consider quantitative game models for the design of reactive systems working in resource-constrained environment. The game is played on a finite weighted graph where some resource (e.g., battery) can be consumed or recharged along the edges of the graph.

In mean-payoff games, the resource usage is computed as the long-run average resource consumption. In energy games, the resource usage is the initial amount of resource necessary to maintain the resource level always positive.

We review fundamental results about mean-payoff games that show the existence of memoryless optimal strategies, and the equivalence of mean-payoff games with finite-duration reachability games, as well as with energy games (which can also be viewed as safety games). These results provide conceptually simple backward-induction algorithms for solving mean-payoff games, and for constructing memoryless optimal strategies. It follows that mean-payoff games can be solved in NP ∩ coNP.

Then we consider games with multiple mean-payoff conditions for systems using multiple resources. In multi-dimension mean-payoff games, memory is necessary for optimal strategies, and the previous equivalence results with reachability and energy (safety) games no longer hold. First, infinite memory is necessary in general for optimal strategies. With infinite memory, the limit of the long-run average resource consumption may not exist, and it is necessary to distinguish between the limsup and the liminf of the long-run average resource consumption. Second, the equivalence with a multi-dimensional version of energy games holds only if the players are restricted to use finite-memory strategies, and in that case the limsup- and the liminf-value coincide.

The complexity of solving multi-dimension mean-payoff games is as follows, depending on which class of strategies is given to the player: NP-complete for memoryless strategies, coNP-complete for finite-memory strategies, NP ∩ coNP for infinite-memory strategies and a conjunction of limsup objectives, and coNP-complete for infinite-memory strategies and a conjunction of liminf objectives.

Contents

The Multiple Dimensions of Mean-Payoff Games
(Extended Abstract)

Laurent Doyen[✉]

LSV, ENS Paris-Saclay and CNRS, Cachan, France
doyen@lsv.fr

Outline. We consider quantitative game models for the design of reactive systems working in resource-constrained environment. The game is played on a finite weighted graph where some resource (e.g., battery) can be consumed or recharged along the edges of the graph.

In mean-payoff games, the resource usage is computed as the long-run average resource consumption. In energy games, the resource usage is the initial amount of resource necessary to maintain the resource level always positive.

We review fundamental results about mean-payoff games that show the existence of memoryless optimal strategies, and the equivalence of mean-payoff games with finite-duration reachability games, as well as with energy games (which can also be viewed as safety games). These results provide conceptually simple backward-induction algorithms for solving mean-payoff games, and for constructing memoryless optimal strategies. It follows that mean-payoff games can be solved in NP ∩ coNP.

Then we consider games with multiple mean-payoff conditions for systems using multiple resources. In multi-dimension mean-payoff games, memory is necessary for optimal strategies, and the previous equivalence results with reachability and energy (safety) games no longer hold. First, infinite memory is necessary in general for optimal strategies. With infinite memory, the limit of the long-run average resource consumption may not exist, and it is necessary to distinguish between the limsup and the liminf of the long-run average resource consumption. Second, the equivalence with a multi-dimensional version of energy games holds only if the players are restricted to use finite-memory strategies, and in that case the limsup- and the liminf-value coincide.

The complexity of solving multi-dimension mean-payoff games is as follows, depending on which class of strategies is given to the player: NP-complete for memoryless strategies, coNP-complete for finite-memory strategies, NP ∩ coNP for infinite-memory strategies and a conjunction of limsup objectives, and coNP-complete for infinite-memory strategies and a conjunction of liminf objectives.

Games. We consider two-player games of infinite duration, as a model of non-terminating reactive systems with controllable and uncontrollable actions. Such models have applications in the verification and synthesis of reactive systems [3, 36,38], and fundamental connections with many areas of computer science, such as logic and automata [24,27,37].

© Springer International Publishing AG 2017
M. Hague and I. Potapov (Eds.): RP 2017, LNCS 10506, pp. 1–8, 2017.
DOI: 10.1007/978-3-319-67089-8_1

The game is played for infinitely many rounds, on a finite graphs $\langle V, E \rangle$ with vertices $V = V_1 \uplus V_2$ partitioned into player-1 and player-2 vertices. Initially a token is placed on a designated vertex $v_0 \in V$. In each round the player owning the vertex v_i where the token lies moves the token to a successor vertex v_{i+1} along an edge $(v_i, v_{i+1}) \in E$ of the graph. The outcome of the game is an infinite path $v_0, v_1, \ldots$ called a *play*. In the traditional qualitative analysis, plays are classified as either winning or losing (for player 1). An *objective* is a set $\Omega \subseteq V^\omega$ of winning plays. The goal of player 1 is to achieve a winning play: the central qualitative question is to decide if there exists a strategy for player 1 such that for all strategies of player 2 the outcome is a winning play in Ω. Sets of winning plays defined by ω-regular conditions are central in verification and synthesis of reactive systems [36,38] and have been extensively studied [10,18,26].

Mean-Payoff and Energy Games. For the design of reactive systems working in resource-constrained environment, we consider weighted graphs $\langle V, E, w \rangle$ where $w : E \to \mathbb{Z}$ is a weight function that assigns a resource consumption to each edge of the graph. The limit-average value (or mean-payoff value) of a play $\rho = v_0, v_1, \ldots$ is defined in two variants, the limsup-average

$$\overline{\mathsf{MP}}(\rho) = \limsup_{n \to \infty} \frac{1}{n} \cdot \sum_{i=0}^{n-1} w(v_i, v_{i+1}),$$

and the liminf-average

$$\underline{\mathsf{MP}}(\rho) = \liminf_{n \to \infty} \frac{1}{n} \cdot \sum_{i=0}^{n-1} w(v_i, v_{i+1}).$$

The goal of player 1 is to maximize the mean-payoff value, and the associated decision problem is to decide, given a threshold value $\nu \in \mathbb{Q}$, whether there exists a winning strategy for player 1 for the mean-payoff objective $\overline{\mathsf{MP}}^{\geq \nu} = \{\rho \mid \overline{\mathsf{MP}}(\rho) \geq \nu\}$ (or, $\underline{\mathsf{MP}}^{\geq \nu} = \{\rho \mid \underline{\mathsf{MP}}(\rho) \geq \nu\}$) with a mean-payoff value at least ν. In the sequel we only consider the case $\nu = 0$, which can be obtained by shifting all weights in the graph by the given value ν (and scaling them to get integers).

Memoryless strategies are sufficient to win mean-payoff games [23] and the associated decision problem lies in NP $\cap$ coNP [32,43]. The solution of mean-payoff games is more intuitive by considering the class of energy games [6,11] where the objective of player 1 is to maintain the accumulated resource level (i.e., the energy level) always nonnegative, given an initial credit value $c_0 \in \mathbb{N}$. The energy level of a finite path with initial credit c_0 is defined by

$$\mathsf{EL}_{c_0}(v_0, v_1, \ldots, v_n) = c_0 + \sum_{i=0}^{n-1} w(v_i, v_{i+1}),$$

and the energy objective is

$$\mathsf{EL}_{c_0}^{\geq 0} = \{v_0, v_1, \ldots \mid \forall n \in \mathbb{N} : \mathsf{EL}_{c_0}(v_0, v_1, \ldots, v_n) \geq 0\}.$$

The associated decision problem asks whether there exists c_0 such that player 1 has a winning strategy for the energy objective with initial credit c_0. It is important that the initial credit c_0 is not fixed to obtain the equivalence with mean-payoff games (see next paragraph). For fixed initial credit we get a variant of energy games (see Related Work). Note that the energy condition is a safety condition [1]: if a finite prefix of a play violates the energy condition, then every continuation violates the energy condition.

Memoryless Determinacy and Equivalence Results. Intuitively, player 1 wins the energy game if he can ensure that whenever a cycle is formed in the play, the cycle has nonnegative sum of weights. The converse is also true [6,39]. Consider a finite-duration game played analogously to the games we considered so far, but that stops whenever a cycle is formed, and declared won by player 1 if and only if the cycle is nonnegative. If player 1 wins the finite-duration game, then we can use his strategy to play the energy game and ensure that all cycles that are formed are nonnegative and therefore a finite initial credit c_0 is sufficient to survive along acyclic portions of the play (thus $c_0 \leq |V| \cdot W$ is sufficient, where W is the largest absolute weight in the graph). Conversely, if player 1 cannot avoid that a negative cycle is formed in the finite-duration game, then it is easy to show that player 2 can fix a strategy to ensure that only negative cycles are formed in the energy game, which would exhaust any arbitrary finite initial credit. Thus player 1 cannot win the energy game.

This argument reduces energy games to a reachability game in the finite tree obtained by unfolding the original graph and stopping a branch whenever a cycle is formed. Each leaf corresponds to the closing of a cycle, and the leaves associated with a positive cycle define the target nodes of a reachability objective for player 1. Using backward induction on the tree it is easy to establish that from all nodes where player 1 has a winning strategy for the reachability objective, finite initial credit is sufficient for the energy objective.

Finally, to establish the equivalence with mean-payoff games [6,23], it is easy to see that if player 1 can ensure that only nonnegative cycles are formed along a play, than the mean-payoff value is nonnegative (both for the limsup and the liminf variants), and otherwise player 2 can ensure that only negative cycles are formed, and the mean-payoff value is negative. It follows that mean-payoff games are determined (i.e., if player 1 does not have a winning strategy for $\overline{\mathsf{MP}}^{\geq 0}$, then player 2 has a winning strategy for the complement $V^\omega \setminus \overline{\mathsf{MP}}^{\geq 0}$). Moreover, viewing energy games as a safety game it is easy to show that memoryless strategies are sufficient to win energy games, and that the same strategy can be used for the mean-payoff objective, showing the memoryless determinacy of mean-payoff games.

We can solve mean-payoff games in NP by guessing a memoryless strategy for player 1 and checking that it induces only nonnegative reachable cycles in the graph game, which can be done in polynomial time using shortest-path algorithms. By memoryless determinacy, a coNP algorithm can guess a memoryless winning strategy for player 2. Hence mean-payoff games are in NP $\cap$ coNP [32,43], which can be improved to UP $\cap$ coUP [30]. Mean-payoff games can be solved in $O(|V| \cdot |E| \cdot W)$, thus in P for weights encoded in unary [9]. It is a long-standing open question to know whether mean-payoff games can be solved in polynomial time for weights encoded in binary.

Multi-Dimension Mean-Payoff Games. In multi-dimension mean-payoff games, the weight function $w : E \to \mathbb{Z}^k$ assigns a vector of resource consumption to each edge of the graph. The objective of player 1 is to ensure the mean-payoff objective in each dimension $1, \ldots, k$, thus a conjunction of k one-dimension mean-payoff objectives with threshold 0. Hence for player 2 the objective is a disjunction of mean-payoff objectives. Simple examples show that infinite memory may be necessary for player 1, for both the limsup and the liminf variants [42]. Moreover, the conjunction of mean-payoff objectives is not equivalent to a conjunction of energy conditions (which requires to maintain the accumulated resource level always nonnegative in every dimension, for some vector of finite initial credit).

Since infinite memory may be necessary for player 1, we consider the problem of deciding the existence of a winning strategy with the following memory restrictions: memoryless strategies, finite-memory strategies, and the general case of infinite-memory strategies [42]. With memoryless strategies, the decision problem is NP-complete. With finite-memory strategies, multi-dimension mean-payoff games are equivalent to energy games, in both the limsup and the liminf variants; memoryless strategies are sufficient for player 2 and the problem is coNP-complete. In the general case with infinite-memory strategies, the problem is in NP ∩ coNP for conjunctions of limsup-average, and coNP-complete for conjunctions of liminf-average. In both cases memoryless strategies are sufficient for player 2. Thus in all cases player 2 does not need memory, but the proofs of the memoryless results rely on different techniques (see next paragraph).

Memoryless Strategies in Mean-Payoff Games. In the results presented above, it is crucial to establish that memoryless strategies are sufficient for one player (and sometimes for both). We emphasize that different techniques can be used to prove those memorylessness results.

Edge induction and shuffling. A general technique is to use edge induction [25, 34]: to prove that a player is memoryless, consider for example a vertex v owned by that player with two outgoing edges, and consider the game G_1 obtained by removing the first outgoing edge, and the game G_2 obtained by removing the second outgoing edge. By induction we argue that memoryless strategies are sufficient for the player owning v in the games G_1 and G_2, and we need to show that no (arbitrary) strategy in the original game can achieve a better value than either the optimal (memoryless) strategy in G_1 or in G_2. Thus switching between the two outgoing transitions when visiting the vertex v does not give a better play (for the owner of v). Roughly, such a play can be decomposed into the appropriate shuffling of a play in G_1 and a play in G_2, and essentially it suffices to show (in case the owner of v is a minimizer, i.e., player 2) that the mean-payoff value of a shuffle of two plays is not smaller than the min of the values of the two plays, which holds for liminf-average (but not for limsup-average [33,42]). Dually, in case the owner of v is a maximizer, i.e., player 1, we need to show that the mean-payoff value of a shuffle of two plays is not greater than the max of the values of the two plays.

This technique can be used to show that player 2 is memoryless in multi-dimension energy games, and in the liminf-average variant of mean-payoff games.

Backward induction. To show memorylessness in one-dimension energy games, a simpler proof uses a monotonicity property that if an outgoing edge is a good choice from a vertex v when the current accumulated resource level is x, then the same outgoing edge is a good choice in v for all accumulated resource levels $x' > x$. Therefore in every vertex there exists a choice of outgoing edge that is independent of the current resource level and defines a memoryless winning strategy. This argument is similar to the proof that safety games admit memoryless winning strategies: to win a safety game it is sufficient to always choose a successor vertex that lies in the winning set.

Nested memoryless objectives. As the edge-induction technique does not work to show that player 2 is memoryless in limsup-average mean-payoff games, we use a specific result, based on nested (iterated) elimination of losing vertices: if from a given vertex v player 1 cannot win for one of the limsup-average mean-payoff objective, then v is a losing vertex for player 1 (and player 2 can use a memoryless strategy to win). Given a set $L \subseteq V$ of such losing vertices, all vertices from which player 2 can ensure to reach L are also losing for player 1. Note that player 2 can use a memoryless strategy to reach L. As long as such losing vertices (for player 1) exist, the above argument shows that player 2 has a memoryless strategy to win. The conclusion of the argument is to show that if no losing vertex remains (for any of the one-dimension objectives), then player 1 wins for the multi-dimension objective from every remaining vertex [42].

Related Work. We give pointers to the literature related to multiple mean-payoff conditions in graphs and games. Deriving a deterministic algorithm from the coNP result for multi-dimension mean-payoff games gives an algorithm that is exponential in the number of vertices. The hyperplane separation technique gives an algorithm that is polynomial for fixed dimension k and bounded weights [21]. The technique has been extended to obtain a pseudo-polynomial algorithm for solving multi-dimension energy games of fixed dimension with a fixed initial credit [31]. Strategy synthesis is studied in [20] showing that exponential memory is sufficient for winning strategies in multi-dimension energy games (and thus in multi-dimension mean-payoff games under finite-memory strategies). Finitary variants of mean-payoff objectives have been considered in [17].

The vector of Pareto-optimal thresholds for multi-dimension mean-payoff games is studied in [8], showing that deciding if there exists a vector of threshold in a given polyhedron that can be ensured by player 1 is complete for

NP^{NP}. Games with a Boolean combination of mean-payoff objectives are undecidable [41], and their restriction to finite-memory strategies is inter-reducible with Hilbert's tenth problem over the rationals [40]. Mean-payoff conditions have been used to define quantitative specification frameworks with appealing expressiveness and closure properties [2,15]. The special case of a Boolean combination of mean-payoff objectives defined by a one-dimension weight function gives rise to interval objectives, solvable in $NP \cap coNP$ [29].

We discuss three directions to extend the model of two-player mean-payoff games. First, the mean-payoff objective has been combined with Boolean objectives such as the parity condition, a canonical form to express ω-regular conditions, in one dimension [13,19] and in multiple dimensions [5,20]. Note that parity games can be reduced to (one-dimension) mean-payoff games [30], which can be reduced to discounted-sum games, themselves reducible to simple stochastic games [43]. Second, the mean-payoff objective has been considered in Markov decision processes [7,12] and stochastic games [4,14], in combination with parity condition [16] and under finite-memory strategies [14]. Third, mean-payoff and energy games (in single dimension) with partial observation have been shown undecidable [22,28]. Special assumptions on the structure of the game lead to decidable subclasses [28]. Partial-observation energy games with fixed initial credit are Ackermann-complete [35].

References

1. Alpern, B., Demers, A.J., Schneider, F.B.: Safety without stuttering. Inform. Process. Lett. **23**(4), 177–180 (1986)
2. Alur, R., Degorre, A., Maler, O., Weiss, G.: On omega-languages defined by mean-payoff conditions. In: Alfaro, L. (ed.) FoSSaCS 2009. LNCS, vol. 5504, pp. 333–347. Springer, Heidelberg (2009). doi:10.1007/978-3-642-00596-1_24
3. Alur, R., Henzinger, T.A., Kupferman, O.: Alternating-time temporal logic. J. ACM **49**, 672–713 (2002)
4. Basset, N., Kwiatkowska, M., Topcu, U., Wiltsche, C.: Strategy synthesis for stochastic games with multiple long-run objectives. In: Baier, C., Tinelli, C. (eds.) TACAS 2015. LNCS, vol. 9035, pp. 256–271. Springer, Heidelberg (2015). doi:10.1007/978-3-662-46681-0_22
5. Bohy, A., Bruyère, V., Filiot, E., Raskin, J.-F.: Synthesis from LTL specifications with mean-payoff objectives. In: Piterman, N., Smolka, S.A. (eds.) TACAS 2013. LNCS, vol. 7795, pp. 169–184. Springer, Heidelberg (2013). doi:10.1007/978-3-642-36742-7_12
6. Bouyer, P., Fahrenberg, U., Larsen, K.G., Markey, N., Srba, J.: Infinite runs in weighted timed automata with energy constraints. In: Cassez, F., Jard, C. (eds.) FORMATS 2008. LNCS, vol. 5215, pp. 33–47. Springer, Heidelberg (2008). doi:10.1007/978-3-540-85778-5_4
7. Brázdil, T., Brožek, V., Chatterjee, K., Forejt, V., Kučera, A.: Markov decision processes with multiple long-run average objectives. Logical Meth. Comput. Sci.**10**(1:13) (2014)
8. Brenguier, R., Raskin, J.-F.: Pareto curves of multidimensional mean-payoff games. In: Kroening, D., Păsăreanu, C.S. (eds.) CAV 2015. LNCS, vol. 9207, pp. 251–267. Springer, Cham (2015). doi:10.1007/978-3-319-21668-3_15

9. Brim, L., Chaloupka, J., Doyen, L., Gentilini, R., Raskin, J.-F.: Faster algorithms for mean-payoff games. Formal Meth. Syst. Des. **38**(2), 97–118 (2011)

10. Büchi, J.R., Landweber, L.H.: Solving sequential conditions by finite-state strategies. Trans. Am. Math. Soc. **138**, 295–311 (1969)

11. Chakrabarti, A., Alfaro, L., Henzinger, T.A., Stoelinga, M.: Resource interfaces. In: Alur, R., Lee, I. (eds.) EMSOFT 2003. LNCS, vol. 2855, pp. 117–133. Springer, Heidelberg (2003). doi:10.1007/978-3-540-45212-6_9

12. Chatterjee, K.: Markov decision processes with multiple long-run average objectives. In: Arvind, V., Prasad, S. (eds.) FSTTCS 2007. LNCS, vol. 4855, pp. 473–484. Springer, Heidelberg (2007). doi:10.1007/978-3-540-77050-3_39

13. Chatterjee, K., Doyen, L.: Energy parity games. In: Abramsky, S., Gavoille, C., Kirchner, C., Meyer auf der Heide, F., Spirakis, P.G. (eds.) ICALP 2010. LNCS, vol. 6199, pp. 599–610. Springer, Heidelberg (2010). doi:10.1007/978-3-642-14162-1_50

14. Chatterjee, K., Doyen, L.: Perfect-information stochastic games with generalized mean-payoff objectives. In: Proceedings of LICS: Logic in Computer Science, pp. 247–256. ACM (2016)

15. Chatterjee, K., Doyen, L., Edelsbrunner, H., Henzinger, T.A., Rannou, P.: Mean-payoff automaton expressions. In: Gastin, P., Laroussinie, F. (eds.) CONCUR 2010. LNCS, vol. 6269, pp. 269–283. Springer, Heidelberg (2010). doi:10.1007/978-3-642-15375-4_19

16. Chatterjee, K., Doyen, L., Gimbert, H., Oualhadj, Y.: Perfect-information stochastic mean-payoff parity games. In: Muscholl, A. (ed.) FoSSaCS 2014. LNCS, vol. 8412, pp. 210–225. Springer, Heidelberg (2014). doi:10.1007/978-3-642-54830-7_14

17. Chatterjee, K., Doyen, L., Randour, M., Raskin, J.-F.: Looking at mean-payoff and total-payoff through windows. In: Hung, D., Ogawa, M. (eds.) ATVA 2013. LNCS, vol. 8172, pp. 118–132. Springer, Cham (2013). doi:10.1007/978-3-319-02444-8_10

18. Chatterjee, K., Henzinger, T.A.: A survey of stochastic ω-regular games. J. Comput. Syst. Sci. **78**(2), 394–413 (2012)

19. Chatterjee, K., Henzinger, T.A., Jurdziński, M.: Mean-payoff parity games. In: Proceedings of LICS: Logic in Computer Science, pp. 178–187. IEEE Computer Society (2005)

20. Chatterjee, K., Randour, M., Raskin, J.-F.: Strategy synthesis for multi-dimensional quantitative objectives. Acta Inf. **51**, 129–163 (2014)

21. Chatterjee, K., Velner, Y.: Hyperplane separation technique for multidimensional mean-payoff games. In: D'Argenio, P.R., Melgratti, H. (eds.) CONCUR 2013. LNCS, vol. 8052, pp. 500–515. Springer, Heidelberg (2013). doi:10.1007/978-3-642-40184-8_35

22. Degorre, A., Doyen, L., Gentilini, R., Raskin, J.-F., Toruńczyk, S.: Energy and mean-payoff games with imperfect information. In: Dawar, A., Veith, H. (eds.) CSL 2010. LNCS, vol. 6247, pp. 260–274. Springer, Heidelberg (2010). doi:10.1007/978-3-642-15205-4_22

23. Ehrenfeucht, A., Mycielski, J.: Positional strategies for mean payoff games. Int. J. Game Theory **8**(2), 109–113 (1979)

24. Emerson, E.A., Jutla, C.: Tree automata, mu-calculus and determinacy. In: Proceedings of FOCS: Foundations of Computer Science, pp. 368–377. IEEE (1991)

25. Gimbert, H., Zielonka, W.: When can you play positionally? In: Fiala, J., Koubek, V., Kratochvíl, J. (eds.) MFCS 2004. LNCS, vol. 3153, pp. 686–697. Springer, Heidelberg (2004). doi:10.1007/978-3-540-28629-5_53

26. Mazala, R.: Infinite games. In: Grädel, E., Thomas, W., Wilke, T. (eds.) Automata Logics, and Infinite Games. LNCS, vol. 2500, pp. 23–38. Springer, Heidelberg (2002). doi:10.1007/3-540-36387-4_2

27. Gurevich, Y., Harrington, L.: Trees, automata, and games. In: Proceedings of STOC: Symposium on Theory of Computing, pp. 60–65. ACM Press (1982)

28. Hunter, P., Pérez, G.A., Raskin, J.-F.: Mean-payoff games with partial-observation. In: Ouaknine, J., Potapov, I., Worrell, J. (eds.) RP 2014. LNCS, vol. 8762, pp. 163–175. Springer, Cham (2014). doi:10.1007/978-3-319-11439-2_13

29. Hunter, P., Raskin, J.-F.: Quantitative games with interval objectives. In: Proceedings of FSTTCS: Foundation of Software Technology and Theoretical Computer Science, vol. 29 of LIPIcs, pp. 365–377. Schloss Dagstuhl - Leibniz-Zentrum fuer Informatik (2014)

30. Jurdziński, M.: Deciding the winner in parity games is in UP ∩ co-UP. Inf. Process. Lett. **68**(3), 119–124 (1998)

31. Jurdziński, M., Lazić, R., Schmitz, S.: Fixed-dimensional energy games are in pseudo-polynomial time. In: Halldórsson, M.M., Iwama, K., Kobayashi, N., Speckmann, B. (eds.) ICALP 2015. LNCS, vol. 9135, pp. 260–272. Springer, Heidelberg (2015). doi:10.1007/978-3-662-47666-6_21

32. Karzanov, A.V., Lebedev, V.N.: Cyclical games with prohibitions. Math. Program. **60**, 277–293 (1993)

33. Kelmendi, E.: Two-Player Stochastic Games with Perfect and Zero Information. Ph.D. thesis, Université de Bordeaux (2016)

34. Kopczyński, E.: Half-positional determinacy of infinite games. In: Bugliesi, M., Preneel, B., Sassone, V., Wegener, I. (eds.) ICALP 2006. LNCS, vol. 4052, pp. 336–347. Springer, Heidelberg (2006). doi:10.1007/11787006_29

35. Pérez, G.A.: The fixed initial credit problem for partial-observation energy games is Ack-complete. Inform. Process. Lett. **118**, 91–99 (2017)

36. Pnueli, A., Rosner R.: On the synthesis of a reactive module. In: Proceedings of POPL, pp. 179–190. ACM Press (1989)

37. Rabin, M.O.: Automata on Infinite Objects and Church's Problem. American Mathematical Society, Boston (1972)

38. Ramadge, P.J., Wonham, W.M.: The control of discrete event systems. Proc. IEEE **77**, 81–98 (1989)

39. Raskin, J.-F.: A tutorial on mean-payoff and energy games. Dependable Softw. Syst. Eng. **45**, 179–201 (2016)

40. Velner, Y.: Finite-memory strategy synthesis for robust multidimensional mean-payoff objectives. In Proceedings of CSL-LICS: Joint Meeting of Computer Science Logic (CSL) and Logic in Computer Science (LICS), pp. 79:1–79:10. ACM (2014)

41. Velner, Y.: Robust multidimensional mean-payoff games are undecidable. In: Pitts, A. (ed.) FoSSaCS 2015. LNCS, vol. 9034, pp. 312–327. Springer, Heidelberg (2015). doi:10.1007/978-3-662-46678-0_20

42. Velner, Y., Chatterjee, K., Doyen, L., Henzinger, T.A., Rabinovich, A.M., Raskin, J.-F.: The complexity of multi-mean-payoff and multi-energy games. Inf. Comput. **241**, 177–196 (2015)

43. Zwick, U., Paterson, M.: The complexity of mean payoff games on graphs. Theor. Comput. Sci. **158**(1&2), 343–359 (1996)

Adding Dense-Timed Stack to Integer Reset Timed Automata

Devendra Bhave[1]([✉]) and Shibashis Guha[2]

[1] Indian Institute of Technology Bombay, Mumbai, India
devendra@cse.iitb.ac.in
[2] The Hebrew University of Jerusalem, Jerusalem, Israel
shibashis@cs.huji.ac.il

Abstract. Integer reset timed automata (IRTA) are known to be a determinizable subclass of timed automata, but it is not known whether they are input-determined, i.e., the clock values are completely determined by an input timed word. We first define a syntactic subclass of IRTA called strict IRTA and show that strict IRTA is equivalent to IRTA. We show that the class of strict IRTA is indeed input-determined. Visibly pushdown automata is another input-determined class of automata with a stack that is also closed under boolean operations and admits a logical characterization. We propose dtIRVPA as a class of timed automata with a dense-timed stack. Similar to strict IRTA, we define strict dtIRVPA and show that strict dtIRVPA is input-determined where both – stack operations and the values of the integer reset clocks – are determined by the input word, and this helps us to get the monadic second-order (MSO) logical characterization of dtIRVPA. We prove the closure properties of dtIRVPA under union, intersection, complementation, and determinization. Further, we show that reachability of dtIRVPA is PSPACE-complete, i.e. the complexity is no more than that of timed automata.

Keywords: Visibly pushdown automata · Dense-timed stack · Integer reset timed automata · Logical characterization · MSO

1 Introduction

Program verification involves ensuring that a program does not exhibit any unintended behavior. Such verification is often done by building a suitable computational model of the program, which needs to be sufficiently powerful to express program semantics, but without losing decidability of several interesting properties. Analysis and verification of such programs amount to checking various language theoretic properties of their corresponding models. For programs involving timed behaviour, timed automaton [4] is a simple yet powerful computational model. They use a finite set of real-valued variables – called *clocks* – all of which increase at the same rate as time elapses. Clocks can be reset as desired, which

S. Guha—Supported by FP7/2007-2013, ERC grant no 278410.

M. Hague and I. Potapov (Eds.): RP 2017, LNCS 10506, pp. 9–25, 2017.
DOI: 10.1007/978-3-319-67089-8_2

is useful to measure the time delay between various events. From a language theoretic perspective, though timed automata are closed under union and intersection, they are not closed under complementation and determinization. For this reason, it is not possible to verify a program modeled as a timed automaton against specifications given by another timed automaton.

Suman et al. [20] identified integer reset timed automata (IRTA), where a clock can be reset only when the value of some clock in an IRTA is an integer, as a *perfect subclass* of timed automata, that are closed under all the language theoretic operations such as union, intersection, complementation and determinization. Naturally, universality checking and inclusion checking are decidable for IRTA. But interestingly, IRTA are shown to be equivalent to their one clock counterpart.

Apart from timing constraints, presence of function calls and interrupts in the programs make the task of their verification difficult. Pushdown automata (PDA) is a popular formalism for modeling function calls. PDA are closed under union, but not under intersection, which limits their use for verification. A visibly pushdown automaton (VPA) [5] is a perfect subclass of deterministic PDA that is closed under union, intersection and complementation leading to decidable language emptiness and inclusion.

Though IRTA forms a relatively restricted class of timed automata, Mohalik el al. [19] have successfully used it in the latency analysis of distributed real-time systems that synchronize on integer global times. They model tasks which run periodically and communicate asynchronously using buffers with IRTA. Here Fig. 1 shows a self recursive procedure P in one such task which implements a boolean lock. Procedure P is a handler routine which is activated periodically by a module that uses integer reset clocks. We do not show that module, but instead discuss the usefulness of dense-timed stack in verifying richer properties. In Fig. 1, the dashed transitions correspond to either call or return transitions in different contexts of P. Now, consider the following specification: "If a lock is acquired in any context of a procedure, it must be released in the same context within 5 time units". Such requirement is enforced by pushing a symbol α on the stack when a lock is acquired and checking whether the age of α is within 5 units of time while releasing the lock.

Contributions. We consider task models as used in [19] augmented with dense-timed stacks. This motivates us to model recursive time-sensitive tasks using dense-timed integer reset visibly pushdown automata (dtIRVPA) as a model for real-time recursive programs. Our model uses integer reset clocks, visible alphabet and a dense-timed stack. Like VPA, an input symbol determines the stack operations, with the difference that we use a dense-timed stack. We show that the formalism of dtIRVPA enjoys all good properties like closure under union, intersection and determinization that paves the way to decidability of language inclusion based model checking, where the specification is given in terms of dtIRVPA. We consider a canonical form of dtIRVPA called the *strict* dtIRVPA that enjoys input determinacy property, *i.e.* when reading a timed word u, the clock values are completely determined by u. For the ease of presentation, we

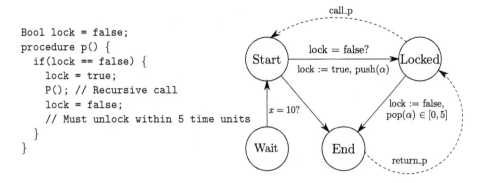

```
Bool lock = false;
procedure p() {
  if(lock == false) {
    lock = true;
    P(); // Recursive call
    lock = false;
    // Must unlock within 5 time units
  }
}
```

Fig. 1. A recursive program and its dtIRVPA model

first define *strict* IRTA and show that it is equivalent to the class of IRTA. A similar construction can be made for dtIRVPA which implies that the class of dtIRVPA is equivalent to the class of strict dtIRVPA. In this work, we also provide the monadic second-order (MSO) logical characterization for strict dtIRVPA. This allows us to check a system modelled as a dtIRVPA against any specification given by such an MSO formula. Another significant contribution of this work is to show that the location reachability checking is PSPACE-complete for dtIRVPA.

Related Work. Various models are known that combine clocks and pushdown stack to model programs with timing constraints on function calls. The earliest such model is a pushdown timed system [9]. It uses a set of global continuous variables and a timeless stack. Reachability of a location in the pushdown timed system is shown to be decidable. Dang [11] studied a model called pushdown timed automata that uses global clocks, but the clocks here are never pushed on the stack. Trivedi and Wojtczak [21] extended timed automata with recursion where they permitted pushing the clocks onto a stack using various mechanisms like pass-by-value and pass-by-reference and studied reachability and termination problems for this model. The model of dense-timed pushdown automata (dtPDA) by Abdulla et al. [1] is also closely related to our work. Whenever a stack symbol is pushed on the stack of a dtPDA, a real value called *age* is associated with the stack symbol. Ages of all symbols present in the stack increase uniformly with time. The problem of checking whether given a dtPDA and a location ℓ in it, there exists a run from an initial location of the dtPDA to location ℓ is shown to be decidable by Abdulla et al. [1] and is EXPTIME-complete. We mention here that in dtPDA, the age of a newly pushed stack symbol is initialized to a non-deterministic value while in the model of dtIRVPA introduced here, the age is initialized to zero. However, this difference is merely syntactic in nature and does not affect expressiveness [10]. Another noteworthy contribution is nested timed automata (NeTA) proposed by Li et al. [16]. In their model, an instance of timed automata can be pushed on the stack along with the clocks. Clocks of timed automata continue to run while on the stack. They have shown the decidability of the reachability problem by reducing it to dtPDA. Recently they have further explored the model of NeTA where clocks on the stack are either frozen or progressing [17]. However reachability for this extension is undecidable for multiple global clocks.

Timed matching logic proposed by Droste and Perevoshchikov [12] is an existential fragment of second-order logic characterizing dtPDA. They effectively reduce a formula in timed matching logic to dtPDA such that it is satisfiable iff the language accepted by the corresponding dtPDA is non-empty. Recently Bhave et al. [7] proposed dense-timed visibly pushdown automata (dtVPA) as a perfect subclass of timed context-free languages in the sense that it is closed under union, intersection, complementation and determinization. Language inclusion is shown to be decidable for dtVPA. Further an equivalent MSO logic has been proposed for dtVPA. In [8], they have also studied a perfect subclass of context-sensitive timed languages called dense-timed multistack visibly pushdown automata (dtMVPA). Informally, a round of multistack computation accesses each stack once. dtMVPA has been shown to enjoy all good properties as that of dtVPA for the words having k-rounds of computations. For multistack dense-timed pushdown systems, Akshay et al. [3] have proposed a tree automata based technique for reachability problem on words with k-rounds.

Organization. We set up the technical definitions in Sect. 2. In Sect. 3, we give an effective construction to convert any IRTA into a language equivalent canonical *strict* IRTA. We show that strict IRTA are input-determined automata (IDA) that implies input determinacy for strict dtIRVPA, a property that we need for the logical characterization of strict dtIRVPA. In Sect. 4, we define dtIRVPA, discuss its closure properties, show that the model is determinizable and discuss the complexity of checking emptiness of dtIRVPA. In Sect. 5, we give a logical characterization of strict dtIRVPA. We conclude in Sect. 6.

We note that the abstract procedure for determinization of timed automata given in [6] identifies IRTA as a subset of timed automata that can be determinized by following the procedure. It constructs an intermediate symbolic infinite timed tree that satisfies the input-determinacy property. The deterministic symbolic infinite tree is folded back to construct the resulting deterministic timed automaton. The folding into a timed automaton is possible only when the number of *active clocks* in each node of the infinite tree is bounded by some $\gamma \in \mathbb{N}$. The folding back requires mapping the clocks of the infinite tree to a finite set of clocks X_γ. Under the γ-clock-boundedness, the only requirement is that each time a new clock in X_γ is needed for mapping a clock of the infinite tree to a clock in X_γ, one free clock is available in X_γ. This renaming, however, does not preserve the input-determinacy property and any relation to input-determinacy cannot be ascertained from the procedure in [6].

Also, once we show that strict IRTA is input-determined, from [13], it automatically implies that there exists an MSO logical characterization for strict IRTA and such a logical characterization can be derived from the framework given in [13] for any generic input-determined timed automaton. In [13], the authors define a timed MSO (TMSO) and show the equivalence between the language of an IDA and a set of timed words satisfying a TMSO formula using a *proper symbolic alphabet*. The logic in [13] uses an input-determined operator Δ that has a semantic function of the signature $\llbracket \Delta \rrbracket : (T\Sigma^\omega \times \mathbb{N}) \mapsto 2^{\mathcal{I}_\mathbb{Q}}$, where $T\Sigma^\omega$ is the set of infinite timed words over an alphabet Σ, and $\mathcal{I}_\mathbb{Q}$ is the set of rational-bounded intervals over the non-negative reals. We use an operator $\zeta^k : \mathbb{N} \mapsto \mathcal{I}_\mathbb{Q} \cup \{\top\}$, where the symbol $\top$ denotes the clock values greater than some integer k.

2   Preliminaries

A timed automaton (TA) is a non-deterministic automaton that allows modeling of events to take place at specific time instants or within a time interval. It allows modeling the passage of time by a finite number of clock variables. All the clocks increase at the same rate. Lower case letters x, y, z will be used to denote clock variables and C will denote the set of clock variables. Clock variables are assigned non-negative real values.

Let $\uplus$ denote the disjoint union of sets. For a given $k \in \mathbb{N}$, let $\mathcal{I}^k = \{(p, p + 1) \mid 0 \le p < k\} \cup \{[p, p] \mid 0 \le p \le k\} \cup \{(k, \infty)\}$, where $p \in \mathbb{N}$, be a set of real disjoint intervals. Let $x \in C$ be a clock variable. Whenever it is clear from the context, we use $\mathcal{I}$ instead of $\mathcal{I}^k$. A clause is of the form $x \in I$. We say that a clause $(x \in I)$ holds true iff the current value of a clock variable x is in the interval I. A guard is a conjunction of finitely many such clauses and its syntax is given as $g := g \wedge g \mid (x \in I)$ where $x \in C$ and $I \in \mathcal{I}$. Let $g[(x + p)/x]$ be an expression obtained by replacing the variable x by the expression $(x + p)$ in the formula g. Let $\Phi(C)$ be the set of all guards.

A clock valuation or simply a valuation is a function $v : C \mapsto \mathbb{R}_{\ge 0}$. For a clock $x \in C$ and a valuation v, we use $v(x)$ to denote the value of clock x in v. We use $\lfloor v(x) \rfloor$ to denote the integer part of $v(x)$ while $frac(v(x))$ is used to denote the fractional part of $v(x)$. We define $\lceil v(x) \rceil = \lfloor v(x) \rfloor + 1$ if $frac(v(x)) \ne 0$, else $\lceil v(x) \rceil = \lfloor v(x) \rfloor$.

For a clock valuation v, we use $v + d$ to denote the clock valuation where every clock is being increased by an amount $d \in \mathbb{R}_{\ge 0}$. Formally, for each $d \in \mathbb{R}_{\ge 0}$, the valuation $v + d$ is defined as $(v + d)(x) = v(x) + d$, for each $x \in C$.

For a clock valuation v, we use $v_{[R \leftarrow \bar{0}]}$ to denote the clock valuation where every clock in $R \subseteq C$ is set to zero, while the value of the remaining clocks remain the same as in v. Formally, for each $R \subseteq C$, the valuation $v_{[R \leftarrow \bar{0}]}$ is defined by $v_{[R \leftarrow \bar{0}]}(x) = 0$ if $x \in R$, else $v_{[R \leftarrow \bar{0}]}(x) = v(x)$. We say that a valuation v satisfies a guard g, denoted $v \models g$, if for each clock x appearing in g, the formula obtained by replacing x with $v(x)$ is valid.

A timed automaton is defined by the tuple $(L, L_0, \Sigma, C, E, L_f)$ where L is a finite set of locations, L_0 is a non-empty set of initial locations, Σ is a finite alphabet disjoint from $\mathbb{R}_{\ge 0}$, C is a finite set of clocks, $E \subseteq L \times \Sigma \times \Phi(C) \times 2^C \times L$ is a finite set of edges and $L_f \subseteq L$ is a set of accepting locations. Note that our definition of guards is not succinct but it is equally expressive as the definition of [4]. The definition that we use in this paper allows us to have cleaner proofs.

A timed transition system [14], (TTS for short), $S = \langle Q, Q_0, \Sigma, \rightarrow, \hookrightarrow, Q_F \rangle$, where Σ is a finite alphabet, Q is a set of states, $q_0 \in Q_0$ is an initial state, $\rightarrow \subseteq Q \times \mathbb{R}_{\geq 0} \times Q$ is a set of delay transition relations, and $\hookrightarrow \subseteq Q \times \Sigma \times Q$ is a set of discrete transition relations. We write $q \xrightarrow{d} q'$ if $(q, d, q') \in \rightarrow$ and $q \xrightarrow{a} q'$ if $(q, a, q') \in \hookrightarrow$.

Let $\mathcal{A} = \langle L, L_0, \Sigma, C, E, L_f \rangle$ be a timed automaton. The semantics of a timed automaton is described by a TTS. The timed transition system $T(\mathcal{A})$ generated by $\mathcal{A}$ is defined as $T(\mathcal{A}) = \langle Q, Q_0, \Sigma, \rightarrow, \hookrightarrow, Q_F \rangle$, where

- $Q = \{(\ell, v) \mid \ell \in L, v \text{ is a clock valuation}\}$, is a set of states. Note that due to the real-valued nature of time, this set is generally uncountable.
- Let v_{init} denote the valuation such that $v_{init}(x) = 0$ for all $x \in C$. Then $Q_0 = \{(\ell_0, v_{init}) \mid l_0 \in L_0\}$.
- $\rightarrow = \{((\ell, v), (\ell, v + d)) \mid (\ell, v), d, (\ell, v + d) \in Q\}$ for all $d \in \mathbb{R}_{\geq 0}$.
- $\hookrightarrow = \{((\ell, v), a, (\ell', v')) \text{ such that } (\ell, v), (\ell', v') \in Q \text{ and there is an edge } e = (\ell, a, g, R, \ell') \in E \text{ and } v \models g \text{ and } v' = v_{[R \leftarrow \bar{0}]}\}$. From a state (ℓ, v), if $v \models g$, then there exists a $a \in \Sigma$ transition to a state (ℓ', v'); after this, the clocks in R are reset while the values of the clocks in $C \backslash R$ remain unchanged.
- $Q_F = \{(\ell, v) \mid l \in L_f \text{ and } v \text{ is a clock valuation}\}$.

For a timed automaton state $p = (\ell, v)$, we denote by $v_x(p)$ the value of clock x for state p. A run of a timed automaton is of the form $\pi = (\ell_0, v_0) \xrightarrow{d_0} (\ell_0, v_0 + d_0) \xrightarrow{a_0} (\ell_1, v_1) \xrightarrow{d_1} (\ell_1, v_1 + d_1) \xrightarrow{a_1} (\ell_2, v_2) \dots \xrightarrow{d_k} (\ell_k, v_k + d_k) \xrightarrow{a_k} (\ell_{k+1}, v_{k+1})$ where for all $i \geq 0$, we have $d_i \in \mathbb{R}_{\geq 0}$ and $a_i \in \Sigma$. Note that π is a continuous run in the sense that for a delay transition $(\ell_i, v_i), \xrightarrow{d_i} (\ell_i, v_i + d_i)$, it includes all states $(\ell_i, v_i + d)$ for all $0 \leq d \leq d_i$. A run is said to be $initial$ if $\ell_0 \in L_0$ and $v_0 = v_{init}$. An initial run is accepting if it ends in an accepting location. A timed word $w = (a_0, t_0)(a_1, t_1) \dots (a_k, t_k)$ is said to be read on π whenever $t_i = \sum_{j=0}^{i} d_j$ for every $1 \leq i \leq k$. The timed word w is said to be accepted by $\mathcal{A}$ if there is an initial and accepting run of $\mathcal{A}$ that reads u. We write $L(\mathcal{A})$ for the set of timed words (or timed language) accepted by $\mathcal{A}$. We say that a TA $\mathcal{A}$ is deterministic whenever every timed word w produces at most one unique run. The set of finite words over Σ is denoted by Σ^*. Additionally, we denote the set of all finite timed words by $T\Sigma^*$.

An *integer reset timed automaton* (IRTA) [20] is a timed automaton $\mathcal{A} = \langle L, L_0, \Sigma, C, E, L_f \rangle$ with the restriction that for every edge $e = \langle \ell, a, g, R, \ell' \rangle$, if $R \neq \emptyset$, then g has a clause of the form $x \in I$ for some $x \in C$ and I is of the form $[p, p]$ for $p \in \mathbb{N}$. Such clauses in the guard ensure that all resets happen at integer time units. A consequence of this is that at any time, for any run of an IRTA, the fractional parts of the values of all the clocks are the same [20].

It is known that given an IRTA $\mathcal{A}$, it can be determinized to produce another IRTA $\mathcal{B}$ whose size is exponential in the number of locations of $\mathcal{A}$ [18]. Further, given an IRTA $\mathcal{A}$ with an arbitrary number of clocks, it can be converted to an IRTA $\mathcal{B}$ such that $\mathcal{B}$ has a single clock and the number of locations in $\mathcal{B}$ is exponential in the number of clocks of $\mathcal{A}$ [18]. In both the above constructions, the timed language accepted by $\mathcal{A}$ is preserved.

A *strong timed simulation* relation between two timed systems $T_i = \langle Q_i, Q_{0,i}, \Sigma, \rightarrow_i, \hookrightarrow_i, Q_{F,i} \rangle$, for $i \in \{1, 2\}$ is a relation $\mathcal{R} \subseteq Q_1 \times Q_2$ such that if $(q_1, q_2) \in \mathcal{R}$, and $q_1 \overset{\alpha}{\rightarrowtail} q_1'$, where $\rightarrowtail = \rightarrow$ and $\alpha \in \mathbb{R}_{\geq 0}$, or $\rightarrowtail = \hookrightarrow$ and $\alpha \in \Sigma$, then there exists $q_2' \in Q_2$ such that $q_2 \overset{\alpha}{\rightarrowtail} q_2'$ and $(q_1', q_2') \in \mathcal{R}$. A strong timed bisimulation relation between two timed systems T_i for $i \in \{1, 2\}$ is a relation $\mathcal{R} \subseteq Q_1 \times Q_2$ such that both $\mathcal{R}$ and $\mathcal{R}^{-1}$ are strong timed simulation relations. We say that two timed automata $\mathcal{A}_1$ and $\mathcal{A}_2$ are timed bisimilar if for every initial state q_1 of $T(\mathcal{A}_1)$, there exists an initial state q_2 of $T(\mathcal{A}_2)$ such that there exists a strong timed bisimulation containing q_1 and q_2, and for every initial state q_2 of $T(\mathcal{A}_2)$, there exists an initial state q_1 of $T(\mathcal{A}_1)$ such that there exists a strong timed bisimulation containing q_1 and q_2.

Visibly pushdown automata [5] are a determinizable subclass of pushdown automata that operate over words that dictate the stack operations. This notion is formalized by giving an explicit partition of the alphabet into three disjoint sets of *call*, *return*, and *local* symbols and the visibly pushdown automata must push one symbol to the stack while reading a call symbol, and must pop one symbol (given the stack is non-empty) while reading a return symbol, and must not touch the stack while reading the local symbol. A *visibly pushdown alphabet* is a tuple $\Sigma = \langle \Sigma_c, \Sigma_r, \Sigma_l \rangle$ where Σ is partitioned into a *call* alphabet Σ_c, a *return* alphabet Σ_r, and a *local* alphabet Σ_l. A visibly pushdown automaton over $\Sigma = \langle \Sigma_c, \Sigma_r, \Sigma_l \rangle$ is a tuple $(L, \Sigma, \Gamma, L^0, E, L_f)$ where L is a finite set of locations including a set $L^0 \subseteq L$ of initial locations, a finite stack alphabet Γ with special end-of-stack symbol $\vdash$, and $E \subseteq (L \times \Sigma_c \times L \times (\Gamma \setminus \vdash)) \cup (L \times \Sigma_r \times \Gamma \times L) \cup (L \times \Sigma_l \times L)$ and $L_f \subseteq L$ is a set of final locations. Alur and Madhusudan [5] showed that visibly pushdown automata are determinizable and closed under Boolean operations, concatenation, Kleene closure, and projection. They also showed that the language accepted by visibly pushdown automata can be characterized by MSO over words augmented with a binary matching predicate first studied in [15].

3   Transformation to Strict IRTA

In this section, we first define strict IRTA and show that the class of strict IRTA is equivalent to IRTA. Then we show that strict IRTA are input-determined automata.

Definition 1. *An IRTA is said to be* strict *iff (i) it has only one clock and (ii) every edge having a guard condition of the form* $[p, p]$ *with* $p \in \mathbb{N}$ *resets the clock.*

Assume wlog that we are given a one-clock (not necessarily deterministic), but non-strict IRTA $\mathcal{A} = (L, L_0, \Sigma, \{x\}, E, L_f)$. We now describe a construction that yields a strict IRTA $\mathcal{B}$ which is timed bisimilar to $\mathcal{A}$. For the following discussion, we assume k to be the maximum constant appearing in the guards of $\mathcal{A}$.

First, we present an intuition behind our construction with some observations. Consider the one clock IRTA $\mathcal{A}$ in Fig. 2 having a single clock x. We do not show the labels on the edges with the letters from Σ in the figure. Clearly $\mathcal{A}$ is not a strict IRTA as the edge from ℓ_2 to ℓ_3 has an integer guard, but it does not reset x. Suppose we forcefully reset x on the ℓ_2 to ℓ_3 edge, then we need to suitably change the guards on all the edges that may be taken thereafter to preserve the timed language. For example, one of the changes that we can immediately identify is to make the guard in the edge from ℓ_3 to ℓ_1 as $x \in (0,1)$ instead of earlier $x \in (3,4)$ as the new value of x lags by 3. Clearly, the other side effects of resetting x must be taken care of appropriately. These side effects are *path sensitive*, *i.e.* for each location the amount of lag in x introduced because of additional reset of x depends completely on the incoming path to that location.

As a general principle, consider an edge $\ell \xrightarrow{a, x \in [m,m], \emptyset} \ell'$ which denotes a transition from a location ℓ to ℓ' on an input symbol a and checks whether the value of the clock x is m, but does not reset x. Suppose we modify it by adding a reset to it, clock x will then lag by m units along the run until x is reset again. Intuitively our construction keeps track of such a time lag introduced along the run in the locations. Let $\mathbb{N}_{\leq m} = \{0, 1, \ldots, m\}$ denote the set of natural numbers less than or equal to m. We maintain sets of lags $X_\ell \subseteq \mathbb{N}_{\leq k}$ for each location $\ell \in L$, where k is the maximum integer appearing in the guards of the IRTA. Let $\gamma : E \mapsto 2^{\mathbb{N}_{\leq k}}$ give the lag introduced by each edge. Recall that a guard I on an edge u of the one clock IRTA $\mathcal{A}$ is of the form $[m,m]$ or $(m, m+1)$ for $m \in \mathbb{N}$.

$$\gamma(u) = \begin{cases} \{m\} & \text{if } u = (\ell_1, x \in [m,m], a, \emptyset, \ell_2) \\ \{0\} & \text{if } u = (\ell_1, x \in [m,m], a, \{x\}, \ell_2) \\ X_{\ell_1} \cap \mathbb{N}_{\leq \inf(I)} & \text{if } u = (\ell_1, x \in I, a, \emptyset, \ell_2), \text{ where } I \neq [m,m] \text{ for } m \in \mathbb{N}_{\leq k} \end{cases}$$

Let $pre(\ell)$ be the set of all incoming edges to location ℓ. For computing the possible set of lags at each location, we write the set of fixed point equations for each location ℓ as $X_\ell = \bigcup_{u \in pre(\ell)} \gamma(u)$. For initial locations, there is no lag initially, so we initialize X_ℓ to $\{0\}$ for $\ell \in L_0$. Fixed point solution to these sets of equations exists as the sets are finite and set union is monotonicity preserving. Note that in each iteration $\gamma(u)$ is computed by intersecting with a constant set. Let $\overline{X}_\ell$ denote the fixed point solutions.

Now we construct a strict IRTA $\mathcal{B} = (L^{\mathcal{B}}, L_0^{\mathcal{B}}, \Sigma, \{x\}, E^{\mathcal{B}}, L_f^{\mathcal{B}})$. We record the time lag along the run in the locations of $\mathcal{B}$ such that $L^{\mathcal{B}} = \{(\ell, p) \mid \ell \in L \text{ and } p \in \overline{X}_\ell\}$ and initial locations are $L^{\mathcal{B}} = L_0 \times \{0\}$. Final locations are $L_f^{\mathcal{B}} = \{(\ell, p) \mid \ell \in L_f \text{ and } (\ell, p) \in L^{\mathcal{B}}\}$. The set of edges of $\mathcal{B}$ are given by

$$E^{\mathcal{B}} = \begin{array}{l} \{((\ell, p), a, (x + p \in I), \emptyset, (\ell', p)) \mid (\ell, x \in I, a, \emptyset, \ell') \in E \\ \quad \text{and } I \neq [m,m] \text{ for } m \in \mathbb{N}_{\leq k} \text{ and } p \leq \inf(I)\} \cup \\ \{((\ell, p), a, (x + p \in [m,m]), \{x\}, (\ell', m)) \mid (\ell, (x \in [m,m]), a, \emptyset, \ell') \in E \\ \quad \text{and } p \leq m\} \cup \\ \{((\ell, p), a, (x + p \in [m,m]), \{x\}, (\ell', 0)) \mid (\ell, (x \in [m,m]), a, \{x\}, \ell') \in E \\ \quad \text{and } p \leq m\} \end{array}$$

Remark 1. Note that since the IRTA $\mathcal{A}$ has only one clock and its guards belong to $\mathcal{I}$, the size of the IRTA $\mathcal{B}$ is polynomial in the size of $\mathcal{A}$. Further, from $E^{\mathcal{B}}$, we note that the maximum constant with which the clock is compared to in $\mathcal{B}$ is no more than the maximum constant with which the clock is compared to in $\mathcal{A}$.

We now apply our construction on the automaton in Fig. 2. We compute the set X_{ℓ_i} for each location ℓ_i where $0 \leq i \leq 3$. Initially X_{ℓ_0} is set to $\{0\}$, while for $i \neq 0$, we set $X_{l_i} = \emptyset$. Next X_{ℓ_1} is set to $\{0\}$ as it propagates from X_{ℓ_0} due to the presence of the edge from ℓ_0 to ℓ_1. Then X_{ℓ_2} is set to $\{0\}$ as it propagates from X_{ℓ_1} because of the edge from ℓ_1 to ℓ_2. Then X_{ℓ_3} is set to $\{3\}$ because of the edge from ℓ_2 to ℓ_3. Again X_{ℓ_1} is modified to $\{0,3\}$ since 3 is propagated from X_{ℓ_3} due to the presence of the edge from ℓ_3 to ℓ_1. Thus we reach the following fixed point: $\overline{X}_{\ell_0} = \{0\}$, $\overline{X}_{\ell_1} = \{0,3\}$, $\overline{X}_{\ell_2} = \{0\}$ and $\overline{X}_{\ell_3} = \{3\}$. Note that 3 is not added to X_{ℓ_2} since 3 is greater than the infimum of the guard on the edge from ℓ_1 to ℓ_2 which is 1. The edges are added following the definition of $E^{\mathcal{B}}$ given above. For example, for the edge from ℓ_3 to ℓ_1, consider the locations $(\ell_3, 3)$ and $(\ell_1, 3)$. In the strict IRTA that is obtained, we have the edge $\big((\ell_3,3),\cdot,x{+}3 \in (3,4),(\ell_1,3)\big)$. The strict IRTA obtained is shown in Fig. 3.

Theorem 1. *Given a one clock IRTA $\mathcal{A}$, the construction presented above produces a strict IRTA $\mathcal{B}$ such that $\mathcal{A}$ and $\mathcal{B}$ are timed bisimilar.*

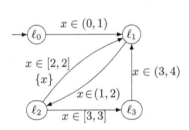

Fig. 2. An IRTA that is not strict.

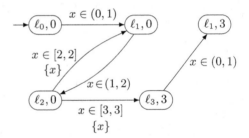

Fig. 3. A strict IRTA obtained from the one in Fig. 2.

We say that the class of timed automata has the property of *input determinacy* if the values of the clocks along a run are completely determined by the input timed word alone and do not depend on any specific instance of a timed automaton. Clearly the class of IRTA as a whole does not have this property, however, we claim that the strict IRTA does have the input determinacy property.

Lemma 1. *Strict IRTA have the input determinacy property.*

4   Dense-Timed Integer Reset Visibly Pushdown Automata

We introduce dense-timed integer reset visibly pushdown automata (dtIRVPA) as an IRTA augmented with a dense-timed stack having a visibly pushdown alphabet. Let an input alphabet $\Sigma = \Sigma_c \uplus \Sigma_r \uplus \Sigma_l$ be partitioned into call, return and local symbols respectively. Let $\vdash$ be the special stack symbol denoting the bottom of the stack. We now formally define dtIRVPA and describe their semantics.

Definition 2 (dtIRVPA). *A dense-timed integer reset visibly pushdown automaton (dtIRVPA) over $\Sigma = \Sigma_c \uplus \Sigma_r \uplus \Sigma_l$ is a tuple $\mathcal{A} = (L, L_0, \Sigma, \Gamma, C, E = E_c \uplus E_r \uplus E_l, L_f)$, where L is the finite set of locations, $L_0, L_f \subseteq L$ are the set of initial and final locations respectively, Γ is the finite stack alphabet with special end-of-stack symbol $\vdash$, $E_c \subseteq (L \times \Sigma_c \times \Phi(C) \times 2^C \times L \times (\Gamma \setminus \vdash))$ is the finite set of call transitions, $E_r \subseteq (L \times \Sigma_r \times \Phi(C) \times 2^C \times \Gamma \times \mathcal{I} \times L)$ is the finite set of return transitions, and $E_l \subseteq (L \times \Sigma_l \times \Phi(C) \times 2^C \times L)$ is the finite set of local transitions. Additionally, the set of clocks that get reset in a transition is nonempty only if its guard condition contains a clause of the form $(x \in [p,p])$ where x is some clock in C and $p \in \mathbb{N}$.*

Each symbol on the stack has an associated clock-like real value (called *age*) which increments uniformly with time. When a symbol is pushed on the stack, its age is initialized to zero. As time elapses, ages of all stack symbols increase uniformly. A pop transition checks the age of the topmost stack symbol. We denote the contents of the stack in a configuration using a timed word itself. Let σ be such a timed word where $untime(\sigma) \in \Gamma^*$ is the string of (untimed) stack symbols while $age(\sigma)$ is the string of real valued ages. We define the age of stack bottom symbol $\vdash$ to be of undefined value, denoted by the special symbol $\perp$ which is not affected by the passage of time. Hence $(\perp + m)$ is defined to be $\perp$ for any $m \in \mathbb{R}_{\geq 0}$. We introduce a string concatenation operation :: for both types of strings for convenience in the next discussion.

Let $w = (a_1, t_1), \cdots, (a_n, t_n)$ be a timed word. A configuration of dtIRVPA is a tuple $(\ell, v, (\gamma\sigma, age(\gamma\sigma)))$, where ℓ is the current location of the dtIRVPA, v is the clock valuation, $\gamma\sigma \in \Gamma\Gamma^*$ is the content of the stack with γ being the topmost symbol and σ is the untimed word representing the stack content below γ, while $age(\gamma\sigma)$ is a string of real numbers encoding the ages of all the stack symbols (the time elapsed since each of them was pushed on to the stack).

The run of a dtIRVPA on a timed word $w = (a_1, t_1), \ldots, (a_n, t_n)$ is a sequence of configurations given as follows: $(\ell_0, v_0, (\langle \vdash \rangle, \langle \perp \rangle)), (\ell_1, v_1, (\sigma_1, age(\sigma_1))), \ldots, (\ell_n, v_n, (\sigma_n, age(\sigma_n)))$ where $\ell_i \in L, \sigma_i \in \Gamma^*, \ell_0 \in L_0, t_0 = 0$, and for each i, $1 \leq i \leq n$, we have:

- If $a_i \in \Sigma_c$, then there is a transition $(\ell_{i-1}, a_i, g, R, \ell_i, \gamma) \in E$ such that $v_{i-1} + (t_i - t_{i-1}) \models g$. The clock valuation $v_i = (v_{i-1} + (t_i - t_{i-1}))_{[R \leftarrow \bar{0}]}$. The symbol $\gamma \in \Gamma \setminus \{\vdash\}$ is then pushed onto the stack, and its age is initialized to zero, obtaining $(\sigma_i, age(\sigma_i)) = (\gamma :: \sigma_{i-1}, 0 :: (age(\sigma_{i-1}) + (t_i - t_{i-1})))$. Note that the age of all symbols in the stack excluding the topmost one increases by $t_i - t_{i-1}$.
- If $a_i \in \Sigma_r$, then there is a transition $(\ell_{i-1}, a_i, g, R, \gamma, I, \ell_i) \in E$. The configuration $(\ell_{i-1}, v_{i-1}, (\sigma_{i-1}, age(\sigma_{i-1})))$ evolves to $(\ell_i, v_i, (\sigma_i, age(\sigma_i)))$ iff $v_{i-1} + (t_i - t_{i-1}) \models g, \sigma_{i-1} = \gamma :: \kappa \in \Gamma\Gamma^*$ and $age(\gamma) + (t_i - t_{i-1}) \in I$. Then

we obtain $\sigma_i = \kappa$, with $age(\sigma_i) = age(\kappa) + (t_i - t_{i-1})$. However, if $\gamma = \vdash$, the symbol is not popped, and the attached interval I is irrelevant. The clock valuation $v_i = (v_{i-1} + (t_i - t_{i-1}))_{[R \leftarrow \bar{0}]}$.

- If $a_i \in \Sigma_l$, then there is a transition $(\ell_{i-1}, a_i, g, R, \ell_i) \in E$ such that $v_{i-1} + (t_i - t_{i-1}) \models g$. The clock valuation $v_i = (v_{i-1} + (t_i - t_{i-1}))_{[R \leftarrow \bar{0}]}$. In this case the stack remains unchanged i.e. $\sigma_i = \sigma_{i-1}$, and $age(\sigma_i) = age(\sigma_{i-1}) + (t_i - t_{i-1})$. All symbols in the stack age by $t_i - t_{i-1}$.

A run ρ of a dtIRVPA $\mathcal{A}$ is accepting if it terminates in a final location. A timed word w is an accepting word if there is an accepting run of $\mathcal{A}$ on w. The language $L(\mathcal{A})$ of a dtIRVPA $\mathcal{A}$, is the set of all timed words w accepted by $\mathcal{A}$.

Definition 3 (Deterministic dtIRVPA). *A dtIRVPA* $\mathcal{A} = (L, L_0, \Sigma, \Gamma, C, E, L_f)$ *is said to be deterministic if it has exactly one start location, and for every location and input symbol pair exactly one transition is enabled at all times. Formally, we have the following conditions: (i) for call transitions* $(\ell, a, g_1, R_1, \ell', \gamma_1), (\ell, a, g_2, R_2, \ell', \gamma_2) \in E_c$, *we have* $g_1 \wedge g_2$ *is unsatisfiable. (ii) for return transitions* $(\ell, a, g_1, R_1, \gamma_1, I_1, \ell'), (\ell, a, g_2, R_2, \gamma_2, I_2, \ell') \in E_r$, *either* $g_1 \wedge g_2$ *is unsatisfiable or* $I_1 \cap I_2 = \emptyset$. *(iii) for local transitions* $(\ell, a, g_1, R_1, \ell'), (\ell, a, g_2, R_2, \ell') \in E_l$, *we have* $g_1 \wedge g_2$ *is unsatisfiable.*

Now we state one of the central results of the paper.

Theorem 2. *dtIRVPA are determinizable and closed under union, intersection and complementation. Also, their language emptiness and inclusion is decidable.*

Determinization. Although IRTA and VPA are individually determinizable, their determinization techniques cannot be easily combined for determinizing dtIRVPA due to the presence of a dense-timed stack. However technique used for determinization of dtVPA in [7] is helpful for handling dense-timed stack. We have the following result about the determinization of dtIRVPA.

Lemma 2. *dtIRVPA are determinizable.*

Closure properties and decision problems. The closure of dtIRVPA under union follows from the non-deterministic union of two dtIRVPA, while the intersection follows from their cross product construction. To obtain a complement of a given dtIRVPA, we first determinize it and then interchange final and non-final locations. We state the following results about the closure properties of dtIRVPA.

Lemma 3. *dtIRVPA are closed under union, intersection and complementation.*

The reachability problem for a dtPDA amounts to checking whether there exists a run starting from an initial configuration to a given configuration in the given dtPDA. If the given configuration is a final one, then this amounts to checking whether the language accepted by the dtPDA is empty. Abdulla et al. [1] proved that the configuration reachability checking problem for dtPDA is EXPTIME-complete. We now state the following theorem for the reachability checking of dtIRVPA.

Theorem 3. *The reachability checking for dtIRVPA is PSPACE-complete.*

PSPACE-hardness follows after a minor change in the initialization edges of the constructed timed automaton to yield an IRTA in the proof of the reachability problem of timed automata as given in [2]. An NPSPACE algorithm for emptiness checking is given below.

We first define the notion of regions for dtIRVPA, then state the construction of a region graph. Let $\mathcal{A} = (L, L_0, \Sigma, \Gamma, C, E, L_f)$ be a dtIRVPA with k as a maximum constant used in the guards. We define the regions for $\mathcal{A}$ as follows: The region is a triple (ℓ, u, b) where $\ell \in L$ is a location, $u : C \mapsto \mathbb{N} \cup \{k^+\}$ is a function that abstracts a clock valuation, and $b \in \{0, 1\}$ is a flag which denotes whether the fractional parts of the values of the clocks is zero. Here k^+ is a special symbol that represents clock values greater than k. We use $b = 0$ to denote that the fractional part of all clocks is zero and $b = 1$ to denote non-zero value of fractional part. Recall that Lemma 5 ensures that the value of fractional parts of all integer reset clocks is the same. For a valuation v, for each clock $x \in C$, we have $u(x) = k^+$ if $v(x) > k$, else $u(x) = \lfloor v(x) \rfloor$. We say that a state (ℓ, v, σ), where σ is the stack content, *belongs* to a region (ℓ, u, b) if for each clock $x \in C$, we have $u(x) = \lfloor v(x) \rfloor$ when $v(x) <= k$, and $u(x) = k^+$ when $v(x) > k$. Let $\mathcal{R}$ be the set of all such regions.

The region graph G induced by $\mathcal{A}$ is a graph in which the vertices are regions in $\mathcal{R}$ and the directed edges are labeled either by symbols in Σ or by intervals in $\mathcal{I}$. Edges are labeled by input symbols for discrete transitions between regions. If there is an edge labeled $I \in \mathcal{I}$ from region r_1 to r_2, it means that for every state $(\ell_1, v_1, \sigma_1) \in r_1$, there exists a $t \in I$ such that there is a concrete run from (ℓ_1, v_1, σ_1) that reaches some state $(\ell_2, v_2, \sigma_2) \in r_2$ after time $t \in I$.

Example 1. Consider a dtIRVPA $\mathcal{A}$ with a maximum constant $k = 2$ in the guards. This yields the set of intervals $\mathcal{I} = \{[0, 0], (0, 1), [1, 1], (1, 2), [2, 2], (2, \infty)\}$. The set of clocks of $\mathcal{A}$ is $C = \{x, y, z\}$. Let the stack symbols be $\Gamma = \{\alpha, \beta\}$. Consider a state $s_1 = (\ell_1, v_1 = \langle 1.2, 2.2, 0.2 \rangle, \sigma_1 = \langle (\alpha, 1.2), (\beta, 0.1) \rangle)$ of $\mathcal{A}$. Recall that all the clocks in an IRTA always have the same fractional part. The region r_1 to which s_1 belongs is $r_1 = (\ell_1, u_1 = \langle 1, 2^+, 0 \rangle, 1)$. Note that the stack contents are not recorded in the regions. Now consider the effect of a time delay of 0.8 units on s_1. We get $s_2 = (\ell_1, v_2 = \langle 2.0, 3.0, 1.0 \rangle, \sigma_2 = \langle (\alpha, 2.0), (\beta, 0.9) \rangle)$. The state s_2 belongs to region $r_2 = (\ell_1, u_2 = \langle 2, 2^+, 1 \rangle, 1)$. This gives us an edge in the region graph $r_1 \xrightarrow{(0,1)} r_2$. In fact for every state $s \in r_1$, we can always choose some $t \in (0, 1)$ such that by delaying time t we reach some state in r_2.

Construction of region graph. We now use an alternative definition of timed words that uses delay intervals instead of global timestamps. For a timed word $w = (a_1, \delta_1) \ldots (a_n, \delta_n)$, duration of w is $\Sigma_{i=1}^{n} \delta_i$. Duration of a run is the duration of the timed word that induces the run. We define an *interval reachability* relation R_I between the regions such that if $(r_1, r_2) \in R_I$ then for every state $s_1 \in r_1$, there exists a $t \in I$ and a concrete run that reaches some state $s_2 \in r_2$ after time t. A region graph is constructed using the reachability relation $R = \bigcup_{I \in \mathcal{I}} R_I$.

Definition 4. *We define interval reachability relation R_I recursively as follows. We say $(r, r') \in R_I$ if one of the following cases holds.*

- $\left[\text{Case } I \right]$ *there are states $(\ell, v_1, \sigma_1) \in r$ and $(\ell, v_2, \sigma_2) \in r'$ and a time delay $t \in I$ such that $v_2 = v_1 + t$ and $\sigma_2 = \sigma_1 + t$. This case is for reachability by delay transition.*
- $\left[\text{Case } I \circ L \right]$ $(r, r_1) \in R_I$ *and there is a local transition from r_1 to r'*
- $\left[\text{Case } C \circ I \circ R \right]$ *all of the following hold*
  - *there is a call transition from r to r_1 that pushes a symbol α on the stack*
  - *there exists some I-labeled edge from r_1 to r_2 i.e. $(r_1, r_2) \in R_I$*
  - *there is a return transition from r_2 to r' with stack condition $pop(\alpha) \in I$*
- $\left[\text{Case } I \circ I \right]$ *there exist $(r, r_1) \in R_{J_1}$ and $(r_1, r') \in R_{J_2}$ and there exist $t_1 \in J_1, t_2 \in J_2$ and $t \in I$ such that $t_1 + t_2 = t$.*

We now give an NPSPACE algorithm to check if a region r_2 is reachable from a region r_1. The size of the input is $O(\log k)$ bits as the input contains the description of a given dtlRVPA. Each abstract value of a clock requires $O(\log k)$ bits and hence the function u needs $|C| \cdot O(\log k)$ bits of memory. Thus a region requires $O(\log k)$ bits which is polynomial in the size of the input. We systematically guess the regions at each transition along the run such that only $O(1)$ regions are stored in each step. Our algorithm performs the following steps until no new relation can be inferred further. (i) It add $(r_1, r_2) \in R_I$ for delay transitions using case I. (ii) It guesses regions r_1, r_2 and r_3 such that $(r_1, r_2) \in R_{I_1}$ and $(r_2, r_3) \in R_{I_2}$. It then concatenates them to get reachability from r_1 to r_3 using case $I \circ I$. (iii) It guesses regions $(r_1, r_2) \in R_I$ and guesses call and return transitions such that $r \to r_1$ is a call transition and $r_2 \to r'$ is return transition. It then infers that $(r, r') \in R_I$ using case $C \circ I \circ R$. (iv) It guesses regions r_1, r_2 and r_3 such that $(r_1, r_2) \in R_{I_1}$ and (r_2, r_3) is a local transition. It then infers the reachability from r_1 to r_3 using case $I \circ L$.

A timed word is called *well-matched* if there is no call position without a matching return position and vice versa. Our reachability algorithm can as well be extended to words that are not well-matched by treating unmatched calls and returns as local variables.

The problem of language inclusion checking for dtlRVPA is stated as whether $L(\mathcal{A}) \subseteq L(\mathcal{B})$ for dtlRVPA $\mathcal{A}$ and $\mathcal{B}$ and this can be done by testing if $L(\mathcal{A}) \cap L(\overline{\mathcal{B}}) = \emptyset$. The language inclusion checking for VPA is EXPTIME-complete [5]. As VPA is a proper subclass of dtlRVPA, we have the following lemma.

Lemma 4. *For dtlRVPA $\mathcal{A}$ and $\mathcal{B}$, checking whether $L(\mathcal{A}) \subseteq L(\mathcal{B})$ is decidable and is EXPTIME-hard.*

5   MSO Characterization for Strict dtlRVPA

We can extend Definition 1 to dtlRVPA to obtain a *strict* dtlRVPAin a straightforward way. We restate the following key lemmas regarding the properties of IRTA that are instrumental in obtaining a strict IRTA from any given IRTA and given a dtlRVPA, we can obtain a strict dtlRVPA analogously.

Lemma 5. *[20] Let $\mathcal{A}$ be an IRTA and v be a clock valuation in any given run in $\mathcal{A}$. Then for all clocks x and y of $\mathcal{A}$, we have $frac(v(x)) = frac(v(y))$.*

Lemma 6. *[18] Given an IRTA $\mathcal{A}$, a deterministic one clock IRTA $\mathcal{B}$ can be constructed such that $L(\mathcal{A}) = L(\mathcal{B})$.*

Using the lemmas stated above and following a construction similar to the one presented in Sect. 3, we have the following lemma.

Lemma 7 (Clock reduction and strictness). *For every dtIRVPA $\mathcal{A}$, there is a strict dtIRVPA $\mathcal{B}$ such that $L(\mathcal{A}) = L(\mathcal{B})$.*

Theorem 4. *Strict dtIRVPA have input determinacy property.*

The above theorem allows us to have an MSO characterization for strict dtIRVPA.

Let $w = (a_1, t_1) \ldots (a_m, t_m)$ be a finite timed word accepted by a strict dtIRVPA $\mathcal{A}$. Let $\mathcal{D}^w = \{1, \ldots, m\}$ be the set of positions in w called the *domain* of w. Owing to Theorem 4, the value of the (only) clock at each position of w can be computed and is given by a function $\zeta^k : \mathcal{D}^w \mapsto [0, k] \cup \top$, where $[0, k]$ is the set of reals from zero to k and $\top$ is an artificially added symbol which intuitively denotes the clock values greater than k. We let $t_0 = 0$ to be the initial timestamp. Formally $\zeta^k(0) = 0$ and for $j > 0$,

$$\zeta^k(j) = \begin{cases} t_j - t_i & \text{if } i \text{ is the largest position with } 0 \leq i < j \text{ and having integer} \\ & t_i \text{ and } t_j - t_i \leq k \text{ and } \zeta^k(i) \neq \top \\ \top & \text{otherwise.} \end{cases}$$

We now define the syntax of $\mathsf{MSO}(\Sigma, k)$ formulas over alphabet Σ and parameter $k \in \mathbb{N}$ using the following syntax.

$$\varphi ::= Q_a(n) \mid \zeta^k_I(n) \mid \mu_I(n_1, n_2) \mid n_1 < n_2 \mid n \in X \mid \neg\varphi \mid (\varphi \vee \varphi) \mid \exists n \, \varphi(n) \mid \exists X \, \varphi(X)$$

For every timed word w, we associate a word model $\underline{w}$ on which $\mathsf{MSO}(\Sigma, k)$ formulas are evaluated. Predicate $Q_a(n)$ checks whether the symbol $a \in \Sigma$ occurs at position n in w. Predicate $\zeta^k_I(n)$ checks whether the value of function ζ^k is in the interval $I \in \mathcal{I} \cup \{\top\}$ at position n. The ordering relation $<$ and the set membership relation $\in$ over the set positions $\mathcal{D}^w$ have their usual meaning. We introduce a stack matching predicate $\mu_I(n_1, n_2)$ which holds true when n_1 is a call position that pushes a stack symbol γ on the stack and n_2 is a matching return position which pops the same γ from the stack. Further, the time delay between the positions n_1 and n_2 is in the interval I. This ensures that the age of the topmost stack symbol at position n_2 is in I.

Consider an $\mathsf{MSO}(\Sigma, k)$ formula $\varphi(n_1, \ldots, n_p, X_1, \ldots, X_q)$ having p first order and q second order free variables. Let Var be the set of variables. Let $\mathbb{I} : Var \mapsto \mathcal{D}^w \cup 2^{\mathcal{D}^w}$ be the function which assigns values to all the free variables in φ. We denote the interpretation $\mathbb{I} = (k_1, k_2, \ldots, k_p, K_1, K_2, \ldots, K_q)$ such that it assigns

k_i to the first order free variable n_i and K_i to the second order free variable X_i in φ respectively.

The model of the formula $\varphi(n_1, \ldots, n_p, X_1, \ldots, X_q)$ is a tuple $\langle w, \mathbb{I} \rangle$ where $w \in T\Sigma^*$ is a finite timed word and $\mathbb{I}$ is an interpretation. This model is obtained by extending $T\Sigma$ with a bit vector of size $p + q$. For this purpose, we let $\Sigma_c^{p+q} = \Sigma_c \times \{0,1\}^{p+q}$, $\Sigma_r^{p+q} = \Sigma_r \times \{0,1\}^{p+q}$, and $\Sigma_l^{p+q} = \Sigma_l \times \{0,1\}^{p+q}$ be extended call, extended return and extended local alphabets respectively. Let $\Sigma^{p+q} = \Sigma_c^{p+q} \cup \Sigma_r^{p+q} \cup \Sigma_l^{p+q}$. Similarly we define $T\Sigma^{p+q} = T\Sigma \times \{0,1\}^{p+q}$. Let $w = (a_1, t_1), \ldots, (a_{|w|}, t_{|w|}) \in T\Sigma^*$ be a timed word. We encode $\mathbb{I}$ into an extended timed word $u = (\alpha_1, t_1), \ldots, (\alpha_{|w|}, t_{|w|}) \in (T\Sigma^{p+q})^*$ whose untimed alphabet set is extended to Σ^{p+q}. This encoding is done as follows.

- Both w and u have the same length.
- for each position $i \in \mathcal{D}^w$, $\alpha_i = (a_i, b_i^1, \ldots, b_i^p, c_i^1, \ldots, c_i^q) \in \Sigma^{p+q}$ such that
  - $b_i^j = 1$ iff $\mathbb{I}(n_j) = i$
  - $c_i^j = 1$ iff $i \in \mathbb{I}(X_j)$

We define the language of φ as $L(\varphi) = \{u \in (T\Sigma^{p+q})^* \mid \langle w, \mathbb{I} \rangle \models \varphi\}$.

The semantics of an $\mathsf{MSO}(\Sigma, k)$ formula in this system is given as follows.

$\langle w, \mathbb{I} \rangle \models Q_a(n)$ iff a occurs at the position $\mathbb{I}(n)$
$\langle w, \mathbb{I} \rangle \models \zeta_I^k(n)$ iff $\zeta^k(\mathbb{I}(n)) \in I$
$\langle w, \mathbb{I} \rangle \models \mu_I(n_1, n_2)$ iff $\mathbb{I}(n_1)$ is a call and $\mathbb{I}(n_2)$ is matching return and
$\qquad\qquad\qquad\qquad (t_{\mathbb{I}(n_2)} - t_{\mathbb{I}(n_1)}) \in I$
$\langle w, \mathbb{I} \rangle \models n_1 < n_2$ iff $\mathbb{I}(n_1) < \mathbb{I}(n_2)$
$\langle w, \mathbb{I} \rangle \models n \in X$ iff $\mathbb{I}(n) \in \mathbb{I}(X)$
$\langle w, \mathbb{I} \rangle \models \neg\varphi$ iff $w, \mathbb{I} \not\models \varphi$
$\langle w, \mathbb{I} \rangle \models \varphi \vee \varphi'$ iff $\langle w, \mathbb{I} \rangle \models \varphi$ or $\langle w, \mathbb{I} \rangle \models \varphi'$
$\langle w, \mathbb{I} \rangle \models \exists n\, \varphi(n)$ iff there exists an $i \in D^w$ such that $\langle w, \mathbb{I}[i/n] \rangle \models \varphi(n)$
$\langle w, \mathbb{I} \rangle \models \exists X\, \varphi(X)$ iff there exists an $S \subseteq D^w$ such that $\langle w, \mathbb{I}[S/X] \rangle \models \varphi(X)$

where $\mathbb{I}[i/n]$ denotes $\mathbb{I}(n) := i$ and $\mathbb{I}[S/X]$ denotes $\mathbb{I}(X) := S$.

Theorem 5. *L is a timed language over Σ accepted by a dtlRVPA with k as a maximum constant used in its guards iff there is an $\mathsf{MSO}(\Sigma, k)$ sentence φ that defines L.*

Let $\mathsf{MSO}^1(\Sigma, k)$ be the MSO logic obtained by removing atom $\mu_I(n_1, n_2)$ from $\mathsf{MSO}(\Sigma, k)$. One proof of the MSO^1 characterization of strict IRTA follows from Lemma 1 and the work by D'Souza and Tabareau [13]. As strict IRTA are a proper subclass of strict dtlRVPA, we get another proof of their MSO^1 characterization based on Theorem 5 and we state it as the following corollary.

Corollary 1. *L is a timed language over Σ accepted by a IRTA with k as a maximum constant used in its guards iff there is an $\mathsf{MSO}^1(\Sigma, k)$ sentence φ that defines L.*

6   Conclusion

The class of dense-timed integer reset timed automata introduced in this paper is a *perfect* subclass of timed context-free languages. The decidability of their inclusion checking paves the way for the model checking programs described as dtlRVPA against the subclass of richer timed context-free specifications. The other novelty is that their emptiness checking is PSPACE-complete which is same as that of timed automata. This is significant as timed automata cannot describe context free specifications.

References

1. Abdulla, P.A., Atig, M.F., Stenman, J.: Dense-timed pushdown automata. In: LICS, pp. 35–44 (2012)
2. Aceto, L., Laroussinie, F.: Is your model checker on time? on the complexity of model checking for timed modal logics. J. Log. Algebr. Program. **52–53**, 7–51 (2002)
3. Akshay, S., Gastin, P., Krishna, S.N.: Analyzing timed systems using tree automata. In: CONCUR, pp. 27:1–27:14 (2016)
4. Alur, R., Dill, D.: A theory of timed automata. Theor. Comput. Sci. **126**, 183–235 (1994)
5. Alur, R., Madhusudan, P.: Visibly pushdown languages. In: STOC, pp. 202–211 (2004)
6. Baier, C., Bertrand, N., Bouyer, P., Brihaye, T.: When are timed automata determinizable? In: Albers, S., Marchetti-Spaccamela, A., Matias, Y., Nikoletseas, S., Thomas, W. (eds.) ICALP 2009. LNCS, vol. 5556, pp. 43–54. Springer, Heidelberg (2009). doi:10.1007/978-3-642-02930-1_4
7. Bhave, D., Dave, V., Krishna, S.N., Phawade, R., Trivedi, A.: A logical characterization for dense-time visibly pushdown automata. In: Dediu, A.-H., Janoušek, J., Martín-Vide, C., Truthe, B. (eds.) LATA 2016. LNCS, vol. 9618, pp. 89–101. Springer, Cham (2016). doi:10.1007/978-3-319-30000-9_7
8. Bhave, D., Dave, V., Krishna, S.N., Phawade, R., Trivedi, A.: A perfect class of context-sensitive timed languages. In: Brlek, S., Reutenauer, C. (eds.) DLT 2016. LNCS, vol. 9840, pp. 38–50. Springer, Heidelberg (2016). doi:10.1007/978-3-662-53132-7_4
9. Bouajjani, A., Echahed, R., Robbana, R.: On the automatic verification of systems with continuous variables and unbounded discrete data structures. Hybrid Syst. **II**, 64–85 (1995)
10. Clemente, L., Lasota, S.: Timed pushdown automata revisited. In: LICS, pp. 738–749 (2015)
11. Dang, Z.: Binary reachability analysis of pushdown timed automata with dense clocks. In: Berry, G., Comon, H., Finkel, A. (eds.) CAV 2001. LNCS, vol. 2102, pp. 506–517. Springer, Heidelberg (2001). doi:10.1007/3-540-44585-4_48
12. Droste, M., Perevoshchikov, V.: A logical characterization of timed pushdown languages. In: Beklemishev, L.D., Musatov, D.V. (eds.) CSR 2015. LNCS, vol. 9139, pp. 189–203. Springer, Cham (2015). doi:10.1007/978-3-319-20297-6_13
13. D'Souza, D., Tabareau, N.: On timed automata with input-determined guards. In: Lakhnech, Y., Yovine, S. (eds.) FORMATS/FTRTFT -2004. LNCS, vol. 3253, pp. 68–83. Springer, Heidelberg (2004). doi:10.1007/978-3-540-30206-3_7

14. Henzinger, T.A., Majumdar, R., Prabhu, V.S.: Quantifying similarities between timed systems. In: Pettersson, P., Yi, W. (eds.) FORMATS 2005. LNCS, vol. 3829, pp. 226–241. Springer, Heidelberg (2005). doi:10.1007/11603009_18

15. Lautemann, C., Schwentick, T., Thérien, D.: Logics for context-free languages. In: Pacholski, L., Tiuryn, J. (eds.) CSL 1994. LNCS, vol. 933, pp. 205–216. Springer, Heidelberg (1995). doi:10.1007/BFb0022257

16. Li, G., Cai, X., Ogawa, M., Yuen, S.: Nested timed automata. In: Braberman, V., Fribourg, L. (eds.) FORMATS 2013. LNCS, vol. 8053, pp. 168–182. Springer, Heidelberg (2013). doi:10.1007/978-3-642-40229-6_12

17. Li, G., Ogawa, M., Yuen, S.: Nested timed automata with frozen clocks. In: Sankaranarayanan, S., Vicario, E. (eds.) FORMATS 2015. LNCS, vol. 9268, pp. 189–205. Springer, Cham (2015). doi:10.1007/978-3-319-22975-1_13

18. Manasa, L., Krishna, S.N.: Integer reset timed automata: clock reduction and determinizability. CoRR, abs/1001.1215 (2010)

19. Mohalik, A., Rajeev, C., Dixit, M.G., Ramesh, S., Suman, P.V., Pandya, P.K., Jiang, S.: Model checking based analysis of end-to-end latency in embedded, real-time systems with clock drifts. In: DAC (2008)

20. Suman, P.V., Pandya, P.K., Krishna, S.N., Manasa, L.: Timed automata with integer resets: language inclusion and expressiveness. In: Cassez, F., Jard, C. (eds.) FORMATS 2008. LNCS, vol. 5215, pp. 78–92. Springer, Heidelberg (2008). doi:10.1007/978-3-540-85778-5_7

21. Trivedi, A., Wojtczak, D.: Recursive timed automata. In: Bouajjani, A., Chin, W.-N. (eds.) ATVA 2010. LNCS, vol. 6252, pp. 306–324. Springer, Heidelberg (2010). doi:10.1007/978-3-642-15643-4_23

Space-Efficient Fragments of Higher-Order Fixpoint Logic

Florian Bruse[1,2][✉], Martin Lange[1], and Etienne Lozes[2]

[1] University of Kassel, Kassel, Germany
florian.bruse@uni-kassel.de
[2] LSV, ENS Paris-Saclay, CNRS, Cachan, France

Abstract. Higher-Order Fixpoint Logic (HFL) is a modal specification language whose expressive power reaches far beyond that of Monadic Second-Order Logic, achieved through an incorporation of a typed λ-calculus into the modal μ-calculus. Its model checking problem on finite transition systems is decidable, albeit of high complexity, namely k-EXPTIME-complete for formulas that use functions of type order at most $k > 0$. In this paper we present a fragment with a presumably easier model checking problem. We show that so-called tail-recursive formulas of type order k can be model checked in $(k - 1)$-EXPSPACE, and also give matching lower bounds. This yields generic results for the complexity of bisimulation-invariant non-regular properties, as these can typically be defined in HFL.

1 Introduction

Higher-Order Modal Fixpoint Logic (HFL) [18] is an extension of the modal μ-calculus [9] by a simply typed λ-calculus. Formulas do not only denote sets of states in labelled transition systems but also functions from such sets to sets, functions from sets to functions on sets, etc. The syntax becomes a bit more complicated because the presence of fixpoint quantifiers requires formulas to be strongly typed in order to guarantee monotonicity of the function transformers (rather than just set transformers) whose fixpoints are quantified over.

HFL is an interesting specification language for reactive systems: the ability to construct functions at arbitrary type levels gives it an enormous expressive power compared to the μ-calculus, the standard yardstick for the expressive power of bisimulation-invariant specification languages [7]. HFL has the power to express non-MSO-definable properties [11,13,18] like certain assume-guarantee properties; all context-free and even some context-sensitive reachability properties; structural properties like being a balanced tree, being bisimilar to a word, etc. As a bisimulation-invariant fixpoint logic, HFL is essentially an extremely powerful logic for specifying complex reachability properties.

F. Bruse—This work was supported by a fellowship within the FITweltweit programme of the German Academic Exchange Service (DAAD).

M. Hague and I. Potapov (Eds.): RP 2017, LNCS 10506, pp. 26–41, 2017.
DOI: 10.1007/978-3-319-67089-8_3

There is a natural hierarchy of fragments HFL^k formed by the maximal function order k of types used in a formula where HFL^0 equals the modal μ-calculus. The aforementioned examples are all expressible in fragments of low order, namely in HFL^1 or in exceptional cases only HFL^2.

Type order is a major factor for model-theoretic and computational properties of HFL. It is known that HFL^{k+1} is strictly more expressive than HFL^k. The case of $k = 0$ is reasonably simple since the expressive power of the modal μ-calculus, i.e. HFL^0 is quite well understood, including examples of properties that are known not to be expressible in it. The aforementioned tree property of being balanced is such an example [4]. For $k > 0$ this follows from considerations in computational complexity: model checking HFL^k is k-EXPTIME-complete [3] and this already holds for the data complexity. I.e. each HFL^k, $k \geq 1$, contains formulas which express some decision problem that is hard for deterministic k-fold exponential time. Expressive strictness of the type order hierarchy is then a direct consequence of the time hierarchy theorem [6] which particularly shows that k-EXPTIME $\subsetneq (k+1)$-EXPTIME.

Here we study the complexity of HFL model checking w.r.t. space usage. We identify a syntactical criterion on formulas – *tail-recursion* – which causes space-efficiency in a relative sense. It has been developed for PHFL, a polyadic extension of HFL, in the context of descriptive complexity. Extending Otto's result showing that a polyadic version of the modal μ-calculus [1] captures the bisimulation-invariant fragment of polynomial time [14], $PHFL^0 \equiv P/\sim$ in short, it was shown that $PHFL^1 \equiv EXPTIME/\sim$ [12], i.e. polyadic HFL formulas of function order at most 1 express exactly the bisimulation-invariant graph properties that can be evaluated in deterministic exponential time. Tail-recursion restricts the allowed combinations of fixpoint types (least or greatest), modality types (existential or universal), Boolean operators (disjunctions and conjunctions) and nestings of function applications. Its name is derived from the fact that a standard top-down evaluation algorithm working on states of a transition system and formulas can be implemented tail-recursively and, hence, intuitively in a rather space-efficient way. In the context of descriptive complexity, it was shown that the tail-recursive fragment of $PHFL^1$ captures polynomial space modulo bisimilarity, $PHFL^1_{\mathsf{tail}} \equiv PSPACE/\sim$ [12].

These results can be seen as an indication that tail-recursion is indeed a synonym for space-efficiency. In this paper we show that this is not restricted to order 1. We prove that the model checking problem for the tail-recursive fragment of HFL^{k+1} is k-EXPSPACE-complete. This already holds for the data complexity which yields a strict hierarchy of expressive power within HFL_{tail}, as a consequence of the space hierarchy theorem [16].

In Sect. 2 we recall HFL and apply the concept of tail-recursion, originally developed for a polyadic extension, to this monadic logic. In Sect. 3 we present upper bounds; matching lower bounds are presented in Sect. 4.

2   Higher-Order Fixpoint Logic

Labeled Transition Systems. Fix a set $\mathcal{P} = \{p, q, \dots\}$ of atomic propositions and a set $\mathcal{A} = \{a, b, \dots\}$ of actions. A labeled transition system (LTS) is a tuple $\mathcal{T} = (\mathcal{S}, \{\overset{a}{\rightarrow}\}_{a \in \mathcal{A}}, \ell)$, where $\mathcal{S}$ is a set of states, $\overset{a}{\rightarrow}$ is a binary relation for each $a \in \mathcal{A}$ and $\ell \colon \mathcal{S} \to \mathfrak{P}(\mathcal{P})$ is a function assigning, to each state, the set of propositions that are satisfied in it. We write $s \overset{a}{\rightarrow} t$ to denote that $(s, t) \in \overset{a}{\rightarrow}$.

Types. The semantics of HFL is defined via complete function lattices over a transition system. In order to guarantee monotonicity (and other well-formedness conditions), formulas representing functions need to be strongly typed according to a simple type system. It defines types inductively from a ground type via function forming: the set of HFL-types is given by the grammar

$$\tau \ ::= \ \bullet \ | \ \tau^v \to \tau$$

where $v \in \{+, -, 0\}$ is called a variance. It indicates whether a function uses its argument in a monotone, antitone or arbitrary way.

The order $\mathsf{ord}(\tau)$ of a type τ is defined inductively as $\mathsf{ord}(\bullet) = 0$, and $\mathsf{ord}(\sigma \to \tau) = \max(1 + \mathsf{ord}(\sigma), \mathsf{ord}(\tau))$.

The function type constructor $\to$ is right-associative. Thus, every type is of the form $\tau_1^{v_1} \to \dots \tau_m^{v_m} \to \bullet$.

Formulas. Let $\mathcal{P}$ and $\mathcal{A}$ be as above. Additionally, let $\mathcal{V}_\lambda = \{x, y, \dots\}$ and $\mathcal{V}_{\mathsf{fp}} = \{X, Y, \dots\}$ be two sets of variables. We only distinguish them in order to increase readability of formulas, referring to $\mathcal{V}_\lambda$ as λ -*variables* and $\mathcal{V}_{\mathsf{fp}}$ as *fixpoint variables*. The set of (possibly non-well-formed) HFL formulas is then given by the grammar

$$\varphi ::= p \mid \varphi \vee \varphi \mid \varphi \wedge \varphi \mid \neg\varphi \mid \langle a \rangle \varphi \mid [a]\varphi \mid x \mid \lambda(x^v \colon \tau).\ \varphi \mid \varphi\,\varphi$$
$$\mid X \mid \mu(X \colon \tau).\ \varphi \mid \nu(X \colon \tau).\ \varphi$$

where $p \in \mathcal{P}, a \in \mathcal{A}, x \in \mathcal{V}_\lambda, X \in \mathcal{V}_{\mathsf{fp}}, \tau$ is an HFL-type and v is a variance. Derived connectives such as $\Rightarrow, \Leftrightarrow, \top, \bot$ can be added in the usual way, but we consider $\wedge, [a]$ and ν to be built-in operators instead of derived connectives. The set of subformulas $\mathsf{sub}(\varphi)$ of a formula φ is defined in the usual way. Note that fixpoint variables need no decoration by a variance since they can only occur in a monotonic fashion.

The intuition for the operators not present in the modal μ-calculus is as follows: $\lambda(x \colon \tau).\ \varphi$ defines a function that consumes an argument x of type τ and returns what φ evaluates to, x returns the value of λ-variable x, and $\varphi\,\psi$ applies ψ as an argument to the function φ. If a formula consists of several consecutive λ abstractions, we compress the argument display in favor of readability. For example, $\lambda(x \colon \tau).\ \lambda(y \colon \sigma).\ \psi$ becomes $\lambda(x \colon \tau, y \colon \sigma).\ \psi$ or even $\lambda(x, y \colon \tau).\ \psi$ if $\tau = \sigma$.

$$\frac{}{\Gamma \vdash p : \bullet} \qquad \frac{\Gamma \vdash \varphi : \bullet}{\Gamma \vdash \langle a \rangle \varphi : \bullet} \qquad \frac{\Gamma \vdash \varphi : \bullet}{\Gamma \vdash [a] \varphi : \bullet} \qquad \frac{\overline{\Gamma} \vdash \varphi : \bullet}{\Gamma \vdash \neg \varphi : \bullet}$$

$$\frac{\Gamma \vdash \varphi : \bullet \qquad \Gamma \vdash \psi : \bullet}{\Gamma \vdash \varphi \vee \psi : \bullet} \qquad \frac{\Gamma \vdash \varphi : \bullet \qquad \Gamma \vdash \psi : \bullet}{\Gamma \vdash \varphi \wedge \psi : \bullet} \qquad \frac{v \in \{+, 0\}}{\Gamma, x^v : \tau \vdash x : \tau}$$

$$\frac{}{\Gamma, X^+ : \tau \vdash X : \tau} \qquad \frac{\Gamma, x^v : \sigma \vdash \varphi : \tau}{\Gamma \vdash \lambda(x^v : \sigma).\, \varphi : \sigma^v \to \tau} \qquad \frac{\Gamma, X^+ : \tau \vdash \varphi : \tau}{\Gamma \vdash \mu(X : \tau).\, \varphi : \tau}$$

$$\frac{\Gamma, X^+ : \tau \vdash \varphi : \tau}{\Gamma \vdash \nu(X : \tau).\, \varphi : \tau} \qquad \frac{\Gamma \vdash \varphi : \sigma^+ \to \tau \qquad \Gamma \vdash \psi : \sigma}{\Gamma \vdash \varphi\, \psi : \tau}$$

$$\frac{\Gamma \vdash \varphi : \sigma^- \to \tau \qquad \overline{\Gamma} \vdash \psi : \sigma}{\Gamma \vdash \varphi\, \psi : \tau} \qquad \frac{\Gamma \vdash \varphi : \sigma^0 \to \tau \qquad \Gamma \vdash \psi : \sigma \qquad \overline{\Gamma} \vdash \psi : \sigma}{\Gamma \vdash \varphi\, \psi : \tau}$$

Fig. 1. The HFL typing system

A sequence of the form $X_1^{v_1} : \tau_1, \ldots, X_n^{v_n} : \tau_n, x_1^{v_1'} : \tau_1', \ldots, x_j^{v_j'} : \tau_j'$ where the X_i are fixpoint variables, the x_j are λ-variables, the τ_i, τ_j' are types and the v_i, v_j' are variances, is called a *context*. We assume that each fixpoint variable and each λ-variable occurs only once per context. The context $\overline{\Gamma}$ is obtained from Γ by replacing all typing hypotheses of the form $X^+ : \tau$ by $X^- : \tau$ and vice versa, and doing the same for λ-variables. An HFL-formula φ has type τ in context Γ if $\Gamma \vdash \varphi : \tau$ can be derived via the typing rules in Fig. 1. A formula φ is *well-formed* if $\Gamma \vdash \varphi : \tau$ can be derived for some Γ and τ. Note that, while fixpoint variables may only be used in a monotonic fashion, contexts with fixpoint variables of negative variance are still necessary to type formulas of the form $\mu(X : \bullet).\, \neg\neg X$. In some examples, we may sometimes omit type and/or variance anotations.

Moreover, we also assume that in a well-formed formula φ, each fixpoint variable $X \in \mathcal{V}_{\mathsf{fp}}$ is bound at most once, i.e., there is at most one subformula of the form $\mu(X : \tau).\, \psi$ or $\nu(X : \tau).\, \psi$. Then there is a function $\mathsf{fp} \colon \mathcal{V}_{\mathsf{fp}} \to \mathsf{sub}(\varphi)$ such that $\mathsf{fp}(X)$ is the unique subformula $\sigma(X : \tau).\, \varphi'$ with $\sigma \in \{\mu, \nu\}$. Note that it is possible to order the fixpoints in such a formula as $X_1, \ldots, X_n$ such that $\mathsf{fp}(X_i) \notin \mathsf{sub}(\mathsf{fp}(X_j))$ for $j > i$.

The *order* of a formula φ is the maximal type order k of any type used in a proof of $\emptyset \vdash \varphi \colon \bullet$. With HFL^k we denote the set of all well-formed HFL formulas of ground type whose order is at most k. In particular, HFL^0 is the modal μ-calculus $\mathcal{L}_\mu$. The notion of order of a formula can straightforwardly be applied to formulas which are not of ground type $\bullet$. We will therefore also speak of the order of some arbitrary subformula of an HFL formula.

Semantics. Given an LTS $\mathcal{T}$, each HFL type τ induces a complete lattice $[\![\tau]\!]^{\mathcal{T}}$ starting with the usual powerset lattice of its state space, and then lifting this to lattices of functions of higher order. When the underlying LTS is clear from the context we only write $[\![\tau]\!]$ rather than $[\![\tau]\!]^{\mathcal{T}}$. We also identify a lattice with its underlying set and write $f \in [\![\tau]\!]$ for instance. These lattices are then inductively defined as follows:

- $[\![\bullet]\!]^{\mathcal{T}}$ is the lattice $\mathfrak{P}(\mathcal{S})$ ordered by the inclusion relation $\subseteq$,
- $[\![\sigma^v \to \tau]\!]^{\mathcal{T}}$ is the lattice whose domain is the set of all (if $v = 0$), resp. monotone (if $v = +$), resp. antitone (if $v = -$) functions of type $[\![\sigma]\!]^{\mathcal{T}} \to [\![\tau]\!]^{\mathcal{T}}$ ordered pointwise, i.e. $f \sqsubseteq_{\sigma^v \to \tau} g$ iff $f(x) \sqsubseteq_\tau g(x)$ for all $x \in [\![\sigma]\!]^{\mathcal{T}}$.

Given a context Γ, an *environment* η that respects Γ is a partial map from $\mathcal{V}_\lambda \cup \mathcal{V}_{\mathsf{fp}}$ such that $\eta(x) \in [\![\tau]\!]$ if $\Gamma \vdash x : \tau$ and $\eta(X) \in [\![\tau']\!]$ if $\Gamma \vdash x : \tau'$. From now on, all environments respect the context in question. The update $\eta[X \mapsto f]$ is defined in the usual way as $\eta[X \mapsto f](x) = \eta(x)$, $\eta[X \mapsto f](Y) = \eta(Y)$ if $Y \neq X$ and $\eta(Y) = f$ if $X = Y$. Updates for λ-variables are defined analogously.

$$[\![\Gamma \vdash p : \bullet]\!]_\eta = \{s \in \mathcal{S} \mid P \in \ell(s)\}$$

$$[\![\Gamma \vdash \varphi \vee \psi : \bullet]\!]_\eta = [\![\Gamma \vdash \varphi : \bullet]\!]_\eta \cup [\![\Gamma \vdash \psi : \bullet]\!]_\eta$$

$$[\![\Gamma \vdash \varphi \wedge \psi : \bullet]\!]_\eta = [\![\Gamma \vdash \varphi : \bullet]\!]_\eta \cap [\![\Gamma \vdash \psi : \bullet]\!]_\eta$$

$$[\![\Gamma \vdash \langle a \rangle \varphi : \bullet]\!]_\eta = \{s \in \mathcal{S} \mid \text{ex. } t \in [\![\Gamma \vdash \varphi : \bullet]\!]_\eta \text{ s.t. } s \xrightarrow{a} t\}$$

$$[\![\Gamma \vdash [a]\varphi : \bullet]\!]_\eta = \{s \in \mathcal{S} \mid \text{f.a. } t \in \mathcal{S} \text{ with } s \xrightarrow{a} t \text{ holds } t \in [\![\Gamma \vdash \varphi : \bullet]\!]_\eta\}$$

$$[\![\Gamma \vdash x : \tau]\!]_\eta = \eta(x)$$

$$[\![\Gamma \vdash X : \tau]\!]_\eta = \eta(X)$$

$$[\![\Gamma \vdash \lambda(x^v : \sigma) : \sigma^v \to \tau]\!]_\eta = f \in [\![\sigma^v \to \tau]\!] \text{ s.t. f.a. } y \in [\![\sigma]\!].\ f(y)$$
$$= [\![\Gamma, x^v : \sigma \vdash \varphi : \tau]\!]_{\eta[x \mapsto y]}$$

$$[\![\Gamma \vdash \varphi\psi : \tau]\!]_\eta = [\![\Gamma \vdash \varphi : \sigma^v \to \sigma]\!]_\eta ([\![\Gamma \vdash \psi : \sigma]\!]_\eta)$$

$$[\![\Gamma \vdash \mu(X : \tau).\varphi : \tau]\!]_\eta = \bigsqcap \{d \in [\![\tau]\!] \mid [\![\Gamma, X : \tau^+ \vdash \varphi : \tau]\!]_{\eta[X \mapsto d]} \sqsubseteq_\tau d\}$$

$$[\![\Gamma \vdash \nu(X : \tau).\varphi : \tau]\!]_\eta = \bigsqcup \{d \in [\![\tau]\!] \mid d \sqsubseteq_\tau [\![\Gamma, X : \tau^+ \vdash \varphi : \tau]\!]_{\eta[X \mapsto d]}\}$$

Fig. 2. Semantics of HFL

The semantics of an HFL formula is defined inductively as per Fig. 2. We write $\mathcal{T}, s \models_\eta \varphi : \tau$ if $s \in [\![\Gamma \vdash \varphi : \tau]\!]_\eta$ for suitable Γ and abbreviate the special case with a closed formula of ground type writing $\mathcal{T}, s \models \varphi$ instead of $\mathcal{T}, s \models_\emptyset \varphi : \bullet$.

The Tail-Recursive Fragment. In general, a tail-recursive function is one that is never called recursively in an intermediate step of the evaluation of its body, either for evaluating a condition on branching, or for evaluating an argument of a function call. Tail-recursive functions are known to be more space-efficient in general as they do not require a call stack for their evaluation.

The notion of tail-recursion has been transposed to the framework of higher-order fixpoint logics, originally for a polyadic extension of HFL [12]. The adaptation to HFL is straight-forward, presented in the following. Intuitively, tail-recursion restricts the syntax of the formulas such that fixpoint variables do not occur freely under the operators $\wedge$ and $[a]$, nor in an operand position.

Definition 1. *An HFL formula φ is* tail-recursive *if the statement* $\mathrm{tail}(\varphi, \emptyset)$ *can be derived via the rules in Fig. 3.* $\mathrm{HFL}^k_{\mathrm{tail}}$ *consists of all tail-recursive formulas in* HFL^k.

$$
\frac{}{\mathrm{tail}(p, \bar{X})} \qquad \frac{}{\mathrm{tail}(x, \bar{X})} \qquad \frac{X \in \bar{X}}{\mathrm{tail}(X, \bar{X})} \qquad \frac{\mathrm{tail}(\varphi, \emptyset)}{\mathrm{tail}(\neg\varphi, \bar{X})} \qquad \frac{\mathrm{tail}(\varphi, \bar{X}) \quad \mathrm{tail}(\psi, \bar{X})}{\mathrm{tail}(\varphi \vee \psi, \bar{X})}
$$

$$
\frac{\mathrm{tail}(\varphi, \emptyset) \quad \mathrm{tail}(\psi, \bar{X})}{\mathrm{tail}(\varphi \wedge \psi, \bar{X})} \qquad \frac{\mathrm{tail}(\varphi, \bar{X})}{\mathrm{tail}(\langle a \rangle \varphi, \bar{X})} \qquad \frac{\mathrm{tail}(\varphi, \emptyset)}{\mathrm{tail}([a]\varphi, \bar{X})} \qquad \frac{\mathrm{tail}(\varphi, \bar{X}) \quad \mathrm{tail}(\psi, \emptyset)}{\mathrm{tail}(\varphi \, \psi, \bar{X})}
$$

$$
\frac{\mathrm{tail}(\varphi, \bar{X})}{\mathrm{tail}(\lambda(x : \tau^v).\varphi, \bar{X})} \qquad \frac{\mathrm{tail}(\varphi, \bar{X} \cup \{Z\})}{\mathrm{tail}(\mu(Z : \tau).\varphi, \bar{X})} \qquad \frac{\mathrm{tail}(\varphi, \bar{X} \cup \{Z\})}{\mathrm{tail}(\nu(Z : \tau).\varphi, \bar{X})}
$$

Fig. 3. Derivation rules for establishing tail-recursiveness. The set $\bar{X}$ denotes the set of allowed free fixpoint variables of the formula in question.

Note that these rules do not treat conjunctions symmetrically. For instance, $\mu X.p \vee (q \wedge \langle - \rangle X)$ – the straight-forward translation of the CTL reachability property $\mathbf{E}(q \, \mathbf{U} \, p)$ – is tail-recursive, but $\mu X.p \vee (\langle - \rangle X \wedge q)$ is *not* tail-recursive because the rule for $\wedge$ in Fig. 3 only allows recursive calls to fixpoint variables via the right conjunct of a conjunction. Of course, adding one more rule to Fig. 3, one could make $\mathrm{HFL}_{\mathrm{tail}}$ closed under commutations of $\wedge$ operands, the only important point is that all of the free recursive variables occur on at most one side of each $\wedge$.

Example 2. The HFL^1 formula

$$
\bigl(\nu F.\lambda x.\lambda y.(x \Rightarrow y) \wedge (F \, \langle a \rangle x \, \langle b \rangle y)\bigr) \top \langle b \rangle \top
$$

has been introduced for expressing a form of assume-guarantee property [18]. This formula is tail-recursive, as one can easily check.

The property of being a balanced tree can also be formalised by a tail-recursive HFL^1 formula: $\bigl(\mu F.\lambda x.[-]\bot \vee (F \, [-]x)\bigr) \bot$.

In the next section, we will see that these properties and any other expressible in $\mathrm{HFL}^1_{\mathrm{tail}}$ can be checked in polynomial space, thus improving a known exponential time upper bound [2,3].

Example 3. Consider reachability properties of the form "there is a maximal path labelled with a word from L" where $L \subseteq \Sigma^*$ is some formal language. For context-free languages the logic formalising such properties is Propositional Dynamic Logic of Context-Free Programs [5]. It can be model checked in polynomial time [10]. However, formal-language constrained reachability is not restricted to context-free languages only. Consider the reachability problem above for $L = \{a^n b^n c^n \mid n \geq 1\}$. It can be formalised by the HFL^2 formula

$$
\bigl(\mu F.\lambda f.\lambda g.\lambda h.\lambda x.f(g(h(x))) \vee (F \, (\lambda x.f \, \langle a \rangle x) \, (\lambda x.g \, \langle b \rangle x) \, (\lambda x.h \, \langle c \rangle x))\bigr)
$$
$$
id \; id \; id \; [-]\bot
$$

with type $x : \bullet$; $f, g, h : \tau_1 := \bullet^+ \to \bullet$ and $F : \tau_1^+ \to \tau_1^+ \to \tau_1^+ \to \bullet^+ \to \bullet$. Again, one can check that it is tail-recursive. Since it is of order 2, Theorem 5 yields that the corresponding reachability problem can be checked using exponential space.

3   Upper Bounds in the Exponential Space Hierarchy

Consider an HFL fixpoint formula of the form $\psi = \sigma(X : \tau).\varphi$ and its finite approximants defined via

$$X^0 := \begin{cases} \bot & , \text{ if } \sigma = \mu, \\ \top & , \text{ otherwise} \end{cases} \quad \text{and} \quad X^{i+1} := \varphi[X^i/X] .$$

where $\varphi[X^i/X]$ denotes the simultaneous replacement of every free occurrence of X by X^i in φ.

It is known that over a finite LTS $\mathcal{T} = (\mathcal{S}, \{\xrightarrow{a}\}, \ell)$, ψ is equivalent to X^m, where m is the height $\mathsf{ht}(\tau)$ of the lattice of τ. Generally, $\mathsf{ht}(\tau)$ is k-fold exponential in the size of $|\mathcal{S}|$ for $k = ord(\tau)$ [3]. Note that a k-fold exponentially large number can be represented by $(k-1)$-fold exponentially many bits.

For an $\mathsf{HFL}^k_{\mathsf{tail}}$ formula φ, we define its *recursion depth* $\mathsf{rd}(\varphi)$:

$$\mathsf{rd}(p) = \mathsf{rd}(X) := 0$$
$$\mathsf{rd}(\varphi_1 \vee \varphi_2) := \max(\mathsf{rd}(\varphi_1), \mathsf{rd}(\varphi_2))$$
$$\mathsf{rd}(\varphi_1 \wedge \varphi_2) := \max(\mathsf{rd}(\varphi_2), 1 + \mathsf{rd}(\varphi_1))$$
$$\mathsf{rd}(\varphi_1 \, \varphi_2) := \max(\mathsf{rd}(\varphi_1, 1 + \mathsf{rd}(\varphi_2))$$
$$\mathsf{rd}(\langle a \rangle \varphi) = \mathsf{rd}(\lambda X.\varphi) = \mathsf{rd}(\mu X.\varphi) = \mathsf{rd}(\nu X.\varphi) := \mathsf{rd}(\varphi)$$
$$\mathsf{rd}(\neg \varphi) = \mathsf{rd}([a]\varphi) := 1 + \mathsf{rd}(\varphi)$$

The recursion depth of a formula measures the number of times that a top-down nondeterministic local model-checking procedure has to maintain calling contexts. For example, when verifying whether a state is a model of a disjunction, it is sufficient to nondeterministically guess a disjunct and continue with it; the other disjunct is irrelevant. For a conjunction, the procedure also descends into one of the conjuncts first, but has to remember, e.g., the environment at the conjunction itself in case the procedure has to backtrack. Note that the recursion depth of a formula is linear in its size.

We combine the bounded number of calling contexts and the above unfolding property into a model-checking algorithm that avoids the enumeration of full function tables for fixpoint definitions of the highest order by only evaluating it at arguments actually occurring in the formula. Unfolding a fixpoint expression is results in the evaluation of the same fixpoint at different arguments, and the unfolding property allows to give an upper bound on the number of unfoldings needed. Tail-recursiveness ensures that this procedure proceeds in a mostly linear fashion, since the number of calling contexts that need to maintained at any given moment during the evaluation is bounded by the recursion depth of the formula in question.

For the remainder we fix a formula $\psi \in \mathrm{HFL}_{\mathsf{tail}}^k$ and an LTS $\mathcal{T} = (\mathcal{S}, \{\xrightarrow{a}\}, \ell)$. We present two mutually recursive functions **check** and **buildFT**. The function **check**$(s, \varphi, (f_1, \ldots, f_n), \eta, \mathsf{cnt})$ consumes a state $s \in \mathcal{S}$, a subformula φ of ψ, a list of function tables, an environment η and a partial function cnt from $\mathcal{V}_{\mathsf{fp}}$ to $\mathbb{N}$ and checks whether $s \models_\eta (\cdots (\varphi\, f_n) \cdots f_1)$ if all free fixpoint variables X of φ are replaced by $X^{\mathsf{cnt}(X)}$ in a suitable order. The function **buildFT**(φ, η) consumes a subformula φ of ψ and an environment η and builds the complete function table of φ with respect to η, i.e., computes $[\![\varphi]\!]_\eta$.

The definition of **check**$(s, \varphi, (f_1, \ldots, f_n), \eta, \mathsf{cnt})$ depends on the form of φ:

- If φ is an atomic formula, return true if $s \models \varphi$ and false otherwise.
- If $\varphi = \varphi_1 \vee \varphi_2$, guess $i \in \{1, 2\}$ and return **check**$(s, \varphi_i, (f_1, \ldots, f_n), \eta, \mathsf{cnt})$.
- If $\varphi = \varphi_1 \wedge \varphi_2$, note that $\mathsf{rd}(\varphi_1) < \mathsf{rd}(\varphi)$ and that φ_1 has no free fixpoint variables. Return false if **check**$(s, \varphi_1, (f_1, \ldots, f_n), \eta, \emptyset)$ returns false. Otherwise, return **check**$(s, \varphi_2, (f_1, \ldots, f_n), \eta, \mathsf{cnt})$.
- If $\varphi = \langle a \rangle \varphi'$, guess t with $s \xrightarrow{a} t$ and return **check**$(t, \varphi', (f_1, \ldots, f_n), \eta, \mathsf{cnt})$.
- If $\varphi = [a]\varphi'$, note that $\mathsf{rd}(\varphi') < \mathsf{rd}(\varphi)$ and that φ' has no free fixpoint variables. Iterate over all t with $s \xrightarrow{a} t$. If **check**$(t, \varphi', (f_1, \ldots, f_n), \eta, \emptyset)$ returns false for at least one such t, return false. Otherwise, return true.
- If $\varphi = \neg\varphi'$, note that $\mathsf{rd}(\varphi') < \mathsf{rd}(\varphi)$ and that φ' has no free fixpoint variables. If **check**$(s, \varphi', (f_1, \ldots, f_n), \eta, \emptyset)$ returns true, return false and vice versa.
- If $\varphi = \varphi' \, \varphi''$, note that $\mathsf{rd}(\varphi'') < \mathsf{rd}(\varphi)$ and that φ'' has no free fixpoint variables. Compute $f_{n+1} = $ **buildFT**(φ'', η) and return **check**$(s, \varphi', (f_1, \ldots, f_n, f_{n+1}), \eta, \mathsf{cnt})$.
- If $\varphi = x$, return true if $s \in (\cdots (\eta(x)\, f_n) \cdots f_1)$, return false otherwise.
- If $\varphi = \lambda x.\varphi'$, return **check**$(s, \varphi', (f_1, \ldots, f_{n-1}), \eta[x \mapsto f_n], \mathsf{cnt})$.
- If $\varphi = \mu(X : \tau).\varphi'$, return **check**$(s, \varphi', (f_1, \ldots, f_n), \eta, \mathsf{cnt}[X \mapsto \mathsf{ht}(\tau)])$.
- If $\varphi = \nu(X : \tau).\varphi'$, return **check**$(s, \varphi', (f_1, \ldots, f_n), \eta, \mathsf{cnt}[X \mapsto \mathsf{ht}(\tau)])$.
- If $\varphi = X$, return false if $\mathsf{cnt}(X) = 0$ and X is a least fixpoint variable, return true if $\mathsf{cnt}(X) = 0$ and X is a greatest fixpoint variable, otherwise, return **check**$(s, \mathsf{fp}(X), (f_1, \ldots, f_n), \eta, \mathsf{cnt}')$, where $\mathsf{cnt}'(Y) = \mathsf{cnt}(Y)$ if $Y \neq X$ and $\mathsf{cnt}'(X) = \mathsf{cnt}(X) - 1$.

The definition of **buildFT**(φ, η) is rather simple: If $\varphi : \tau_n \to \cdots \to \tau_1 \to \bullet$, iterate over all $s \in \mathcal{S}$ and all $(f_n, \ldots, f_1) \in [\![\tau_n]\!] \times \cdots \times [\![\tau_1]\!]$ and call **check**$(s, \varphi, (f_1, \ldots, f_n), \eta, \emptyset)$ for each combination. This will yield the function table $[\![\varphi]\!]_\eta$ via $[\![\varphi]\!]_\eta = \{f \in [\![\tau_n \to \cdots \to \tau_1 \to \bullet]\!] \mid (\cdots (f\, f_n) \cdots f_1) = \{s \in \mathcal{S} \mid$ **check**$(s, \varphi, (f_1, \ldots, f_n), \eta, \emptyset) = \mathsf{true}\}\}$.

Theorem 4. *Let* $\psi \in \mathrm{HFL}_{\mathsf{tail}}$. *Then* **check**$(s, \psi, \epsilon, \emptyset, \emptyset)$ *returns* true *iff* $\mathcal{T}, s \models \psi$.

Proof (Sketch). Fix an order of the fixpoint variables of ψ as $X_1, \ldots, X_m$ such that $\mathsf{fp}(X_i) \notin \mathsf{sub}(\mathsf{fp}(X_j))$ if $j > i$. Note that this also orders the possible values of cnt by ordering them lexicographically and assuming that undefined values are larger than $\mathsf{ht}(\tau)$ for any τ appearing in ψ.

Consider a subformula φ of ψ. Given a partial map cnt made total as in the previous paragraph, we write φ^{cnt} to denote $\varphi[X_1^{\mathsf{cnt}(X_1)}/X_1, \ldots, X_n^{\mathsf{cnt}(X_n)}/X_n]$, i.e., the result of simultaneously replacing free fixpoint variables of φ by their approximants as per cnt such that none of them occur free anymore.

In fact, $\mathbf{check}(s, \varphi, (f_1, \ldots, f_n), \eta, \mathsf{cnt})$ returns true iff $s \in [\![\varphi^{\mathsf{cnt}}]\!]_\eta\, f_n \cdots f_1$ assuming that $\mathbf{buildFT}(\varphi, \eta)$ computes $[\![\varphi]\!]_\eta$. It is easy to see that the statement in the theorem follows from this. The proof itself is a routine induction over the syntax of ψ to show that the above invariant is maintained. In each step, the procedure either passes to a proper subformula and maintains the value of cnt and recursion depth, or, in case of fixpoint unfoldings, properly decreases cnt but keeps recursion depth, or, in case of calls that are not tail-recursive, passes to a formula with properly reduced recursion depth. Moreover, in the case of function application, the call to $\mathbf{buildFT}$ will result in calls to $\mathbf{check}$ with properly reduced recursion depth, and $\mathbf{buildFT}$ just computes a tabular representation of the HFL semantics. Hence, the procedure eventually halts and works correctly. □

Theorem 5. *The model checking problem for* $\mathrm{HFL}_{\mathsf{tail}}^{k+1}$ *is in k-EXPSPACE.*

Proof. By Savitch's Theorem [15] and Theorem 4, it suffices to show that the nondeterministic procedure $\mathbf{check}$ can be implemented to use at most k-fold exponential space for formulas in $\mathrm{HFL}_{\mathsf{tail}}^{k+1}$.

The information required to evaluate $\mathbf{check}(s, \varphi, (f_1, \ldots, f_n), \eta, \mathsf{cnt})$ takes k-fold exponential space: references to a state and a subformula take linear space, each of the function tables $f_1, \ldots, f_n$ appears in operand position and, hence, is a function of order at most k, which takes k-fold exponential space. An environment is just a partial map from $\mathcal{V}_\lambda$ to more function tables, also of order at most k. Finally, cnt stores $|\mathcal{V}_{\mathsf{fp}}|$ many numbers whose values are bounded by an $(k+1)$-fold exponential. Hence, they can be represented as k-fold exponentially long bit strings.

During evaluation, $\mathbf{check}$ operates in a tail-recursive fashion for most operators, which means that no stack has to be maintained and the space needed is restricted to what is described in the previous paragraph. A calling context (which is just an instance of $\mathbf{check}$ as described above, with an added logarithmically sized counter in case of $[a]\varphi$) has to be preserved only at the steps where the recursion depth decreases. In the case of negation, it is not necessary to maintain the complete calling context. Instead, the nondeterministic procedure for the negated subformula is called and the return value is inverted. By Savitch's Theorem, the procedure can actually be implemented to run deterministically with the same space requirements, and, hence, is safe to call in a nondeterministic procedure.

Since the recursion depth of an $\mathrm{HFL}_{\mathsf{tail}}^k$-formula is linear in the size of the formula, only linearly many such calling contexts have to be stored at any given point during the evaluation, which does not exceed nondeterministic k-fold exponential space. Moreover, Savitch's Theorem has to be applied only linearly often on any computation path. □

Note that occurrences of negation do not lead to proper backtracking to a calling context, but rather mark an invocation of Savitch's Theorem. Hence, the definition of recursion depth could be changed to not increase at negation. We chose to include applications of Savitch's Theorem into the definition of recursion depth for reasons of clarity.

4   Matching Lower Bounds

A typical k-EXPSPACE-complete problem (for $k \geq 0$) is the order-k corridor tiling problem [17]: A tiling system is of the form $\mathcal{K} = (T, H, V, t_I, t_\square, t_F)$ where T is a finite set of tile types, $H, V \subseteq T \times T$ are the so-called horizontal and vertical matching relations, and $t_I, t_\square, t_F \in T$ are three designated tiles called initial, blank and final.

Let $2_0^n = n$ and $2_{k+1}^n = 2^{2_k^n}$. The *order-k corridor tiling problem* is the following: given a tiling system $\mathcal{K}$ as above and a natural number n encoded unarily, decide whether or not there is some m and a sequence $\rho_0, \ldots, \rho_{m-1}$ of words over the alphabet T, with $|\rho_i| = 2_k^n$ for all $i \in \{0, \ldots, m-1\}$, and such that the following four conditions hold. We write $\rho(j)$ for the j-th letter of the word ρ, beginning with $j = 0$.

- $\rho_0 = t_I t_\square \ldots t_\square$
- For each $i = 0, \ldots, m-1$ and $j = 0, \ldots, 2_k^n - 2$ we have $(\rho_i(j), \rho_i(j+1)) \in H$.
- For each $i = 0, \ldots, m-2$ and $j = 0, \ldots, 2_k^n - 1$ we have $(\rho_i(j), \rho_{i+1}(j)) \in V$.
- $\rho_{m-1}(0) = t_F$

Such a sequence of words is also called a *solution* to the order-k corridor tiling problem on input $\mathcal{K}$ and n. The i-th word in this sequence is also called the *i-th row*.

Proposition 6 ([17]). *For each $k \geq 0$, the order-k corridor tiling problem is k-EXPSPACE-hard.*

In the following we construct a polynomial reduction from the order-k corridor tiling problem to the model checking problem for $\mathrm{HFL}_{\mathrm{tail}}^{k+1}$. Fix a tiling system $\mathcal{K} = (T, H, V, t_I, t_F)$ and an $n \geq 1$. W.l.o.g. we assume $|T| \leq n$, and we fix an enumeration $T = \{t_0, \ldots, t_{|T|-1}\}$ of the tiles such that $t_0 = t_I$, $t_{|T|-2} = t_\square$, and $t_{|T|-1} = t_F$.

We define the transition system $\mathcal{T}_{\mathcal{K},n} = (\mathcal{S}, \{\overset{a}{\longrightarrow}\}_{a \in \mathcal{A}}, \ell)$ as follows:

- $\mathcal{S} = \{0, \ldots, n-1\}$,
- $\mathcal{A} = \{\mathsf{h}, \mathsf{v}, \mathsf{e}, \mathsf{u}, \mathsf{d}\}$ with $\overset{\mathsf{h}}{\longrightarrow} = \{(i, j) \mid (t_i, t_j) \in H\}$ (for "horizontal"), $\overset{\mathsf{v}}{\longrightarrow} = \{(i, j) \mid (t_i, t_j) \in V\}$ (for "vertical"), $\overset{\mathsf{e}}{\longrightarrow} = \{0, \ldots, n-1\} \times \{0, \ldots, n-1\}$ (for "everywhere"), $\overset{\mathsf{u}}{\longrightarrow} = \{(i, j) \mid 0 \leq i < j \leq n-1\}$ (for "up") and $\overset{\mathsf{d}}{\longrightarrow} = \{(i, j) \mid 0 \leq j < i \leq n-1\}$ (for "down").
- $\ell(0) = \{p_I\}$, $\ell(|T| - 2) = \{p_\square\}$, and $\ell(|T| - 1) = p_F$.

The states of this transition system appear in two roles. On one hand, they encode the different tiles of the tiling problem $\mathcal{K}$, with the generic tiles $t_I, t_\square, t_F$ identified by propositional labeling, while the rest remain anonymous. The horizontal and vertical matching relations are encoded by the accessibility relations h and v, respectively. On the other hand, the states double as the digits of the representation of large numbers. The relation u connects a digit to all digits of higher significance, d connects to all digits of lower significance, and e is the global accessibility relation.

Next we construct, for all $k \geq 1$, an $\mathrm{HFL}_{\mathrm{tail}}^{k+1}$ formula φ_k such that $\mathcal{T}_{\mathcal{K},n} \models \varphi_k$ holds iff $(\mathcal{K}, n)$ admits a solution to the order-k corridor tiling problem. We encode the rows of a tiling as functions of order k. Column numbers in $\{0, \ldots, 2_k^n - 1\}$ are encoded as functions of order $k-1$, following an approach similar to Jones [8].

Let $\tau_0 = \bullet$ and $\tau_{k+1} = \tau_k \to \bullet$ for all $k \geq 0$. For all $k \geq 0$ and $i \in \{0, \ldots, 2_{k+1}^n - 1\}$, let $\mathrm{jones}_k(i)$ be the function in the space $[\![\tau_k]\!]^{\mathcal{T}_{\mathcal{K},n}}$ defined as follows:

- $\mathrm{jones}_0(i)$ is the set of bits equal to 1 in the binary representation of i, i.e. $\mathrm{jones}_0(i) = S \subseteq \{0, \ldots, n-1\}$ where S is such that $i = \sum_{j \in S} 2^j$
- $\mathrm{jones}_{k+1}(i)$ maps $\mathrm{jones}_k(j)$ (for all $j \in \{0, \ldots, 2_{k+1}^n - 1\}$) to $\{0, \ldots, n-1\}$ if the j-th bit of i is 1, otherwise $\mathrm{jones}_{k+1}(i)$ maps $\mathrm{jones}_k(j)$ to $\emptyset$.

Consider the following formulas.

$$\mathrm{ite} \quad = \quad \lambda(b\colon \bullet), (x\colon \bullet), (y\colon \bullet).\ (b \wedge x) \vee (\neg b \wedge y)$$

$$\mathrm{zero}_0 \quad = \quad \bot$$

$$\mathrm{zero}_{k+1} \quad = \quad \lambda(m\colon \tau_k).\ \bot$$

$$\mathrm{gt}_0 \quad = \quad \lambda(m_1, m_2\colon \tau_0).\ \langle \mathrm{e} \rangle \big(m_2 \wedge \neg m_1 \wedge [\mathrm{u}](m_1 \Rightarrow m_2)\big)$$

$$\mathrm{gt}_{k+1} \quad = \quad \lambda(m_1, m_2\colon \tau_{k+1}).\ \mathrm{exists}_k \Big(\lambda(i\colon \tau_k).\ (m_2\ i) \wedge \neg(m_1\ i) \wedge$$

$$\mathrm{forall}_k \big(\lambda(j\colon \tau_k).\ (\mathrm{gt}_k\ i\ j) \Rightarrow (m_1\ j) \Rightarrow (m_2\ j)\big)\Big)$$

$$\mathrm{next}_0 \quad = \quad \lambda(m\colon \bullet).\ \mathrm{ite}\ m\ (\langle \mathrm{d} \rangle \neg m)\ ([\mathrm{d}]m)$$

$$\mathrm{next}_{k+1} \quad = \quad \lambda(m\colon \tau_{k+1}, i\colon \tau_k).\ \mathrm{ite}\ (m\ i)$$

$$\Big(\mathrm{exists}_k \big(\lambda(j_1\colon \tau_k).\ (\mathrm{gt}_k\ i\ j_1) \wedge \neg(m\ j_1)\big)\Big)$$

$$\Big(\mathrm{forall}_k \big(\lambda(j_2\colon \tau_k).\ (\mathrm{gt}_k\ i\ j_2) \Rightarrow (m\ j_2)\big)\Big)$$

$$\mathrm{exists}_k \quad = \quad \lambda(p\colon \tau_{k+1}).\ \Big(\big(\mu(F\colon \tau_k \to \bullet).\ \lambda(m\colon \tau_k).\ ([\mathrm{e}](p\ m)) \vee$$

$$F\ (\mathrm{next}_k\ m)\big)\ \mathrm{zero}_k\Big)$$

$$\mathrm{forall}_k \quad = \quad \lambda(p\colon \tau_{k+1}).\ \neg \mathrm{exists}_k\ (\neg p)$$

Let $\top_{\mathcal{S}} = [\![\top]\!]^{\mathcal{T}_{\mathcal{K},n}} = \{0, \ldots, n-1\}$ and $\bot_{\mathcal{S}} = [\![\bot]\!]^{\mathcal{T}_{\mathcal{K},n}} = \emptyset$. The functions above encode the if-then-else-operator, respectively arithmetic functions on Jones encodings of large natural numbers. The function gt_k allows to compare two integers : for all $m_1, m_2 \in \{0, \ldots, 2_{k+1}^n - 1\}$, $m_1 < m_2$ iff $\mathrm{gt}_k\ \mathrm{jones}_{m_1}(k)\ \mathrm{jones}_{m_2}(k)$ evaluates to $\top_{\mathcal{S}}$. Level 0 Jones encodings of numbers m_1 and m_2 are in relation gt_0 if, there is a bit that is set in $\mathrm{jones}_0(m_2)$ but not in $\mathrm{jones}_0(m_1)$, and all more significant bits that are set in $\mathsf{jones}_0(m_1)$ are also set in $\mathsf{jones}_0(m_2)$. The function gt_{k+1} operates on the same principle, except that bit positions are now level k Jones encodings of numbers, and the bit at position j is set in $\mathsf{jones}_{k+1}(m_i)$ iff $(m_i\ j)$ returns $\top_S$. Moreover, quantification over all bit positions uses the functions forall_k and exists_k instead of the relation e.

The function next_k returns the level k Jones encoding of the number encoded by its input, incremented by one: If a bit is set in the encoding of the input, it stays set if and only if there is a bit of lesser significance that is not set. If it was not set in the input, it is set if and only if all lower bits were set in the input. For example, if m is the set $\{0, 1, 3\}$ that encodes the number 11, then next_0 returns the set $\{2, 3\}$ which encodes 12. Encoding of bits and quantification over them works as in the case of gt_k.

Finally, the function exists_k checks for the existence of (the level k Jones encoding of) a number such that parameter p returns $\top_S$ with this number as an argument. This is achieved by iterating over all level k Jones encodings of numbers between 0 and $2^n_{k+1} - 1$. Consequently, exists_k expects an argument p of type τ_{k+1}, i.e., a function consuming an argument of type τ_k.

Lemma 7. *The following hold:*

1. *Assume $\eta(b) \in \{\top_S, \bot_S\}$. If $\eta(b) = \top_S$, then $[\![\mathsf{ite}\ b\ x\ y]\!]_\eta$ is $\eta(x)$, else it is $\eta(y)$.*
2. *$[\![\mathsf{zero}_k]\!] = \mathsf{jones}_k(0)$ for all $k \geq 0$.*
3. *If $[\![\mathsf{next}_k\ m]\!]_\eta = \mathsf{jones}_k(i)$ and $\eta(m) = \mathsf{jones}_k(j)$, then $i = j + 1$ modulo 2^m_{k+1}.*
4. *$[\![\mathsf{exists}_k\ p]\!]_\eta = \top_S$ if there exists $\mathcal{X} \in [\![\tau_k]\!]^{T_{\mathcal{K},n}}$ such that $[\![p\ x]\!]_{\eta[x \mapsto \mathcal{X}]} = \top_S$, otherwise $[\![\mathsf{exists}_k\ p]\!]_\eta = \bot_S$*

We are now ready to define the encoding of rows of width 2^n_k as functions in the space $[\![\tau_k]\!]^{T_{\mathcal{K},n}}$. Let $\rho = \rho_0 \ldots \rho_{2^n_k} \in T^*$ be a row of width 2^n_k for some $k \geq 1$. The coding $\mathsf{row}_k(\rho)$ of ρ is the function that maps $\mathsf{jones}_{k-1}(i)$ to $\{j\}$ where j is the number of i-th tile of the row, *i.e.* $\rho_i = t_j$. For example, the initial row of a tiling problem has the form $t_I\ t_\square \cdots t_\square$, i.e., the initial tile followed by $2^n_k - 1$ instances of $t_\square$. The function encoding it would return the set $\{0\}$ of tiles labeled by t_I at argument $\mathsf{jones}_{k-1}(0)$ and return the set $\{|T| - 2\}$ of tiles labeled by $t_\square$ at arguments $\mathsf{jones}_{k-1}(1), \ldots, \mathsf{jones}_{k-1}(2^n_k - 1)$.

Consider then the following formulas.

$$
\begin{aligned}
\mathsf{isTile} &= \lambda(x\colon \bullet),.\ [\mathsf{e}]\Big(x \Rightarrow \big(([\mathsf{u}]\neg x) \wedge ([\mathsf{d}]\neg x) \wedge (p_F \vee \langle \mathsf{u}\rangle p_F)\big)\Big)\\
\mathsf{isRow}_k &= \lambda(r\colon \tau_k).\ \mathsf{forall}_{k-1}\big(\lambda(m\colon \tau_{k-1}).\ \mathsf{isTile}\ (r\ m)\big)\\
\mathsf{isZero}_0 &= \lambda(m\colon \tau_0).\ [\mathsf{e}]\neg m\\
\mathsf{isZero}_{k+1} &= \lambda(m\colon \tau_{k+1}).\ \mathsf{forall}_k\ \big(\lambda(o\colon \tau_k).\ \mathsf{isZero}_0(m\ o)\big)\\
\mathsf{init}_k &= \lambda(m\colon \tau_{k-1}).\ \mathsf{ite}\ (\mathsf{isZero}_k\ m)\ p_I\ p_\square\\
\mathsf{isFinal}_k &= \lambda(r\colon \tau_k).\ [\mathsf{e}]\big((r\ \mathsf{zero}_{k-1}) \Rightarrow p_F\big)\\
\mathsf{horiz}_k &= \lambda(r\colon \tau_k).\ \mathsf{forall}_{k-1}\ \Big(\lambda(m\colon \tau_{k-1}).\\
&\quad [\mathsf{e}]\big((r\ m) \Rightarrow \big((\mathsf{isZero}_{k-1}\ (\mathsf{next}_{k-1}\ m)) \vee \langle \mathsf{h}\rangle(r\ (\mathsf{next}_{k-1}\ m))\big)\big)\Big)\\
\mathsf{vert}_k &= \lambda(r_1, r_2\colon \tau_k).\ \mathsf{forall}_{k-1}\ \Big(\lambda(m\colon \tau_{k-1}).\ [\mathsf{e}]\big((r_1\ m) \Rightarrow \langle \mathsf{v}\rangle(r_2\ m)\big)\Big)
\end{aligned}
$$

The function isTile checks whether its argument uniquely identifies a tile by verifying that it is a singleton set, and that it is not a state of index greater than $|T| - 1$. The function isRow checks whether its argument r is a proper encoding of a row by verifying that $r\,m$ returns the encoding of a tile for each $m \in \{\mathsf{jones}_{k-1}(0), \ldots, \mathsf{jones}_{k-1}(2^n_k - 1)\}$. The function init_k returns the initial row encoded as described in the previous paragraph, while $\mathsf{isFinal}_k$ verifies that its argument is a final row, i.e., a row where the tile in position 0 is t_F. Moreover, the function horiz_k verifies that the row r satisfies the horizontal matching condition. This is achieved by checking that, for each $m \in \{\mathsf{jones}_{k-1}(0), \ldots, \mathsf{jones}_{k-1}(2^n_k - 1)\}$, either m is $\mathsf{jones}_{k-1}(2^n_k)$ (whence the value $\mathsf{isZero}_{k-1}(\mathsf{next}_{k-1}\,m)$ is $\top_{\mathcal{S}}$) or that there is a h-transition from the singleton set $(r\,m)$ into the singleton set $r\,(\mathsf{next}_{k-1}\,m)$. Finally, vert_k verifies that two rows satisfy the vertical matching condition in a similar way.

Lemma 8. *The following hold:*

1. $[\![\mathsf{isTile}\,x]\!]_\eta$ *evaluates to* $\top_{\mathcal{S}}$ *if* $\eta(x) = \{i\}$ *for some* $i \in \{0, \ldots, |T| - 1\}$, *otherwise it evaluates to* $\bot_{\mathcal{S}}$.
2. $[\![\mathsf{isRow}_k\,x]\!]_\eta$ *evaluates to* $\top_{\mathcal{S}}$ *iff* $\eta(x) = \mathsf{row}_k(\rho)$ *for some row* ρ *of width* 2^n_k, *otherwise it evaluates to* $\bot_{\mathcal{S}}$.
3. $[\![\mathsf{init}_k]\!]$ *evaluates to* $\mathsf{row}_k(t_I \cdot t_\square \cdots t_\square)$.
4. *Assume* $\eta(r) = \mathsf{row}_k(\rho)$ *and* $\eta(r') = \mathsf{row}_k(\rho')$ *for some rows* $\rho = \rho_0 \ldots \rho_{2^n_k}$ *and* $\rho' = \rho'_0 \ldots \rho'_{2^n_k}$. *Then*
   (a) $[\![\mathsf{isFinal}_k\,r]\!]_\eta$ *evaluates to* $\top_{\mathcal{S}}$ *if* $\rho_0 = t_F$, *otherwise it evaluates to* $\bot_{\mathcal{S}}$.
   (b) $[\![\mathsf{horiz}_k\,r]\!]_\eta$ *evaluates to* $\top_{\mathcal{S}}$ *if* $(\rho_i, \rho_{i+1}) \in H$ *for all* $i \in \{0, \ldots, 2^n_k - 1\}$, *otherwise it evaluates to* $\bot_{\mathcal{S}}$.
   (c) $[\![\mathsf{vert}_k\,r\,r']\!]_\eta$ *evaluates to* $\top_{\mathcal{S}}$ *if* $(\rho_i, \rho'_i) \in V$ *for all* $i \in \{0, \ldots, 2^n_k - 1\}$, *otherwise it evaluates to* $\bot_{\mathcal{S}}$.

We now have introduced all the pieces we need for defining φ_k. Intuitively, φ_k should check for the existence of a solution to the order-k corridor tiling problem by performing an iteration that starts with a representation of the initial row in a solution and then guesses the next rows, each time checking that they match the previous one vertically. The iteration stops when a row is found that begins with the final tile. Let

$$\varphi_k = \big(\mu(P\colon \tau_{k+1}).\,\lambda(r_1\colon \tau_k).(\mathsf{isFinal}_k\,r_1) \vee (\mathsf{exists\_succ}_k\,r_1\,P)\big)\,\mathsf{init}_k$$

where

$$\mathsf{exists\_succ}_k = \lambda(r_1\colon \tau_k, p\colon \tau_{k+1}).\,\mathsf{exists}_k\,\big(\lambda(r_2\colon \tau_k).\,(\mathsf{horiz}_k\,r_2) \wedge (\mathsf{vert}_k\,r_1\,r_2) \wedge (p\,r_2).$$

Here, $\mathsf{exists\_succ}$ consumes a row r_1 of type τ_k, and a function p of type τ_{k+1}. It guesses a row r_2 using exists_k, verifies that it matches r_1 vertically from above, and then applies p to r_2. Of course, p in this setting is the fixpoint P which generates new rows using $\mathsf{exists\_succ}$ until one of them is a final row, or ad infinitum, if the tiling problem is unsolvable.

Theorem 9. *The model-checking problem of* $\text{HFL}_{\text{tail}}^{k+1}$ *is k-EXPSPACE-hard in data complexity for $k \geq 0$.*

Proof. For $k = 0$ this is already known: there is a simple and fixed HFL^1 formula φ_0 that expresses the universality problem for NFA [2], a problem known to be PSPACE-hard, i.e. 0-EXPSPACE-hard. It is easy to check that this φ_0 is in fact tail-recursive.

Let $k \geq 1$. The problem of deciding whether $\mathcal{T}_{n,\mathcal{K}} \models \varphi_k$ is equivalent to the problem of deciding whether $(\mathcal{K}, n)$ has a solution to the order-k corridor tiling problem. Therefore, we only need to give a formula ψ_k that is tail-recursive and equivalent to φ_k. Note indeed that φ_k is *not* tail recursive, because the recursive variable P of type τ_{k+1} appears as an argument of exists_succ_k. However, after β-reduction of $\text{exists\_succ}_k \ r_1 \ P$ and then $\text{exists}_k(\lambda r_2 \ldots)$, we get a formula ψ_k equivalent to φ_k and of the form

$$\Big(\mu(P : \tau_{k+1}). \lambda(r_1 : \tau_k).$$
$$(\ldots) \vee \big(\mu(F : \tau_{k+1}).\lambda(r_2 : \tau_k) \ ((\ldots) \wedge (P \ r_2)) \vee (F \ (\text{next}_k \ r_2))\big) \ r_1\Big) \ \text{init}_k$$

where the $(\ldots)$ parts do not contain the recursive variables P and F, hence this formula is tail-recursive. ▯

The upper bound and the fact that the lower one holds for the data complexity already yield a hierarchy of expressive power within HFL_{tail}.

Corollary 10. *For all $k \geq 0$, $\text{HFL}_{\text{tail}}^k \lneq \text{HFL}_{\text{tail}}^{k+1}$.*

Proof. Suppose this was not the case. Then there would be a $k \geq 0$ such that $\text{HFL}_{\text{tail}}^k \equiv \text{HFL}_{\text{tail}}^{k+1}$. We need to distinguish the cases $k = 0$ and $k > 0$.

Let $k = 0$. Note that $\text{HFL}_{\text{tail}}^0$ is a fragment of the modal μ-calculus which can only express regular properties. On the other hand, $\text{HFL}_{\text{tail}}^1$ contains formulas that express non-regular properties, for instance uniform inevitability [2].

Now let $k > 0$ and suppose that for every $\varphi \in \text{HFL}_{\text{tail}}^{k+1}$ there would exist a $\widehat{\varphi} \in \text{HFL}_{\text{tail}}^k$ such that $\widehat{\varphi} \equiv \varphi$. Take the formula φ_{k+1} as constructed above and used in the proof of Theorem 9. Fix some function *enc* which represents a transition system and a state as a string over some suitable alphabet. According to Theorem 9, $L := \{enc(\mathcal{T}, s) \mid \mathcal{T}, s \models \varphi_{k+1}\}$ is a k-EXPSPACE-hard language.

On the other hand, consider $\widehat{\varphi_{k+1}}$ which, by assumption, belongs to $\text{HFL}_{\text{tail}}^k$ and is equivalent to φ_{k+1}. Hence, $L = \{enc(\mathcal{T}, s) \mid \mathcal{T}, s \models \widehat{\varphi_{k+1}}\}$. According to Theorem 5, we have $L \in (k{-}1)$-EXPSPACE and therefore k-EXPSPACE $= (k - 1)$-EXPSPACE which contradicts the space hierarchy theorem [16]. ▯

5   Conclusion

We have presented a fragment of HFL that, given equal type order, is more efficient to model-check than regular HFL: Instead of $(k + 1)$-fold exponential time, model-checking an order $k + 1$ tail-recursive formula requires only k-fold exponential space. We have shown that this is optimal. Moreover, since the result already holds for data complexity, the space hierarchy theorem yields a strict hierarchy of expressive power within HFL_{tail}.

The definition of tail recursion presented in this paper was designed for clarity and can be extended with some syntactic sugar. For example, we take advantage of the free nondeterminism available due to Savitch's Theorem to resolve disjunctions and modal diamonds. One can, of course, also design a tail-recursive fragment that uses co-nondeterminism, allows unrestricted use of conjunctions and modal boxes, but restricts use of their duals. For symmetry reasons this fragment enjoys the same complexity theoretic properties as the fragment presented here. In fact, it is even possible to mix both fragments: tail recursion demands that (some) subformulas under operators that are not covered by Savitch's Theorem be *safe* in the sense that they have no free fixpoint variables. It is completely reasonable to allow a switch from nondeterministic tail recursion to co-nondeterministic tail recursion, and vice versa, at such safe points. Since clever use of negation can emulate this in the fragment presented in this paper, we have chosen not to introduce such switches in this paper for reasons of clarity. Making co-nondeterminism available can be helpful if formulas in negation normal form, which HFL admits, are needed.

An open question is how much the restrictions of tail recursion can be lifted for fixpoint definitions of order below the maximal order in a formula. A naïve approach would conclude that one can lift tail recursion for fixpoints of low order, since there is enough space available to compute their semantics via traditional fixpoint iteration. However, this can have undesired effects when lower-order fixpoints are nested with higher-order ones, breaking tail recursion. Outlining the definite border on what is possible with respect to lower-order fixpoints is a direction for future work.

References

1. Andersen, H.R.: A polyadic modal μ-calculus. Technical Report ID-TR: 1994-195, Dept. of Computer Science, Technical University of Denmark, Copenhagen (1994)
2. Axelsson, R., Lange, M.: Model checking the first-order fragment of higher-order fixpoint logic. In: Dershowitz, N., Voronkov, A. (eds.) LPAR 2007. LNCS (LNAI), vol. 4790, pp. 62–76. Springer, Heidelberg (2007). doi:10.1007/978-3-540-75560-9_7
3. Axelsson, R., Lange, M., Somla, R.: The complexity of model checking higher-order fixpoint logic. Logical Meth. Comput. Sci. **3**, 1–33 (2007)
4. Emerson, E.A.: Uniform inevitability is tree automaton ineffable. Inf. Process. Lett. **24**(2), 77–79 (1987)
5. Harel, D., Pnueli, A., Stavi, J.: Propositional dynamic logic of nonregular programs. J. Comput. Syst. Sci. **26**(2), 222–243 (1983)
6. Hartmanis, J., Stearns, R.E.: On the computational complexity of algorithms. Trans. AMS **117**, 285–306 (1965)
7. Janin, D., Walukiewicz, I.: On the expressive completeness of the propositional μ-calculus with respect to monadic second order logic. In: CONCUR, pp. 263–277 (1996)

8. Jones, N.D.: The expressive power of higher-order types or, life without CONS. J. Funct. Progm. **11**(1), 5–94 (2001)
9. Kozen, D.: Results on the propositional μ-calculus. TCS **27**, 333–354 (1983)
10. Lange, M.: Model checking propositional dynamic logic with all extras. J. Appl. Logic **4**(1), 39–49 (2005)
11. Lange, M.: Temporal logics beyond regularity. Habilitation thesis, University of Munich, BRICS research report RS-07-13 (2007)
12. Lange, M., Lozes, E.: Capturing bisimulation-invariant complexity classes with higher-order modal fixpoint logic. In: Diaz, J., Lanese, I., Sangiorgi, D. (eds.) TCS 2014. LNCS, vol. 8705, pp. 90–103. Springer, Heidelberg (2014). doi:10.1007/978-3-662-44602-7_8
13. Lange, M., Somla, R.: Propositional dynamic logic of context-free programs and fixpoint logic with chop. Inf. Process. Lett. **100**(2), 72–75 (2006)
14. Otto, M.: Bisimulation-invariant PTIME and higher-dimensional μ-calculus. Theor. Comput. Sci. **224**(1–2), 237–265 (1999)
15. Savitch, W.J.: Relationships between nondeterministic and deterministic tape complexities. J. Comput. Syst. Sci. **4**, 177–192 (1970)
16. Stearns, R.E., Hartmanis, J., Lewis II, P.M.: Hierarchies of memory limited computations. In: Proceedings of the 6th Annual Symposium on Switching Circuit Theory and Logical Design, pp. 179–190. IEEE (1965)
17. van Emde Boas, P.: The convenience of tilings. In: Sorbi, A. (ed.) Complexity, Logic, and Recursion Theory, vol. 187 of Lecture Notes in Pure and Applied Mathematics, pp. 331–363. Marcel Dekker Inc (1997)
18. Viswanathan, M., Viswanathan, R.: A higher order modal fixed point logic. In: Gardner, P., Yoshida, N. (eds.) CONCUR 2004. LNCS, vol. 3170, pp. 512–528. Springer, Heidelberg (2004). doi:10.1007/978-3-540-28644-8_33

Refinement of Trace Abstraction for Real-Time Programs

Franck Cassez[1], Peter Gjøl Jensen[1,2(✉)], and Kim Guldstrand Larsen[2]

[1] Department of Computing, Macquarie University, Sydney, Australia
[2] Department of Computer Science, Aalborg University, Aalborg, Denmark
pgj@cs.aau.dk

Abstract. Real-time programs are made of instructions that can perform assignments to discrete and real-valued variables. They are general enough to capture interesting classes of timed systems such as timed automata, stopwatch automata, time(d) Petri nets and hybrid automata. We propose a semi-algorithm using refinement of trace abstractions to solve both the reachability verification problem and the parameter synthesis problem for real-time programs. We report on the implementation of our algorithm and we show that our new method provides solutions to problems which are unsolvable by the current state-of-the-art tools.

1 Introduction

Model-checking is a widely used formal method to assist in verifying software systems. A wide range of model-checking techniques and tools are available and there are numerous successful applications in the safety-critical industry and the hardware industry – in addition the approach is seeing an increasing adoption in the general software engineering community. The main limitation of this formal verification technique is the so-called *state explosion problem. Abstraction refinement techniques* were introduced to overcome this problem. The most well-known technique is probably the *Counter Example Guided Abstraction Refinement* (CEGAR) method pioneered by Clarke *et al.* [12]. In this method the state space is abstracted with predicates on the concrete values of the program variables. The (counter-example guided) *refinement of trace abstraction* (TAR) method was proposed recently by Heizmann *et al.* [17,18] and is based on abstracting the set of traces of a program rather than the set of states. These two techniques have been widely used in the context of software verification. Their effectiveness and versatility in verifying *qualitative* (or functional) properties of C programs is reflected in the most recent *Software Verification* competition results [6,11].

Analysis of Timed Systems. Reasoning about *quantitative* properties of programs requires extended modeling features like real-time clocks. *Timed Automata* [1] (TA), introduced by Alur and Dill in 1989, is a very popular formalism to model real-time systems with dense-time clocks. Efficient symbolic model-checking techniques for TA are implemented in the real-time model-checker UPPAAL [4]. Extending TA, e.g., with the ability to stop and resume

© Springer International Publishing AG 2017
M. Hague and I. Potapov (Eds.): RP 2017, LNCS 10506, pp. 42–58, 2017.
DOI: 10.1007/978-3-319-67089-8_4

clocks (stopwatches), leads to undecidability of the reachability problem [9,20]. Semi-algorithms have been designed to verify *hybrid systems* (extended classes of TA) and are implemented in a number of dedicated tools [15,16,19]. However, a common difficulty with the analysis of quantitative properties of timed automata and extensions thereof is that ad-hoc data-structures are needed for each extension and each type of problem. As a consequence, the analysis tools have special-purpose efficient algorithms and data-structures suited and optimized only towards their specific problem and extension.

In this work we aim to provide a uniform solution to the analysis of timed systems by designing a generic semi-algorithm to analyze real-time programs which semantically captures a wide range of specification formalisms, including hybrid automata. We demonstrate that our new method provides solutions to problems which are unsolvable by the current state-of-the-art tools. We also show that our technique can be extended to solve specific problems like robustness and parameter synthesis.

Related Work. The *refinement of trace abstractions* (TAR) was proposed by Heizmann *et al.* [17,18]. It has not been extended to the verification of real-time systems. Wang *et al.* [23] proposed the use of TAR for the analysis of timed automata. However, their approach is based on the computation of the standard *zones* which comes with usual limitations: it is not applicable to extensions of TA (e.g., stopwatch automata) and can only discover predicates that are zones. Their approach has not been implemented and it is not clear whether it can outperform state-of-the-art techniques e.g., as implemented in UPPAAL. Dierks *et al.* [14] proposed a CEGAR based method for Timed Systems. To the best of our knowledge, this method got limited attention in the community.

Tools such as UPPAAL [4], SPACEEX [16], HYTECH [19], PHAVER [15], VERIFIX [21], SYMROB [22] and IMITATOR [2] all rely on special-purpose polyhedra libraries to realize their computation.

Our technique is radically different to previous approaches and leverages the power of SMT-solvers to discover non-trivial invariants for the class of hybrid automata. All the previous analysis techniques compute, reduce and check the state-space either up-front or on-the-fly, leading to the construction of significant parts of the statespace. In contrast our approach is an abstraction refinement method and the refinements are built by discovering non-trivial program invariants that are not always expressible using zones, or polyehdra. This enables us to successfully analyze (terminate) instances of non-decidable classes like stopwatch automata. A simple example is discussed in Sect. 2.

Our Contribution. In this paper, we propose a refinement of trace abstractions (TAR) technique to solve the reachability problem and the parameter synthesis problem for real-time programs.

Our approach combines an automata-theoretic framework and state-of-the-art Satisfiability Modulo Theory (SMT) techniques for discovering program invariants. We demonstrate on a number of case-studies that this new approach can compute answers to problems unsolvable by special-purpose tools and algorithms in their respective domain.

2   Motivating Example

The finite automaton A_1 (Fig. 1), accepts the regular language $\mathcal{L}(A_1) = i.t_0.t_1^*.t_2$.
By interpreting the labels of A_1 according to the Table in Fig. 1, we can view it
as a stopwatch automaton with 2 clocks, x and z, and one stopwatch y (the variables). Each label defines a *guard* g (a Boolean constraint on the variables), an
update u which is a (discrete)
assignment to the variables, and
a *rate* (vector) r that defines the
derivatives of the variables.[1] We
associate with a sequence $w =$
$a_0.a_1.\cdots.a_n \in \mathcal{L}(A_1)$, a (possibly
empty) set of *timed words*, $\tau(w)$,
of the form $(a_0, \delta_0).\cdots (a_n, \delta_n)$
where $\delta_i \geq 0, i \in [0 \dots n]$. For
instance, the timed words associ-
ated with $i.t_0.t_2$ are of the form
$(i, \delta_0).(t_0, \delta_1).(t_2, \delta_2)$, for all $\delta_i \in$

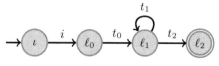

Edge	Guard	Update	Rate
i	*True*	x:=y:=z:=0	dy/dt=1
t_0	*True*	z:=0	dy/dt=0
t_1	x==1	x:=0	dy/dt=0
t_2	x-y>=1 and z<1	-	dy/dt=0

Fig. 1. Finite automaton A_1

$\mathbb{R}_{\geq 0}, i \in \{0, 1, 2\}$ such that following constraints can be satisfied:

$$x_0 = y_0 = z_0 = \delta_0 \wedge \delta_0 \geq 0 \tag{P_0}$$

$$x_1 = x_0 + \delta_1 \wedge y_1 = y_0 \wedge z_1 = \delta_1 \wedge \delta_1 \geq 0 \tag{P_1}$$

$$x_1 - y_1 \geq 1 \wedge z_1 < 1 \wedge x_2 = x_1 + \delta_2 \wedge y_2 = y_1 \wedge z_2 = z_1 + \delta_2 \wedge \delta_2 \geq 0 \tag{P_2}$$

The initial values of the variables x, y, z (in location ι, source of edge i) are
denoted x_{-1}, y_{-1}, z_{-1} and are unconstrained. Hence we assume that the initial
predicate on the variables x_{-1}, y_{-1}, z_{-1} is $P_{-1} = True$. P_0 must be satisfied after
taking i and letting time progress for $\delta_0 \geq 0$ time units, which is enforced by
a constraint on the variables[2] x_0, y_0, z_0 that stand for the values of x, y, z after
taking i; similarly $P_0 \wedge P_1$ must hold after $i.t_0$ and $P_0 \wedge P_1 \wedge P_2$ after $i.t_0.t_2$. Hence
the set of timed words associated with $i.t_0.t_2$ is not empty iff $P_0 \wedge P_1 \wedge P_2$ is
satisfiable. The *timed language*, $\mathcal{TL}(A_1)$, accepted by A_1 is the set of timed words
associated with all the words w accepted by A_1 i.e., $\mathcal{TL}(A_1) = \cup_{w \in \mathcal{L}(A_1)} \tau(w)$.

The *language emptiness problem* is a standard problem in Timed Automata
theory and is stated as follows [1]: "given a (Timed) Automaton A, is $\mathcal{TL}(A)$
empty?". It is known that the emptiness problem is decidable for some classes
of real-time programs (e.g., Timed Automata [1]), but undecidable for slightly
more expressive classes (e.g., Stopwatch Automata [20]). It is usually possible to
compute symbolic representations of sets of *reachable* valuations after a sequence
of labels. However, to compute the set of reachable valuations we may need to
explore an arbitrary and unbounded number of sequences. Hence only semi-
algorithms exist to compute the set of reachable valuations. For instance, using
PHAVER to compute the set of reachable valuations for A_1 does not terminate

---

[1] As x and z are clocks their rate is always 1 and omitted in the Table.

[2] If x was not reset by i, we would have a constraint $x_0 = x_{-1}$, with x_{-1} unconstrained.

(Table 1). To force termination, we can compute an over-approximation of the set of reachable valuations. Computing an over-approximation is sound (if we declare a timed language to be empty it is empty) but incomplete i.e., it may result in *false positives* (we declare a timed language non empty whereas it is empty). This is witnessed by the column "UPPAAL" in Table 1 where UPPAAL over-approximates sets of valuations in the stopwatch automaton with DBMs. After $i.t_0$, the over-approximation is $0 \leq y \leq x \wedge 0 \leq z \leq x$. This over-approximation intersects the guard $x - y \geq 1 \wedge z - y < 1$ of t_2 and ℓ_2 is reachable but this is an artifact of the over-approximation.[3]

Table 1. Symbolic representation of reachable states after a sequence of instructions. UPPAAL concludes that $\mathcal{TL}(A_1) \neq \varnothing$ due to the over-approximation using DBMs. PHAVER does not terminate.

Sequence	PHAVER	UPPAAL
$i.t_0$	$z = x - y \wedge 0 \leq z \leq x$	$0 \leq y \leq x \wedge 0 \leq z \leq x$
$i.t_0.t_1$	$z = x - y + 1 \wedge 0 \leq x \leq z \leq x + 1$	$0 \leq z - x \leq 1 \wedge 0 \leq y$
$i.t_0.(t_1)^2$	$z = x - y + 2 \wedge 0 \leq x \leq z - 1 \leq x + 1$	$1 \leq z - x \leq 2 \wedge 0 \leq y$
$i.t_0.(t_1)^3$	$z = x - y + 3 \wedge 0 \leq x \leq z - 2 \leq x + 1$	$2 \leq z - x \leq 3 \wedge 0 \leq y$
...	...	...
$i.t_0.(t_1)^k$	$z = x - y + k \wedge 0 \leq x \leq z - k + 1 \leq x + 1$	$k - 1 \leq z - x \leq k \wedge 0 \leq y$
...	...	...

Neither UPPAAL nor PHAVER can prove that $\mathcal{TL}(A_1) = \varnothing$. The technique we introduce in this paper enables us to discover arbitrary abstractions and invariants that enable us to prove $\mathcal{TL}(A_1) = \varnothing$. Our method is a version of the *Trace Abstraction Refinement* (TAR) technique introduced in [17]. Let us demonstrate how the method works on the stopwatch automaton A_1:

- find a (untimed) word accepted by A_1. Let $w_1 = i.t_0.t_2$ be such a word. We check whether $\tau(w_1) = \varnothing$ by encoding the corresponding associated timed traces as described by Eqs. (P_0)–(P_2) and then check whether $P_0 \wedge P_1 \wedge P_2$ is satisfiable[4]. As $P_0 \wedge P_1 \wedge P_2$ is not satisfiable we have $\tau(w_1) = \varnothing$.
- from the proof that $P_0 \wedge P_1 \wedge P_2$ is not satisfiable, we can obtain an *inductive interpolant* that comprises of two predicates I_0, I_1 – one for each conjunction – over the clocks x, y, z. An example of inductive interpolant[5] is $I_0 = x \leq y$ and $I_1 = x - y \leq z$. These predicates are *invariants* of any timed word of the untimed word w_1, and can be used to annotate w_1 with pre- and post-conditions (Eq. 1), which are Hoare triples of the form $\{P\}\ a\ \{Q\}$:

---

[3] UPPAAL terminates with the result "the language may not be empty".
[4] This can be done using an SMT-solver e.g., Z3.
[5] This is the pair returned by Z3 for $P_0 \wedge P_1 \wedge P_2$.

$$\{\mathit{True}\} \quad i \quad \{I_0\} \quad t_0 \quad \{I_1\} \quad t_2 \quad \{\mathit{False}\} \tag{1}$$

$$\{\mathit{True}\} \quad i \quad \{I_0\} \quad t_0 \quad \mathbf{\{I_1\}} \quad \mathbf{(t_1)^*} \quad \mathbf{\{I_1\}} \quad t_2 \quad \{\mathit{False}\} \tag{2}$$

We can also prove that $\{I_1\} \, (t_1)^* \, \{I_1\}$ is a valid Hoare triple and combined with Eq. 1 this gives Eq. 2. For each word $w \in i.t_0.(t_1)^*.t_2$, $\tau(w) = \varnothing$ and as $\mathcal{L}(A_1) \subseteq i.t_0.(t_1)^*.t_2$ we can conclude that $\mathcal{TL}(A_1) = \varnothing$.

3 Real-Time Programs

Our approach is general enough and applicable to a wide range of timed systems called *real-time programs*. As an example, timed, stopwatch, hybrid automata and time Petri nets are special cases of real-time programs.

In this section we define *real-time programs*. Real-time programs define the control flow of *instructions*, just as standard imperative programs do. The instructions can update *variables* by assigning new values to them. Each instruction has a semantics and together with the control flow this precisely defines the semantics of real-time programs.

Notations. A finite automaton over an alphabet Σ is a tuple $\mathcal{A} = (Q, \iota, \Sigma, \Delta, F)$ where Q is a finite set of locations s.t. $\iota \in Q$ is the initial location, Σ is a finite alphabet of actions, $\Delta \subseteq (Q \times \Sigma \times Q)$ is a finite transition relation, $F \subseteq Q$ is the set of *accepting* locations. A word $w = \alpha_0.\alpha_1. \cdots .\alpha_n$ is a finite sequence of letters from Σ; we let $w[i] = \alpha_i$ the i-th letter, $|w|$ be the length of w which is $n + 1$. Let ϵ be the empty word and $|\epsilon| = 0$, Σ^* is the set of finite words over Σ. The *language*, $\mathcal{L}(\mathcal{A})$, accepted by $\mathcal{A}$ is defined in the usual manner as the set of words that can lead to F from ι.

Let V be a finite set of real-valued variables. A *valuation* is a function $\nu : V \to \mathbb{R}$. The set of valuations is $[V \to \mathbb{R}]$. We denote by $\beta(V)$ a set of *constraints* on the variables in V. Given $\varphi \in \beta(V)$, we let $\mathit{Vars}(\varphi)$ be the set of free variables in φ. The truth value of a constraint φ given a valuation ν is denoted by $\varphi(\nu)$ and we write $\nu \models \varphi$ when $\varphi(\nu) = \mathit{True}$. We let $\llbracket \varphi \rrbracket = \{\nu \mid \nu \models \varphi\}$. An *update* of the variables in V is a binary relation $\mu \subseteq [V \to \mathbb{R}] \times [V \to \mathbb{R}]$. Given an update μ and a set of valuations $\mathcal{V}$, we let $\mu(\mathcal{V}) = \{\nu' \mid \exists \nu \in \mathcal{V} \text{ and } (\nu, \nu') \in \mu\}$. We let $\mathcal{U}(V)$ be the set of updates on the variables in V. A *rate* ρ is a function from V to $\mathbb{Q}$ (rates can be negative), i.e., an element of $\mathbb{Q}^V$. We let $\mathcal{R}(V) \subseteq \mathbb{Q}^V$ be a set of *valid* rates – that is, rates that can be written (syntactically) as a predicate on an edge. Given a valuation ν, a valid rate $\rho \in \mathbb{Q}(V)$ and a timestep $\delta \in \mathbb{R}_{\geq 0}$ the valuation $\nu + \rho \times \delta$ is defined by: $(\nu + \rho \times \delta)(v) = \nu(v) + \rho(v) \times \delta$ for $v \in V$.

Real-Time Instructions. Let $\mathcal{I} = \beta(V) \times \mathcal{U}(V) \times \mathcal{R}(V)$ be a countable set of instructions. Each $\alpha \in \mathcal{I}$ is a tuple (*guard, update, rates*) denoted by $(\gamma_\alpha, \mu_\alpha, \rho_\alpha)$. Let $\nu : V \to \mathbb{R}$ and $\nu' : V \to \mathbb{R}$ be two valuations. For each pair $(\alpha, \delta) \in \mathcal{I} \times \mathbb{R}_{\geq 0}$ we define the following transition relation:

$$\nu \xrightarrow{\alpha, \delta} \nu' \iff \begin{cases} 1. & \nu \models \gamma_\alpha \text{ (guard of } \alpha \text{ is satisfied in } \nu\text{),} \\ 2. & \exists \nu'' \text{ s.t. } (\nu, \nu'') \in \mu_\alpha \text{ (discrete update allowed by } \alpha\text{) and} \\ 3. & \nu' = \nu'' + \delta \times \rho_\alpha \text{ (continuous update as defined by } \alpha\text{).} \end{cases}$$

The semantics of $\alpha \in \mathcal{I}$ is a mapping $[\![\alpha]\!] : [V \to \mathbb{R}] \to [V \to \mathbb{R}]$ that can be extended to sets of valuations as follows:

$$\nu \in [V \to \mathbb{R}], \ [\![\alpha]\!](\nu) = \{\nu' \mid \exists \delta \geq 0, \nu \xrightarrow{\alpha, \delta} \nu'\}$$
$$K \subseteq [V \to \mathbb{R}], \ [\![\alpha]\!](K) = \bigcup_{\nu \in K} [\![\alpha]\!](\nu).$$

Let K be a set of valuations, $\alpha \in \mathcal{I}$ and $w \in \mathcal{I}^*$. We inductively define the *post operator* Post as follows:

$$Post(K, \epsilon) = K$$
$$Post(K, \alpha.w) = Post([\![\alpha]\!](K), w)$$

The post operator extends to logical constraints $\varphi \in \beta(V)$ by defining $Post(\varphi, w) = Post([\![\varphi]\!], w)$. In the sequel, we assume that, when $\varphi \in \beta(V)$,

then $[\![\alpha]\!]([\![\varphi]\!])$ is also definable as a constraint in $\beta(V)$. This inductively implies that $Post(\varphi, w)$ can also be expressed as a constraint in $\beta(V)$ for sequences of instructions $w \in \mathcal{I}^*$.

Timed Words and Feasible Words. A *timed word* (over alphabet $\mathcal{I}$) is a finite sequence $\sigma = (\alpha_0, \delta_0).(\alpha_1, \delta_1). \cdots .(\alpha_n, \delta_n)$ such that for each $0 \leq i \leq n$, $\delta_i \in \mathbb{R}_{\geq 0}$ and $\alpha_i \in \mathcal{I}$. The timed word σ is *feasible* if and only if there exists a set of valuations $\{\nu_0, \ldots, \nu_{n+1}\} \subseteq [V \to \mathbb{R}]$ such that:

$$\nu_0 \xrightarrow{\alpha_0, \delta_0} \nu_1 \xrightarrow{\alpha_1, \delta_1} \nu_2 \cdots \nu_n \xrightarrow{\alpha_n, \delta_n} \nu_{n+1}.$$

We let $Unt(\sigma) = \alpha_0.\alpha_1. \cdots .\alpha_n$ be the *untimed* version of σ. We overload the term *feasible* as follows: an untimed word $w \in \mathcal{I}^*$ is feasible iff $w = Unt(\sigma)$ for some feasible timed word σ.

Lemma 1. *An untimed word $w \in \mathcal{I}^*$ is feasible iff $Post(True, w) \neq False$.*

Proof. The lemma follows trivially from the inductive definition of Post. □

Real-Time Programs. The specification of a real-time program decouples the *control* (e.g., for Timed Automata, the locations) and the *data* (the clocks). A *real-time program* is a pair $P = (A_P, [\![\cdot]\!])$ where A_P is a finite automaton $A_P = (Q, \iota, I, \Delta, F)$ over the finite alphabet[6] $I \subseteq \mathcal{I}$, Δ defines the control-flow graph of the program and $[\![\cdot]\!]$ (as defined previously for $\mathcal{I}$) provides the semantics of each instruction. A timed word σ is *accepted* by P if and only if:

1. $Unt(\sigma)$ is accepted by A_P ($Unt(\sigma) \in \mathcal{L}(A_P)$) and
2. σ is feasible.

---

[6] $\mathcal{I}$ can be infinite but we require the control-flow graph Δ (transition relation) of A_P to be finite.

Notice that the definition of feasibility of a timed word σ is independent from the acceptance of $Unt(\sigma)$ by A_P.

The *timed language*, $\mathcal{TL}(P)$, of a real-time program P is the set of timed words accepted by P, i.e., $\sigma \in \mathcal{TL}(P)$ if and only if $Unt(\sigma) \in \mathcal{L}(A_P)$ and σ is feasible.

Remark 1. We do not assume any particular values initially for the variables of a real-time program (the variables that appear in I). This is reflected by the definition of *feasibility* that only requires the existence of valuations without containing the initial one ν_0. When specifying a real-time program, initial values can be set by regular instructions. This is similar to standard programs where the first instructions can set the values of some variables.

Timed Language Emptiness Problem. The *(timed) language emptiness problem* asks the following:

Given a real-time program P, is $\mathcal{TL}(P)$ empty?

Theorem 1. $\mathcal{TL}(P) \neq \varnothing$ iff $\exists w \in \mathcal{L}(A_P)$ such that $Post(True, w) \not\subseteq False$.

Proof. $\mathcal{TL}(P) \neq \varnothing$ iff there exists a feasible timed word σ such that $Unt(\sigma)$ is accepted by A_P. This is equivalent to the existence of a feasible word $w \in \mathcal{L}(A_P)$, and by Lemma 1, feasibility of w is equivalent to $Post(True, w) \not\subseteq False$. □

Useful Classes of Real-Time Programs. *Timed Automata* are a special case of real-time programs. The variables are called clocks. $\beta(V)$ is restricted to constraints on individual clocks or *difference constraints* generated by the grammar:

$$b_1, b_2 ::= True \mid False \mid x - y \bowtie k \mid x \bowtie k \mid b_1 \wedge b_2 \qquad (3)$$

where $x, y \in V$, $k \in \mathbb{Q}_{\geq 0}$ and $\bowtie \in \{<, \leq, =, \geq, >\}$[7]. We note that wlog. we omit *location invariants* as for the language emptiness problem, these can be implemented as guards. An update in $\mu \in \mathcal{U}(V)$ is defined by a set of clocks to be *reset*. Each pair $(\nu, \nu') \in \mu$ is such that $\nu'(x) = \nu(x)$ or $\nu'(x) = 0$ for each $x \in V$. The valid rates are fixed to 1, and thus $\mathcal{R}(V) = \{1\}^V$.

Stopwatch Automata can also be defined as a special case of real-time programs. As defined in [9], Stopwatch Automata are Timed Automata extended with *stopwatches* which are clocks that can be stopped. $\beta(V)$ and $\mathcal{U}(V)$ are the same as for Timed Automata but the set of valid rates is defined by the functions of the form $\mathcal{R}(V) = \{0, 1\}^V$ (the clock rates can be either 0 or 1). An example of a Stopwatch Automaton is given by the timed system $\mathcal{A}_1$ in Fig. 1.

As there exists syntactic translations (preserving reachability) that maps hybrid automata to stopwatch automata [9], and translations that map time Petri nets [5,10] and extensions [7,8] thereof to timed automata, it follows that time Petri nets and hybrid automata are also special cases of real-time programs. This shows that the method we present in the next section is applicable to wide range of timed systems.

---

[7] While difference constraints are strictly disallowed in most definitions of Timed Automata, the method we propose retain its properties regardless of their presence.

What is remarkable as well, is that it is not restricted to timed systems that have a finite number of discrete states but can also accommodate infinite discrete state spaces. For example, the automaton in Fig. 2 has two clocks x and y and an unbounded integer variable k. Even though k is unbounded, our technique discovers the invariant $y \geq k$ at location 1 which is over a real-time clock y and the integer variable k. It allows us to prove that $\mathcal{TL}(P_2) = \varnothing$.

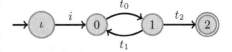

Edge	Guard	Update
i	$True$	x:=y:=k:=0
t_0	$x \geq 1$	—
t_1	$True$	x:=0; k++
t_2	$y < k$	—

Fig. 2. Real-time program P_2

4   Trace Abstraction Refinement for Real-Time Programs

In this section we propose a semi-algorithm to solve the language emptiness problem for real-time programs. The semi-algorithm is a version of the *refinement of trace abstractions* (TAR) approach [17] for timed systems.

Refinement of Trace Abstraction for Real-Time Programs. Figure 3 gives a precise description of the TAR semi-algorithm for real-time programs. This is the standard trace abstraction refinement semi-algorithm as introduced in [17] – we therefore omit theorems of completeness and soundness as these will be equivalent to the theorems in [17] and are proved in the exact same manner. The input to the semi-algorithm is a real-time program $P = (A_P, \llbracket \cdot \rrbracket)$. An invariant of the semi-algorithm is that R is empty or contains only infeasible traces.

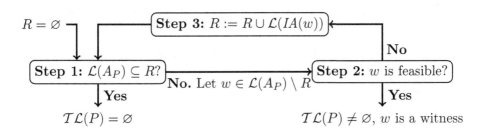

Fig. 3. Trace abstraction refinement semi-algorithm for real-time programs

Initially the refinement R is the empty set. The semi-algorithm works as follows:

Step 1. Check whether all the (untimed) traces in $\mathcal{L}(A_P)$ are in R. If this is the case, $\mathcal{TL}(P)$ is empty and the semi-algorithm terminates. Otherwise, there is a sequence $w \in \mathcal{L}(A_P) \setminus R$, goto Step 2;

Step 2. If w is feasible i.e., there is a feasible timed word σ such that $Unt(\sigma) = w$, then $\sigma \in T\mathcal{L}(P)$ and $T\mathcal{L}(P) \neq \varnothing$ and the semi-algorithm terminates. Otherwise w is not feasible, goto Step 3;

Step 3. w is infeasible and given the reason for infeasibility we can construct a finite *interpolant automaton*, $IA(w)$, that accepts w and other words that are infeasible for the same reason. How $IA(w)$ is computed is addressed in the sequel. The automaton $IA(w)$ is added to the previous refinement R and the semi-algorithm starts a new round at Step 1.

Checking Feasibility. Given a word $w \in \mathcal{I}^*$, we can check whether w is feasible by encoding the side-effects of each instruction in w, similar to a Static Single Assignment (SSA) form in programming languages.

Let us define a function for constructing such a constraint-system characterizing the feasibility of a given trace. We shall assume that constraints in $\beta(V)$ and updates in $\mathcal{U}(V)$ are syntactically defined. Let $P = (Q, q_0, \mathcal{I}, \Delta, F)$ be a real-time program and $w \in \mathcal{I}^*$ be a word over $\mathcal{I}$. Let $V^n = \{x^n, x_\mu^n \mid x \in V\} \cup \{\delta^n\}$ be a set of variables extended with an index $n \in \mathbb{N}_{>0}$. For a given constraint-system $\varphi \in \beta(V)$ write $\varphi_{[V/V^n]}$ for replacing all occurrences of V with their indexed occurrence in V^n (implying that $\varphi_{[V/V^n]} \in \beta(V^n)$). We assume that the relation $\mu \in \mathcal{U}(V)$ is of SSA form, and let $\mu_{[V/(V^n,V^m)]}$ be the replacement of all occurrences of variables $x \in V$ with their indexes and sub-scripted occurrence in V^n if x is assigned to and from V^m if x is read from. As an example, $(v \leftarrow v+w)_{[V/(V^n,V^m)]} = v_\mu^n \leftarrow v^m+w^m$ where $\leftarrow$ denotes assignment. Given this we can now recursively define the function $Enc : \mathcal{I}^* \to \beta(\{V^n \mid 0 \leq n \leq |w|\})$

$$Enc(\epsilon) = True$$
$$Enc(w.\alpha) = Enc(w) \wedge \delta^n \geq 0 \wedge \varphi_{[V/V^{n-1}]} \wedge \delta^n \geq 0 \wedge \mu_{[V/(V_\mu^n, V^{n-1})]}$$
$$\wedge \bigwedge_{v \in V} v^n = v_\mu^n + \rho(v) \times \delta^n \text{ where } n = |w| - 1 \text{ and } (\varphi, \mu, \rho) = \alpha$$

The function $Enc : \mathcal{I}^* \to \beta(V^{\mathbb{N}_{\geq 0}})$ constructs a constraint-system characterizing exactly the feasibility of a word w:

Lemma 2. *A word w is feasible i.e., $Post(True, w) \not\subseteq False$ iff $Enc(w)$ is satisfiable.*

We shall frequently refer to such a constraints system $C = Enc(w)$ for some word w where $|w| = n$ as a sequence of conjunctions $P_0 \wedge \cdots \wedge P_m \wedge \cdots \wedge P_n = C$ where $P_m \in \beta(V^{m-1} \cup V^m)$ refers to the encoding of the m'th instruction, and we shall call such an element P_m a predicate.

An example of an encoding for the real-time program A_1 (Fig. 1) is given by the predicates in Eqs. (P_0)–(P_2). The variables x_k, y_k, z_k denote the values of x, y, z after k steps (initially the variables can have arbitrary values). The sequence $w_1 = i.t_0.t_2$ is feasible iff $Enc(w_1) = P_0 \wedge P_1 \wedge P_2$ is satisfiable.

From such a sequence we can use interpolating SMT-solvers to construct a sequence of *craig-interpolants*.

Construction of Interpolant Automata. When it is determined that a trace w is infeasible, we can easily discard such a single trace and continue searching. However, the power of the TAR method is to generalize the infeasibility of a single trace w into a family (regular set) of traces. This regular set of infeasible traces is computed from the reason of infeasibility of w and is formally specified by an *interpolant automaton*, $IA(w)$. The reason for infeasibility itself has the form of an *inductive interpolant*.

Given a conjunctive formula $f = P_0 \wedge \cdots \wedge P_m$, if f is unsatisfiable, an *interpolating* SMT-solver is capable of producing inductive arguments for the unsatisfiability reason. This argument is an *inductive interpolant* $I_0, \ldots, I_{m-1}$ s.t. for each $0 \leq n \leq m - 1$, $I_n \wedge P_{n+1}$ implies I_{n+1} (with $I_m = False$), and for each $0 \leq n \leq m - 1$, the variables in I_n appear in both P_n and P_{n+1}.

One can intuitively think of each interpolant as a *sufficient* condition for infeasibility of the post-fix of the trace and this can be represented by a sequence of Hoare triples of the form $\{P\}\ a\ \{Q\}$:

$$\{True\}\quad a_0\quad \{I_0\}\quad a_1\quad \{I_1\}\quad \cdots \quad \{I_{m-1}\}\quad a_m\quad \{False\}$$

Consider the real-time program P_2 of Fig. 2 and the two infeasible untimed words $w_1 = i.t_0.t_2$ and $w_2 = i.t_0.t_1.t_0.t_2$. The Hoare triples for w_1 and w_2 are given by Eq. 4 and 5 where the predicates are: $I_1 = y \geq x \wedge (k = 0)$, $I_2 = y \geq k$, $I_3 = y \geq x \wedge k \leq 0$, $I_4 = y \geq 1 \wedge k \leq 0$, $I_5 = y \geq k + x$, $I_6 = y \geq k + 1$.

$$\{True\}\quad i\quad \{I_1\}\quad t_0\quad \{I_2\}\quad t_2\quad \{False\} \tag{4}$$

$$\{True\}\quad i\quad \{I_3\}\quad t_0\quad \{I_4\}\quad t_1\quad \{I_5\}\quad t_0\quad \{I_6\}\quad t_2\quad \{False\} \tag{5}$$

As can be seen in Eq. 5, the sequence contains two occurrences of t_0: this suggests that a loop occurs in the program, and this loop may be infeasible as well. Formally, because $Post(I_6, t_1) \subseteq I_5$, any trace of the form $i.t_0.t_1.(t_0.t_1.t_0)^*.t_2$ is infeasible. This enables us to construct $IA(w_2)$ as accepting the regular set of infeasible traces $i.t_0.t_1.(t_0.t_1.t_0)^*.t_2$. Overall, because w_1 is also infeasible, we obtain a refinement which is $\mathcal{L}(IA(w_1)) \cup \mathcal{L}(IA(w_2))$, Fig. 4.

Let us formalize the interpolant-automata construction. Given the interpolants $I_0, \ldots I_k$ for the constraint-system $P_0 \wedge \cdots \wedge P_{k+1} = Enc(w)$ for some word w where $k = |w| - 1$ and given the automata description of our Real Time Program $\mathcal{A} = (Q, q_0, \Sigma, \Delta, F)$, then we can construct an interpolant automaton $\mathcal{A}^I = (Q^I, q_0^I, \Sigma^I, \Delta^I, F^I)$ s.t. $w \in \mathcal{L}(\mathcal{A}^I)$ and for all $w' \in \mathcal{L}(\mathcal{A}^I)$ we have that w'

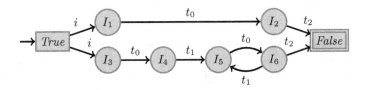

Fig. 4. Interpolant automaton for $\mathcal{L}(IA(w_1)) \cup \mathcal{L}(IA(w2))$.

is infeasible. Let $Q = \{\mathit{True}, \mathit{False}, I_0, \ldots, I_k\}$, $q_0 = \mathit{True}$, $\Sigma^I = \Sigma$, $F = \{\mathit{False}\}$, then we let the transition-function be the largest transition-function satisfying the following.

1. $(\mathit{True}, w[0], I_0) \in \Delta^I$,
2. $(I_k, w[k], \mathit{False}) \in \Delta^I$,
3. $(I_{n-1}, w[n-1], I_n) \in \Delta^I$ for $1 < n \leq k$, and
4. for each $1 \leq n, m \leq k$, if $I_m \subset_V I_n$ then $(I_{n-1}, w[n-1], I_m) \in \Delta^I$ where $\subset_V$ is subset-checking, modulo variable indexing.

The above conditions induce an algorithm IA for constructing interpolant automata from an untimed word w.

Theorem 2 (Interpolant Automata). *Let w be an infeasible word over P, then for all $w' \in \mathcal{L}(IA(w))$, w' is infeasible.*

We can verify that the construction using rules 1–3 is correct as these come directly from the feasibility-check of the trace and the definition of interpolants.

The *pumping*-rule (rule 4) utilizes that if by firing some transition labeled α from some interpolant I_{n-1} gives us a "stronger" argument for infeasibility than in I_m, then surely every sequence which is infeasible from I_m is also infeasible from I_{n-1} after firing α.

Feasibility Beyond Timed Automata. Satisfiability can be checked with an SMT-solver (and decision procedures exist for useful theories). In the case of timed automata and stopwatch automata, the feasibility of a trace can be encoded as a linear program. The corresponding theory, Linear Real Arithmetic (LRA) is decidable and supported by most SMT-solvers. It is also possible to encode non-linear constraints (non-linear guards and assignments). In the latter cases, the SMT-solver may not be able to provide an answer to the SAT problem as non-linear theories are undecidable. However, we can still build on a semi-decision procedure of the SMT-solver, and if it provides an answer, get the status of a trace (feasible or not).

5   Parameter Synthesis for Real-Time Programs

In this section we show how to use the trace abstraction refinement semi-algorithm presented in Sect. 4 to synthesize *good initial values* for some of the program variables. Given a real-time program P, the objective is to determine a set of *initial valuations* $I \subseteq [V \to \mathbb{R}]$ such that, when we start the program in I, P does not accept any timed word.

Given a constraint $I \in \beta(V)$, we define the associated *assume* guard-transformer for instructions that for a letter $\alpha = (\gamma, \rho, \mu)$ defines $Assume(\alpha, I) = (\gamma', \rho, \mu)$ s.t. $\gamma' = \gamma \wedge I$. Let $P = (Q, \iota, \mathcal{I}, \Delta, F)$ be a real-time program. Then we can define the real-time program $Assume(I).P = (Q, \iota, \mathcal{I}, (\Delta \setminus \{(\iota, i, q_0)\}) \cup \{(\iota, Assume(i, I), q_0)\}, F)$.

Safe Initial Set Problem. The *safe initial state problem* asks the following:

> Given a real-time program P, is there $I \in \beta(V)$ s.t. $\mathcal{TL}(Assume(I).P) = \varnothing$?

Semi-Algorithm for the Safe Initial State Problem. Let $w \in \mathcal{L}(P)$. When $Enc(w)$ is satisfiable, we define the (existentially quantified) constraint $\exists\, Vars(Enc(w)) \setminus V_{-1}.Enc(w)$ i.e., the projection of the set of solutions on the initial values of the variables. We let $\exists_i(w)$ be $\exists\, Vars(Enc(w)) \setminus V_{-1}.Enc(w)$ with all the free occurrences of x_{-1} replaced by x (remove index for each var). $\exists_i(w)$ is a constraint over the set of variables V (and existential quantifiers)[8].

The semi-algorithm in Fig. 5 works as follows: (1) initially $I = True$ (2) using the semi-algorithm from Fig. 3, test if $\mathcal{TL}(Assume(I).P)$ is empty – if so P does not accept any timed word when we start from $[\![I]\!]$ (3) Otherwise, there is a witness word $\sigma \in \mathcal{TL}(Assume(I).P)$, implying that $I \wedge Enc(Unt(\sigma))$ is satisfiable. We can then determine a sufficient condition $I' = \exists_i(Unt(\sigma))$ for the feasibility s.t. $(\neg I') \wedge Enc(Unt(\sigma))$ is unsatisfiable and use this to strengthen the constraint I (step 2).

If the semi-algorithm terminates, it computes exactly the set of parameters for which the system is not safe (I), captured formally by Theorem 3.

Theorem 3. *If the semi-algorithm SafeInit terminates and outputs I, then for any $I' \in \beta(V)$, $\mathcal{TL}(Assume(I').P) = \varnothing$ if and only if $I' \subseteq I$.*

Proof ($\Longrightarrow$). Let us assume by contradiction that upon termination we have $\mathcal{TL}(Assume(I).P) \neq \varnothing$. This violates the termination critirion of either Fig. 3 or 5.   □

Proof ($\Longleftarrow$). Let us assume by contradiction that upon termination there exists some $I' \neq \varnothing$ for which $I' \cap I = \varnothing$ and $\mathcal{TL}(Assume(I').P) = \varnothing$. Then let us prove inductively that no such I' can ever exist.

In the base-case in step 1, if the algorithm terminates, clearly $I' = \varnothing$ violating our requirements for the contradiction. For our contradiction to be valid, we must instead look at how we modify I in step 2. For I' to be non-empty, the quantification over parameter-values for σ must construct a larger-than-needed set of parameter value, i.e., that $I' \subseteq \neg\exists_i Enc(Unt(\sigma))$. This contradicts the definition of existential quantification. As we never over-approximate the parameter-set needed for the valuation in step 2, we can conclude that I' cannot exist.   □

6   Experiments

We have conducted two sets of experiments, each testing the applicability of our proposed method (denoted by RTTAR) compared to state-of-the-art tools with

---

[8] Existential quantification for the theory of Linear Real Arithmetic is within the theory via Fourier-Motzkin-elimination – hence the solver only needs support for Linear Real Arithmetic for Parameter Synthesis for Stopwatch and Timed Automata.

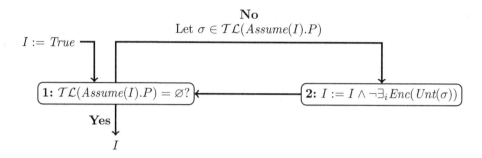

Fig. 5. Semi-algorithm *SafeInit*.

specialized data-structures and algorithms for the given setting. All experiments were conducted on AMD Opteron 6376 Processors and limited to 1 hour of computation. The RTTAR tool uses the UPPAAL parsing-library, but relies on Z3 [13] for the interpolant computation.

Verification of Timed and Stopwatch Automata. The real-time programs, P_1 of Fig. 1 and P_2 of Fig. 2 can be analyzed with our technique. The analysis (RTTAR algorithm, Fig. 3) terminates in two iterations for the program P_1, a stopwatch automaton. As emphasized in the introduction, neither UPPAAL (over-approximation with DBMs) nor PHAVER can provide the correct answer to reachability problem for P_1.

To prove that location 2 is unreachable in program P_2 requires to discover an invariant that mixes integers (discrete part of the state) and clocks (continuous part). Our technique successfully discovers the program invariants I_5 and I_6 (thanks to the interpolating SMT-solver). As a result the refinement depicted in Fig. 2 is constructed and as it contains $\mathcal{L}(A_{P_2})$ the refinement algorithm terminates and proves that 2 is not reachable. A_{P_2} can only be analyzed in UPPAAL with significant computational effort and bounded integers.

Robustness of Timed Automata. Another remarkable feature of our technique is that it can readily be used to check *robustness* of timed automata. In essence, checking robustness amounts to enlarging the guards of an TA A by an $\varepsilon > 0$. The resulting TA is A_ε. The automaton A is (safety) robust iff there is some $\varepsilon > 0$ such $\mathcal{TL}(A_\epsilon) = \varnothing$.

To address the robustness problem for a real-time program P, we use the semi-algorithm presented in Sect. 5 and reduce the robustness-checking problem to that of parameter-synthesis. Assuming P is robust[9] i.e., there exists some $\epsilon > 0$ such that $\mathcal{TL}(A_\epsilon) = \varnothing$ and the previous process terminates we can compute the largest set of parameters for which P is robust.

---

[9] Proving that a system is non-robust requires proving *feasibility* of infinite traces for ever decreasing ϵ. We have developed some techniques to do so but this is outside of the scope of this paper.

As Table 2 demonstrates, SYM-ROB [22] and RTTAR do not always agree on the results. Notably, since the TA M3 contains strict guards, SYMROB is unable to compute the robustness of it. Furthermore, SYM-ROB over-approximates ϵ, an artifact of the so-called "loop-acceleration"-technique and the polyhedra-based algorithm. This can be observed in the modified model M3c, which is now analyzable by SYMROB, but differ in results compared to RTTAR. This is the same case with the model denoted a. We experimented with ϵ-values to confirm that M3 is safe for all the values tested – while a is safe only for values tested respecting $\epsilon < \frac{1}{2}$. We can also see that our proposed method is sig-

Test	Time	$\epsilon <$	Time	$\epsilon <$
	SYMROB		RTTAR	
`csma_05`	0.43	1/3	68.23	1/3
`csma_06`	2.44	1/3	227.15	1/3
`csma_07`	8.15	1/3	1031.72	1/3
`fischer_04`	0.16	1/2	45.24	1/2
`fischer_05`	0.65	1/2	249.45	1/2
`fischer_06`	3.71	1/2	1550.89	1/2
M3c	4.34	250/3	43.10	∞
M3	**N/A**	**N/A**	43.07	∞
a	27.90	1/4	15661.14	1/2

Table 2. Results for robustness analysis comparing RTTAR with SYMROB. Time is given in seconds. N/A indicates that SYM-ROB was unable to compute the robustness for the given model.

nificantly slower than SYMROB. As our tool is currently only a prototype with rudimentary state-space-reduction-techniques, this is to be expected.

Parametric Stopwatch Automata. In our last series of tests, we compare the RTTAR tool to IMITATOR [2] – the state-of-the-art parameter synthesis tool for reachability[10]. We shall here use the semi-algorithm is presented in Sect. 5 For the test-cases we use the gadget presented initially in Fig. 1, a few of the test-cases used in [3], as well as two modified version of Fischers Protocol, shown in Fig. 6. In the first version we replace the constants in the model with parameters. In the second version (marked by robust), we wish to compute an expression, that given an arbitrary upper and lower bound yields the robustness of the system – in the same style as the experiments presented in Sect. 6, but here for arbitrary guard-values.

As illustrated by Table 3 the performance of RTTAR is slower than IMITATOR when IMITATORis able to compute the results. On the other hand, when using IMITATOR to verify our motivating example from Fig. 1, we observe that IMI-TATOR never terminates, due to the divergence of the polyhedra-computation. This is the effect illustrated in Table 1.

When trying to synthesize the parameters for Fischers algorithm, in all cases, IMITATOR times out and never computes a result. For both two and four processes in Fischers algorithm, our tool detects that the system is safe if and only if $a < 0 \vee b < 0 \vee b - a > 0$. Notice that $a < 0 \vee b < 0$ is a trivial constraint preventing the system from doing anything. The constraint $b - a > 0$ is the only useful one. Our technique provides a formal proof that the algorithm is correct for $b - a > 0$.

---

[10] We compare with the `EFSynth`-algorithm in the IMITATOR tool as this yielded the lowest computation time in the two terminating instances.

Table 3. Results for parameter-synthesis comparing RTTAR with IMITATOR. Time is given in seconds. DNF marks that the tool did not complete the computation within an hour.

Test	IMITATOR	RTTAR
Sched2.50.0	201.95	1656.00
Sched2.100.0	225.07	656.26
A_1	DNF	0.1
fischer_2	DNF	0.23
fischer_4	DNF	40.13
fischer_2_robust	DNF	0.38
fischer_4_robust	DNF	118.11

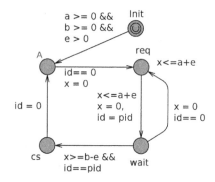

Fig. 6. A UPPAAL template for a single process in Fischers Algorithm. The variables e, a and b are parameters for ϵ, lower and upper bounds for clock-values respectively.

In the same manner, our technique can compute the most general constraint ensuring that Fischers algorithm is robust.

The result of RTTAR algorithm is that the system is robust iff $\epsilon \leq 0 \vee a < 0 \vee b < 0 \vee b - a - 2\epsilon > 0$ – which for $\epsilon = 0$ (modulo the initial non-zero constraint on ϵ) reduces to the constraint-system obtained in the non-robust case.

7   Conclusion

We have proposed a version of the trace abstraction refinement approach to real-time programs. We have demonstrated that our semi-algorithm can be used to solve the reachability problem for instances which are not solvable by state-of-the-art analysis tools.

Our algorithms can handle the general class of real-time programs that comprises of classical models for real-time systems including timed automata, stopwatch automata, hybrid automata and time(d) Petri nets.

As demonstrated in Sect. 6, our tool is capable of solving instances of reachability problems problems, robustness, parameter synthesis, that current tools are incapable of handling.

For future work we would like to improve the scalability of the proposed method, utilizing well known techniques such as extrapolations, partial order reduction and compositional verification. Furthermore, we would like to extend our approach from reachability to more expressive temporal logics.

Acknowledgments. The research leading to these results was made possible by an external stay partially funded by Otto Mønsted Fonden.

References

1. Alur, R., Dill, D.L.: A theory of timed automata. Theor. Comput. Sci. **126**(2), 183–235 (1994)
2. André, É., Fribourg, L., Kühne, U., Soulat, R.: IMITATOR 2.5: a tool for analyzing robustness in scheduling problems. In: Giannakopoulou, D., Méry, D. (eds.) FM 2012. LNCS, vol. 7436, pp. 33–36. Springer, Heidelberg (2012). doi:10.1007/978-3-642-32759-9_6
3. André, É., Lipari, G., Nguyen, H.G., Sun, Y.: Reachability preservation based parameter synthesis for timed automata. In: Havelund, K., Holzmann, G., Joshi, R. (eds.) NFM 2015. LNCS, vol. 9058, pp. 50–65. Springer, Cham (2015). doi:10.1007/978-3-319-17524-9_5
4. Behrmann, G., David, A., Larsen, K.G., Hakansson, J., Petterson, P., Yi, W., Hendriks, M.: Uppaal 4.0. In: QEST 2006, pp. 125–126 (2006)
5. Bérard, B., Cassez, F., Haddad, S., Lime, D., Roux, O.H.: Comparison of the expressiveness of timed automata and time Petri nets. In: Pettersson, P., Yi, W. (eds.) FORMATS 2005. LNCS, vol. 3829, pp. 211–225. Springer, Heidelberg (2005). doi:10.1007/11603009_17
6. Beyer, D.: Competition on software verification. In: Flanagan, C., König, B. (eds.) TACAS 2012. LNCS, vol. 7214, pp. 504–524. Springer, Heidelberg (2012). doi:10.1007/978-3-642-28756-5_38
7. Bérard, B., Cassez, F., Haddad, S., Lime, D., Roux, O.H.: The expressive power of time Petri nets. Theor. Comput. Sci. **474**, 1–20 (2013)
8. Byg, J., Jacobsen, M., Jacobsen, L., Jørgensen, K.Y., Møller, M.H., Srba, J.: TCTL-preserving translations from timed-arc Petri nets to networks of timed automata. TCS (2013). doi:10.1016/j.tcs.2013.07.011
9. Cassez, F., Larsen, K.: The impressive power of stopwatches. In: Palamidessi, C. (ed.) CONCUR 2000. LNCS, vol. 1877, pp. 138–152. Springer, Heidelberg (2000). doi:10.1007/3-540-44618-4_12
10. Cassez, F., Roux, O.H.: Structural translation from time Petri nets to timed automata. J. Softw. Syst. **79**(10), 1456–1468 (2006)
11. Cassez, F., Sloane, A.M., Roberts, M., Pigram, M., Suvanpong, P., de Aledo, P.G.: Skink: static analysis of programs in LLVM intermediate representation - (Competition Contribution). In: Legay, A., Margaria, T. (eds.) TACAS 2017. LNCS, vol. 10206, pp. 380–384. Springer, Heidelberg (2017). doi:10.1007/978-3-662-54580-5_27
12. Clarke, E., Grumberg, O., Jha, S., Lu, Y., Veith, H.: Counterexample-guided abstraction refinement. In: Emerson, E.A., Sistla, A.P. (eds.) CAV 2000. LNCS, vol. 1855, pp. 154–169. Springer, Heidelberg (2000). doi:10.1007/10722167_15
13. Moura, L., Bjørner, N.: Z3: an efficient SMT solver. In: Ramakrishnan, C.R., Rehof, J. (eds.) TACAS 2008. LNCS, vol. 4963, pp. 337–340. Springer, Heidelberg (2008). doi:10.1007/978-3-540-78800-3_24
14. Dierks, H., Kupferschmid, S., Larsen, K.G.: Automatic abstraction refinement for timed automata. In: Raskin, J.-F., Thiagarajan, P.S. (eds.) FORMATS 2007. LNCS, vol. 4763, pp. 114–129. Springer, Heidelberg (2007). doi:10.1007/978-3-540-75454-1_10
15. Frehse, G.: PHAVer: algorithmic verification of hybrid systems past HyTech. In: Morari, M., Thiele, L. (eds.) HSCC 2005. LNCS, vol. 3414, pp. 258–273. Springer, Heidelberg (2005). doi:10.1007/978-3-540-31954-2_17

16. Frehse, G., Guernic, C., Donzé, A., Cotton, S., Ray, R., Lebeltel, O., Ripado, R., Girard, A., Dang, T., Maler, O.: SpaceEx: scalable verification of hybrid systems. In: Gopalakrishnan, G., Qadeer, S. (eds.) CAV 2011. LNCS, vol. 6806, pp. 379–395. Springer, Heidelberg (2011). doi:10.1007/978-3-642-22110-1_30

17. Heizmann, M., Hoenicke, J., Podelski, A.: Refinement of trace abstraction. In: Palsberg, J., Su, Z. (eds.) SAS 2009. LNCS, vol. 5673, pp. 69–85. Springer, Heidelberg (2009). doi:10.1007/978-3-642-03237-0_7

18. Heizmann, M., Hoenicke, J., Podelski, A.: Software model checking for people who love automata. In: Sharygina, N., Veith, H. (eds.) CAV 2013. LNCS, vol. 8044, pp. 36–52. Springer, Heidelberg (2013). doi:10.1007/978-3-642-39799-8_2

19. Henzinger, T.A., Ho, P.-H., Wong-toi, H.: HyTech: a model checker for hybrid systems. Softw. Tools Technol. Transf. 1, 460–463 (1997)

20. Henzinger, T.A., Kopke, P.W., Puri, A., Varaiya, P.: What's decidable about hybrid automata? J. Comput. Syst. Sci. 57(1), 94–124 (1998)

21. Kordy, P., Langerak, R., Mauw, S., Polderman, J.W.: A symbolic algorithm for the analysis of robust timed automata. In: Jones, C., Pihlajasaari, P., Sun, J. (eds.) FM 2014. LNCS, vol. 8442, pp. 351–366. Springer, Cham (2014). doi:10.1007/978-3-319-06410-9_25

22. Sankur, O.: Symbolic quantitative robustness analysis of timed automata. In: Baier, C., Tinelli, C. (eds.) TACAS 2015. LNCS, vol. 9035, pp. 484–498. Springer, Heidelberg (2015). doi:10.1007/978-3-662-46681-0_48

23. Wang, W., Jiao, L.: Trace abstraction refinement for timed automata. In: Cassez, F., Raskin, J.-F. (eds.) ATVA 2014. LNCS, vol. 8837, pp. 396–410. Springer, Cham (2014). doi:10.1007/978-3-319-11936-6_28

An Abstract Machine for Asynchronous Programs with Closures and Priority Queues

Davide Ancona, Giorgio Delzanno[(✉)], Luca Franceschini, Maurizio Leotta, Enrico Prampolini, Marina Ribaudo, and Filippo Ricca

Dip. di Informatica, Bioingegneria, Robotica e Ingegneria dei Sistemi (DIBRIS), Università di Genova, Genoa, Italy
giorgio.delzanno@dibris.unige.it

Abstract. We present the operational semantics of an abstract machine that models computations of event-based asynchronous programs inspired to the Node.js server-side system, a convenient platform for developing Internet of Things applications. The goal of the formal description of Node.js internals is twofold: (1) integrating the existing documentation with a more rigorous semantics and (2) validating widely used programming and transformation patterns by means of mathematical tools like transition systems. Our operational semantics is parametric in the transition system of the host scripting language to mimic the infrastructure of the V8 virtual machine where Javascript code is executed on top of the event-based engine provided by the C++ libuv concurrency library. In this work we focus our attention on priority callback queues, nested callbacks, and closures; these are widely used Node.js programming features which, however, may render programs difficult to understand, manipulate, and validate.

1 Introduction

Asynchronous programming is getting more and more popular thanks to emergent server-side platforms like Node.js and operating systems for applications that require a constant interaction with the user interface; this programming paradigm reduces the need of controlling concurrency using synchronization primitives like lock and monitors. As an example, the execution model of Node.js is based on a single threaded loop used to poll events with different priorities and to serialize the execution of pending tasks by means of callbacks. Accordingly, I/O operations are performed through calls to asynchronous functions where callbacks are passed to specify how the computation continues once the corresponding I/O operations completed asynchronously.

Taking inspiration from previous work [1,2,4–8,10], in this paper we focus our attention on a formal semantics of asynchronous programs with the following features: Priority callback queues; Nested callback definitions to model anonymous callbacks; Closures used to propagate the caller scope to the postponed callback invocation. The formal semantics of the resulting system is given in a

© Springer International Publishing AG 2017
M. Hague and I. Potapov (Eds.): RP 2017, LNCS 10506, pp. 59–74, 2017.
DOI: 10.1007/978-3-319-67089-8_5

parametric form. Namely, we give a presentation that is modular in the transition system of the host programming language. We use callbacks as a bridge between the two layers as in implementation of scripting languages like Node.js running on virtual machines like Chrome V8. In our framework a callback is a procedure whose execution is associated with a given event. When the event is triggered by the program or by an external agent, the corresponding callback is added to a queue of pending tasks. In our model the execution of callbacks is controlled by an event-loop. After the complete execution of a callback, the event loop polls the queue and selects the next callback to execute.

This kind of behavior is typically supported via concurrent executions of I/O bound operations on a pool of worker threads. To get closer to the Node.js execution model, we model the behavior of the event loop using different phases. More precisely, we provide continuations as a means to define pending tasks with highest priority (they are executed at the end of a callback) as for the process.nextTick[1] operation in Node.js. Furthermore, we provide postponed callbacks as a means to postpone a callback after the poll phase of standard callbacks (internal, I/O, and networking events). This mechanism is similar to the setImmediate operation provided in Node.js. As in Node.js, nested continuations (a continuation that invokes a continuation) or the enqueuing of tasks during the poll phase are potential sources of starvation for the event loop. In actual implementations non termination in the poll phase is avoided by imposing a hard limit on the number of callbacks to be executed in each tick. All pending postponed callbacks are executed when the poll phase is quiescent.

Examples. To illustrate all above mentioned concepts, let us consider some examples taken from the standard fs module supporting file system operations in Node.js.

```
var fs = require('fs');
fs.readFile('abc.txt',function(err,data){err||console.log(data);});
console.log('ok');
```

Function readFile is asynchronous; once the read operation has completed, its continuation is defined by an anonymous callback with two parameters err and data holding, respectively, an optional error object and the data read from the file (in case no error occurred err contains null). If the read operation completes successfully, then the callback will print the read data on the standard output, but only after string ok. Let us now consider an example that uses the events module in Node.js for emitting events and registering associated callbacks.

```
var EventEmitter = require('events');
var Emitter = new EventEmitter();
var msg = function msg() { console.log('ok'); }
Emitter.on('evt1', msg);
Emitter.emit('evt1');
while (true);
```

---

[1] Despite of the name, this is the current semantics of Node.js.

On line 4 the callback msg is registered and associated with events of type 'evt1', then on the subsequent line an event of type msg is emitted; since method emit exhibits a synchronous behaviour, the associated callback is immediately executed and the message ok is printed before the program enters an infinite loop where no other callback will ever be executed. We now modify the program above as follows.

```
eventEmitter.on('evt1', function () { setImmediate(msg); });
eventEmitter.emit('evt1');
while (true);
```

Also in this case, after the event has been emitted, the associated callback is synchronously executed, but then setImmediate is used to postpone the execution of function msg to the next loop iteration, and therefore the program enters immediately the infinite loop without printing ok. System functions like setImmediate are used to interleave the main thread and callbacks. While there exists a rigorous semantics for Javascript, see e.g. [9], the Node.js on-line documentation [12] has not a formal counterpart and contains several ambiguities as can be read in [13], and in several discussions on the meaning of operations like setImmediate, nextTick, etc. see e.g. [11,14,15].

The combination of asynchronous programming with nested callbacks and closures may lead to programs with a quite intricate semantics; let us consider, for instance, the following fragment.

```
function test(){
    var d = 5;
    var foo = function(){ d = 10; }
    process.nextTick(foo);
    setImmediate(() => { console.log(d) })
}
test();
```

Function test defines a local variable d, which, however, is global to the inner function foo which is passed as callback to process.nextTick; technically, foo is called a closure, since it depends on the global variable d, which is updated by foo itself. Function process.nextTick postpones the execution of foo to the next loop iteration, however foo has higher priority over the callback passed to setImmediate on the following line. After the call to test is executed, the variable d local to the call is still allocated in the heap since it is referenced by the closure foo; when foo is called, the value of d is updated to 10, therefore the execution of console.log(d) will print 10 as result.

In the paper we propose a formal model for describing computations and to clarify the semantics of this kind of programs.

Plan of the paper. In Sect. 2 we present the formal definitions of the operational semantics of a scripting language and of the abstract machine that captures the event-driven behavior of our scripts. Both components are inspired to Node.js. Section 3 illustrates how to apply the operational semantics to reason about asynchronous programs. In Sect. 4 we define a specification language for reasoning about computations of the resulting combined framework (abstract machine and semantics of scripting language). Finally, in Sect. 5 we address related work and future research directions.

2   Abstract Machine for Asynchronous Programs

In this section we define the formal semantics of the abstract machine. We will first try to use a compositional method with respect to the semantics of the host language. We will instantiate the language with a simplified scripting language.

Preliminaries. In the rest of the paper we will use the following notation. $A^* = \{v_1 \ldots v_n | v_i \in A, i : 1, \ldots, n, \ n \geq 0\}$ denotes the set of words with elements in A. We use $w_1 \cdot w_2$ to denote concatenation of two lists and ϵ to denote the empty word. $A^{\otimes} = \{\{v_1 \ldots v_n\} | v_i \in A, \ i : 1, \ldots, n, \ n \geq 0\}$ denotes the set of multisets of elements in A. We use $m_1 \oplus m_2$ to denote multiset union of m_1 and m_2. We also use $a \oplus m$ to denote the addition of element $a \in A$ to m. $A^n = \{v = \langle v_1, \ldots, v_n \rangle | v_i \in A, \ i : 1, \ldots, n \ n \geq 1\}$ denotes set of tuples with elements in A. $[A \rightarrow B]$ denotes the set of maps from A to B. We use $[x/a]$ to denote the sequence of substitutions or maps $[x_1/a_1, \ldots, x_n/a_n]$ for $i : 1, \ldots, n$, $n \geq 1$. We use $t[s/x]$ to denote the term obtained from t by substituting every free occurrence of x with s. Furthermore, $m[v/x]$ denotes the maps m' defined as $m'(x) = v$ and $m'(y) = m(y)$ for every $y \neq x$. To manipulate callbacks we will use lambda-terms. A variable x, a value v and the constant *any* are lambda-terms. For a variable x and a lambda term t, $\lambda x.t$ is a lambda-term. If t and t' are lambda-terms, then $t(t')$ is a lambda-term. A variable x is free in t if there are occurrences of x in t that are not in the scope of a binder λx. Lambda terms are usually considered modulo renaming of bounded variable, i.e., all free occurrences under the scope of the same binder can be renamed without changing the abstract structure of the term. If x does not occur free in t', the application $(\lambda x.t)(t')$ reduces to the term $t[t'/x]$ obtained by substituting all free occurrences of x in t with the term t'.

2.1   Host Language

We assume here that programs are defined starting from *sequential* programs in a host language L with basic constructs and (recursive) procedures. Let F be a denumerable set of function names. Let us consider a denumerable set Val of primitive values (pure names in our example) and a denumerable set Var of variables. Expressions are either values or variables. We will also use the special term *any* to denote a non-deterministically selected value and in some example consider natural numbers and expression with standard semantics. To simplify the presentation, we will represent programs as words over the alphabet of program instructions I with variables in Var. An (anonymous) callback definition is a lambda-term $\lambda x.s$, where $x \in Var^k$ is the set of formal parameters, and $s \in I^*$. Now let A be a finite set of names of asynchronous operations. *Events* is a finite set of (internal and external) event labels s.t. $Events = Events_i \cup Events_e$ and $Events_i \cap Events_e = \emptyset$. Var may contain variable and function names in F. In order to define environments we will extend Val in order to contain closures, i.e., pairs in $Env \times Callback$ where $Callback$ is the set of lambda terms that denotes callback (function) definitions.

Furthermore, we introduce a denumerable set Loc of locations that we use to denote memory references so as to obtain a semantics with stateful closures. The association between locations and values will be defined via a global heap memory H that will be part of the system configuration. The heap memory H is a list of maps $[l_1/v_1, \ldots, l_k/v_k]$ s.t. l_i is a location and v_i is a value (primitive value or closure). We will use $Heap$ to denote the set of possible heaps.

The set of environments Env consists of list of substitutions $[x_1/l_1, \ldots, x_n/l_n]$ s.t. $x_i \in Var$ and $l_i \in Val$ for $i : 1, \ldots, n$. Given $\ell = [x_1/l_1, \ldots, x_n/l_n]$, $\ell(x) = l$ if there exists i s.t. $x_i = x$, $l_i = l$, and $x_j \neq x$ for $j > i$. In other words to evaluate x in ℓ we search the first occurrence of x from right to left and return its value. Given an environment ℓ and the heap memory H, we use ℓ_H to denote the function defined as $\ell_H(v) = H(\ell(v))$ for $v \in Var$.

In this way we can use an environment as a stack and represent therein nested scopes of variables. $Listener$ is the finite set maps $Events \rightarrow (Env \times F^*)^*$. A listener maps an event to a sequence of pairs each one consisting of an environment (the current environment of the caller) and a list of callback names (defined in the corresponding environment). $Call_F$ is the set of callback calls $\{f(v)|f \in F, v \in Val^k, k \geq 0\}$. $Call_A$ is the set of asynchronous calls $\{call(a, cb)|a \in A, cb \in F\}$ where A is a set of labels. Finally, a frame (a record of the call stack of the main program) is a pair $\langle \ell, u \rangle$ s.t. $\ell \in Env$ and $u \in I^*$.

The host language provides a denumerable set of global variables Var_G and an operation $store(x, e)$ to write the evaluation of expression e in the global variable x. We assume here that store operations on undefined variables add the variable to the environment (i.e. global environment can only be extended). Furthermore, we provide a special operation obs to label specific control points with the current value of an expression. The label is made observable by labeling the transition relation with it. The proposed instance of the host language allows us to design an assertional language to specify properties of computations in the abstract machine.

A program expression has either the structure $let\ x = e\ in\ B$ where x is a local variables and e an expression denoting a primitive value (not a function), or $let\ f_1 = \lambda y_1.P_1, \ldots, f_k = \lambda y_k.P_k\ in\ B$ where $P_1, \ldots, P_k$ are program expressions (they may contain let declarations). In both cases B is a finite sequence of instructions built on top of the above mentioned instruction set. We consider then the following types of instructions.

- $obs(e)$ is used to observe a certain event (a value)
- $store(x, e)$ is used to store a value (the evaluation of e) in the global or local variable x. We use the expression any to denote a value non deterministically selected from the set of values.

– $f(e)$ is used to synchronously invoke a callback f with the vector of parameters e. Actual parameters are global or local variables.

We assume that all necessary procedure definitions are declared in the program (we will introduce an example language with *let* declarations) so that their names are always defined in the current local environment. We now define the set of configurations C_L of the host language. C_L consists of tuples of the form $\langle G, H, S \rangle$, where $G \in Env$, H is the global heap, and $S \in Frame^*$. In other words S has the form $\langle \ell_1, S_1 \rangle \dots \langle \ell_n, S_n \rangle$ for $i : 1, \dots, n$. A word of frames will be interpreted as the stack of procedure calls. In a pair $\langle \ell, w \rangle$ ℓ is the local environment and w is the corresponding program to be executed.

$$\frac{\ell' = \ell[x/l], \; l_H(e) = v, \; H' = H[l/v], \; l \notin dom(H)}{\langle G, H, \langle \ell, let \; x = e \; in \; B \rangle \cdot S \rangle \rightarrow_L \langle G, H', \langle \ell', B \rangle \cdot S \rangle} \; s1v$$

$$\frac{\ell' = \ell[f_1/l_1, \dots, f_k/l_k], \; H' = H[l_1/\langle \ell, \lambda \boldsymbol{x}_1.P_1 \rangle, \dots, l_k/\langle \ell, \lambda \boldsymbol{x}_k.P_k \rangle]}{l_i \notin dom(H), \; l_i \neq l_j, \; for \; i, j : 1, \dots, k, \; i \neq j}{\langle G, H, \langle \ell, let \; f_1 = \lambda \boldsymbol{x}_1.P_1, \dots, f_k = \lambda \boldsymbol{x}_k.P_k \; in \; B \rangle \cdot S \rangle \rightarrow_L \langle G, H', \langle \ell', B \rangle \cdot S \rangle} \; s1f$$

$$\frac{}{\langle G, H, \langle \ell, obs(e) \cdot B \rangle \cdot S \rangle \rightarrow_L^{\widehat{\ell_H}(e)} \langle G, H, \langle \ell, B \rangle \cdot S \rangle} \; s2$$

$$\frac{x \notin dom(\ell) \quad G \cdot \ell_H(e) = w \neq \lambda y.e}{\langle G, H, \langle \ell, store(x, e) \cdot B \rangle \cdot S \rangle \rightarrow_L \langle G[x/w], H, \langle \ell, B \rangle \cdot S \rangle} \; s3g$$

$$\frac{x \in dom(\ell) \quad \ell_H(e) = w \neq \lambda y.e \quad \ell(x) = l}{\langle G, H, \langle \ell, store(x, e) \cdot B \rangle \cdot S \rangle \rightarrow_L \langle G, H[l/w], \langle \ell, B \rangle \cdot S \rangle} \; s3l$$

$$\frac{\ell_H(f) = \langle \ell', \lambda \boldsymbol{y}.u \rangle, \; G \cdot (\ell_H) \cdot (\ell'_H)(\boldsymbol{v}) = \boldsymbol{v}', \; H' = H[l/\boldsymbol{v}'], \; \ell'' = \ell[\boldsymbol{y}/\boldsymbol{l}],}{for \; \boldsymbol{l} = l_1, \dots, l_k, \; l_i \notin dom(H), \; l_i \neq l_j, \; for \; i, j : 1, \dots, k, \; i \neq j}{\langle G, H, \langle \ell, f(\boldsymbol{v}) \cdot B \rangle \cdot S \rangle \rightarrow_L \langle G, H', \langle \ell'', u \rangle \cdot \langle \ell, B \rangle \cdot S \rangle} \; s4$$

$$\frac{}{\langle G, H, \langle \ell, \epsilon \rangle \cdot S \rangle \rightarrow_L \langle G, H, S \rangle} \; s5$$

Fig. 1. Operational semantics of the host language

2.2   Operational Semantics

We assume that the operational semantics of programs in L is defined via a transition system $\langle C_L, \rightarrow_L \rangle$, where $\rightarrow_L \subseteq (C_L \times C_L)$ defines small step operational semantics of generic statements of programs in L. We will use λ-terms to represent callbacks in the local environment during program evaluation. In the semantics of our language, lambda terms are used as values for function names. Indeed, a local environment ℓ is a map that associates function names to locations, and H associates locations to lambda expressions. By using location for both variables and function names we obtain a more general semantics open to extensions in which variables can contain functions (as in Javascript) that can be dynamically updates. The transition system is obtained as the minimal set satisfying the rule schemes defined in Fig. 1. Rule $s1v$ models the semantics of the *let* expression for variables with primitive values (we assume here that e is not a function nor a function call). Its effect is to update the local environment with a new substitution between the variable name and a fresh location, and the heap with an association between the new location and the value of the expression. Rule $s1f$ models the semantics of the *let* expression. Its effect is to update the local environment with new substitutions between function names and locations, and the heap with associations between locations of pairs that represent the current environment and the lambda term that represents the body of the callback definition. Rule $s2$ models the semantics of instructions. This rule captures the effect of observing an event by exporting the label to the meta-level (i.e. as a label of the transition step). We assume here that if an expression a is not defined in ℓ_H (and it is not a function name) than it is simply viewed as a constant, i.e., $\widehat{\ell_H}(e) = e$ if $\ell_H(e)$ is not defined. Rule $s3$ captures the effect of a *store*(x, e) operation. We assume that *store* is defined only if x is a global variable and e evaluates to a value that is not a function. Furthermore, $\ell(any) \in Val$ (non deterministically selected). Rule $s4$ models synchronous calls. In this rule we first evaluate f in the current local environment to retrieve its definition. We then evaluate the parameters in the concatenation of global and local environments. We push a new frame onto the call stack containing a copy of the current environment (so as to transport the scope information from the current frame to the new one) concatenated with the evaluation of the parameters and the body of the function definition. Finally, rule $s5$ models the return from a call by eliminating the frame on top of the stack when its body is empty. In our host language, we can define a stronger rule by observing that local environments are copied from old to new frames and that local environments are not used as state by other frames. In other words, we can reason modulo the following equivalence between stack expressions: $(S_1 \cdot \langle \ell, \epsilon \rangle \cdot S_2) \equiv (S_1 \cdot S_2)$.

2.3   Abstract Machine

In this section we define the formal semantics of an abstract machine that can handle programs as those specified in the previous section extended with built-in instructions for associating event-handlers (callbacks) to event names, and to control the priority queues via special enqueues built-in primitives. More precisely, programs are defined by enriching the language L with the following control instructions:

- $reg(e, u)$: registers callbacks in the word (list) $u \in F^*$ for event e, we use a list since the callbacks must be processed in order.
- $unreg(e, P)$: unregisters all callbacks in the set $P \in \mathcal{P}(F)$ for event e.
- $call(op, cb)$: invokes an asynchronous operation op and registers the callback cb to be executed upon its termination. We assume here that the operation

generates a vector of input values that are passed, upon termination of op, to the callback cb.

- $nexttick(f, \boldsymbol{v})$: enqueues the call to f with parameters $\boldsymbol{v}$ in the nextTick queue.
- $setimmediate(f, \boldsymbol{v})$: postpones the call to function f with parameters $\boldsymbol{v}$ to the next tick of the event loop.
- $trigger(e, \boldsymbol{v})$: generates event $e \in Events_i$ (pushing callbacks in the poll queue) with actual parameters $\boldsymbol{v}$.

We now define the operational semantics of programs. We first define the set of configurations C_L of the host language. C_L consists of tuples of the form $\langle G, H, S \rangle$ where $G \in Env$, H is the heap memory, and $S \in Frame^*$. In other words S has the form $\langle \ell_1, S_1 \rangle \ldots \langle \ell_n, S_n \rangle$ for $i : 1, \ldots, n$. A word of frames will be interpreted as the stack of procedure calls. In a pair $\langle \ell, w \rangle$ ℓ is the local environment and w is the corresponding program to be executed. We assume that the operational semantics of programs in L are defined via a transition system $\langle C_L, \rightarrow_L \rangle$, where $\rightarrow_L \subseteq (C_L \times C_L)$ defines small step operational semantics of generic statements of programs in L.

A configuration is a tuple $\langle G, H, E, S, C, Q, P, R \rangle$, where $G \in Env$, $H \in Heap$, $E \in Listener$, $S \in Frame^*$, $C, Q, P \in (Env \times Call_F)^*$, and $R \in (Env \times Call_A)^{\otimes}$. C, Q, P and R are sequences of pairs consisting of a local environment and of a function invocation. C is the (nexttick) queue of pending callback invocations generated by $nexttick$, Q is the (poll) queue of pending callback invocations generated by $trigger$ and by external events. P is the (setimmediate) queue of pending callback invocations generated by $setimmediate$. Local environments are used to evaluate variables defined in the body of a callback at the moment of registration, synchronous or asynchronous invocation.

We associate to every L-program Π enriched with control instructions a transition system $T_\Pi = \langle Conf, \rightarrow \rangle$ in which $Conf$ is the set of configurations, and $\rightarrow$ is a relation in $Conf \times Conf$. Furthermore, we will use labeled versions of the transition relations, namely, $\rightarrow^\alpha$ and $\rightarrow^\alpha_L$, in order to keep track of observations generated by the evaluation of programs instructions. Labels are either values, variable or function names. For simplicity, we will use $\rightarrow$ [resp. $\rightarrow_L$] to denote $\rightarrow^\epsilon$ [resp. $\rightarrow^\epsilon_L$].

The initial configuration is the tuple

$$\gamma_0 = \langle \emptyset, \emptyset, \emptyset, \langle \epsilon, P \rangle, \epsilon, \epsilon, \epsilon, \emptyset \rangle$$

where we use $\emptyset$ to denote an empty map or multiset, ϵ to denote empty queues and local environments (both treated as words). In the rest of the paper we will use $\perp$ to denote the empty call stack (it helps in reading configurations). In order to evaluate expressions we need to combine G and a local environment ℓ. We use $G \cdot \ell$ to indicate the concatenations of the substitutions contained in G and ℓ. As for environments, to evaluate x we inspect the list of substitutions in $G \cdot \ell$ from right to left (a local variable can hide a global one with the same name). In the rest of the section we assume that procedure names occurring in a rule are always defined in the corresponding local environment. The transition system is obtained as the minimal set satisfying the rule schemes defined in Fig. 2. Rule $r1$ is used to embed the semantics of L into the semantics of the abstract machine. Rule $r2$ associates the current environment and the ordered list of callbacks u to the event evt. Everytime evt is triggered, the callbacks in u will be added to the queue of pending tasks together with the environment in the same order as they occur in u. Rule $r3$ unregisters all callbacks in P for event evt. We use $\ominus$ to denote this operation. Rule $r4$ assigns a semantics to the *trigger* instruction. It corresponds to the combination of emit and setImmediate discussed in the introduction. The rationale behind this definition is that when evt is triggered, all registered callbacks are added to the pending queue. The current local environment is stored together with the callback invocation. The formal parameters are instantiated with the actual parameters defined in the *trigger* statement. The environment can be used to evaluate variables occurring in the body of the callback definition. The actual parameters v are evaluated using the composition of the global and local environment.

We now consider asynchronous calls of built-in libraries to be executed in a thread pool. Rule $r5$ adds the call to a pool of pending tasks submitted to the pool thread. We do not model the internal behavior of asynchronous calls. The only information maintained in R is a pointer to the callback cb that has to be executed upon termination of the thread execution. The pool R is used to keep track of the operations that have been submitted to the thread pool. Since the termination order of these calls is not known a priori and, at least in principle, the calls might be processed in parallel by different threads, we abstract from the order and use a multiset for modeling the pool. According to this idea, rule $r6$ models the termination of a thread and the invocation of the corresponding callback cb. We assume here that cb expects k parameters. The callback is invoked with k non-deterministically generated values (they model the result returned by the asynchronous call). We remark that the constant a is used as a label and has no specific semantics (it helps in the examples).

In order to handle the response to external events (e.g. connections, etc.) we use the non-deterministic rule $r7$. We assume here that the data generated by the operation are non-deterministically selected from the set of values and associated with the formal parameters of the callback functions $p_1, \ldots, p_k$. Every callback invocation is stored together with the corresponding local environment.

Rule $r8$ deals with nextTick callbacks. Invocation of such an operation is defined as follows. The callback invocation is stored together with the current local environment. Rule $r9$ is used to deal with setImmediate invocations. The callback invocation is stored together with the current local environment. In $r8$ and $r9$ the actual parameters are evaluated using the composition of the global and local environment.

Rule $r10$ and $r11$ define the selection of pending tasks. The selection phase is defined according with the following priority order: nextTick, poll, setImmediate. nextTick callbacks are selected every time the call stack becomes empty (at the end of a callback execution). Poll callbacks are selected only when the call stack is empty and there are no nextTick callbacks to execute. The local envi-

$$\frac{\langle G, H, S\rangle \to_L^\alpha \langle G', H', S'\rangle}{\langle G, H, E, S, C, Q, P, R\rangle \to^\alpha \langle G', H', E, S', C, Q, P, R\rangle} \; r1$$

$$\frac{E' = E[evt/(E(evt) \cdot \langle \ell, u\rangle)]}{\langle G, H, E, \langle \ell, reg(evt, u)\rangle \cdot w\rangle \cdot S, C, Q, P, R\rangle \to \langle G, H, E', \langle \ell, w\rangle \cdot S, C, Q, P, R\rangle} \; r2$$

$$\frac{E' = E[evt/(E(evt) \ominus u)]}{\langle G, H, E, \langle \ell, unreg(evt, u)\rangle \cdot w\rangle \cdot S, C, Q, P, R\rangle \to \langle G, H, E', \langle \ell, w\rangle \cdot S, C, Q, P, R\rangle} \; r3$$

$$\frac{\begin{array}{c} evt \in Events_i \quad E(evt) = \langle \ell_1, u_1\rangle \ldots \langle \ell_m, u_m\rangle \quad u_i = p_1^i \cdot \ldots \cdot p_{k_i}^i \; for \; i:1,\ldots,m \\ r = \langle \ell_1, p_1^1(\boldsymbol{v})\rangle \cdot \ldots \cdot \langle \ell_1, p_{k_1}^1(\boldsymbol{v})\rangle \ldots \langle \ell_m, p_1^m(\boldsymbol{v})\rangle \cdot \ldots \cdot \langle \ell_m, p_{k_m}^m(\boldsymbol{v})\rangle \quad \boldsymbol{v} \in Val^k \end{array}}{\langle G, H, E, \langle \ell, trigger(evt, \boldsymbol{v})\rangle \cdot w\rangle \cdot S, C, Q, P, R\rangle \to \langle G, H, E, \langle \ell, w\rangle \cdot S, C, Q \cdot r, P, R\rangle} \; r4$$

$$\frac{R' = R \oplus \{\langle \ell, call(a, cb)\rangle\}}{\langle G, H, E, \langle \ell, call(a, cb)\rangle \cdot w\rangle \cdot S, C, Q, P, R\rangle \to \langle G, H, E, \langle \ell, w\rangle \cdot S, C, Q, P, R'\rangle} \; r5$$

$$\frac{u = \langle \ell, cb(\boldsymbol{v})\rangle \quad \boldsymbol{v} \in Val^k \quad R' = R \setminus \{\langle \ell, call(a, cb)\rangle\}}{\langle G, H, E, S, C, Q, P, R\rangle \to \langle G, H, E, S, C, Q \cdot u, P, R'\rangle} \; r6$$

$$\frac{\begin{array}{c} evt \in Events_e \quad E(evt) = \langle \ell_1, u_1\rangle \ldots \langle \ell_m, u_m\rangle \quad u_i = p_1^i \cdot \ldots \cdot p_{k_i}^i \; for \; i:1,\ldots,m \\ r = \langle \ell_1, p_1^1(\boldsymbol{v})\rangle \cdot \ldots \cdot \langle \ell_1, p_{k_1}^1(\boldsymbol{v})\rangle \ldots \langle \ell_m, p_1^m(\boldsymbol{v})\rangle \cdot \ldots \cdot \langle \ell_m, p_{k_m}^m(\boldsymbol{v})\rangle \quad \boldsymbol{v} \in Val^k \end{array}}{\langle G, H, E, S, C, Q, P, R\rangle \to \langle G, H, E, S, C, Q \cdot r, P, R\rangle} \; r7$$

$$\frac{G \cdot \ell_H(\boldsymbol{v}) = \boldsymbol{v}'}{\langle G, H, E, \langle \ell, nexttick(f, \boldsymbol{v})\rangle \cdot w\rangle \cdot S, C, Q, P, R\rangle \to \langle G, H, E, \langle \ell, w\rangle \cdot S, C \cdot \langle \ell, f(\boldsymbol{v}')\rangle, Q, P, R\rangle} \; r8$$

$$\frac{G \cdot \ell_H(\boldsymbol{v}) = \boldsymbol{v}'}{\langle G, H, E, \langle \ell, setimmediate(f, \boldsymbol{v})\rangle \cdot w\rangle \cdot S, C, Q, P, R\rangle \to \langle G, H, E, \langle \ell, w\rangle \cdot S, C, Q, P \cdot \langle \ell, f(\boldsymbol{v}')\rangle, R\rangle} \; r9$$

$$\frac{\begin{array}{c} \ell_H(p) = \langle \ell', \lambda\boldsymbol{y}.s\rangle, \; G \cdot (\ell_H) \cdot (\ell_H')(\boldsymbol{v}) = \boldsymbol{v}', \; H' = H[\boldsymbol{l}/\boldsymbol{v}'], \; \ell'' = \ell[\boldsymbol{y}/\boldsymbol{l}], \\ for \; \boldsymbol{l} = l_1, \ldots, l_k, \; l_i \notin dom(H), \; l_i \neq l_j, \; for \; i, j : 1, \ldots, k, \; i \neq j \end{array}}{\langle G, H, E, \bot, \langle \ell, p(\boldsymbol{v})\rangle \cdot C, Q, P, R\rangle \to \langle G, H', E, \langle \ell', s\rangle, C, Q, P, R\rangle} \; r10$$

$$\frac{\begin{array}{c} \ell_H(f) = \langle \ell', \lambda\boldsymbol{y}.s\rangle, \; G \cdot (\ell_H) \cdot (\ell_H')(\boldsymbol{v}) = \boldsymbol{v}', \; H' = H[\boldsymbol{l}/\boldsymbol{v}'], \; \ell'' = \ell[\boldsymbol{y}/\boldsymbol{l}], \\ for \; \boldsymbol{l} = l_1, \ldots, l_k, \; l_i \notin dom(H), \; l_i \neq l_j, \; for \; i, j : 1, \ldots, k, \; i \neq j \end{array}}{\langle G, H, E, \bot, \epsilon, p(\boldsymbol{v}) \cdot Q, P, R\rangle \to \langle G, H', E, \langle \ell', s\rangle, \epsilon, Q, P, R\rangle} \; r11$$

$$\frac{}{\langle G, H, E, \bot, \epsilon, \epsilon, P, R\rangle \to \langle G, H, E, \bot, \epsilon, P, \epsilon, R\rangle} \; r12$$

Fig. 2. Operational semantics of the abstract machine

ronment is initialized with the stored environment ℓ and the map that associates parameters to actual values. SetImmediate callbacks are selected only when both the call stack and the nextTick queue are empty. We assume that the definition of p is available in the local environment stored with the callback (the global environment does not contain function definitions). The local environment is initialized with the stored environment ℓ and the map that associates parameters to actual values. Finally, in rule r12 all (pending) setImmediate callbacks are executed before passing to the next tick of the event loop.

Given a program P with initial state γ_0 and transition relation $\to$, we use $\to^*$ to denote the reflexive and transitive closure of $\to$. The sequence of labels generated during the unfolding of the transition relation $\to$ gives rise to possibly infinite words in $Labels^*$ that we will use to observe the behavior of a given instance of the host language when executed in the abstract machine. Starting from an initial state γ_0, a program can give rise to several different computations obtained by considering every possible reordering of asynchronous operations. This feature, in combination with the callback mechanism that can delay the execution of a function, makes our programs a non trivial computational model even in the simple case of Boolean programs, i.e., programs in which all data are abstracted into a finite set of possible values.

We will restrict our attention to infinite executions under fairness conditions to ensure the termination of asynchronous callbacks after finitely many steps. Indeed, asynchronous callbacks are typically built-in operations that terminate with an error if something goes wrong in their execution. Similarly, we might restrict our attention to infinite executions in which external events, for which there are registered callbacks, occur infinitely often.

3   Formal Reasoning

In this section we will consider some example of formal reasoning via the transition systems introduced in the previous sections. For the sake of simplicity, in all examples but the last one on closures with state, we will omit the heap component and consider only environments mapping variables to values. We will use the complete semantics when considering side effects on closures.

Let us first consider the program defined as follows.

$$P = let\ f = (let\ (cb = \lambda x.\ obs(x))\ in\ call(read, cb) \cdot f)\ in\ f()$$

A possible computation, in which we apply the reduction $\langle \ell, f \rangle \cdot \langle \ell, \epsilon \rangle \equiv \langle \ell, f \rangle$, is given below.

$$\rho_1 = \langle \emptyset, \emptyset, \emptyset, \langle \epsilon, P \rangle, \epsilon, \epsilon, \epsilon, \emptyset \rangle \rightarrow$$
$$\rho_2 = \langle \emptyset, \emptyset, \emptyset, \langle \ell, f \rangle, \epsilon, \epsilon, \epsilon, \emptyset \rangle\ s.t.\ \ell\ defines\ f \rightarrow$$
$$\rho_3 = \langle \emptyset, \emptyset, \emptyset, \langle \ell, f \rangle, \epsilon, \epsilon, \epsilon, \emptyset \rangle \rightarrow$$
$$\rho_4 = \langle \emptyset, \emptyset, \emptyset, \langle \ell, let\ cb = \lambda x.obs(x)\ in\ call(read, cb) \cdot f \rangle, \epsilon, \epsilon, \epsilon, \emptyset \rangle \rightarrow$$
$$\rho_5 = \langle \emptyset, \emptyset, \emptyset, \langle \ell', call(read, cb) \cdot f \rangle, \epsilon, \epsilon, \epsilon, \emptyset \rangle\ s.t.\ \ell'\ defines\ cb \rightarrow$$
$$\rho_6 = \langle \emptyset, \emptyset, \emptyset, \langle \ell', f \rangle, \epsilon, \epsilon, \epsilon, \{\langle \ell', call(read, cb) \rangle\} \rangle$$

In the configuration ρ_6 we can either assume that the asynchronous call is already terminated or continue with the execution of the current callback. In the former case we have the following continuation.

$$\rho_6 \rightarrow \rho_7 = \langle \emptyset, \emptyset, \emptyset, \langle \ell', f \rangle, \epsilon, \epsilon, \langle \ell', cb(d) \rangle, \emptyset \rangle\ for\ d \in Val$$

In the latter case we will add a new frame to the call stack with the body of f. We now observe that, in both cases, the callback stack will never get empty again. Therefore, the callback cb, defined in the local environment ℓ', will never be selected for execution even under additional fairness conditions. As a consequence, the transition system will never generate observations during any of its infinitely many possible computations (the termination of the asynchronous call can happen anytime). This formally explains why in systems like Node.js everytime the main application has a recursive structure (e.g. to model an infinite loop) in order to make it responsive to external events, it is necessary to encapsulate the recursive call into invocations of primitives like setImmediate and nextTick. To illustrate this idea, let us consider the following modified program.

$$P_1 = let\ f = (let\ cb = \lambda x.\ obs(x)\ in\ call(read, cb) \cdot setimmediate(f))\ in\ f()$$

We obtain the following behavior.

$$\rho_1 = \langle \emptyset, \emptyset, \emptyset, \langle \epsilon, P_1 \rangle, \epsilon, \epsilon, \epsilon, \emptyset \rangle \rightarrow$$
$$\rho_2 = \langle \emptyset, \emptyset, \emptyset, \langle \ell, f \rangle, \epsilon, \epsilon, \epsilon, \emptyset \rangle s.t.\ \ell\ defines\ f \rightarrow^*$$
$$\rho_3 = \langle \emptyset, \emptyset, \emptyset, \langle \ell', setimmediate(f) \rangle, \epsilon, \epsilon, \epsilon, \{\langle \ell', call(read, cb) \rangle\} \rangle\ s.t.\ \ell'\ def.\ f, cb$$

Again we have a bifurcation here. For instance, let us assume that *read* terminates. We obtain then the following computation.

$$\rho_3 \rightarrow \rho_4 = \langle \emptyset, \emptyset, \emptyset, \langle \ell, setimmediate(f) \rangle, \epsilon, cb(d), \epsilon, \emptyset \rangle \rightarrow^*$$
$$\rho_5 = \langle \emptyset, \emptyset, \emptyset, \bot, \epsilon, \langle \ell', cb(d) \rangle, \langle \ell', f \rangle, \emptyset \rangle \rightarrow$$
$$\rho_6 = \langle \emptyset, \emptyset, \emptyset, \langle \ell', cb(d) \rangle, \epsilon, \langle \ell', f \rangle, \emptyset \rangle \rightarrow$$
$$\rho_7 = \langle \emptyset, \emptyset, \emptyset, \langle \ell'[x/d], obs(x) \rangle, \epsilon, \langle \ell', f \rangle, \emptyset \rangle \rightarrow^d$$
$$\rho_8 = \langle \emptyset, \emptyset, \emptyset, \langle \ell'[x/d], \epsilon \rangle, \epsilon, \langle \ell', f \rangle, \emptyset \rangle \ldots$$

It is interesting to observe here that callbacks are evaluated in the environment of the caller. For instance, in this example function cb and f are both defined in ℓ', the local environment used to initialize the frame associated to the invocation $cb(d)$. In other words, under fairness conditions on the termination of asynchronous callbacks, the execution of program P_1 generates infinite traces labeled with an arbitrary sequence of values that correspond to successful termination of read operations.

To understand the difference between nextTick and setImmediate, let us first consider the nextTick operation.

$$NT = let\ f_1 = (\lambda d_1.obs(a)),\ f_2 = (\lambda d_2.obs(b)),\ f_3 = (\lambda z.obs(c))$$
$$in\ nexttick(f_1) \cdot call(b, f_2) \cdot call(c, f_3)$$

We then apply our operational semantics to study its behavior.

$$\rho_1 = \langle \emptyset, \emptyset, \emptyset, \langle \epsilon, W \rangle, \epsilon, \epsilon, \epsilon, \emptyset \rangle \rightarrow$$
$$\rho_2 = \langle \emptyset, \emptyset, \emptyset, \langle \ell, nexttick(f_1) \cdot call(b, f_2) \cdot call(c, f_3) \rangle, \epsilon, \epsilon, \epsilon, \emptyset \rangle$$
$$s.t.\ \ell\ cont.\ all\ def. \rightarrow$$
$$\rho_3 = \langle \emptyset, \emptyset, \emptyset, \langle \ell, call(b, f_2) \cdot call(c, f_3) \rangle, \langle \ell, f_1 \rangle, \epsilon, \epsilon, \emptyset \rangle \rightarrow$$
$$\rho_4 = \langle \emptyset, \emptyset, \emptyset, \langle \ell, call(b, f_2) \rangle, \langle \ell, f \rangle, \epsilon, \epsilon, \{call(c, f_3)\} \rangle$$

We now have possible bifurcations due delays in the termination of c. We could for instance reach one of the following two configurations:

$$\rho_5 = \langle \emptyset, \emptyset, \emptyset, \langle \ell, call(c, f_3) \rangle, \langle \ell, f_1 \rangle, call(b, f_2), \epsilon, \emptyset \rangle$$
$$\rho_5' = \langle \emptyset, \emptyset, \emptyset, \bot, \langle \ell, f_1 \rangle, \epsilon, \epsilon, \{call(b, f_2), call(c, f_3)\} \rangle$$

From the latter we can obtain

$$\rho_6' = \langle \emptyset, \emptyset, \emptyset, \bot, \langle \ell, f_1 \rangle, call(b, f_2) \cdot call(c, f_3), \epsilon, \emptyset \rangle$$
$$\rho_6'' = \langle \emptyset, \emptyset, \emptyset, \bot, \langle \ell, f_1 \rangle, call(b, f_3) \cdot call(c, f_2), \epsilon, \emptyset \rangle$$

In all cases f_1 will be executed before f_2 and f_3 because of the priority order used to inspect the queue of pending calls when the call stack becomes empty, i.e., neither f_2 nor f_3 can overtake f_1.

Now let us consider the same program with *setimmediate* replacing *nexttick*.

$$NT = let \;\; f_1 = (\lambda d_1.obs(a)), \;\; f_2 = (\lambda d_2.obs(b)), \;\; f_3 = (\lambda z.obs(c))$$
$$in \; setimmediate(f_1) \cdot call(b, f_2) \cdot call(c, f_3)$$

We then apply our operational semantics to study its behavior.

$$\rho_1 = \langle \emptyset, \emptyset, \emptyset, \langle \epsilon, W \rangle, \epsilon, \epsilon, \epsilon, \emptyset \rangle \rightarrow$$
$$\rho_2 = \langle \emptyset, \emptyset, \emptyset, \langle \ell, setimmediate(f_1) \cdot call(b, f_2) \cdot call(c, f_3) \rangle, \epsilon, \epsilon, \epsilon, \emptyset \rangle$$
$$s.t. \;\ell \; cont. \; all \; def. \rightarrow$$
$$\rho_3 = \langle \emptyset, \emptyset, \emptyset, \langle \ell, call(b, f_2) \cdot call(c, f_3) \rangle, \epsilon, \epsilon, \langle \ell, f_1 \rangle, \emptyset \rangle \rightarrow$$
$$\rho_4 = \langle \emptyset, \emptyset, \emptyset, \langle \ell, call(b, f_2) \rangle, \epsilon, \epsilon, \langle \ell, f_1 \rangle, \{call(c, f_3)\} \rangle$$

We now have possible bifurcations due delays in the termination of c. We could for instance reach one of the following two configurations:

$$\rho_5 = \langle \emptyset, \emptyset, \emptyset, \langle \ell, call(c, f_3) \rangle, \epsilon, call(b, f_2), \langle \ell, f_1 \rangle, \emptyset \rangle$$
$$\rho_5' = \langle \emptyset, \emptyset, \emptyset, \bot, \epsilon, \epsilon, \langle \ell, f_1 \rangle, \{\langle \ell, call(b, f_2) \rangle, \langle \ell, call(c, f_3) \rangle\} \rangle$$

From the latter we can obtain one of the following configurations:

$$\rho_6 = \langle \emptyset, \emptyset, \emptyset, \langle \ell, f_1 \rangle, \epsilon, \epsilon, \{\langle \ell, call(b, f_2) \rangle \cdot \langle \ell, call(c, f_3) \rangle\} \rangle$$
$$\rho_7 = \langle \emptyset, \emptyset, \emptyset, \bot, \langle \ell, call(b, f_2) \rangle \cdot \langle \ell, call(c, f_3) \rangle, \langle \ell, f_1 \rangle, \emptyset \rangle$$
$$\rho_8 = \langle \emptyset, \emptyset, \emptyset, \bot, \langle \ell, call(c, f_3) \rangle \cdot \langle \ell, call(b, f_2) \rangle, \langle \ell, f_1 \rangle, \emptyset \rangle$$

4   Property Specification Language

The formalization of the operational semantics for an abstract machine for even-loop based programs has several possible applications. First of all, it gives a formal meaning to complex computational models underlying widely used systems like Node.js. The informal documentation of operations like nextTick, setImmediate, etc. that we found in the dev site [12] is ambiguous and difficult to parse. A transition system like the one presented in this paper gives a precise mathematical meaning to each operation in terms of evolution of configurations. Based on this, we can use the operational semantics as a formal tool to reason about computations in the abstract machines. For this purpose, we introduce an extension of regular expressions in order to handle values from an infinite domain, i.e., represent labels associated to values. A finite state automata is a tuple $A = \langle Q, \Sigma, \delta, q_0 \rangle$ in which Q is a finite set of states, $\delta : Q \times \Sigma \rightarrow Q$ is the transition relation and q_0 is an initial state. A computation is a (possibly infinite) sequence $q_0 a_0 q_1 a_1 q_2 \ldots$ s.t. $q_{i+1} = \delta(q_i, a_i)$ for $i \geq 0$. The observation of a computation $q_0 a_0 q_1 a_1 q_2 \ldots$ is the possibly infinite word $a_0 a_1 a_2 \ldots$ of labels occurring along the computation.

For an alphabet Σ, let $\widehat{\Sigma} = \{\widehat{a}|a \in \Sigma\}$. An extended automata EA is an automata $A = \langle Q, \Sigma \cup \widehat{\Sigma}, \delta, q_0 \rangle$. We use $\widehat{x}$ as a sort of variable. The effect of $\widehat{x}$ is to associate a value v, non deterministically chosen, to x and to instantiate x with v in every successive transition labeled with x until the next $\widehat{x}$ label is encountered and so on. If there are no occurrences of $\widehat{a}$ then the label is interpreted as a. In other words during the unfolding of the transition relation of an extended automata for each label we maintain its current state. The initial state of label a is a itself. However everytime we encounter $\widehat{a}$ its state is updated with some value taken from D. More precisely, the configuration of an extended automata is a tuple $\langle q, \rho \rangle$ where $\rho : \Sigma \to D$. The initial state is defined as $\langle q_0, id_\Sigma \rangle$, where $id_\Sigma(a) = a$ for each $a \in \Sigma$. Given a configuration $\langle q, \rho \rangle$, $a \in \Sigma$ and $\delta(q, a) = q'$, we have that $\langle q, \rho \rangle \to^a \langle q', \rho \rangle$. Given a configuration $\langle q, \rho \rangle$, $a \in \Sigma$ and $\delta(q, \widehat{a}) = q'$, we have that $\langle q, \rho \rangle \to^v \langle q', \rho' \rangle$ where $\rho'(a) = v$ for some $v \in D$ and $\rho'(b) = \rho(b)$ for $b \neq a, b \in \Sigma$. A computation is a sequence $\langle q_0, \rho_0 \rangle \alpha_0 \langle q_1, \rho_1 \rangle \alpha_1 \ldots$ such that $\langle q_i, \rho_i \rangle \to_i^\alpha \langle q_{i+1}, \rho_{i+1} \rangle$ for $i \geq 0$. The sequence of labels $\alpha_0 \alpha_1 \ldots$ is called here observation. This simple extension of finite automata allows us to represent observations of value non-deterministically generated during a computation and passed from one callback to another. By definition, we consider only a finite number of variables in order to keep the model as simplest as possible. Finally, we say that a program P conforms to specification given as an extended automata A iff for every computation c of program P in the abstract machine that generates a sequence of labels σ, there exists a computation in the extended automata with observation σ.

To validate examples extracted from Node.js code, we have written a meta-interpreter in Prolog that can explore all possible bounded executions of the proposed model and catch unexpected execution orders with respect to specifications given in a sublanguage of the automata based language proposed in this section. The interpreter [16] exploits the search mechanism of the Prolog runtime system in order to analyze sets of executions of a given input program. We remark that, although Node.js are at first sight sequential programs, their computation is often highly non- deterministic due to the heavy use of asynchronous operations and internal and external events.

5   Conclusions and Related Work

We have presented a first attempt of formalizing the operational semantics of the Node.js event-loop asynchronous computation model including some of the more intricate elements (priority callback queues, nested callbacks, closures) of such a programming system. Following the underlying structured of the event-based loop (inspired to the V8 engine), we have formulated the semantics in terms of an abstract machine operating on a parametric transition system describing the semantics of the host scripting language. We believe that formal specification and verification of this kind of systems will be more and more important in order to improve the development process of Internet of Things applications, their reliability, and in order to provide non ambiguous documentations of low level details of primitives like those described in this paper. More work has still to be done concerning automation of the verification task e.g. by exploiting approximated algorithms and abstraction for both procedural and functional scripting languages.

There exist several works on formal models of asynchronous programs. In [10] the authors provide verification algorithms for asynchronous systems modeled as pushdown systems with external memory. The external memory is defined as a multiset of pending procedure calls. Theoretical results on recognizability of Parikh images of context-free language are used to obtain an algorithmic characterization of the reachable set of the resulting model. The algorithms have been extended to other types of external memory in [2]. Algorithms for liveness properties are studied in [7] and for real-time extensions are given in [5]. A complexity analysis of decidable fragments is given in [6]. In [8] the authors consider a general model of event-based systems in which task are maintained in FIFO queues. The focus of their analysis again is providing algorithmic techniques for different types of restrictions of the model via reductions to Petri Nets, PDS, and Lossy channel systems. In [3] the authors define a model for asynchronous programs with task buffers in which events and buffers are dynamically created. Decidable fragments are obtained via reductions to Data nets. Differently from the above mentioned work, the goal of the present paper is not that of isolating decidable fragments. We are interested instead in giving a precise semantics to the interplay between asynchronous architecture like Node.js and scripting languages executed on top of them see e.g. more empirical works like [1,4]. In this sense we think that, more than restrictions, our framework needs further . extensions in order to capture for instance objects and dynamic memory allocation as done in formal semantics of languages like Javascript [9]. Our validation approach is based on enumeration techniques and partial search similar to tools used for concurrent systems.

References

1. Alimadadi, S., Sequeira, S., Mesbah, A., Pattabiraman, K.: Understanding javascript event-based interactions with clematis. ACM Trans. Softw. Eng. Methodol. **25**(2), 12:1–12:38 (2016)
2. Chadha, R., Viswanathan, M.: Decidability results for well-structured transition systems with auxiliary storage. In: Caires, L., Vasconcelos, V.T. (eds.) CONCUR 2007. LNCS, vol. 4703, pp. 136–150. Springer, Heidelberg (2007). doi:10.1007/978-3-540-74407-8_10
3. Emmi, M., Ganty, P., Majumdar, R., Rosa-Velardo, F.: Analysis of asynchronous programs with event-based synchronization. In: Vitek, J. (ed.) ESOP 2015. LNCS, vol. 9032, pp. 535–559. Springer, Heidelberg (2015). doi:10.1007/978-3-662-46669-8_22

4. Gallaba, K., Mesbah, A., Beschastnikh, I.: Don't call us, we'll call you: characterizing callbacks in Javascript. In: 2015 ACM/IEEE International Symposium on Empirical Software Engineering and Measurement, ESEM 2015, Beijing, China, 22–23 October 2015, pp. 247–256 (2015)

5. Ganty, P., Majumdar, R.: Analyzing real-time event-driven programs. In: Ouaknine, J., Vaandrager, F.W. (eds.) FORMATS 2009. LNCS, vol. 5813, pp. 164–178. Springer, Heidelberg (2009). doi:10.1007/978-3-642-04368-0_14

6. Ganty, P., Majumdar, R.: Algorithmic verification of asynchronous programs. ACM Trans. Program. Lang. Syst. **34**(1), 6:1–6:48 (2012)

7. Ganty, P., Majumdar, R., Rybalchenko, A.: Verifying liveness for asynchronous programs. POPL **2009**, 102–113 (2009)

8. Geeraerts, G., Heußner, A., Raskin, J.-F.: On the verification of concurrent, asynchronous programs with waiting queues. ACM Trans. Embedded Comput. Syst. **14**(3), 58:1–58:26 (2015)

9. Park, D., Stefanescu, A., Rosu, G.: KJS: a complete formal semantics of javascript. PLDI **2015**, 346–356 (2015)

10. Sen, K., Viswanathan, M.: Model checking multithreaded programs with asynchronous atomic methods. In: Ball, T., Jones, R.B. (eds.) CAV 2006. LNCS, vol. 4144, pp. 300–314. Springer, Heidelberg (2006). doi:10.1007/11817963_29

11. https://howtonode.org/understanding-process-next-tick

12. https://nodejs.org/en/docs/

13. https://nodejs.org/en/docs/guides/event-loop-timers-and-nexttick/

14. http://stackoverflow.com/questions/15349733/setimmediate-vs-nexttick

15. https://www.quora.com/

16. http://www.disi.unige.it/person/DelzannoG/NODE/

Copyful Streaming String Transducers

Emmanuel Filiot[1] and Pierre-Alain Reynier[2(✉)]

[1] Computer Science Department, Université Libre de Bruxelles, Brussels, Belgium
[2] Aix-Marseille Univ, LIF, CNRS, Marseille, France
`pierre-alain.reynier@lif.univ-mrs.fr`

Abstract. Copyless streaming string transducers (copyless SST) have
been introduced by R. Alur and P. Černý in 2010 as a one-way deterministic automata model to define transductions of finite strings. Copyless
SST extend deterministic finite state automata with a set of variables
in which to store intermediate output strings, and those variables can
be combined and updated all along the run, in a linear manner, i.e., no
variable content can be copied on transitions. It is known that copyless
SST capture exactly the class of MSO-definable string-to-string transductions, and are as expressive as deterministic two-way transducers.
They enjoy good algorithmic properties. Most notably, they have decidable equivalence problem (in PSpace).

On the other hand, HDT0L systems have been introduced for a while,
the most prominent result being the decidability of the equivalence problem. In this paper, we propose a semantics of HDT0L systems in terms
of transductions, and use it to study the class of deterministic copyful
SST. Our contributions are as follows:

(i) HDT0L systems and total deterministic copyful SST have the same
expressive power,
(ii) the equivalence problem for deterministic copyful SST and the equivalence problem for HDT0L systems are inter-reducible, in linear
time. As a consequence, equivalence of deterministic SST is decidable,
(iii) the functionality of non-deterministic copyful SST is decidable,
(iv) determining whether a deterministic copyful SST can be transformed
into an equivalent deterministic copyless SST is decidable in polynomial time.

1 Introduction

The theory of languages is extremely rich and important automata-logic corre-
spondances have been shown for various classes of logics, automata, and structures. There are less known automata-logic connections in the theory of transductions. Nevertheless, important results have been obtained for the class of

The work of Emmanuel Filiot was funded by the ARC project Transform (Federation
Wallonia-Brussels) and the Belgian FNRS CDR project Flare. Emmanuel Filiot is
research associate at F.R.S.-FNRS. The work of Pierre-Alain Reynier was funded by
the DeLTA project (ANR-16-CE40-0007).

M. Hague and I. Potapov (Eds.): RP 2017, LNCS 10506, pp. 75–86, 2017.
DOI: 10.1007/978-3-319-67089-8_6

MSO-definable transductions, as defined by Courcelle. Most notably, it has been shown by J. Engelfriet and H.J. Hoogeboom that MSO-definable (finite) string to string transductions are exactly those transductions defined by deterministic two-way transducers [12]. This result has then been extended to ordered ranked trees by J. Engelfriet and S. Maneth, for the class of linear-size increase macro tree transducers [13] and recently to nested words-to-words transductions [10]. MSO-definable transductions of finite strings have also been characterized by a new automata model, that of (copyless) streaming string transducers, by R. Alur and P. Černý [2].

Copyless streaming string transducers (SST) extend deterministic finite state automata with a finite set of string variables $X, Y, \ldots$. Each variable stores an intermediate string output and can be combined and updated with other variables. Along the transitions, a finite string can be appended or prepended to a variable, and variables can be reset or concatenated. The variable updates along the transitions are formally defined by variable substitutions and the copyless restriction is defined by considering only linear substitutions. Therefore, variable update such as $X := XX$ are forbidden by the copyless restriction. The SST model has then been extended to other structures such as infinite strings [7], trees [4], and quantitative languages [5].

Two examples of SST are depicted in Fig. 1:

- The SST T_0 depicted on the left realizes the function f_0 mapping any input word $u \in \Sigma^*$ to the word $u\bar{u}$, where $\bar{u}$ is the mirror image of the word u. Indeed, when the input word u has been read by the automaton, the variable X contains the word u, while the variable Y contains the word $\bar{u}$. Hence, the final output, defined as XY, is equal to the concatenation $u\bar{u}$. It is worth noting that this SST is copyless.
- The SST T_1 depicted on the right realizes the function f_1 mapping any input word $u = a^n$, with $n \geq 1$, to the output word a^{2^n}. This SST is copyful.

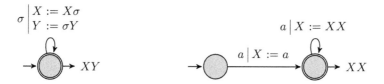

Fig. 1. Two streaming string transducers T_0 (left) and T_1 (right).

One of the most important and fundamental problem in the theory of transducers is the *equivalence problem*, which asks, given two transducers, whether they realize the same transduction. This problem is well known to be decidable for rational functions, and more generally for MSO-definable transductions [14], and hence for copyless SST (in PSpace, as shown in [1]). The problem gets undecidable when the transducers define binary relations instead of functions:

it is already undecidable for rational transducers [17], a strict subclass of non-deterministic SST. However, it was unknown whether, in the functional case, decidability still holds without the copyless restriction, as mentioned in [3], an extended version of [4].

HDT0L systems allow to define languages by means of morphism iteration: a sequence of indices $i_1, \ldots, i_k$ induces a composition of morphisms (one morphism for each index i_j) which, applied on an initial and fixed word, produces a new word. An important result related to HDT0L systems has been obtained in the 80's, see [9]. It states that the equivalence of finite-valued transducers over HDT0L languages is decidable, with unknown complexity.

In this paper, we build a tight connection between HDT0L systems and streaming string transducers. To this end, we introduce a new semantics of HDT0L systems, viewed as transducers. This allows us to prove that (total) copyful SST and HDT0L systems (seen as transducers) have the same expressive power, with back and forth transformations of linear complexity. As a corollary of this result, we obtain that the equivalence problem of copyful SST and the equivalence problem of HDT0L systems are inter-reducible, in linear time. This result has two consequences:

- first, the decidability of SST equivalence directly follows from [9],
- second, the functionality problem for non-deterministic (copyful) SST is decidable.

Note that the decidability of SST equivalence also follows from the two recent results [8,21].

Last, we study the following subclass definability problem: given a (copyful) SST, does there exist an equivalent copyless SST? We show that this problem is decidable in polynomial time, using a reduction to a boundedness problem for products of matrices studied by Mandel and Simon [20], and show that when possible, we can build an equivalent copyless SST.

Organization of the paper. We introduce the models of streaming string transducers and HDT0L systems in Sect. 2. In Sect. 3, we prove that these two models are equi-expressive. We apply this result to prove the decidability of the equivalence of copyful SST and of the functionality of non-deterministic SST in Sect. 4. Last, in Sect. 5, we study the subclass definability problem for copyless SST.

2   Preliminaries

For all finite alphabets Σ, we denote by Σ^* the set of finite words over Σ, and by ϵ the empty word. Given two alphabets Σ and Γ, a *transduction* R from Σ^* to Γ^* is a subset of $\Sigma^* \times \Gamma^*$. It is *functional* if it defines a function, i.e. for all $w \in \Sigma^*$, there exists at most one $v \in \Gamma^*$ such that $(w, v) \in R$. The domain of R, denoted by $Dom(R)$, is the set $Dom(R) = \{w \in \Sigma^* \mid \exists v \in \Gamma^*, (w, v) \in R\}$. A transduction is *total* if $Dom(R) = \Sigma^*$. Given two finite alphabets Σ, Γ, a morphim from Σ^* to Γ^* is a mapping $h : \Sigma^* \to \Gamma^*$ such that $h(uv) = h(u)h(v)$ for any two words $u, v \in \Sigma^*$.

2.1   Streaming String Transducers

Let $\mathcal{X}$ be a finite set of variables denoted by $X, Y, \ldots$ and Γ be a finite alphabet. A substitution s is defined as a mapping $s : \mathcal{X} \to (\Gamma \cup \mathcal{X})^*$. Let $\mathcal{S}_{\mathcal{X},\Gamma}$ be the set of all substitutions. Any substitution s can be extended to $\hat{s} : (\Gamma \cup \mathcal{X})^* \to (\Gamma \cup \mathcal{X})^*$ in a straightforward manner. The composition $s_1 \circ s_2$ (or $s_1 s_2$ for short) of two substitutions $s_1, s_2 \in \mathcal{S}_{\mathcal{X},\Gamma}$ is defined as the standard function composition $\hat{s}_1 \circ s_2$, i.e. $(s_1 s_2)(X) = (\hat{s}_1 s_2)(X) = \hat{s}_1(s_2(X))$ for all $X \in \mathcal{X}$.

Definition 1. *A non-deterministic streaming string transducer (NSST for short) is a tuple $T = (\Sigma, \Gamma, Q, Q_0, Q_f, \Delta, \mathcal{X}, \rho, s_0, s_f)$ where:*

- *Σ and Γ are finite alphabets of input and output symbols,*
- *Q is a finite set of states,*
- *$Q_0 \subseteq Q$ is a set of initial states,*
- *$Q_f \subseteq Q$ is a set of final states,*
- *$\Delta \subseteq Q \times \Sigma \times Q$ is a transition relation,*
- *$\mathcal{X}$ is a finite set of variables,*
- *$\rho : \Delta \to 2^{\mathcal{S}_{\mathcal{X},\Gamma}}$ is a variable update function such that $\rho(t)$ is finite, for all $t \in \Delta$,*
- *$s_0 : \mathcal{X} \to \Gamma^*$ is the initial function that gives the initial content of the variables,*
- *$s_f : Q_f \to (\mathcal{X} \cup \Gamma)^*$ is the final output function, which gives what is output for each final state.*

The concept of a run of an NSST is defined in an analogous manner to that of a finite state automaton: it is a finite sequence $r \in (Q\Sigma)^* Q$, denoted $r = q_0 \xrightarrow{\sigma_1} q_1 \xrightarrow{\sigma_2} q_2 \ldots q_{n-1} \xrightarrow{\sigma_n} q_n$, such that $(q_i, \sigma_{i+1}, q_{i+1}) \in \Delta$ for all $0 \le i < n$. It is accepting if $q_0 \in Q_0$ and $q_n \in Q_f$. A sequence of substitutions $\bar{s} = \langle s_i \rangle_{1 \le i \le n}$ in $\mathcal{S}_{\mathcal{X},\Gamma}$ is *compatible* with r if for all $1 \le i \le n$, $s_i \in \rho(q_{i-1}, \sigma_i, q_i)$. If r is accepting, the output of r, denoted by $Out(r) \subseteq \Gamma^*$, is defined as

$$Out(r) = \{ s_0 s_1 \ldots s_n s_f(q_n) \mid \langle s_i \rangle_{1 \le i \le n} \in (\mathcal{S}_{\mathcal{X},\Gamma})^* \text{ is compatible with } r \}.$$

For all words $w \in \Sigma^*$, the output of w by T, denoted by $T(w)$, is $T(w) = \{ Out(r) \mid r \text{ is an accepting run on } w \}$. The *domain* of T, denoted by $Dom(T)$, is defined as the set of words w such that $T(w) \neq \emptyset$. The transduction $[\![T]\!]$ defined by T is the relation from Σ^* to Γ^* given by the set of pairs (w, v) such that $v \in T(w)$.

Deterministic and functional SST. A deterministic SST (SST for short) is an NSST such that $|Q_0| = 1$ and for all $p \in Q, \sigma \in \Sigma$, there exists at most one $q \in Q$ such that $(p, \sigma, q) \in \Delta$, and such that for all $t \in \Delta$, $|\rho(t)| = 1$. When an SST is deterministic, we identify Q_0 with q_0, and given $t \in \Delta$, we write $\rho(t) = s$ instead of $\rho(t) = \{s\}$.

In the following, the streaming string transducers we consider are deterministic, unless they are explicitly stated to be non deterministic.

In [2,6], the variable updates are required to be *copyless*, i.e. for every variable $X \in \mathcal{X}$, and for every transition $t \in \Delta$, X occurs at most once in $\rho(t)(X_1), \ldots, \rho(t)(X_n)$ where $\{X_1, \ldots, X_n\} = \mathcal{X}$. One of the main result of [2] is to show that this restriction, as well as determinism, allows one to capture exactly the class of MSO-definable transductions.

It is worth noting that any SST, since it is deterministic, defines a functional transduction. More generally, we say that an NSST T is *functional* if $[\![T]\!]$ is functional. It is known that functional NSST with copyless update are no more expressive than (deterministic) SST with copyless update [6]. We show a similar result for (copyful) SST:

Proposition 1. *Functional* NSST *and* SST *are equi-expressive.*

Proof. Let $T = (\Sigma, \Gamma, Q, Q_0, Q_f, \Delta, \mathcal{X}, \rho, s_0, s_f)$ be a functional NSST. Without loss of generality, we assume that T is trim, *i.e.* every state of T is reachable from some initial state, and co-reachable from an accepting state. Any SST can be made trim by filtering out the states that do not have this property (which is decidable in PTime).

The main idea is to realize a subset construction on T (a similar construction was given in [7]). On states, the subset construction is just as the subset construction for NFA. On variables, one needs to duplicate each variable as many times as the number of states. The invariant property is the following: after reading a word w, if there exists a run ρ of T on w leading to q, then for all $X \in \mathcal{X}$ such that there exists an accepting continuation w' of w (*i.e.* $ww' \in Dom(T)$) whose output uses the content of X after ρ, then X_q and X have the same content after reading w. There might be several runs of T leading to q, but since T is trim and functional, then content of F does not depend on the chosen run. Hence the invariant is well-defined.

Formally, we define an equivalent SST $T' = (\Sigma, \Gamma, Q', q_0', Q_f', \Delta', \mathcal{X}', \rho', s_0', s_f')$ such that $(\Sigma, \Gamma, Q', q_0', Q_f', \Delta')$ is the DFA resulting from the classical subset construction (in particular $Q' = 2^Q$) and such that:

- $\mathcal{X}' = \mathcal{X} \times Q$ (each variable is denoted by X_q)
- $\forall t' = (Q_1, \sigma, Q_2) \in \Delta', \forall q_2 \in Q_2, \forall X \in \mathcal{X}$, $\rho'(t')(X_{q_2}) = \text{rename}_{q_1}(\rho(t)(X))$ for some $q_1 \in Q_1$ such that $t = (q_1, \sigma, q_2) \in \Delta$, where rename_{q_1} is the identity morphism on Σ and replaces any $Y \in \mathcal{X}$ by Y_{q_1}. As explained before, the functionality of T entails that the choice of q_1 is not important (a different choice would give the same value to X_{q_2}). This choice can be made canonical by using some order on the states of T.
- $\forall P \in Q_f'$, $\rho'(P) = \text{rename}_q(\rho(q))$ for some $q \in P \cap Q_f$. Once again, by functionality of T, the choice of q does not matter and can be made canonical.   □

We say that a SST T is *total* if $[\![T]\!]$ is total. We also show that regarding the equivalence problem, considering total SST is harmless, as one can modify a SST in linear time in order to make it total.

Proposition 2. *Given two SST T, T', one can build in linear time two total SST T_{tot} and T'_{tot} such that $[\![T]\!] = [\![T']\!]$ iff $[\![T_{tot}]\!] = [\![T'_{tot}]\!]$.*

Proof. Indeed, let $\# \notin \Gamma$. Any (partial) SST T can be transformed into an SST T_{tot} that defines the following transduction: $[\![T_{tot}]\!](u) = [\![T]\!](u)$ if $u \in Dom(T)$, and $[\![T_{tot}]\!](u) = \#$ otherwise. This is achieved using a new variable $X_\#$ whose content is always $\#$, and by completing the rules of T by adding an accepting sink state q_{sink}. We also modify final states and the final output function: states that were not final are declared final, and the final output function associates with these states the variable $X_\#$.   □

2.2   HDT0L Systems

Lindenmayer introduced in the sixties a formal grammar in order to model the developement process of some biological systems [19]. We consider here a particular class of these systems, called HDT0L systems (HDT0L stands for Deterministic 0-context Lindenmayer systems with Tables and with an additional Homomorphism).

Definition 2 (HDT0L System). *An HDT0L system over Σ and Γ is defined as a tuple $H = (\Sigma, A, \Gamma, v, h, (h_\sigma)_{\sigma \in \Sigma})$ where:*

- *Σ, A and Γ are finite alphabets,*
- *$v \in A^*$ is the initial word,*
- *h is a morphism from A^* to Γ^*,*
- *for each $\sigma \in \Sigma$, h_σ is a morphism from A^* to A^*.*

The equivalence problem for HDT0L systems asks, given two such systems $H = (\Sigma, A, \Gamma, v, h, (h_\sigma)_{\sigma \in \Sigma})$ and $G = (\Sigma, A, \Gamma, w, g, (g_\sigma)_{\sigma \in \Sigma})$, whether, for every $\sigma_1 \ldots \sigma_k \in \Sigma^*$, we have $h(h_{\sigma_1} \ldots h_{\sigma_k}(v)) = g(g_{\sigma_1} \ldots g_{\sigma_k}(w))$. This problem is known to be decidable [9], with unknown complexity. The original proof of [9] is based on Ehrenfeucht's conjecture and Makanin's algorithm. Honkala provided a simpler proof in [18], based on Hilbert's Basis Theorem.

In order to transfer this decidability result to SST, we introduce a semantics of HDT0L systems in terms of transductions.

Definition 3 (Transduction realized by an HDT0L system). *Let $H = (\Sigma, A, \Gamma, v, h, (h_\sigma)_{\sigma \in \Sigma})$ be an HDT0L system. We define $[\![H]\!]$ as a (total) transduction from Σ^* to Γ^* defined by $[\![H]\!](\sigma_1 \ldots \sigma_k) = h(h_{\sigma_1} \ldots h_{\sigma_k}(v))$.*

Example 1. Let us consider the function f_0 introduced in the introduction. We define an HDT0L $H_0 = (\Sigma, A, \Sigma, v_0, h, (h_\sigma)_{\sigma \in \Sigma})$ such that $[\![H_0]\!] = f_0$, with $A = \{\$_1, \$_2, a, b\}$, $\Sigma = \{a, b\}$, $v_0 = \$_1\$_2$, and the morphisms are defined as follows:

$$
\begin{array}{lll}
h: a \to a & h_a: a \to a & h_b: a \to a \\
 b \to b & b \to b & b \to b \\
 \$_1 \to \epsilon & \$_1 \to \$_1 a & \$_1 \to \$_1 b \\
 \$_2 \to \epsilon & \$_2 \to a\$_2 & \$_2 \to b\$_2
\end{array}
$$

For instance, we have the following derivation:

$$\llbracket H_0 \rrbracket(abb) = hh_{abb}(\$_1\$_2) = hh_{ab} \circ h_b(\$_1\$_2) = hh_{ab}(\$_1 bb\$_2) = hh_a(\$_1 bbbb\$_2)$$
$$= h(\$_1 abbbba\$_2) = abbbba$$

We can now rephrase the result of [9] as follows:

Theorem 1 [9]. *Given two HDT0L systems H_1, H_2 over Σ and Γ, it is decidable whether $\llbracket H_1 \rrbracket = \llbracket H_2 \rrbracket$.*

In the next section, we show that HDT0L systems and SST define the same class of transductions.

3   SST and HDT0L Systems Are Equi-Expressive

Let Σ and Γ two alphabets. In this section, we always consider that SST and HDT0L systems are over Σ and Γ. We prove the following theorem:

Theorem 2. HDT0L *systems over Σ and Γ and total SST define the same class of transductions. Moreover, the constructions are effective in both directions, in linear-time.*

A direct consequence of this result is:

Corollary 1. *The equivalence problems for HDT0L systems and for (copyful) streaming string transducers are inter-reducible in linear time.*

We prove successively the two directions of Theorem 2.

Lemma 1. *For all HDT0L systems H, there exists an equivalent (total) SST T with only one state.*

Proof. Let $H = (\Sigma, A, \Gamma, v, h, (h_\sigma)_{\sigma \in \Sigma})$ be an HDT0L system. We construct a total SST T over Σ and Γ such that $\llbracket T \rrbracket = \llbracket H \rrbracket$. The SST has one state q, both initial and accepting. Its set of variables is the set $\mathcal{X} = \{X_a \mid a \in A\}$. Its transitions are defined by $q \xrightarrow{\sigma} q$ for all $\sigma \in \Sigma$.

To define the update functions, we first introduce the morphism $\mathrm{rename}_\mathcal{X} : A^* \to \mathcal{X}^*$ defined for all $a \in A$ by $\mathrm{rename}_\mathcal{X}(a) = X_a$. Then, the update function ρ is defined, for all $\sigma \in \Sigma$ and $a \in A$ by $\rho((q, \sigma, q))(X_a) = \mathrm{rename}_\mathcal{X}(h_\sigma(a))$.

Finally, the initial function is defined by $s_0(X_a) = h(a)$ for all $a \in A$, and the final function s_f by $s_f(q) = \mathrm{rename}_\mathcal{X}(v)$. $\qquad\square$

Example 2. For the HDT0L system H_0 of Example 1, we obtain the SST T_2 depicted in Fig. 2.

We now prove the converse.

Lemma 2. *For all total SST T, there exists an equivalent HDT0L system H.*

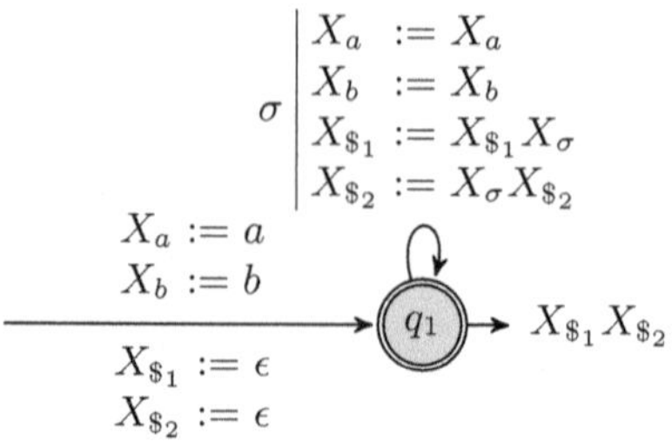

$$\sigma \begin{vmatrix} X_a & := X_a \\ X_b & := X_b \\ X_{\$_1} & := X_{\$_1} X_\sigma \\ X_{\$_2} & := X_\sigma X_{\$_2} \end{vmatrix}$$

$$\begin{aligned} X_a &:= a \\ X_b &:= b \end{aligned}$$

$$\xrightarrow{} \;\; (q_1) \longrightarrow X_{\$_1} X_{\$_2}$$

$$\begin{aligned} X_{\$_1} &:= \epsilon \\ X_{\$_2} &:= \epsilon \end{aligned}$$

Fig. 2. A SST T_2.

Proof. Let $T = (\Sigma, \Gamma, Q, q_0, Q_f, \Delta, \mathcal{X}, \rho, s_0, s_f)$ be a total SST (remember that by default an SST is deterministic). We define an equivalent HDT0L H as follows.

We consider the finite alphabet $A = \{\alpha_q \mid \alpha \in \Gamma \cup \mathcal{X}, q \in Q\}$. For every $q \in Q$, we consider the morphism $\mathrm{subscript}_q : (\Gamma \cup \mathcal{X})^* \rightarrow A^*$ defined for all $\alpha \in \Gamma \cup \mathcal{X}$ by $\mathrm{subscript}_q(\alpha) = \alpha_q$.

As T is total, we have that $Q_f = Q$. We consider an enumeration $q_1, \ldots, q_n$ of Q. We define the initial word v as follows:

$$v = \mathrm{subscript}_{q_1}(s_f(q_1)) \ldots \mathrm{subscript}_{q_n}(s_f(q_n))$$

We define the morphim $h : A^* \rightarrow \Gamma^*$ as follows:

$$\begin{aligned} h : \gamma_{q_0} &\rightarrow \gamma && \text{with } \gamma \in \Gamma \\ X_{q_0} &\rightarrow s_0(X) && \text{with } X \in \mathcal{X} \\ \alpha_q &\rightarrow \epsilon && \text{with } q \neq q_0 \text{ and } \alpha \in \Gamma \cup \mathcal{X} \end{aligned}$$

Last, given $\sigma \in \Sigma$ we define the morphism $h_\sigma : A^* \rightarrow A^*$ as follows. Given a state q, we define the set $Pre_q^\sigma \subseteq Q$ as the set of states p such that $(p, \sigma, q) \in \Delta$.

We define: (by convention, the product over the empty set gives the empty word)

$$\begin{aligned} \forall \gamma \in \Gamma, \; h_\sigma(\gamma_q) &= \Pi_{p \in Pre_q^\sigma} \mathrm{subscript}_p(\gamma) \\ \forall X \in \mathcal{X}, h_\sigma(X_q) &= \Pi_{p \in Pre_q^\sigma} \mathrm{subscript}_p(\rho(p, \sigma, q)(X)) \end{aligned}$$

Intuitively, the HDT0L system simulates the computations of the SST in a backward manner, starting from the final states. These computations are encoded using the labelling of symbols by states. One can easily prove by induction on the length of some input word w that after reading w, for every state q, the projection of $h_w(v)$ on the subalphabet $\mathrm{subscript}_q(\Gamma \cup \mathcal{X})$ encodes the run of the SST on w starting in state q, which is unique since T is deterministic. The morphism h then simply erases parts of the computations that did not reach the initial state q_0. □

We point out the following result, which follows from Lemmas 1 and 2:

Corollary 2. *For all SST T, one can construct in polynomial time an equivalent SST T' such that the underlying input DFA of T' is the minimal complete DFA recognizing $Dom(T)$.*

Proof. If T is total, then the result is a direct consequence of the successive application of Lemmas 2 and 1. Note that in this case, T' has only one state.

If T is not total, we make it total as in the proof of Proposition 2, and obtain a total SST S which can be converted into a single state SST S'. Then, we minimize the underlying input DFA of T (which recognizes $Dom(T)$) into a minimal complete DFA A_{min}. Finally, T' is defined as a kind of product of S' and A_{min}: if $A_{min} = (\Sigma, P, p_0, P_f, \delta)$ and $S' = (\Sigma, \Gamma, \{q\}, q, \{q\}, \{(q, \sigma, q) \mid \sigma \in \Sigma\}, \mathcal{X}, \rho, s_0, s_f)$, then we let $T' = (\Sigma, \Gamma, P, p_0, P_f, \delta, \mathcal{X}, \rho', s_0, s'_f)$ where:

- $\rho'(p, \sigma, p') = \rho(q, \sigma, q)$ for all $(p, \sigma, p') \in \delta$,
- $s'_f(p_f) = s_f(q)$ for all $p_f \in P_f$. $\qquad\square$

Remark 1. By this corollary, any total SST is equivalent to some single state SST.

4 Applications: SST Equivalence and Functionality of NSST

Based on the correspondence between SST and HDT0L systems, and the fact that the HDT0L system equivalence problem is decidable, we show that that the SST equivalence and functionality problems are decidable.

Theorem 3. *1. Given two SST T and T', it is decidable whether they are equivalent, i.e. $[\![T]\!] = [\![T']\!]$.*
2. Given an NSST T, it is decidable whether T is functional.

Proof. The first statement is straightforward by Theorems 1, 2 and Proposition 2.

To prove the second statement, we reduce the functionality problem to the equivalence of two (deterministic) SST T_1 and T_2. Let $T = (\Sigma, \Gamma, Q, Q_0, Q_f, \Delta, \mathcal{X}, \rho, s_0, s_f)$ be an NSST. We extend the alphabet Σ with pairs of rules of T as follows: $\Sigma' = \Sigma \times \Delta^2$. Now, T_1 and T_2 are defined as the square of T: they run on words w' over Σ', and make sure that the sequence of transitions are valid runs of T on the Σ-projections of w'. In addition, T_i simulates T on the $(i+1)$-th component, for all $i = 1, 2$, by following the transitions defined on the input letters. Clearly, T_1 and T_2 have the same domain, are deterministic, and are equivalent iff all pairs of accepting runs of T on the same input word produce the same output, i.e., iff T is functional. The conclusion follows from statement 1. $\qquad\square$

5 Deciding the Subclass of Copyless SST

The subclass of copyless SST is of great interest, as it exactly corresponds to the class of regular functions which enjoys multiple characterizations (MSO transductions and deterministic two-way transducers for instance) and has been widely studied in the literature (see for instance [16] for a survey). Given a copyful SST, it is thus a natural question whether there exists an equivalent copyless SST and if so, whether one can actually compute such an equivalent machine. In this section, we answer these questions positively:

Theorem 4. *Given an SST T, it is decidable in PTime whether there exists an equivalent copyless SST. If this is the case, one can build an equivalent copyless SST.*

It is well-known that copyless SST define transductions f that are linear-size increase (LSI for short), *i.e.* there exists some constant M such that for every w, we have $|f(w)| \leq M|w|$ (this can be observed for instance using the MSOT presentation). We will use this semantical condition in order to solve the above problem.

Proof. Let $T = (\Sigma, \Gamma, Q, q_0, Q_f, \Delta, \mathcal{X}, \rho, s_0, s_f)$ be an SST. Consider a run $q_0 \xrightarrow{\sigma_1} q_1 \ldots q_{n-1} \xrightarrow{\sigma_n} q_n = p$ of T starting in the initial state. By definition of the semantics of T, after this run, one can associate, in state p, with variable X the content $\nu(X) \in \Gamma^*$ defined as $s_0 s_1 \ldots s_n(X)$ where $s_i = \rho(q_{i-1}, \sigma_i, q_i)$. We use the notation $q_0 \xrightarrow{\sigma_1 \ldots \sigma_n} (p, \nu)$ to describe this fact, and may remove the label $\sigma_1 \ldots \sigma_n$ when it is useless.

We also say that a pair $(p, X) \in Q \times \mathcal{X}$ is *co-accessible* whenever there exists a run starting in state p reaching a final state q_f such that the final output $s_f(q_f)$ involves a variable whose content depends on the content of X at the beginning of the run. In other words, the content of X at configuration (p, X) flows into $s_f(q_f)$, *i.e.* X is "useful" for $s_f(q_f)$. This intuitive notion of variable flow is formally defined in [15].

We introduce the following objects:

- we let $val(p, X) = \{\nu(X) \in \Gamma^* \mid \text{ there exists a run } q_0 \to (p, \nu)\}$
- we let $INF = \{(p, X) \mid (p, X) \text{ is co-accessible and } val(p, X) \text{ is infinite}\}$
- we define $(p, X) \xrightarrow{u|n} (q, Y)$ if there exists a run from p to q on word u on which X flows n times in Y. We may omit u when it is useless.

Claim: $[\![T]\!]$ is definable by a copyless SST iff there exists $K \in \mathbb{N}$ such that for all $(p, X) \xrightarrow{n} (q, Y)$ with $(p, X), (q, Y) \in INF$, we have $n \leq K$.

Before proving the claim, we show that it implies decidability. First, the set INF is computable in polynomial time (fixpoint computation in the set of pairs $(p, X) \in Q \times \mathcal{X}$). Second, we define the following set $\mathcal{M}$ of square matrices indexed by elements of INF with coefficients in $\mathbb{N} \cup \{\bot\}$. We suppose that $\bot$ behaves as 0: for every integer $n \in \mathbb{N}$, we have $n.\bot = \bot.n = \bot$ and $n + \bot = \bot + n = n$. The set $\mathcal{M}$ is defined as the set of finite products of matrices $\{M_a \mid a \in \Sigma\}$, where, for each letter $a \in \Sigma$, we define matrix M_a by:

$$M_a[(p, X), (q, Y)] = \begin{cases} n & \text{if } (p, a, q) \in \Delta \text{ and } |\rho(p, a, q)(Y)|_X = n \\ \bot & \text{if } (p, a, q) \notin \Delta \end{cases}$$

We then observe that the right property of the claim is satisfied iff the set $\mathcal{M}$ is finite. By Mandel and Simon [20], this last property is decidable in polynomial time.

We turn to the proof of the claim:

$\Rightarrow$ We prove the contraposition, by showing that if the right property of the claim is not satisfied, then $[\![T]\!]$ is not LSI, which implies that $[\![T]\!]$ is not definable by a copyless SST as copyless SST are LSI. We thus assume that the set of flow matrices defined previously is not bounded. By the characterization proven in Mandel and Simon of this property, two cases may occur:

1. there exists $(p, X) \in INF$ such that $(p, X) \xrightarrow{n} (p, X)$ with $n \geq 2$,
2. there exist $(p, X), (q, Y) \in INF$ such that $(p, X) \xrightarrow{u|n_1} (p, X)$, $(p, X) \xrightarrow{u|n_2} (q, Y)$ and $(q, Y) \xrightarrow{u|n_3} (q, Y)$, with $n_1, n_2, n_3 \geq 1$, for some word u.

In the first case, using the fact that $(p, X) \in INF$, one can prove that $[\![T]\!]$ is not LSI.

In the second case, for every $n \geq 1$, one has $(p, X) \xrightarrow{u^n|m} (q, Y)$ for some $m \geq n$. Again, one can use this property to show that $[\![T]\!]$ is not LSI.

$\Leftarrow$ The constraint expressed by the right property of the claim precisely states that, with respect to pairs $(p, X) \in INF$, the SST is bounded copy. One can then easily remove variables (p, X) that do not belong to INF, so as to obtain a bounded copy SST, and it is known that every bounded copy SST can be turned into an equivalent copyless SST [7, 11]. $\qquad\square$

6 Conclusion

Our results establish a bridge between the theory of SST and the theory of systems of iterated morphisms. It allows to solve an interesting open problem for copyful streaming string transducers, namely the decidability of the equivalence problem. We have also proven the decidability of functionality for nondeterministic SST, and that of the subclass of copyless SST, using a reduction to a boundedness problem.

We hope that these positive decidability results will pave the way to a further study of the class of copyful SST. As future work, we want to investigate what the theory of iterated morphisms can bring to the theory of SST, and conversely, in terms of tight complexity results. For instance, the class of copyless SST, for which equivalence is PSpace-complete, could have an interesting interpretation in terms of HDT0L systems.

References

1. Alur, A., Černý, P.: Streaming transducers for algorithmic verification of single-pass list-processing programs. In: POPL, pp. 599–610 (2011)
2. Alur, R., Černý, P.: Expressiveness of streaming string transducers. In: FSTTCS, vol. 8, pp. 1–12 (2010)

3. Alur, R., D'Antoni, L.: Streaming tree transducers. CoRR, abs/1104.2599 (2011)
4. Alur, R., D'Antoni, L.: Streaming tree transducers. In: Czumaj, A., Mehlhorn, K., Pitts, A., Wattenhofer, R. (eds.) ICALP 2012. LNCS, vol. 7392, pp. 42–53. Springer, Heidelberg (2012). doi:10.1007/978-3-642-31585-5_8
5. Alur, R., D'Antoni, L., Deshmukh, J.V., Raghothaman, M., Yuan, Y.: Regular functions and cost register automata. In: 28th Annual ACM/IEEE Symposium on Logic in Computer Science, LICS 2013, pp. 13–22. IEEE Computer Society (2013)
6. Alur, R., Deshmukh, J.V.: Nondeterministic streaming string transducers. In: Aceto, L., Henzinger, M., Sgall, J. (eds.) ICALP 2011. LNCS, vol. 6756, pp. 1–20. Springer, Heidelberg (2011). doi:10.1007/978-3-642-22012-8_1
7. Alur, R., Filiot, E., Trivedi, A.: Regular transformations of infinite strings. In: LICS, pp. 65–74. IEEE (2012)
8. Benedikt, M., Duff, T., Sharad, A., Worrell, J.: Polynomial automata: zeroness and applications. In: Proceedings of the 32nd Annual ACM/IEEE Symposium on Logic in Computer Science, LICS 2017. ACM (2017, to appear)
9. Culik, K., Karhumäki, J.: The equivalence of finite valued transducers (on HDT0L languages) is decidable. Theor. Comput. Sci. 47(3), 71–84 (1986)
10. Dartois, L., Filiot, E., Reynier, P.-A., Talbot, J.-M.: Two-way visibly pushdown automata and transducers. In: Proceedings of the 31st Annual ACM/IEEE Symposium on Logic in Computer Science, LICS 2016, pp. 217–226. ACM (2016)
11. Dartois, L., Jecker, I., Reynier, P.-A.: Aperiodic string transducers. In: Brlek, S., Reutenauer, C. (eds.) DLT 2016. LNCS, vol. 9840, pp. 125–137. Springer, Heidelberg (2016). doi:10.1007/978-3-662-53132-7_11
12. Engelfriet, J., Hoogeboom, H.J.: MSO definable string transductions and two-way finite-state transducers. ACM Trans. Comput. Logic 2, 216–254 (2001)
13. Engelfriet, J., Maneth, S.: Macro tree transducers, attribute grammars, and MSO definable tree translations. Inf. Comput. 154(1), 34–91 (1999)
14. Engelfriet, J., Maneth, S.: The equivalence problem for deterministic MSO tree transducers is decidable. Inf. Process. Lett. 100(5), 206–212 (2006)
15. Filiot, E., Krishna, S.N., Trivedi, A.: First-order definable string transformations. In: 34th International Conference on Foundation of Software Technology and Theoretical Computer Science, FSTTCS 2014. LIPIcs, vol. 29, pp. 147–159. Schloss Dagstuhl - Leibniz-Zentrum fuer Informatik (2014)
16. Filiot, E., Reynier, P.-A.: Transducers, logic and algebra for functions of finite words. SIGLOG News 3(3), 4–19 (2016)
17. Griffiths, T.V.: The unsolvability of the equivalence problem for lambda-free nondeterministic generalized machines. J. ACM 15(3), 409–413 (1968)
18. Honkala, J.: A short solution for the HDT0L sequence equivalence problem. Theor. Comput. Sci. 244(1–2), 267–270 (2000)
19. Lindenmayer, A.: Mathematical models for cellular interaction in development. J. Theoret. Biol. 18, 280–315 (1968)
20. Mandel, A., Simon, I.: On finite semigroups of matrices. Theor. Comput. Sci. 5(2), 101–111 (1977)
21. Seidl, H., Maneth, S., Kemper, G.: Equivalence of deterministic top-down tree-to-string transducers is decidable. In: IEEE 56th Annual Symposium on Foundations of Computer Science, FOCS 2015, pp. 943–962. IEEE Computer Society (2015)

Model Checking CTL over Restricted Classes of Automatic Structures

Norbert Hundeshagen$^{(\boxtimes)}$ and Martin Lange

University of Kassel, Kassel, Germany
`hundeshagen@uni-kassel.de`

Abstract. Interpreting formulas over infinite-state relational structures whose states are words over some alphabet and whose relations are recognised by transducers is known under the term "automatic structures" in the world of predicate logic, or as "regular model checking" in formal verification. Both approaches use synchronised transducers, i.e. finite automata reading tuples of letters in each step. This is a strong transducer model with high expressive power leading to undecidability of model checking for any specification language that can express transitive closure.

We develop conditions on a class of binary word relations which are sufficient for the CTL model checking problem to be computable over the class of automatic structures generated by such relations. As an example, we consider recognisable relations. This is an interesting model from an algebraic point of view but it is also far less expressive than those given by synchronised transducers. As a consequence of the weaker expressive power we obtain that this class satisfies the aforementioned sufficient conditions, hence we obtain a decidability result for CTL model checking over a restricted class of infinite-state automatic structures.

1 Introduction

Model checking is a well-known model-based method for proving correctness of the behaviour of dynamic systems [4]. The earliest approaches were confined to finite-state systems [15], limited by the rather obvious undecidability of checking even the simplest temporal properties – namely reachability – on arbitrary infinite-state spaces. The ability to also model check infinite-state systems is indispensable for the verification of software systems, though. Much effort has therefore gone into the design and study of model checking procedures for infinite-state systems, mainly focussing on particular classes of finitely representable infinite-state systems like pushdown systems [10,34], Petri nets [28], process algebraic descriptions of infinite-state systems [20,25], recursion schemes [26], etc.

A rich formalism that gives rise to particular infinite-state systems is known as *automatic structures* [6]. The name is derived from the fact that (finite-state) automata play a major role in the construction of such systems: their states are represented as finite words, and the relations in these structures are recognised by

© Springer International Publishing AG 2017
M. Hague and I. Potapov (Eds.): RP 2017, LNCS 10506, pp. 87–100, 2017.
DOI: 10.1007/978-3-319-67089-8_7

synchronous transducers. Standard automata-theoretic constructions can then be used to show that the model checking problem for First-Order Logic (FO) is decidable over such structures [7]. It is also not difficult to see that model checking for Transitive Closure Logic already – the extension of FO with an operator to express inclusion in the transitive closure of some binary relation – becomes undecidable as the configuration graph of a Turing Machine can be modelled as an automatic structure.

The richness and flexibility of this framework makes it interesting for verification purposes, despite the fact that even the simplest specification languages for typical correctness properties in verification incorporate transitive closures in some form or other [14]. This has led to the study of *regular model checking* [9], a term describing the framework of verifying labelled transition systems (i.e. relational structures with unary and binary relations only) represented as automatic structures. Interestingly, the use of such structures in the rather difficult domain of verification of temporal properties has started a while before the positive and elegant results on FO model checking were discovered [22,36].

Research on regular model checking has seen a great amount of effort spent on the computation of transitive closures [12,31] using various techniques that circumvent undecidability issues, for instance by giving up completeness or precision, like fixpoint acceleration [1,21], widening [32], abstraction [8], inference [18], etc.

One can argue that the restriction to the computation of transitive closures still facilitates "doing model checking", at least for relatively simple temporal properties like safety or liveness. The approximative nature of procedures like the ones cited above usually prohibits the study of combinations of such properties, as safety verification typically requires over-approximations whereas liveness verification needs under-approximations.

In this paper we want to study the possibility to do model checking for a richer class of temporal properties than just safety or liveness. The simple branching-time temporal logic CTL [11] provides a framework for the specification of combinations of such properties. Our object of interest is therefore the model checking problem for CTL over automatic structures. As stated above, this problem is clearly undecidable, and the multitude of work that has gone into studying the subproblem of verifying liveness or safety properties shows that one cannot expect to find many positive results for regular CTL model checking unless one gives up completeness, precision, or expressive power. We aim to retain completeness and precision and study the case where expressive power is limited on the side of the automatic structures rather than the temporal specification language. We consider a particular case of automatic structures for which the accessibility relation is *recognisable*. The concept of recognisability, defined via morphisms onto a finite monoid, is central in the field of algebraic automata theory. An overview over the classes of relations in focus and the notion of recognisability and synchronisation can be found in [5,29].

The class of recognisable relations is a proper subclass of the synchronous ones. Hence, the class of automatic structures defined over them is significantly smaller than the class of automatic structures over synchronous transducers. It remains to be seen whether this class includes families of structures that are interesting for software verification purposes for instance. On the other hand, a consequence of this loss in expressive power is – as we show here – that CTL model checking, i.e. including the verification of simple safety or liveness properties, as well as combinations thereof, is decidable over this class of infinite-state systems.

The paper is organised as follows. In Sect. 2 we recall CTL and transition systems as its standard model of interpretation. CTL model checking over automatic structures defined by recognisable relations is not meant to be the ultimate goal in infinite-state verification; instead we want to provide the basis for the study of temporal logic model checking over restricted classes of automatic structures here. We therefore present a generic description of automatic structures as transition systems, parametrised by the machinery used to define its transition relation; recognisable relations and their corresponding automaton model are one example of such machinery that falls into this framework, and it is the one studied in further detail here.

Section 3 recalls the generic bottom-up global CTL model checking algorithm, and it then develops necessary criteria on the underlying structures for this algorithm to be terminating and correct. In Sect. 4 we then consider the aforementioned recognisable relations, resp. the automatic structures generated by them and show that they satisfy the necessary conditions laid out before. Hence, we get decidability of CTL model checking over this class of automatic structures. Finally, Sect. 5 concludes with remarks on further work in this area.

2 Preliminaries

2.1 Labelled Transition Systems

Let $\mathcal{P} = \{p, q, \ldots\}$ be a set of proposition symbols. A *labelled transition system* (LTS) is a $\mathcal{T} = (\mathcal{S}, \rightarrow, \ell)$ where $\mathcal{S}$ is a (possibly infinite) set of states, $\rightarrow \subseteq \mathcal{S} \times \mathcal{S}$ is the transition relation which is always assumed to be total, i.e. for every $s \in \mathcal{S}$ there is a $t \in \mathcal{S}$ with $(s, t) \in \rightarrow$. We usually write $s \rightarrow t$ instead of $(s, t) \in \rightarrow$. Finally, $\ell : \mathcal{P} \rightarrow 2^{\mathcal{S}}$ is a partial labelling function which assigns sets $\ell(p)$ of states in which p is true, to some propositions p. We assume that $\ell(p)$ is defined for finitely many p only, for otherwise it is not clear how an LTS should be finitely representable as (part of the) input to an algorithm solving some computation problem.

Let $S \subseteq \mathcal{S}$. We write $Pre_{\mathcal{T}}(S)$ for the set of predecessors of S, i.e. $\{t \in \mathcal{S} \mid \exists s \in S \text{ s.t. } t \rightarrow s\}$.

A *path* in $\mathcal{T}$ starting in state s is an infinite sequence $\pi = s_0, s_1, \ldots$ such that $s_0 = s$ and $s_i \rightarrow s_{i+1}$ for all $i \geq 0$. For such a path π and $i \in \mathbb{N}$ let $\pi(i)$ denote its i-th state, i.e. s_i. Let $\Pi_{\mathcal{T}}(s)$ denote the set of all paths in $\mathcal{T}$ that start in s.

2.2 The Branching-Time Logic CTL

Let $\mathcal{P}$ be as above. Formulas of the branching-time logic CTL are built according to the following grammar.

$$\varphi \ ::= \ p \mid \varphi \vee \varphi \mid \neg\varphi \mid \mathsf{EX}\varphi \mid \mathsf{E}(\varphi\mathsf{U}\varphi) \mid \mathsf{EG}\varphi$$

where $p \in \mathcal{P}$.

Besides the usual abbreviations for the Boolean operators like $\wedge, \rightarrow, \mathsf{tt}, \mathsf{ff}$ we also introduce the standard temporal operators via $\mathsf{E}(\varphi\,\mathsf{R}\,\psi) := \mathsf{E}(\psi\,\mathsf{U}\,(\varphi \wedge \psi)) \vee \mathsf{EG}\psi$, $\mathsf{AX}\varphi := \neg\mathsf{EX}\neg\varphi$, $\mathsf{A}(\varphi\,\mathsf{R}\,\psi) := \neg\mathsf{E}(\neg\varphi\,\mathsf{U}\,\neg\psi)$, $\mathsf{EF}\varphi := \mathsf{E}(\mathsf{tt}\,\mathsf{U}\,\varphi)$, $\mathsf{AG}\varphi := \neg\mathsf{EF}\neg\varphi$, and $\mathsf{AF}\varphi := \neg\mathsf{EG}\neg\varphi$.

Formulas of CTL are interpreted over labelled transition systems $\mathcal{T} = (\mathcal{S}, \rightarrow, \ell)$. The semantics inductively defines the set of states at which each subformula is true.

$$
\begin{aligned}
[\![p]\!]^{\mathcal{T}} \ &:= \ \ell(p) \\
[\![\varphi \vee \psi]\!]^{\mathcal{T}} \ &:= \ [\![\varphi]\!]^{\mathcal{T}} \cup [\![\psi]\!]^{\mathcal{T}} \\
[\![\neg\varphi]\!]^{\mathcal{T}} \ &:= \ \mathcal{S} \setminus [\![\varphi]\!]^{\mathcal{T}} \\
[\![\mathsf{EX}\varphi]\!]^{\mathcal{T}} \ &:= \ \{s \in \mathcal{S} \mid \exists t \in \mathcal{S} \text{ s.t. } s \rightarrow t \text{ and } t \in [\![\varphi]\!]^{\mathcal{T}}\} \\
[\![\mathsf{E}(\varphi\,\mathsf{U}\,\psi)]\!]^{\mathcal{T}} \ &:= \ \{s \in \mathcal{S} \mid \exists \pi \in \Pi_{\mathcal{T}}(s), i \geq 0 \text{ s.t. } \pi(i) \in [\![\psi]\!]^{\mathcal{T}} \\
& \qquad\qquad \text{and for all } j < i : \pi(j) \in [\![\varphi]\!]^{\mathcal{T}}\} \\
[\![\mathsf{EG}\varphi]\!]^{\mathcal{T}} \ &:= \ \{s \in \mathcal{S} \mid \exists \pi \in \Pi_{\mathcal{T}}(s) \text{ s.t. for all } i \geq 0 : \pi(i) \in [\![\varphi]\!]^{\mathcal{T}}\}
\end{aligned}
$$

The (global) model checking problem for CTL and a class of labelled transition systems $\mathfrak{K}$ is: given a $\mathcal{T} \in \mathfrak{K}$ and a $\varphi \in \mathrm{CTL}$ (over the same set of atomic propositions), compute $[\![\varphi]\!]^{\mathcal{T}}$. It is well-known that the model checking problem for CTL over finite LTS is computable in polynomial time [15].

2.3 Automatic Structures

We are interested in particular LTS over infinite state spaces, known as *automatic structures* [6]. Originally, the term refers to (possibly infinite) relational structures that can be represented using automata. Here we consider a slightly modified variant that does not bear any essential differences. First, we restrict our attention to unary and binary relations – note that LTS are specific relational structures such that the arities of their relations are two (for the transition relation) and one (for all the atomic propositions).

Second, we consider a slight generalisation, owed to the limits that the original proposal faces in terms of decidability issues. In the original definition of automatic structures, relations are recognised by synchronous transducers, i.e. finite automata over alphabets of the form Σ^k for some $k \geq 1$ (which equals the arity of the underlying relation). This makes the concept of an automatic structure a syntactic definition.

The aim of this work is to find (restricted) classes of automatic structures for which the CTL model checking problem is computable. One way to obtain this is to study restricted mechanisms for defining the relations in an LTS. We therefore prefer a semantic definition of automatic structures here, allowing the representation mechanism to become a parameter for a class of infinite-state structures.

We assume the reader to be familiar with the basic notions of formal language theory and the theory of finite-state automata. We use Σ for a finite alphabet and Σ^* for the set of all finite words over Σ. The empty word is denoted by ε.

A nondeterministic finite automaton (NFA) over Σ is a $\mathcal{A} = (Q, \Sigma, q_I, \delta, F)$ with finite state set Q, initial state $q_I \in Q$, final states $F \subseteq Q$ and transition relation $\delta : Q \times \Sigma \to 2^Q$. The language of $\mathcal{A}$ is denoted $L(\mathcal{A})$, and it consists of all words $w \in \Sigma^*$ for which there is an accepting run of $\mathcal{A}$ on w. We use the standard homomorphic extension $\hat{\delta}$ of δ to words via $\hat{\delta}(q, \varepsilon) = \{q\}$ and $\hat{\delta}(q, wa) = \{q' \mid \exists q'' \in \hat{\delta}(q, w) \text{ s.t. } q' \in \delta(q'', a)\}$. Hence, $L(\mathcal{A}) = \{w \mid \exists f \in \hat{\delta}(q_I, w)\}$.

For our notion of automatic structure we need an abstract concept of a mechanism that represents binary relations over words.

Definition 1. A *binary acceptor* $\mathcal{A}$ is any finite representation of a binary relation $R(\mathcal{A}) \subseteq \Sigma^* \times \Sigma^*$.

This yields a parametric notion of automatic structures.

Definition 2. Let $\mathfrak{A}$ be a class of binary acceptors over some alphabet Σ. An LTS $\mathcal{T} = (\mathcal{S}, \to, \ell)$ is said to be an $\mathfrak{A}$-*automatic transition system*, or $\mathfrak{A}$-automatic in short, if

- $\mathcal{S} = \Sigma^*$,
- for each $p \in \mathcal{P}$ with $\ell(p) \neq$ undef there is an NFA $\mathcal{A}_p$ s.t. $L(\mathcal{A}_p) = \ell(p)$,
- there is a binary acceptor $\mathcal{A}_{\mathrm{tr}} \in \mathfrak{A}$ s.t. $R(\mathcal{A}_{\mathrm{tr}}) = \{(s, t) \mid s \to t\}$.

Thus, roughly speaking, a transition system is automatic, if the labels are represented by an NFA and the transition relation by a binary acceptor. The size of an $\mathfrak{A}$-automatic structure $\mathcal{T}$, denoted $|\mathcal{T}|$, is the sum of the sizes of the NFA used to define the interpretation of the atomic propositions plus the size of the binary acceptor, assuming that some sensible notion of representation size is given for it.

The standard notion of an automatic structure as known from [6] – at least when restricted to one binary and otherwise only unary relations – is obtained in this setting as a $\mathfrak{T}_{\mathsf{sync}}$-automatic transition system with $\mathfrak{T}_{\mathsf{sync}}$ being the class of synchronous transducers, i.e. NFA over the alphabet $\Sigma^2 \cup \{(a, \#), (\#, a) \mid a \in \Sigma\}$. The relation of such a transducer $\mathcal{A}$ is then defined as $R(\mathcal{A}) = \{(u, v) \mid zip(u, v) \in L(\mathcal{A})\}$ where zip merges the two words $u, v \in \Sigma^*$ into a two-tracked word over Σ^2, possibly appending the padding symbol $\#$ in case their lengths are not equal. It is inductively defined via

$$zip(au, bv) := \begin{pmatrix} a \\ b \end{pmatrix} zip(u, v), \qquad zip(\varepsilon, bv) := \begin{pmatrix} \# \\ b \end{pmatrix} zip(\varepsilon, v),$$

$$zip(au, \varepsilon) := \begin{pmatrix} a \\ \# \end{pmatrix} zip(u, \varepsilon), \qquad zip(\varepsilon, \varepsilon) := \varepsilon,$$

where $a, b \in \Sigma$ and $u, v \in \Sigma^*$.

Another example of a binary acceptor is given by the notion of recognisable relations, to be looked at in detail in Sect. 4 as a mechanism to define a class of automatic structures we call *recognisable automatic structures*. The notion of binary acceptor is flexible enough, though, to incorporate all sorts of other mechanisms for defining binary relations. For instance a pair of two NFAs $(\mathcal{A}, \mathcal{B})$ with $R(\mathcal{A}, \mathcal{B}) = L(\mathcal{A}) \times L(\mathcal{B})$ would also be a very simple case of a binary acceptor, leading to what one may call *fully asynchronous automatic structures*. In fact, such a pair yields a very special case of a recognisable relation.

3   Model Checking CTL

We describe the generic and well-known procedure that can be used to compute the set of states in a transition system which satisfy a given CTL formula [10]. It can immediately be derived from the semantics and the fixpoint principle, stating that the set of states satisfying $E(\varphi U \psi)$, resp. $EG\varphi$, can be computed iteratively in a least, resp. greatest fixpoint recursion.

Note that the procedure MODELCHECK as given in Algorithm 1 is not an algorithm strictly speaking: if $|\mathcal{S}| < \infty$ then clearly $Pre_{\mathcal{T}}(\cdot)$ is computable, and termination of the `repeat-until`-loops is guaranteed by monotonicity and boundedness of the values of the variable T in both cases. Hence, procedure MODELCHECK can safely be called an algorithm for CTL model checking on finite structures.

In case of $|\mathcal{S}| = \infty$, termination is not necessarily guaranteed. This does not mean, though, that computability of the model checking problem is not given. As in the case of FO model checking on automatic structures which only uses computable operations on possibly infinite sets, a thorough look at MODELCHECK reveals some sufficient conditions under which CTL model checking becomes computable. For this, we assume the given LTS to be $\mathfrak{A}$-automatic for some class $\mathfrak{A}$. Then the computability of the Boolean operations is guaranteed for as long as they are applied to sets of states which form a regular language. Moreover, computability of the $Pre(\cdot)$-predicate is needed, which is the counterpart to closure under projections in the decidability proof for FO model checking on automatic structures. At last, we need one more property which has no counterpart in FO model checking, since FO has no recursion mechanism but CTL has one in the form of the temporal operators EU and EG.

Definition 3. Let $\mathfrak{A}$ be a class of binary acceptors and $\mathfrak{T}$ be a class of $\mathfrak{A}$-automatic structures. We say that $\mathfrak{T}$ has *finite U-closure ordinals* if for any

Algorithm 1. The standard procedure for model checking CTL.

procedure MODELCHECK(φ)   ▷ assume LTS $\mathcal{T} = (\mathcal{S}, \rightarrow, \ell)$ fixed
    case φ **of**
    p: **return** $\ell(p)$ ▷ $p \in \mathcal{P}$
    $\neg\psi$:
      return $\mathcal{S} \backslash$ MODELCHECK(ψ)
    $\psi_1 \vee \psi_2$:
      return MODELCHECK(ψ_1) $\cup$ MODELCHECK(ψ_2)
    EXψ:
      return $Pre_\mathcal{T}$(MODELCHECK(ψ))
    E(ψ**U**χ):
      $L_1 \leftarrow$ MODELCHECK(ψ); $L_2 \leftarrow$ MODELCHECK(χ); $M \leftarrow \emptyset$
      repeat
        $M' \leftarrow M$; $M \leftarrow L_2 \cup (L_1 \cap Pre_\mathcal{T}(M))$
      until $M = M'$
      return M
    EGψ:
      $L \leftarrow$ MODELCHECK(ψ); $M \leftarrow \mathcal{S}$
      repeat
        $M' \leftarrow M$; $M \leftarrow L \cap Pre_\mathcal{T}(M)$
      until $M = M'$
      return M
    end case
  end procedure

$\mathcal{T} \in \mathfrak{T}$ and any regular languages L_1, L_2 the increasing chain $M_0 \subseteq M_1 \subseteq \ldots$ becomes stationary where

$$M_0 := \emptyset, \quad M_{i+1} := L_2 \cup (L_1 \cap Pre_\mathcal{T}(M_i)).$$

Likewise, we say that $\mathfrak{T}$ has *finite* G-*closure ordinals* if for any $\mathcal{T} \in \mathfrak{T}$ and any regular language L the decreasing chain $M_0 \supseteq M_1 \supseteq \ldots$ becomes stationary where

$$M_0 := \Sigma^*, \quad M_{i+1} := L \cap Pre_\mathcal{T}(M_i).$$

We say that $\mathfrak{T}$ has *finite closure ordinals* if it has finite U- and finite G-closure ordinals.

Here, becoming stationary means that there is an $n \in \mathbb{N}$ such that $M_{n+1} = M_n$. It is a simple consequence of the monotonicity of the operators $Pre_\mathcal{T}(\cdot)$, union and intersection that the series $(M_i)_{i \geq 0}$ indeed forms an increasing, resp. decreasing chain.

Lemma 4. *The model checking problem for* CTL *over the class* $\mathfrak{T}$ *of* $\mathfrak{A}$-*automatic transition systems is computable if*

(a) for any LTS $\mathcal{T} \in \mathfrak{T}$ and any regular language L, the set $Pre_\mathcal{T}(L)$ is effectively regular, i.e. an NFA can be computed for it from an NFA for L, and
(b) $\mathfrak{T}$ has finite closure ordinals.

Proof. It is a standard exercise to show by induction on the structure of φ that calling MODELCHECK(φ) on $\mathcal{T}$ returns $[\![\varphi]\!]^{\mathcal{T}}$ [4, Theorem 6.23] [13, Lemma 7.3.4], provided that it terminates. It then only remains to see that termination is guaranteed when each call to any of the two repeat-until loops terminates.

First we note that by assumption (a), each subcall to MODELCHECK returns a regular language. Then assumption (b) is applicable and guarantees termination of the loops since they iterate through the values of the chains from Definition 3 in their variables M and M' until they become stable. $\square$

4   CTL Model Checking over Recognisable Automatic Transition Systems

In this section we examine a particular class of binary acceptor and the computability of the CTL model checking problem over automatic structures generated by this class. Semantically, it consists of the class of recognisable relations which forms a proper subclass of the relations represented by synchronous transducers. These, in turn, are included in the well-known class of rational relations [29, Theorem 6.4].

An automaton model for the class of recognisable relations can immediately be derived from the fact that every recognisable relation can be expressed as the finite union of the product of some regular languages [5, Theorem 1.5]. This gives rise to a syntactic transducer model for these relations.

Definition 5. An *input-output-independent (IOI) automaton* is a triple $\mathcal{A} = (I, O, F)$ such that $I = (Q^I, \Sigma, q_I^I, \delta^I, \emptyset)$ and $O = (Q^O, \Sigma, q_I^O, \delta^O, \emptyset)$ are NFAs and $F \subseteq Q^I \times Q^O$.

The relation defined by an IOI automaton is

$$R(\mathcal{A}) := \{(u, v) \in \Sigma^* \times \Sigma^* \mid \exists (p, q) \in F \text{ s.t. } p \in \hat{\delta}_i^I(q_I^I, u) \text{ and } q \in \hat{\delta}_i^O(q_I^O, v)\}.$$

Intuitively, an IOI automaton is a pair of NFAs which are only synchronised via final states. They read the input and output word independently, and the acceptance condition prescribes which pairs of states their runs need to end in for the pair of words to be accepted. Clearly, IOI automata are a special form of binary acceptors according to Definition 1. Hence, they give rise to a class of automatic structures, henceforth called *recognisable automatic structures*.

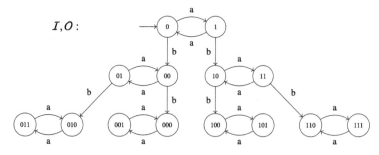

Example 6. Let $\mathcal{A} = (I, O, F)$ be the IOI automaton such that I and O are both the following NFA.

A state at the bottom is reached by a word that contains exactly two b's, hence, it is of the form $a^{n_1} b a^{n_2} b a^{n_3}$ for some $n_1, n_2, n_3 \geq 0$. Such a state $x_1 x_2 x_3$ then indicates the parities (even/odd) of n_1, n_2 and n_3.

The final state pairs of $\mathcal{A}$ are those of the row at the bottom that differ in at least two positions, i.e.

$$F := \{(x_1 x_2 x_3, y_1 y_2 y_3) \mid x_i \neq y_i \text{ for at least two } i \in \{1, 2, 3\}\}.$$

Thus, a pair of words $(a^{n_1} b a^{n_2} b a^{n_3}, a^{m_1} b a^{m_2} b a^{m_3})$ is in $R(\mathcal{A})$, iff $n_i = m_i \mod 2$ for at most one $i \in \{1, 2, 3\}$.

$\mathcal{A}$ generates a recognisable automatic structure with state space $\{a, b\}^*$ that is partly shown in Fig. 1. The grey circles denote subgraphs of nodes of the form $a^{n_1} b a^{n_2} b a^{n_3}$ for which the values of $n_1 + n_2 + n_3$ do not differ. The dashed line abbreviates edges from every node in the left subgraph to the node on the right. Note that $R(\mathcal{A})$ is symmetric in this case, simply because $I = O$ and F happens to be symmetric.

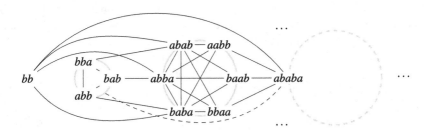

Fig. 1. An excerpt of the relation $R(\mathcal{A})$ for the IOI automaton $\mathcal{A}$ from Example 6.

In order to prove computability of the model checking problem for CTL over recognisable automatic structures it suffices to show that this class satisfies the two conditions laid out in Lemma 4.

Lemma 7. *Let L be a regular language and $\mathcal{T}$ be a recognisable automatic structure. Then $\mathrm{Pre}_{\mathcal{T}}(L)$ is effectively regular.*

Proof. Let L be a regular language accepted, e.g., by some NFA $\mathcal{B} = (Q^{\mathcal{B}}, \Sigma, q_I^{\mathcal{B}}, \delta^{\mathcal{B}}, F^{\mathcal{B}})$ and let $\mathcal{A} = (I, O, F^{\mathcal{A}})$ be the IOI automaton that recognises the transition relation of some recognisable automatic structure $\mathcal{T}$. Consider the IOI automaton $\mathcal{A} \bowtie \mathcal{B} := (I, O', F)$ with $O' = (Q^O \times Q^{\mathcal{B}}, \Sigma, (q_I^O, q_I^{\mathcal{B}}), \delta, \emptyset)$,

$$\delta((p, q), a) = \{(p', q') \mid p' \in \delta^O(p, a), q' \in \delta^{\mathcal{B}}(q, a)\}$$

and $F := \{(f_1, (f_2, f)) \mid (f_1, f_2) \in F^{\mathcal{A}}, f \in F^{\mathcal{B}}\}$. It has the same input component as $\mathcal{A}$, but its output component O' is the synchronous product of the one of $\mathcal{A}$ and $\mathcal{B}$. Hence, it recognises the relation $R(\mathcal{A} \bowtie \mathcal{B}) = \{(u,v) \mid (u,v) \in R(\mathcal{A})$ and $v \in L(\mathcal{B})\}$.

Next, consider the NFA $\mathcal{I}' := (Q^I, \Sigma, q_I^I, \delta^I, F')$ with $F' := \{f_1 \mid \exists(f_2, f)$ s.t. $(f_1, (f_2, f)) \in F\}$. We then have $L(\mathcal{I}') = \{u \mid \exists v$ s.t. $(u,v) \in R(\mathcal{A} \bowtie \mathcal{B})\} = Pre_{\mathcal{T}}(L)$.   □

This is of course a standard construction of forming the intersection of the automaton's second component with a regular language and then projecting it onto its first component. We have spelled out the construction in detail because of an important observation to be made: note that the transition table of the NFA for $Pre_{\mathcal{T}}(L)$ does not depend on L; instead, L only determines its accepting states. This can be seen as an indication of the weakness of IOI automata as a model for automatic structures; however, some sort of weakness is necessary in order to obtain computability.

Lemma 8. *The class of recognisable automatic structures has finite closure ordinals.*

Proof. We will only prove the claim for finite U-closure ordinals. The case of G-closure ordinals is analogous.

Let $\mathcal{A} = (I, O, F)$ be the IOI automaton underlying some recognisable automatic structure $\mathcal{T}$, and let L_1, L_2 be two regular languages. Consider the chain $M_0 \subseteq M_1 \subseteq \ldots$ approximating the set of states in $\mathcal{T}$ that satisfy – by slight abuse of notation – $\mathrm{E}(L_1 \mathbin{\mathsf{U}} L_2)$, as constructed in Definition 3.

By the observation following the previous lemma, we have that $Pre_{\mathcal{T}}(L)$ is recognised by an NFA of the form $(Q^I, \Sigma, q_I^I, \delta^I, F)$ for some $F \subseteq Q^I$. Thus, the graph structure of the NFA does not depend on the input language L, only the set of final states does. Therefore, there are at most $2^{|Q^I|}$ many different languages $Pre_{\mathcal{T}}(L)$ for arbitrary regular L.

Now consider the chain $M_0 \subseteq M_1 \ldots$. Each M_i with $i > 0$ is obtained as $L_2 \cup (L_1 \cap Pre_{\mathcal{T}}(M_{i-1}))$. Assuming that union and intersection are always formed using the same procedure on the same fixed NFA for L_1 and L_2, we get that there are at most $2^{|Q^I|}$ many different NFA for the M_i. With union and intersection being monotone operations, the chain $M_0 \subseteq M_1 \subseteq \ldots$ has to become stable after at most $2^{|Q^I|}$ many steps.   □

Putting Lemmas 4, 7 and 8 together, we immediately obtain the following.

Theorem 9. *The model checking problem for* CTL *over the class of recognisable automatic structures is computable.*

An immediate question arising from such a decidability result concerns the worst-case complexity of the model checking problem for CTL over recognisable automatic transition systems. We note that the time needed to compute $[\![\varphi]\!]^{\mathcal{T}}$ for some such $\mathcal{T}$ and arbitrary CTL formula φ is determined by several factors: (1) the use of intersection and complementation constructions arising from conjunctions and negated subformulas; (2) upper bounds on the number of iterations needed to obtain stability in the in-/decreasing chains of Definition 3. The following lemma shows that stability is reached after a small number of iterations.

Lemma 10. *Consider an IOI automaton $\mathcal{A} = (I, O, F)$ and two regular languages $L_1, L_2 \subseteq \Sigma^*$ represented by NFA $\mathcal{B}_1, \mathcal{B}_2$. Let $\mathcal{A}_0, \mathcal{A}_1, \ldots$ be the sequence of NFA recognising the languages $M_0, M_1, \ldots$ in an in-/decreasing chain according to Definition 3, and let $F_0, F_1, \ldots$ be their final states respectively. Then $F_0, F_1, \ldots$ also forms an increasing, resp. decreasing chain.*

Proof. We assume that in each step of building the $\mathcal{A}_i$, $i \geq 1$, the standard constructions for forming the union and intersection of two languages are being used. Hence, for every final state f in some F_i we have that f is either a final state of $\mathcal{B}_2$, or it is of the form (f', f'') such that f' is a final state of $\mathcal{B}_1$ and f'' is a final state of the NFA constructed in the proof of Lemma 7 by projecting the automaton $\mathcal{A} \bowtie \mathcal{A}_{i-1}$ accordingly.

Now consider the case in which $M_0 \subseteq M_1 \subseteq \ldots$ forms an increasing chain. The case of a decreasing chain is entirely analogous. W.l.o.g. we can assume that $F_0 = \emptyset$ since $M_0 = \emptyset$. Clearly, we have $F_0 \subseteq F_1$. Now let $i > 0$ and assume that $F_{i-1} \subseteq F_i$. We want to show that $F_i \subseteq F_{i+1}$ holds.

Take some $f \in F_i$. If f is a final state of $\mathcal{B}_2$ then it clearly also belongs to F_{i+1}. Hence, suppose that $f = (f', f'')$ with f' being a final state of $\mathcal{B}_1$ and f'' being a final state of the NFA for $Pre_{\mathcal{T}}(M_{i-1})$. According to the construction of the automaton $\mathcal{A} \bowtie \mathcal{A}_{i-1}$ as in the proof of Lemma 7 there must exist some g, g' such that $(f'', (g, g'))$ is a final state of $\mathcal{A} \bowtie \mathcal{A}_{i-1}$. This is only possible if (f'', g) is a final state of the automaton $\mathcal{A}$ and g' is a final state of the NFA $\mathcal{A}_{i-1}$, thus $g' \in F_{i-1}$. Then we can apply the induction hypothesis and get $g' \in F_i$ and therefore $(f'', (g, g'))$ as a final state of $\mathcal{A} \bowtie \mathcal{A}_i$. Then f'' is also a final state of the NFA for $Pre_{\mathcal{T}}(M_i)$ and therefore f is a final state of the NFA for $L_1 \cap Pre_{\mathcal{T}}(M_i)$ and, hence, $f \in F_{i+1}$. □

Note that this does not necessarily yield a polynomial bound on the number of iterations needed to compute $[\![E(\varphi U \psi)]\!]^{\mathcal{T}}$ for instance. Lemma 10 shows that the fixpoint will be reached after after at most $n_\varphi + n_\psi \cdot n$ steps where n_φ, n_ψ are the number of states of an NFA recognising $[\![\varphi]\!]^{\mathcal{T}}$ and $[\![\psi]\!]^{\mathcal{T}}$, respectively. Again, similar considerations can be made for the decreasing chains in Definition 3 and formulas of the form $EG\varphi$. In any case, n equals the number of states of the output component of the IOI automaton recognising the accessibility relation of the underlying recognisable transition system. Hence, n is clearly bounded by $|\mathcal{T}|$, the size of a representation of $\mathcal{T}$. However, n_φ and n_ψ are not a priori bounded since these subformulas can be arbitrary and in particular make use of expensive intersection and complementation constructions.

5 Conclusion and Further Work

We have defined a simple framework for the study of restricted classes of automatic structures in which the binary relations are defined by weaker automata than synchronous ones. This can of course be extended to relations of arbitrary arity, but automatic structures that represent transition systems (i.e. have relations of arity at most two) are most interesting for purposes of verification of reactive and concurrent systems. This also motivates the choice of specification language, here the branching-time temporal logic CTL.

There are plenty of ways that this work can be extended to in the future. The exact complexity of CTL model checking over recognisable automatic transition systems needs to be established. It also remains to be seen whether the sufficient conditions (or similar ones) on IOI automata can be used to prove decidability of model checking problems for richer or similar specification languages like PDL [17] with various extensions [30], regular extensions of CTL [3, 19, 24] or even the modal μ-calculus [23]. Note that these logics are all state-based in the sense that typical global model checking procedures can proceed in a bottom-up fashion similar to Algorithm 1.

The next question that comes up in terms of investigations w.r.t. specification languages concerns linear-time logics like LTL [27] and PSL [2] and then combinations with branching-time features resulting in something like CTL* [16]. Note that model checking for such logics typically requires very different techniques like automata- [33] or tableau-based [35] ones. It therefore remains to see if the sufficient conditions laid out in Lemma 4 would also yield computability of model checking problems for linear-time properties, or whether other conditions can be found similarly.

Another obvious direction for future work is of course to find further instantiations of the relaxed framework of binary acceptors which preferably leads to richer classes of automatic structures but still satisfies the conditions of Lemma 4. One way to go about this is to give up working with essentially two-tracked words since this is one of the main course of undecidability. A simple suggestion for a binary acceptor that is based in the world of one-tracked words is, for instance, the following: given an NFA $\mathcal{A}$, let $R(\mathcal{A}) = \{(u, v) \mid uv \in L(\mathcal{A})\}$. Hence, it defines a relation by cutting words in a regular language apart. It is a simple exercise, though, to see that this model of binary acceptor is effectively equivalent to the IOI automata studied here. Hence, it does not generate a new class. We therefore propose a slight variant and leave it open whether this model of binary acceptor satisfies the conditions of Lemma 4: given an NFA $\mathcal{A}$, let $R(\mathcal{A}) = \{(u, v) \mid$ there is $w \in L(\mathcal{A})$ such that u is a prefix of w and v is a suffix of $w\}$. We suspect that CTL model checking is computable for the class of automatic structures defined by such binary acceptors but have no formal proof at the moment.

We also suspect that recognisable relations may form the largest class of syntactically definable relations for which CTL model checking, or even model checking for some weaker logic like EF, is decidable. It remains to be seen whether it is possible to encode some undecidable reachability problem using an arbitrary relation that incorporates only the slightest form of synchronisation between the runs on the input and the output word.

References

1. Abdulla, P.A., Jonsson, B., Nilsson, M., d'Orso, J.: Regular model checking made simple and effcient. In: Brim, L., Křetínský, M., Kučera, A., Jančar, P. (eds.) CONCUR 2002. LNCS, vol. 2421, pp. 116–131. Springer, Heidelberg (2002). doi:10. 1007/3-540-45694-5_9
2. I. Accellera Organization. Formal semantics of Accellera property specification language (2004). In Appendix B. http://www.eda.org/vfv/docs/PSL-v1.1.pdf
3. Axelsson, R., Hague, M., Kreutzer, S., Lange, M., Latte, M.: Extended computation tree logic. In: Fermüller, C.G., Voronkov, A. (eds.) LPAR 2010. LNCS, vol. 6397, pp. 67–81. Springer, Heidelberg (2010). doi:10.1007/978-3-642-16242-8_6
4. Baier, C., Katoen, J.-P.: Principles of Model Checking. MIT Press, Cambridge (2008)
5. Berstel, J.: Transductions and Context-Free Languages. Leitfäden der angewandten Mathematik und Mechanik. Teubner (1979)
6. Blumensath, A.: Automatic structures. Master's thesis, RWTH Aachen (1999)
7. Blumensath, A., Grädel, E.: Automatic structures. In: Proceedings of the 15th Symposium on Logic in Computer Science, LICS 2000, pp. 51–62. IEEE (2000)
8. Bouajjani, A., Habermehl, P., Vojnar, T.: Abstract regular model checking. In: Alur, R., Peled, D.A. (eds.) CAV 2004. LNCS, vol. 3114, pp. 372–386. Springer, Heidelberg (2004). doi:10.1007/978-3-540-27813-9_29
9. Bouajjani, A., Jonsson, B., Nilsson, M., Touili, T.: Regular model checking. In: Emerson, E.A., Sistla, A.P. (eds.) CAV 2000. LNCS, vol. 1855, pp. 403–418. Springer, Heidelberg (2000). doi:10.1007/10722167_31
10. Burkart, O., Steffen, B.: Model checking the full modal mu-calculus for infinite sequential processes. In: Degano, P., Gorrieri, R., Marchetti-Spaccamela, A. (eds.) ICALP 1997. LNCS, vol. 1256, pp. 419–429. Springer, Heidelberg (1997). doi:10. 1007/3-540-63165-8_198
11. Clarke, E.M., Emerson, E.A.: Design and synthesis of synchronization skeletons using branching time temporal logic. In: Kozen, D. (ed.) Logic of Programs 1981. LNCS, vol. 131, pp. 52–71. Springer, Heidelberg (1982). doi:10.1007/BFb0025774
12. Dams, D., Lakhnech, Y., Steffen, M.: Iterating transducers. J. Log. Algebr. Program 52–53, 109–127 (2002)
13. Demri, S., Goranko, V., Lange, M.: Temporal Logics in Computer Science, volume I - Finite State Systems of Cambridge Tracts in Theor. Comp. Sc. Cambridge Univ. Press (2016)
14. Emerson, E.A., Clarke, E.M.: Characterizing correctness properties of parallel programs using fixpoints. In: Bakker, J., Leeuwen, J. (eds.) ICALP 1980. LNCS, vol. 85, pp. 169–181. Springer, Heidelberg (1980). doi:10.1007/3-540-10003-2_69
15. Emerson, E.A., Clarke, E.M.: Using branching time temporal logic to synthesize synchronization skeletons. Sci. Comput. Program. 2(3), 241–266 (1982)
16. Emerson, E.A., Halpern, J.Y.: "Sometimes" and "not never" revisited: On branching versus linear time temporal logic. J. ACM 33(1), 151–178 (1986)
17. Fischer, M.J., Ladner, R.E.: Propositional dynamic logic of regular programs. J. Comput. Syst. Sci. 18(2), 194–211 (1979)
18. Habermehl, P., Vojnar, T.: Regular model checking using inference of regular languages. In: Proceedings of the 6th International Workshop on Verification of Infinite-State Systems, INFINITY 2004, vol. 138(3), pp. 21–36 (2005)

19. Hamaguchi, K., Hiraishi, H., Yajima, S.: Branching time regular temporal logic for model checking with linear time complexity. In: Clarke, E.M., Kurshan, R.P. (eds.) CAV 1990. LNCS, vol. 531, pp. 253–262. Springer, Heidelberg (1991). doi:10.1007/BFb0023739

20. Hoare, C.A.R.: Communicating sequential processes. Commun. ACM **21**(8), 666–677 (1978)

21. Jonsson, B., Nilsson, M.: Transitive closures of regular relations for verifying infinite-state systems. In: Graf, S., Schwartzbach, M. (eds.) TACAS 2000. LNCS, vol. 1785, pp. 220–235. Springer, Heidelberg (2000). doi:10.1007/3-540-46419-0_16

22. Resten, Y., Maler, O., Marcus, M., Pnueli, A., Shahar, E.: Symbolic model checking with rich assertional languages. In: Grumberg, O. (ed.) CAV 1997. LNCS, vol. 1254, pp. 424–435. Springer, Heidelberg (1997). doi:10.1007/3-540-63166-6_41

23. Kozen, D.: Results on the propositional μ-calculus. TCS **27**, 333–354 (1983)

24. Mateescu, R., Monteiro, P.T., Dumas, E., Jong, H.: Computation tree regular logic for genetic regulatory networks. In: Cha, S.S., Choi, J.-Y., Kim, M., Lee, I., Viswanathan, M. (eds.) ATVA 2008. LNCS, vol. 5311, pp. 48–63. Springer, Heidelberg (2008). doi:10.1007/978-3-540-88387-6_6

25. Milner, R. (ed.): A Calculus of Communicating Systems. LNCS, vol. 92. Springer, Heidelberg (1980)

26. Ong, C.-H.L.: Higher-order model checking: an overview. In: Proceedings of the 30th IEEE Symposium on Logic in Computer Science, LICS 2015, pp. 1–15. IEEE Computer Society (2015)

27. Pnueli, A.: The temporal logic of programs. In: Proceedings of the 18th Symposium on Foundations of Computer Science, FOCS 1977, pp. 46–57. IEEE, Providence (1977)

28. Reisig, W.: Petri Nets (An Introduction). EATCS Monographs on Theoretical Computer Science, vol. 4. Springer, Heidelberg (1985)

29. Sakarovitch, J.: Elements of Automata Theory. Cambridge University Press, Cambridge (2009)

30. Streett, R.S.: Propositional dynamic logic of looping and converse is elementarily decidable. Inf. Control **54**(1/2), 121–141 (1982)

31. Sutner, K.: Iterating transducers. Fundam. Inf. **138**(1–2), 259–272 (2015)

32. Touili, T.: Regular model checking using widening techniques. In: Proceedings of the Workshop on Verification of Parameterized Systems, VEPAS 2001. Electr. Notes Theor. Comput. Sci., vol. 50(4), pp. 342–356. Elsevier (2001)

33. Vardi, M.Y., Wolper, P.: Reasoning about infinite computations. Inf. Comput. **115**(1), 1–37 (1994)

34. Walukiewicz, I.: Pushdown processes: games and model-checking. Inf. Comput. **164**(2), 234–263 (2001)

35. Wolper, P.: The tableau method for temporal logic: an overview. Logique Anal. **28**(110–111), 119–136 (1985)

36. Wolper, P., Boigelot, B.: Verifying systems with infinite but regular state spaces. In: Hu, A.J., Vardi, M.Y. (eds.) CAV 1998. LNCS, vol. 1427, pp. 88–97. Springer, Heidelberg (1998). doi:10.1007/BFb0028736

Topological Characterisation of Multi-buffer Simulation

Milka Hutagalung$^{(\boxtimes)}$

University of Kassel, Kassel, Germany
milka.hutagalung@uni-kassel.de

Abstract. Multi-buffer simulation is an extension of simulation pre-order that can be used to approximate inclusion of languages recognised by Büchi automata up to their trace closures. It has been shown that multi-buffer simulation with unbounded buffers can be characterised with the existence of a continuous function f that witnesses trace closure inclusion. In this paper, we show that such a characterisation can be refined to the case where we only consider bounded buffers by requiring the function f to be Lipschitz continuous. This characterisation only holds for some restricted classes of automata. One of the automata should only produce words where each letter does not commute unboundedly to the left or right. We will show that such an automaton can be characterised with a cyclic-path-connected automaton, which is a refinement of a syntactic characterisation of an automaton that has a regular trace closure.

1 Introduction

Simulation is a pre-order relation that relates two automata $\mathcal{A}$, $\mathcal{B}$ in the sense that one automaton simulates the other. It is used to minimise and approximate language inclusion between automata on words and trees [1,3,4,6].

Multi-buffer simulation is introduced in [9] as an extension of simulation for non-deterministic Büchi automata [7]. It extends the framework of the standard simulation with n FIFO buffers of capacities $k_1, \ldots, k_n \in \mathbb{N} \cup \{\omega\}$. The buffers are associated with the alphabets $\Sigma_1, \ldots, \Sigma_n \subseteq \Sigma$, respectively. SPOILER plays as in the standard simulation. He moves his pebble by reading a letter one by one. However, DUPLICATOR can skip her turn, and push the letter that is chosen by SPOILER to the associated buffers. DUPLICATOR can move and pop some letters from the buffers in some round later. In [9], it is shown that multi-buffer simulation is undecidable in general but decidable if all buffers have bounded capacities, i.e. when $k_1, \ldots, k_n \in \mathbb{N}$. Multi-buffer simulation can be used to approximate inclusion of Mazurkiewicz trace closure. If we have multi-buffer simulation $\mathcal{A} \sqsubseteq^{k, \ldots, k} \mathcal{B}$ for some $k \in \mathbb{N} \cup \{\omega\}$, then we have $L(\mathcal{A}) \subseteq [L(\mathcal{B})]_I$ that is equivalent to the inclusion of Mazurkiewicz trace closure $[L(\mathcal{A})]_I \subseteq [L(\mathcal{B})]_I$, which is known to be undecidable [11] and even highly undecidable [5].

The winning strategy for DUPLICATOR in multi-buffer simulation game can be characterised with a continuous function [9]. We have multi-buffer simulation

© Springer International Publishing AG 2017
M. Hague and I. Potapov (Eds.): RP 2017, LNCS 10506, pp. 101–117, 2017.
DOI: 10.1007/978-3-319-67089-8_8

$\mathcal{A} \sqsubseteq^{\omega,\dots,\omega} \mathcal{B}$ iff there exists a continuous function f that maps the accepting runs of $\mathcal{A}$ to the ones of $\mathcal{B}$ over trace equivalent words. Intuitively, this characterisation could also be lifted to the case of bounded buffer: $\mathcal{A} \sqsubseteq^{k,\dots,k} \mathcal{B}$, for some $k \in \mathbb{N}$ iff there exists such a Lipschitz continuous function f. Unfortunately this is not the case. There are $\mathcal{A}$, $\mathcal{B}$ in which such a Lipschitz continuous function f exists but buffered simulation with bounded buffers does not hold, i.e. $\mathcal{A} \not\sqsubseteq^{k,\dots,k} \mathcal{B}$ for any $k \in \mathbb{N}$. Hence one may ask whether we can add some restriction on the structure of $\mathcal{A}$, $\mathcal{B}$ such that the characterisation holds. This would give a good theoretical justification for multi-buffer simulation with bounded buffers.

We answer this question in this work. We first show that the characterisation with Lipschitz continuity fails in two cases. The first one is the case where SPOILER can form a non-accepting run that cannot be mimicked by DUPLICATOR, which is irrelevant to the use of multi-buffer simulation. We can avoid this by restricting DUPLICATOR's automaton to be complete. The second one is the case where SPOILER can produce a word, in which one of its letters, suppose a, can commute unboundedly to the left or right. SPOILER might read a word where a occurs at a very late position, but in a trace equivalent word that should be produced by DUPLICATOR, a occurs at a very early position. In this case, DUPLICATOR needs to store unboundedly many irrelevant letters before she can read a, and eventually violates the capacity constraint. We will show that we can avoid this by restricting SPOILER's automaton to only produce words where each of its letters cannot commute unboundedly, i.e. there exists a bound $k \in \mathbb{N}$, such that each letter commutes at most k steps to the left or right.

Note that the first restriction is a syntactic restriction, but the second one is not. We cannot check syntactically whether SPOILER's automaton $\mathcal{A}$ admits such a bound k by looking at the structure of $\mathcal{A}$. Hence, it is reasonable to ask whether we can have an equivalent syntactic restriction. For this purpose, we will show that we can lift the syntactic characterisation of *loop-connected* automaton, a syntactic characterisation of an automaton that has a regular trace closure [2].

2   Preliminaries

For any alphabet Σ, we denote the set of finite words over Σ with Σ^*, the set of infinite words over Σ with Σ^ω, and $\Sigma^\infty = \Sigma^* \cup \Sigma^\omega$. For any word $w \in \Sigma^\infty$ of length $n \in \mathbb{N} \cup \{\infty\}$, we denote with $|w| = n$ the length of w, $|w|_a$ the number of a in w, $\mathsf{Pos}(w) \subseteq \mathbb{N}$ the set of positions in w, $w(i)$ the letter of w at position i, and $\Sigma_w = \{w(i) \mid i \in \mathsf{Pos}(w)\}$ the alphabet of w.

A *non-deterministic Büchi automaton* (NBA) is a tuple $\mathcal{A} = (Q, \Sigma, q_I, E, F)$, where Q is a finite set of *states*, Σ is an alphabet, $q_I \in Q$ is the *initial state*, $E \subseteq Q \times \Sigma \times Q$ is the *transition relation*, and $F \subseteq Q$ is the set of *final states*. We denote with $|\mathcal{A}|$ the number of states of $\mathcal{A}$. We sometimes write $p \xrightarrow{a} p'$ if $(p, a, p') \in E$. A *run* of $\mathcal{A}$ on $a_0 a_1 \dots \in \Sigma^\infty$ is an alternating sequence of states and letters $\rho = q_0 a_0 q_1 a_1 \dots$ with q_0 being the initial state of $\mathcal{A}$ and $(q_i, a_i, q_{i+1}) \in E$ for all $i \geq 0$. The run ρ is *accepting* if $q_i \in F$ for infinitely many $i \in \mathbb{N}$. The set of runs and accepting runs are respectively denoted with $\mathsf{Run}(\mathcal{A})$ and

AccRun($\mathcal{A}$). For any run $\rho = q_0 a_0 q_1 a_1 \ldots$, the word of ρ is word$(\rho) = a_0 a_1 \ldots \in \Sigma^\infty$, and the *language* of $\mathcal{A}$ is $L(\mathcal{A}) = \{\text{word}(\rho) \mid \rho \in \text{AccRun}(\mathcal{A})\}$. Moreover, for any finite run $r = q_0 a_0 q_1 a_1 \ldots q_n$, the length of r is $|r| = n$.

2.1 Mazurkiewicz Traces

An *independence alphabet* is a pair (Σ, I), where Σ is a finite alphabet and $I \subseteq \Sigma \times \Sigma$ is an irreflexive and symmetric relation, called *independence relation*. The relation $D = \Sigma \times \Sigma \setminus I$ is called the *dependence relation*, and the graph $G = (\Sigma, E)$, where $E = \{(a, b) \mid (a, b) \in D \text{ and } a \neq b\}$ is called the *dependency graph* of (Σ, I). The tuple $\hat{\Sigma} = (\Sigma_1, \ldots, \Sigma_n)$ where the set $\{\Sigma_1, \ldots, \Sigma_n\}$ is the set of maximal cliques in G is called the *distributed alphabet* of (Σ, I).

Given an independence alphabet (Σ, I), let $\hat{\Sigma} = (\Sigma_1, \ldots, \Sigma_n)$ be the corresponding distributed alphabet, and let $\pi_i : \Sigma^\infty \rightarrow \Sigma_i^\infty$ be a projection from the word over Σ to the word over Σ_i for all $i \in \{1, \ldots, n\}$. The projection $\pi_i(w)$ is obtained by deleting from w all letters that do not belong to Σ_i. For any $w, w' \in \Sigma^\infty$ over (Σ, I), we say w is *trace equivalent* with w', i.e. $w \sim_I w'$, iff $\pi_i(w) = \pi_i(w')$ for all $i \in \{1, \ldots, n\}$. For example if $\Sigma = \{a, b, c\}$, $I = \{(b, c), (c, b)\}$ then $\hat{\Sigma} = (\{a, b\}, \{a, c\})$, and we have $a(bc)^\omega \sim_I a(cb)^\omega$. For any NBA $\mathcal{A}$ over (Σ, I), the *trace closure* of $\mathcal{A}$ is the language $[L(\mathcal{A})]_I = \{w \in \Sigma^\omega \mid \exists w' \in L(\mathcal{A}): w \sim_I w'\}$.

Given an NBA $\mathcal{A}$ over (Σ, I), there is an important result regarding the regularity of $[L(\mathcal{A})]_I$. This result uses the notion of *connected word*. A word $w \in \Sigma^\infty$ over (Σ, I) is called *connected* if the subgraph of the dependency graph induced by Σ_w is connected [10]. We denote such a subgraph with G_w, and call it the *dependency graph of w*. For example, the word $w = a(bc)^\omega$ over $\Sigma = \{a, b, c\}$ and $I = \{(b, c), (c, b)\}$, is connected, but its infinite suffix $(bc)^\omega$ is not. The automaton $\mathcal{A}$ is called *loop-connected* if every cycle in $\mathcal{A}$ produces a connected word. For any NBA $\mathcal{A}$ over (Σ, I), $[L(\mathcal{A})]_I$ is regular iff $\mathcal{A}$ is loop-connected [2].

2.2 Multi-buffer Simulation

Given two NBA $\mathcal{A}$, $\mathcal{B}$ over (Σ, I), let $\hat{\Sigma} = (\Sigma_1, \ldots, \Sigma_n)$ be the distributed alphabet of (Σ, I), and $\kappa = (k_1, \ldots, k_n)$ a vector over $\mathbb{N} \cup \{\omega\}$, the *multi-buffer simulation game* $\mathcal{G}^{\kappa, \hat{\Sigma}}(\mathcal{A}, \mathcal{B})$, or simply $\mathcal{G}^\kappa(\mathcal{A}, \mathcal{B})$ is played between SPOILER and DUPLICATOR in the automata $\mathcal{A}$, $\mathcal{B}$ with n buffers of capacity $k_1, \ldots, k_n$, and the buffers are associated with the alphabets $\Sigma_1, \ldots, \Sigma_n$, respectively. Initially, two pebbles are placed each on the initial states of $\mathcal{A}$ and $\mathcal{B}$. SPOILER moves the pebble in $\mathcal{A}$ by reading a letter $a \in \Sigma$, and pushes a copy of the a-symbol to each buffer i, in which $a \in \Sigma_i$. DUPLICATOR either skips her turn or moves the pebble in $\mathcal{B}$ by reading a word $b_1 \ldots b_m$. While doing so, for every $i \in \{1, \ldots, m\}$, starting from $i = 1$, she pops b_i from each buffer that is associated with b_i. More formally, a configuration is a tuple $(p, \beta_1, \ldots, \beta_n, q) \in Q^\mathcal{A} \times \Sigma_1^* \times \ldots \times \Sigma_n^* \times Q^\mathcal{B}$, where $|\beta_i| \leq k_i$ for all $i \in \{1, \ldots, n\}$. The initial configuration is $(p_0, \epsilon, \ldots, \epsilon, q_0)$, where p_0, q_0 are the initial states of $\mathcal{A}$, $\mathcal{B}$, and in every configuration $(p, \beta_1, \ldots, \beta_n, q)$,

- SPOILER chooses a letter $a \in \Sigma$, a state $p' \in Q^{\mathcal{A}}$, such that $p \xrightarrow{a} p'$,

- DUPLICATOR chooses a finite path $q \xrightarrow{b_1} q_1 \xrightarrow{b_2} q_2 \ldots \xrightarrow{b_m} q_m$ from q in $\mathcal{B}$, such that $\pi_i(a\beta_i) = \pi_i(\beta'_i b_1 \ldots b_m)$ for all $i \in \{1, \ldots, n\}$. The next configuration is $(p', \beta'_1, \ldots, \beta'_k, q')$.

If one of the players gets stuck, then the opponent wins, otherwise SPOILER and DUPLICATOR respectively form infinite runs ρ in $\mathcal{A}$ and ρ' in $\mathcal{B}$. In this case, DUPLICATOR wins iff ρ is not accepting or ρ' is accepting and every letter that is pushed by SPOILER into a buffer is eventually popped by DUPLICATOR. We write $\mathcal{A} \sqsubseteq^{\kappa} \mathcal{B}$ if DUPLICATOR wins $\mathcal{G}^{\kappa}(\mathcal{A}, \mathcal{B})$, and in this case it implies $L(\mathcal{A}) \subseteq [L(\mathcal{B})]_I$.

Example 1. Consider the following two NBA $\mathcal{A}$, $\mathcal{B}$ over the independence alphabet (Σ, I), in which $\hat{\Sigma} = (\{a\}, \{b\})$, i.e. $\Sigma = \{a, b\}$, $I = \{(a, b), (b, a)\}$.

We have $\mathcal{A} \sqsubseteq^{0,\omega} \mathcal{B}$, since DUPLICATOR has the following winning strategy in $\mathcal{G}^{0,\omega}(\mathcal{A}, \mathcal{B})$: she skips her moves, except when SPOILER reads a. In this case, DUPLICATOR goes to q_1: she pops all the bs from the second buffer, and a from the first buffer. From this state, if SPOILER reads b then DUPLICATOR also reads b by looping in q_1 and pops b from the buffer. DUPLICATOR wins since either SPOILER forms a non-accepting run, or DUPLICATOR forms an accepting run and every letter that is pushed by SPOILER into a buffer is eventually popped by DUPLICATOR. DUPLICATOR however loses the game $\mathcal{G}^{0,k}(\mathcal{A}, \mathcal{B})$ for any $k \in \mathbb{N}$, since SPOILER can loop in p_0 indefinitely and push unboundedly many b before he goes to p_1. In this case, DUPLICATOR eventually violates the buffer constraint.

3   Topological Characterisation

Given two NBA $\mathcal{A}$, $\mathcal{B}$, and a function $f : R_1 \to R_2$, $R_1 \subseteq \mathsf{Run}(\mathcal{A})$, $R_2 \subseteq \mathsf{Run}(\mathcal{B})$, let us call f *trace preserving* if for all $\rho \in \mathsf{Dom}(f)$, $\mathsf{word}(\rho) \sim_I \mathsf{word}(f(\rho))$. Trace closure inclusion $L(\mathcal{A}) \subseteq [L(\mathcal{B})]_I$ can be characterised with a trace preserving $f : \mathsf{AccRun}(\mathcal{A}) \to \mathsf{AccRun}(\mathcal{B})$. This is because such a function f exists iff for every $\rho \in \mathsf{AccRun}(\mathcal{A})$, there exists $\rho' \in \mathsf{AccRun}(\mathcal{B})$ over trace equivalent words.

Proposition 1. $L(\mathcal{A}) \subseteq [L(\mathcal{B})]_I$ *iff there exists a trace preserving function* $f : \mathsf{AccRun}(\mathcal{A}) \to \mathsf{AccRun}(\mathcal{B})$.

For such a function $f : R_1 \to R_2$, we can define its continuity by considering the standard metric for infinite words. This is because every run $\rho \in \mathsf{Run}(\mathcal{A})$ can be seen as an infinite word over $\Sigma' = Q^{\mathcal{A}} \cdot \Sigma$. We consider the metric $d : \mathsf{AccRun}(\mathcal{A})^2 \to [0, 1]$, where $d(\rho, \rho') = 0$ if $\rho = \rho'$, and

$d(\rho, \rho') = 2^{-min\{i \mid p_i a_i \neq q_i b_i\}}$ if $\rho = p_0 a_0 \, p_1 a_1 \, \ldots$, $\rho' = q_0 b_0 \, q_1 b_1 \, \ldots$ are different. Intuitively, the distance between two runs is small if they share a long common prefix.

In [9], it is shown that we can refine the characterisation in Proposition 1 for multi-buffer simulation $\mathcal{A} \sqsubseteq^{\omega,\ldots,\omega} \mathcal{B}$ by requiring the function f to be continuous. Recall that f is continuous if for any two distinct runs $\rho, \rho' \in \mathsf{Dom}(f)$ that are very close, they are mapped into two runs $f(\rho), f(\rho')$ that are also very close.

Proposition 2 [9]. $\mathcal{A} \sqsubseteq^{\omega,\ldots,\omega} \mathcal{B}$ *iff there exists a continuous trace preserving function* $f : \mathsf{AccRun}(\mathcal{A}) \to \mathsf{AccRun}(\mathcal{B})$.

Consider again the NBA $\mathcal{A}$, $\mathcal{B}$ from Example 1. We have a continuous trace preserving function $f : \mathsf{AccRun}(\mathcal{A}) \to \mathsf{AccRun}(\mathcal{B})$ that maps every accepting run of $\mathcal{A}$, i.e. over $b^* a b^\omega$, to the one of $\mathcal{B}$ over $a b^\omega$. This function is trace preserving since for every $n \geq 0$, $b^n a b^\omega \sim_I a b^\omega$. It is also continuous since there is only one accepting run in $\mathcal{B}$, therefore the distance between two outputs of f is always 0, i.e. trivially very small.

Such a characterisation of winning strategies with continuous functions is far from new. For example, in the *delay game* [8], it is shown that the winning strategy for DUPLICATOR can be characterised with a continuous function, and in the case of finite delay, the characterisation can be lifted to the one that consider a Lipschitz continuous function. Recall that a function is Lipschitz continuous if there exists a constant $C \in \mathbb{R}$, such that for any two inputs of distance d, their outputs' distance is at most $C \cdot d$.

We would like to have such a topological characterisation for multi-buffer simulation. The characterisation with a continuous function holds for multi-buffer simulation as we can see in Proposition 2. However, the characterisation with a Lipschitz continuous function fails.

Example 2. Consider the following two automata $\mathcal{A}, \mathcal{B}$ over the independence alphabet (Σ, I) with $\hat{\Sigma} = (\{a, b\})$, i.e. $\Sigma = \{a, b\}$ and $I = \emptyset$,

In this case, we have a Lipschitz continuous and trace preserving function $f : \mathsf{AccRun}(\mathcal{A}) \to \mathsf{AccRun}(\mathcal{B})$ that maps the only accepting run of $\mathcal{A}$ to the one of $\mathcal{B}$. This function is trace preserving and also Lipschitz continuous with constant 0. However, SPOILER wins the game $\mathcal{G}^k(\mathcal{A}, \mathcal{B})$ for any $k \in \mathbb{N}$. He wins by playing the word b^ω. For every $k \in \mathbb{N}$, DUPLICATOR eventually fills the buffer more than its capacity in round $k + 1$, and loses the game $\mathcal{G}^k(\mathcal{A}, \mathcal{B})$.

Example 3. Consider again the NBA $\mathcal{A}$, $\mathcal{B}$ from Example 1. We have a trace preserving and continuous function $f : \mathsf{AccRun}(\mathcal{A}) \to \mathsf{AccRun}(\mathcal{B})$ as shown before. It is also Lipschitz continuous with Lipschitz constant 0. However, SPOILER wins the game $\mathcal{G}^{k,k}(\mathcal{A}, \mathcal{B})$ for all $k \in \mathbb{N}$. He wins by first reading $bbb \ldots$ indefinitely. DUPLICATOR either skips her move forever, or eventually moves by reading b. If DUPLICATOR eventually moves by reading b, she would never form an accepting run, and SPOILER can continue read ab^ω and form an accepting run. However if DUPLICATOR never moves, then she violates the buffer constraint in round $k+1$. Hence in both cases DUPLICATOR loses.

We will show that there are some restricted classes of $\mathcal{A}$, $\mathcal{B}$ where we can lift the characterisation in Proposition 2 to the case of bounded buffers by considering a Lipschitz continuous function.

4   Characterisation of $\sqsubseteq^{k,\ldots,k}$, $k \in \mathbb{N}$

First note that if multi-buffer simulation $\mathcal{A} \sqsubseteq^{k,\ldots,k} \mathcal{B}$ holds with some bounded capacity $k \in \mathbb{N}$, then we can construct a Lipschitz continuous trace preserving function $f : \mathsf{AccRun}(\mathcal{A}) \to \mathsf{AccRun}(\mathcal{B})$. For every $\rho \in \mathsf{AccRun}(\mathcal{A})$, we define $f(\rho)$ as the run that is formed by DUPLICATOR in $\mathcal{G}^{k,\ldots,k}(\mathcal{A},\mathcal{B})$, assuming that SPOILER plays ρ and DUPLICATOR plays according to the winning strategy. Such a function is trace preserving since it is derived from a winning strategy of DUPLICATOR, and it is Lipschitz continuous with Lipschitz constant $C = k + \ldots + k$ since for any output run $f(\rho)$ the i-th letter of $f(\rho)$ is determined by the first $C + i$ letters of ρ.

Lemma 1. *If $\mathcal{A} \sqsubseteq^{k,\ldots,k} \mathcal{B}$ for some $k \in \mathbb{N}$, then there exists a Lipschitz continuous trace preserving function $f : \mathsf{AccRun}(\mathcal{A}) \to \mathsf{AccRun}(\mathcal{B})$.*

Proof. For every $\rho \in \mathsf{AccRun}(\mathcal{A})$, we define $f(\rho)$ as the run that is formed by DUPLICATOR in $\mathcal{G}^{k,\ldots,k}(\mathcal{A},\mathcal{B})$, assuming that SPOILER plays ρ and DUPLICATOR plays according to the winning strategy. The function f is trace preserving since it is derived from a winning strategy of DUPLICATOR.

Let $n \in \mathbb{N}$ be some number and $C = k + \ldots + k$. If SPOILER plays $\rho \in \mathsf{AccRun}(\mathcal{A})$, then since DUPLICATOR wins $\mathcal{G}^{k,\ldots,k}(\mathcal{A},\mathcal{B})$, in round $n + C$, DUPLICATOR forms a finite run of length at least n. If there is $\rho' \in \mathsf{AccRun}(\mathcal{A})$ with $d(\rho,\rho') \leq 2^{-(n+C+1)}$, then in the first $n + C$ rounds, DUPLICATOR does not see any difference whether SPOILER actually plays ρ or ρ'. DUPLICATOR makes the same moves in response to ρ or ρ'. The output runs $f(\rho)$ and $f(\rho')$ share the same prefix of length n, i.e. $d(f(\rho), f(\rho')) \leq 2^{-(n+1)}$. This implies $d(f(\rho), f(\rho')) \leq 2^C \cdot d(\rho,\rho')$. The function f is Lipschitz continuous with Lipschitz constant 2^C.

As we can see in the previous section, the reverse direction of this lemma does not hold. In Example 2, the reason why DUPLICATOR loses is because SPOILER can play a non-accepting run that cannot be mimicked by DUPLICATOR. We can easily avoid this by assuming that DUPLICATOR's automaton is complete: for every $q \in Q^{\mathcal{B}}$ and $a \in \Sigma$, there is $q' \in Q^{\mathcal{B}}$ such that $(q,a,q') \in E^{\mathcal{B}}$.

In Example 3, the reason why DUPLICATOR loses is different. The automaton of DUPLICATOR is complete. But in this case, SPOILER can produce b^*ab^ω, in which the letter a can commute unboundedly to the left or right. The letter a can be read by SPOILER in a very late round, but has to be read by DUPLICATOR in an early round. In order to read its trace equivalent word: ab^ω, DUPLICATOR first needs to store indefinitely many bs that are read by SPOILER. To avoid this, we need to restrict words that are produced by SPOILER. He should only produce words, in which each letter cannot commute unboundedly to the left or right. To formalise this restriction we introduce the notion of *corresponding relation*.

For any two words $w, v \in \Sigma^\infty$, the corresponding relation $\mathsf{Corr}_{w,v}$ relates the position of w and v that are over the same letter and have the same order with respect to the letter.

Definition 1. *For any $w, v \in \Sigma^\infty$, the corresponding relation $\mathsf{Corr}_{w,v} \subseteq \mathsf{Pos}(w) \times \mathsf{Pos}(v)$ is defined as $\mathsf{Corr}_{w,v} = \{(i,j) \mid \exists a \in \Sigma, w(i) = v(j) = a, |w(1)\dots w(i)|_a = |v(1)\dots v(j)|_a\}$.*

Consider (Σ, I) where $\Sigma = \{a, b, c\}$, $I = \{(b,c), (c,b)\}$. $w = a(bc)^\omega$ and $v = a(cb)^\omega$. We have $\mathsf{Corr}_{w,v} = \{(1,1)\} \cup \{(i, i+1) \mid i > 1 \text{ is even}\} \cup \{(i, i-1) \mid i > 1 \text{ is odd}\}$.

If w, v are two words over (Σ, I) and $w \sim_I v$, then $\mathsf{Corr}_{w,v}$ is a bijection. This is because for every $a \in \Sigma$, the number of a in w and v are the same. We will use the relation $\mathsf{Corr}_{w,v}$, in which $w \sim_I v$, to determine how long a letter in w or v can commute.

Definition 2. *Given a word $w \in \Sigma^\infty$ over an independence alphabet (Σ, I), and $i \in \mathsf{Pos}(w)$, let $S_w(i) = \{j - i \mid (i,j) \in \mathsf{Corr}_{w,v}, w \sim_I v\}$. We define $\mathsf{Deg}_w^+(i) = \max\{k \in \mathbb{N} \cup \{\infty\} : k \in S_w(i)\}$ and $\mathsf{Deg}_w^-(i) = \max\{k \in \mathbb{N} \cup \{\infty\} : -k \in S_w(i)\}$. The corresponding degree of a letter at position i in w is $\mathsf{Deg}_w(i) = \max\{\mathsf{Deg}_w^+(i), \mathsf{Deg}_w^-(i)\}$.*

Consider the word $w = a(bc)^\omega$ over $\Sigma = \{a, b, c\}$, $I = \{(b,c), (c,b)\}$. We have $\mathsf{Deg}_w(1) = 0$ since for all $v \sim_I w$, $(1,1) \in \mathsf{Corr}_{w,v}$. We have $\mathsf{Deg}_w(2) = \infty$ since for all $k \in \mathbb{N}$, there is $v_k = ac^{k+1}(bc)^\omega$, such that $v_k \sim_I w$ and $(2, k+3) \in \mathsf{Corr}_{w,v_k}$. This implies $\mathsf{Deg}_w^+(2) > k$ for all $k \in \mathbb{N}$, and hence $\mathsf{Deg}_w^+(2) = \infty$.

The corresponding degree $\mathsf{Deg}_w(i)$ tells us the maximum length of how long the letter at position i in w can commute. Moreover, for a set of words $L \in \Sigma^\infty$, we define the corresponding degree of L as $\mathsf{Deg}(L) = \max\{k \in \mathbb{N} \cup \{\infty\} \mid w \in L, i \in \mathsf{Pos}(w), k \in \mathsf{Deg}_w(i)\}$. If $\mathsf{Deg}(L) = \infty$, then for any $k \in \mathbb{N}$, there is a word w_k in L such that one letter of w can commute more than k steps to the left or right. For example, consider the automaton $\mathcal{A}$ in Example 1. We have $\mathsf{Deg}(L(\mathcal{A})) = \infty$ since there is $w = ab^\omega \in L(\mathcal{A})$ and its first letter can commute more than k steps to the right for any $k \in \mathbb{N}$.

For any NBA $\mathcal{A}$ over (Σ, I), let $\mathsf{Tr}(\mathcal{A})$ be the set of words over a finite or infinite path of $\mathcal{A}$, i.e. $\mathsf{Tr}(\mathcal{A}) = \{a_1 a_2 \dots \in \Sigma^\infty \mid \exists p_1, p_2, \dots \in Q^{\mathcal{A}} : (p_1, a_1, p_2), (p_2, a_2, p_3), \dots \in E^{\mathcal{A}}\}$. We will show that for any two NBA $\mathcal{A}, \mathcal{B}$, if the corresponding degree of $\mathsf{Tr}(\mathcal{A})$ is finite and $\mathcal{B}$ is complete, then the reverse direction of Lemma 1 also holds. We will show this by using the *delay* game from [8] as an intermediate game. The delay game is similar to the multi-buffer simulation game. However the winning condition is given by a function $f : R_1 \to R_2$, where $R_1 \subseteq \mathsf{Run}(\mathcal{A})$ and $R_2 \subseteq \mathsf{Run}(\mathcal{B})$. In this game, DUPLICATOR can read any letter freely, even the one that is not yet read by SPOILER.

A *delay game* $\Gamma^k(\mathcal{A}, \mathcal{B}, f)$ is played between SPOILER and DUPLICATOR in $\mathcal{A}$, $\mathcal{B}$ in which the configuration is a pair $(r_\mathcal{A}, r_\mathcal{B})$ of finite runs of $\mathcal{A}$, $\mathcal{B}$ with $0 \le |r_\mathcal{A}| - |r_\mathcal{B}| \le k$. The initial configuration is the pair (p_I, q_I) of the initial states of $\mathcal{A}$, $\mathcal{B}$. In every round $i > 0$ with a configuration $(r_\mathcal{A}, r_\mathcal{B})$,

- SPOILER extends $r_\mathcal{A}$ to some finite run $r'_\mathcal{A} := r_\mathcal{A} a p$ in $\mathcal{A}$, and
- DUPLICATOR extends $r_\mathcal{B}$ to some finite run $r'_\mathcal{B} := r_\mathcal{B} b_1 q_1 b_2 \ldots b_n q_n$ in $\mathcal{B}$.

The next configuration is $(r'_\mathcal{A}, r'_\mathcal{B})$. If one of the players gets stuck, then the opponent wins. Otherwise, the play goes on infinitely many rounds and produces two infinite runs ρ, ρ' of $\mathcal{A}$, $\mathcal{B}$, respectively. DUPLICATOR wins iff whenever $\rho \in \mathsf{Dom}(f)$ then $\rho' = f(\rho)$.

Example 4. Consider the automata $\mathcal{A}$, $\mathcal{B}$ from Example 1. Let $f : \mathsf{AccRun}(\mathcal{A}) \to \mathsf{AccRun}(\mathcal{B})$ be a trace preserving function. In this case, there is such a unique f, i.e. $f(\rho) = q_0 a (q_1 b)^\omega$ for all $\rho \in \mathsf{AccRun}(\mathcal{A})$. DUPLICATOR wins the delay game $\Gamma^0(\mathcal{A}, \mathcal{B}, f)$ with the following winning strategy: first she reads a, then she reads $bbb \ldots$ for the rest of the play. Since DUPLICATOR always forms the image of SPOILER's run without any delay, she wins $\Gamma^0(\mathcal{A}, \mathcal{B}, f)$.

The existence of winning strategy for the DUPLICATOR in the delay game with finite delay basically corresponds to the Lipschitz continuity of the function that defines the winning condition.

Lemma 2. *For any two NBA $\mathcal{A}$, $\mathcal{B}$ in which $\mathcal{B}$ is complete, DUPLICATOR wins $\Gamma^C(\mathcal{A}, \mathcal{B}, f)$ iff f is Lipschitz continuous with constant 2^C.*

Proof ($\Leftarrow$). Consider the following winning strategy for DUPLICATOR. Suppose we are at configuration $(r_\mathcal{A}, r_\mathcal{B})$ and SPOILER extends his run to $r'_\mathcal{A} := r_\mathcal{A} a p$. If $r'_\mathcal{A}$ cannot be extended to any $\rho \in \mathsf{Dom}(f)$, then DUPLICATOR extends her run to $r'_\mathcal{B}$, such that $\mathsf{word}(r'_\mathcal{A}) \sim_I \mathsf{word}(r'_\mathcal{B})$. This is possible since $\mathcal{B}$ is complete. If $r'_\mathcal{A}$ can be extended to some $\rho \in \mathsf{Dom}(f)$ and there exists $r'_\mathcal{B} := r_\mathcal{B} b_1 q_1 \ldots b_n q_n$, such that for every such a run ρ, $f(\rho)$ is started with $r'_\mathcal{B}$, then DUPLICATOR extends her run to such a maximal $r'_\mathcal{B}$. Otherwise, DUPLICATOR skips her turn.

If DUPLICATOR plays according to this strategy, then there is no round with a configuration $(r_\mathcal{A}, r_\mathcal{B})$, in which $|r_\mathcal{A}| - |r_\mathcal{B}| > C$. Suppose there is such a round m. DUPLICATOR does not extend her run to some run longer than $r_\mathcal{B}$ in round m, because there exist two runs $\rho_1, \rho_2 \in \mathsf{Dom}(f)$ that can be extended from $r_\mathcal{A}$, i.e. $d(\rho_1, \rho_2) \le 2^{-(|r_\mathcal{A}|+1)}$, and both $f(\rho_1), f(\rho_2)$ can be extended from $r_\mathcal{B}$, but not from any run longer than $r_\mathcal{B}$, i.e. $d(f(\rho_1), f(\rho_2)) = 2^{-(|r_\mathcal{B}|+1)}$. Since $|r_\mathcal{A}| - |r_\mathcal{B}| > C$, we have $d(f(\rho_1), f(\rho_2)) > 2^C \cdot d(\rho_1, \rho_2)$. This contradicts that f is Lipschitz continuous with constant 2^C.

Since in every round the length difference between SPOILER and DUPLICATOR's runs is at most $C \in \mathbb{N}$, then if SPOILER forms an infinite run, DUPLICATOR also forms an infinite run. Moreover, since the invariant holds that in any round i with a configuration $(r_\mathcal{A}^{(i)}, r_\mathcal{B}^{(i)})$, if ρ is started with $r_\mathcal{A}^{(i)}$ then ρ' is started with $r_\mathcal{B}^{(i)}$, then whenever SPOILER plays $\rho \in \mathsf{Dom}(f)$, DUPLICATOR forms the f-image of ρ, i.e. $\rho' = f(\rho)$. DUPLICATOR wins $\Gamma^C(\mathcal{A}, \mathcal{B}, f)$.

($\Rightarrow$) Let $k \in \mathbb{N}$ be some number. If f is not Lipschitz continuous, then there exist $\rho_1, \rho_2 \in \mathsf{AccRun}(\mathcal{A})$, such that $d(f(\rho_1), f(\rho_2)) > 2^k \cdot d(\rho_1, \rho_2)$. Otherwise, f is Lipschitz continuous and k is a Lipschitz constant of f. Let $n \in \mathbb{N}$, such that $2^{-n} = d(\rho_1, \rho_2)$. The winning strategy for SPOILER is to first play ρ_1. On round $n - k + 1$, if DUPLICATOR forms a finite run r' that is not a prefix of $f(\rho_1)$, then SPOILER keeps playing ρ_1 for the rest of the play. Otherwise, he continues by playing ρ_2. This is possible, since ρ_1, ρ_2 share the same prefix of length n. In the first case, SPOILER wins because DUPLICATOR does not form the f-image of ρ_1. In the second case, since $d(f(\rho_1), f(\rho_2)) > 2^{k-n}$, i.e. $f(\rho_1), f(\rho_2)$ share the same prefix of length less than $n - k$, and $|r'| > n - k$, so r' is not a prefix of $f(\rho_0)$. In this case, DUPLICATOR does not form the f-image of ρ_2.

Unfortunately, the winning strategy for DUPLICATOR in the delay game may not be suitable for the buffer game. Consider DUPLICATOR's winning strategy in Example 4. It is not winning in $\mathcal{G}^{\omega,\omega}(\mathcal{A}, \mathcal{B})$, because in the first round, SPOILER might not read a, and hence DUPLICATOR cannot pop a from the buffer. In the multi-buffer game over $\hat{\Sigma} = (\Sigma_1, \ldots, \Sigma_n)$, if w, w' are the words produced by SPOILER and DUPLICATOR in some round, then $\pi_i(w)$ is a prefix of $\pi_i(w')$ for all $i \in \{1, \ldots, n\}$. This is not always the case in the delay game. DUPLICATOR can read letters that are not yet read by SPOILER. We need to translate the winning strategy from the delay to the buffer game. DUPLICATOR should just take the longest output in the delay game that is allowed in the buffer game.

Lemma 3. *Let $f : \mathsf{AccRun}(\mathcal{A}) \to \mathsf{AccRun}(\mathcal{B})$ be a trace preserving function for two NBA $\mathcal{A}$, $\mathcal{B}$, in which $\mathcal{A}$ is complete. If DUPLICATOR wins $\Gamma^k(\mathcal{A}, \mathcal{B}, f)$ for some $k \in \mathbb{N}$, then she wins $\mathcal{G}^{\omega,\ldots,\omega}(\mathcal{A}, \mathcal{B})$.*

Proof. Suppose the NBA $\mathcal{A}$, $\mathcal{B}$ are over (Σ, I) with distributed alphabet $\hat{\Sigma} = (\Sigma_1, \ldots, \Sigma_n)$. The translation is as follows. Suppose in $\mathcal{G}^{\omega,\ldots,\omega}(\mathcal{A}, \mathcal{B})$, SPOILER and DUPLICATOR form finite runs $r_\mathcal{A}$ and $r_\mathcal{B}$. Let $w = \mathsf{word}(r_\mathcal{A})$ and $w' = \mathsf{word}(r_\mathcal{B})$. If the strategy in the delay game tells DUPLICATOR to extend $r_\mathcal{B}$ to $r'_\mathcal{B} := r_\mathcal{B} b_1 p_1 \ldots b_m p_m$, $m \geq 0$, then in the buffer game, we extend $r_\mathcal{B}$ to $r_\mathcal{B} b_1 q_1 \ldots b_{m'} q_{m'}$, $m' \leq m$, the maximal prefix of $r'_\mathcal{B}$, such that $\pi_i(w'b_1 \ldots b_{m'})$ is a prefix of $\pi_i(w)$ for all $i \in \{1, \ldots, n\}$.

Let ρ, ρ_1 be the accepting runs that are formed by SPOILER and DUPLICATOR in $\Gamma^k(\mathcal{A}, \mathcal{B}, f)$, and ρ, ρ_2 be the runs that are formed in $\mathcal{G}^{\omega,\ldots,\omega}(\mathcal{A}, \mathcal{B})$ according to the translation. Since we always extend DUPLICATOR's run in the buffer game by taking the prefix of the original extension in the delay game, any finite prefix of ρ_2 is also a prefix of ρ_1. The converse also holds: any finite prefix of ρ_1 is a prefix of ρ_2. Suppose $r_\mathcal{B}$ is a finite prefix of ρ_1. There is $r_\mathcal{A}$, a finite prefix of ρ, such that in the delay game, when SPOILER extends his run to $r_\mathcal{A}$, DUPLICATOR extends her run to $r_\mathcal{B}$. Let $w = \mathsf{word}(r_\mathcal{A})$ and $w' = \mathsf{word}(r_\mathcal{B})$. Since f is trace preserving, there is $r'_\mathcal{A} := r_\mathcal{A} a_1 p_1 \ldots a_k p_k$, $k \geq 0$, a finite prefix of ρ, such that $\pi_i(w')$ is a prefix of $\pi_i(wa_1 \ldots a_k)$ for all $i \in \{1, \ldots, n\}$. Hence when SPOILER forms $r'_\mathcal{A}$, DUPLICATOR extends her run to $r_\mathcal{B}$ in the delay game. This implies that r_B is also a prefix of ρ_2. We have $\rho_1 = \rho_2$. Thus, whenever SPOILER plays an accepting run ρ in $\mathcal{G}^{\omega,\dots,\omega}(\mathcal{A}, \mathcal{B})$, then DUPLICATOR forms an accepting run $\rho' = f(\rho)$.

If we additionally assume that the corresponding degree of $\mathsf{Tr}(\mathcal{A})$ is finite, then we can show that DUPLICATOR also wins the buffer game with some bounded capacity. Such an assumption is needed to avoid the case where SPOILER produces a word in which one of its letter commutes unboundedly, and makes DUPLICATOR store unboundedly many irrelevant letters before she reads the corresponding one, as we exemplify in Example 3.

Lemma 4. *Let $f : \mathsf{AccRun}(\mathcal{A}) \to \mathsf{AccRun}(\mathcal{B})$ be a trace preserving function for two NBA $\mathcal{A}$, $\mathcal{B}$, in which the corresponding degree of $\mathsf{Tr}(\mathcal{A})$ is finite, and $\mathcal{B}$ is complete. If DUPLICATOR wins $\Gamma^k(\mathcal{A}, \mathcal{B}, f)$ for some $k \in \mathbb{N}$, then she wins $\mathcal{G}^\kappa(\mathcal{A}, \mathcal{B})$ for some $\kappa \in \mathbb{N}^*$.*

Proof. Let $k' \in \mathbb{N}$ be the corresponding degree of $\mathsf{Tr}(\mathcal{A})$, i.e. $k' = \mathsf{Deg}(\mathsf{Tr}(\mathcal{A}))$. Suppose DUPLICATOR wins for some $k \in \mathbb{N}$. By Lemma 2 we can assume that DUPLICATOR wins $\Gamma^k(\mathcal{A}, \mathcal{B}, f)$ with the winning strategy as defined before. Consider the translation in which DUPLICATOR output the maximal prefix that is allowed in the buffer game. We will show that the translated winning strategy in Lemma 3 is not only winning in $\mathcal{G}^{\omega,\dots,\omega}(\mathcal{A}, \mathcal{B})$, but also in $\mathcal{G}^{k'+k,\dots,k'+k}(\mathcal{A}, \mathcal{B})$. We will show this by contradiction. Suppose while playing in $\mathcal{G}^{\omega,\dots,\omega}(\mathcal{A}, \mathcal{B})$, there exists a round, such that one of the buffers is filled with $k + k' + 1$ letters. Let r_A, r_B be the runs that are formed by SPOILER and DUPLICATOR in this round. We have $|r_A| - |r_B| > k + k'$. DUPLICATOR does not extend her run longer than r_B, because either the winning strategy in $\Gamma^k(\mathcal{A}, \mathcal{B}, f)$ tells her to extend to r_B, or it actually tells her to extend to some run r'_B longer than r_B, but r_B is the maximal prefix of r'_B that satisfies

$$\pi_i(\mathsf{word}(r_B)) \text{ is a prefix of } \pi_i(\mathsf{word}(r_A)), \tag{1}$$

for all $i \in \{1, \dots, n\}$. In the first case, since it implies $|r_A| - |r_B| > k$, this contradicts the strategy is winning in $\Gamma^k(\mathcal{A}, \mathcal{B}, f)$. In the second case, suppose r'_B is extended from r_B by reading u, i.e. $r'_B = r_B u(1) p_1 \dots u(\ell) p_\ell$, $\ell > 0$, and suppose $u(1) = a$. Since (1) holds, we have $|\mathsf{word}(r_B)|_a \leq |\mathsf{word}(r_A)|_a$. However since r_B is the maximal prefix of r'_B that satisfies (1), we have $|\mathsf{word}(r_B)|_a = |\mathsf{word}(r_A)|_a$, since otherwise $r_B a p_1$ also satisfies (1) and contradicts the maximality of r_B. Let w, w' be the words that are produced respectively by SPOILER and DUPLICATOR in $\mathcal{G}^{\omega,\dots,\omega}(\mathcal{A}, \mathcal{B})$. Hence $\mathsf{word}(r_A)$ and $\mathsf{word}(r'_B)$ are prefixes of w and w', respectively. Since we assume f is trace preserving and DUPLICATOR plays according to the winning strategy in Lemma 2, we have $w \sim_I w'$. Let $n_0 = |\mathsf{word}(r_A)|_a = |\mathsf{word}(r_B)|_a$, $i_0 \in \mathsf{Pos}(w)$, and $i_1 \in \mathsf{Pos}(w')$, such that $w(i_0) = w'(i_1) = a$ and $|w(1) \dots w(i_0)|_a = |w'(1) \dots w'(i_1)|_a = n_0 + 1$. Hence $i_0 > |r_A|$ and $i_1 = |r_B| + 1$. This implies $i_0 - i_1 > k'$ since $|r_A| - |r_B| > k'$. Since $(i_0, i_1) \in \mathsf{Corr}_{w,w'}$ and $w \in \mathsf{Tr}(\mathcal{A})$, this contradicts $\mathsf{Deg}(\mathsf{Tr}(\mathcal{A})) = k'$.

Hence if the corresponding degree of $\mathsf{Tr}(\mathcal{A})$ is finite and $\mathcal{B}$ is complete, the existence of a Lipschitz continuous trace preserving function implies that multi-buffer simulation holds for some bounded buffers. Together with Lemma 1, we have the following characterisation.

Theorem 1. *Let $\mathcal{A}$, $\mathcal{B}$ be two NBA, in which the corresponding degree of $\mathsf{Tr}(\mathcal{A})$ is finite and $\mathcal{B}$ is complete. $\mathcal{A} \sqsubseteq^{k,\ldots,k} \mathcal{B}$ for some $k \in \mathbb{N}$ iff there exists a Lipschitz continuous trace preserving function $f : \mathsf{AccRun}(\mathcal{A}) \to \mathsf{AccRun}(\mathcal{B})$.*

5 Cyclic-Path-Connected Automata

Recall that an automaton $\mathcal{A}$ is loop-connected if every cycle in $\mathcal{A}$ produces a connected word. If $\mathcal{A}$ is not loop-connected, then the corresponding degree of $\mathsf{Tr}(\mathcal{A})$ is not finite. For example, consider the automaton $\mathcal{A}$ with two states q_0, q_1, over $\Sigma = \{a, b\}$ and $I = \{(a, b), (b, a)\}$, i.e. a, b is independent with each other. Suppose $E^{\mathcal{A}} = \{(q_0, a, q_1), (q_1, b, q_0)\}$. Hence, $\mathcal{A}$ is not loop-connected since ab is not connected. The corresponding degree of $\mathsf{Tr}(\mathcal{A})$ is also not finite since for every $k \in \mathbb{N}$, we can consider the word $(ab)^{k+1} \in \mathsf{Tr}(\mathcal{A})$, in which its first letter can commute more than k steps to the right. Hence $\mathsf{Deg}(\mathsf{Tr}(\mathcal{A})) = \infty$.

Lemma 5. *If the corresponding degree of $\mathsf{Tr}(\mathcal{A})$ is finite, then $\mathcal{A}$ is loop-connected.*

Proof. Suppose $\mathcal{A}$ is not loop-connected. There exists a cycle c in $\mathcal{A}$ over a non-connected word w. For any $k \in \mathbb{N}$, let $v = w^{k+1}$. Since w is not connected, there exists $\langle \Sigma_1, \Sigma_2 \rangle$ a partition of Σ_w, such that the dependency graph G_w consists of two non-connected components Σ_1 and Σ_2. Every letter in Σ_1 and Σ_2 commutes with each other, i.e. $w \sim_I \pi_1(w)\pi_2(w) \sim_I \pi_2(w)\pi_1(w)$, where π_i is the projection to Σ_i for $i \in \{1, 2\}$. This implies $v \sim_I \pi_1(w)^{k+1}\pi_2(w)^{k+1} \sim_I \pi_2(w)^{k+1}\pi_1(w)^{k+1}$. Let $\mathsf{b} \in \{1, 2\}$, such that $v(1) \in \Sigma_{\mathsf{b}}$. Let $v' = \pi_{\bar{\mathsf{b}}}(w)^{k+1}\pi_{\mathsf{b}}(w)^{k+1}$ and $n = |\pi_{\bar{\mathsf{b}}}(w)^{k+1}|$. We have $n > k$ since at least one letter of w belongs to $\Sigma_{\bar{\mathsf{b}}}$. The first letter of v corresponds to the $(n + 1)$-th letter of v', i.e. $(1, n + 1) \in \mathsf{Corr}_{v,v'}$. Hence for every $k \in \mathbb{N}$, there exists $v \in \mathsf{Tr}(\mathcal{A})$, such that $\mathsf{Deg}_v^+(1) > k$. This implies $\mathsf{Deg}_v^+(1) = \infty$, and hence $\mathsf{Deg}(\mathsf{Tr}(\mathcal{A})) = \infty$.

The converse of this lemma, however, does not hold. Consider the automaton $\mathcal{A}$ from Example 1. It is loop-connected, but we have seen that the corresponding degree of $\mathsf{Tr}(\mathcal{A})$ is not finite. We will show that we can characterise $\mathcal{A}$, in which the corresponding degree of $\mathsf{Tr}(\mathcal{A})$ is finite, by considering a more restrictive condition than loop-connected. Instead of only for the cycle, we require every path in $\mathcal{A}$ that contains a cycle to produce a connected word. We call such an automaton *cyclic-path-connected*.

Definition 3. *An automaton $\mathcal{A}$ over (Σ, I) is cyclic-path-connected if for every path $p \xrightarrow{u} q \xrightarrow{v} q \xrightarrow{w} r$, where $u, w \in \Sigma^*$ and $v \in \Sigma^+$, the word uvw is connected.*

Note that the automaton $\mathcal{A}$ in Example 1 is loop-connected, but not cyclic-path-connected. The word ba is over a cyclic-path of $\mathcal{A}$ but not connected with respect to the given independence alphabet. Note that the corresponding degree of $\mathsf{Tr}(\mathcal{A})$ is also not finite. This is because for every $k \in \mathbb{N}$ we can consider the word $b^{k+1}a \in \mathsf{Tr}(\mathcal{A})$. The last letter of such a word can commute more than k steps to the left, and hence $\mathsf{Deg}(\mathsf{Tr}(\mathcal{A})) = \infty$. This actually also holds in general.

Theorem 2. *If the corresponding degree of $\mathsf{Tr}(\mathcal{A})$ is finite, then $\mathcal{A}$ is cyclic-path-connected.*

Proof. Suppose $\mathcal{A}$ is not cyclic-path-connected. If $\mathcal{A}$ is also not loop-connected, then by Lemma 5, the corresponding degree of $\mathsf{Tr}(\mathcal{A})$ is not finite. Suppose $\mathcal{A}$ is loop-connected but not cyclic-path-connected. There exists a cyclic-path r over a non-connected word w. Without loss of generality, let $w = w'w''$, where w' is produced by a cycle. For any $k \in \mathbb{N}$, let $v = w'^{k+1}w''$. Since w is not connected, there exists $\langle \Sigma_1, \Sigma_2 \rangle$ a non-empty partition of Σ_w, such that $w \sim_I \pi_1(w)\pi_2(w) \sim_I \pi_2(w)\pi_1(w)$. This implies $v \sim_I w'^k\pi_1(w)\pi_2(w) \sim_I w'^k\pi_2(w)\ \pi_1(w)$. Let $\mathsf{b} \in \{1,2\}$, such that $\Sigma_{w'} \subseteq \Sigma_{\mathsf{b}}$. There exists such a b since w' is connected. Let i_0 be the smallest position in v, such that $v(i_0) \in \Sigma_{\bar{\mathsf{b}}}$. Since $w' \neq \epsilon$ and $\Sigma_{w'} \cap \Sigma_{\bar{\mathsf{b}}} = \emptyset$, we have $i_0 > |w'^{k+1}| > k$. Since every letter in Σ_1 and Σ_2 commutes with each other, we have $v \sim_I \pi_{\bar{\mathsf{b}}}(w)w'^k\pi_{\mathsf{b}}(w)$. Let $v' = \pi_{\bar{\mathsf{b}}}(w)w'^k\pi_{\mathsf{b}}(w)$. The first letter of v' corresponds to the i_0-th letter of v i.e. $(i_0, 1) \in \mathsf{Corr}_{v,v'}$. Hence for every $k \in \mathbb{N}$, there exist $v \in \mathsf{Tr}(\mathcal{A})$ and $i_0 \in \mathsf{Pos}(v)$, such that $\mathsf{Deg}_v^-(i_0) > k$. This implies $\mathsf{Deg}_v^-(i_0) = \infty$, and hence $\mathsf{Deg}(\mathsf{Tr}(\mathcal{A})) = \infty$. $\qquad\square$

The converse of Theorem 2 also holds. However, we need a more involved technique. We will show this by considering a relation $\mathsf{Block}_w \subseteq \mathsf{Pos}(w) \times \mathsf{Pos}(w)$. This relation tells us positions of two letters in w that do not commute with each other.

Definition 4. *Let $w \in \Sigma^\infty$ be a word over an independence alphabet (Σ, I). The relation $\mathsf{Block}_w \subseteq \mathsf{Pos}(w) \times \mathsf{Pos}(w)$ is the transitive closure of $D_w = \{(i,j) \mid i \leq j,\ (w(i), w(j)) \in D\}$, where $D = \Sigma^2 \setminus I$.*

Consider the word $w = cdbca$ over an independence alphabet (Σ, I) with dependency graph $G : a-b-c-d$. We have $(1,3), (3,5) \in \mathsf{Block}_w$ since $(c,b) \in D$ and $(b,a) \in D$. By transitivity, we also have $(1,5) \in \mathsf{Block}_w$.

If we have $(i,j) \in \mathsf{Block}_w$ for some two positions i, j of w over (Σ, I), then the letters at positions i and j in w do not commute with each other. This implies that their corresponding positions in some word w' that is trace equivalent with w, do not change order, since otherwise the letter at position i in w commute with the one at position j.

Lemma 6. *Let $w \in \Sigma^\infty$ be a word over (Σ, I). If $(i,j) \in \mathsf{Block}_w$ then $\mathsf{Corr}_{w,w'}(i) \leq \mathsf{Corr}_{w,w'}(j)$ for all $w' \sim_I w$.*

Proof. Suppose $(i, j) \in \mathsf{Block}_w$. Let $k \in \mathsf{Pos}(w)$, such that $i \leq k < j$, $(i, k) \in \mathsf{Block}_w$, and $(w(k), w(j)) \in D$. Suppose there exists w', such that $\mathsf{Corr}_{w,w'}(k) > \mathsf{Corr}_{w,w'}(j)$. Let $k' = \mathsf{Corr}_{w,w'}(k)$ and $j' = \mathsf{Corr}_{w,w'}(j)$. Let $a, b \in \Sigma$, such that $w(k) = w'(k') = a$, $w(j) = w'(j') = b$, and let $\hat{\Sigma} = (\Sigma_1, \ldots, \Sigma_m)$ be the corresponding distributed alphabet of (Σ, I). Since we assume $(a, b) \in D$, there exists $\ell \in \{1, \ldots, m\}$, such that $a, b \in \Sigma_\ell$. Let $n_1 = |w(1) \ldots w(k)|_a = |w'(1) \ldots w'(k')|_a$ and $n_2 = |w(1) \ldots w(j)|_b = |w'(1) \ldots w'(j')|_b$. Note that in the projection of w to Σ_ℓ, i.e. $\pi_\ell(w)$, since $k < j$, there exist at least n_1 many as that occur before the n_2-th b. However, in the projection of w' to Σ_ℓ, i.e. $\pi_\ell(w')$, since $k' > j'$, the n_1-th a occurs after the n_2-th b. There are less than n_1 many as that occur before the n_2-th b. Hence, $\pi_\ell(w) \neq \pi_\ell(w')$. This contradicts $w' \sim_I w$. For all $w' \sim_I w$, we have $\mathsf{Corr}_{w,w'}(k) \leq \mathsf{Corr}_{w,w'}(j)$. By induction hypothesis, we also have $\mathsf{Corr}_{w,w'}(i) \leq \mathsf{Corr}_{w,w'}(k)$ for all $w' \sim_I w$. Thus, $\mathsf{Corr}_{w,w'}(i) \leq \mathsf{Corr}_{w,w'}(j)$ for all $w' \sim_I w$. $\quad\square$

In contrast, if we have $(i, j) \notin \mathsf{Block}_w$ for some position $i < j$ in w over (Σ, I), then the letters at positions i and j commute with each other. If there are n many positions of such i then the letter at position j can commute n many steps to the left.

Lemma 7. *Let $w \in \Sigma^\infty$ be a word over (Σ, I). If there are positions $i_1, \ldots, i_n < j_0 \in \mathsf{Pos}(w)$, such that $(i_1, j_0), \ldots, (i_n, j_0) \notin \mathsf{Block}_w$, then there exists $w' \sim_I w$, such that $(j_0, j_0 - n) \in \mathsf{Corr}_{w,w'}$.*

Proof. Let $i_1, \ldots, i_n$ and j_0 be such positions in w. Without loss of generality, we can assume that i_n is the largest position such that $i_n < j_0$ and $(i_n, j_0) \notin \mathsf{Block}_w$. Hence for all k, $i_n < k < j_0$, $(k, j_0) \in \mathsf{Block}_w$. This implies $(w(i_n), w(k)) \notin D$ for all k, $i_n < k < j_0$, since otherwise $(i_n, j_0) \in \mathsf{Block}_w$. Let $u_1 = w(1)w(2) \ldots w(i_n - 1)$, $u_2 = w(i_n)w(i_n + 1) \ldots w(j_0)$, and $u_3 = w(j_0 + 1)w(j_0 + 2) \ldots$, such that $w = u_1 u_2 u_3$. Let $u_2' = w(i_n + 1) \ldots w(j_0) w(i_n)$. We have $u_2 \sim_I u_2'$ since $(w(i_n), w(k)) \notin D$ for all k, $i_n + 1 \leq k \leq j_0$. Hence we have $w \sim_I u_1 u_2' u_3$. Let $w' = u_1 u_2' u_3$. The letter at position j_0 in w corresponds to the one at position $j_0 - 1$ in w', i.e. $(j_0, j_0 - 1) \in \mathsf{Corr}_{w,w'}$. By induction hypothesis, there exists $w'' \sim w'$, such that $(j_0 - 1, j_0 - n) \in \mathsf{Corr}_{w',w''}$. Hence we have $(j_0, j_0 - n) \in \mathsf{Corr}_{w,w''}$. $\quad\square$

Let us define $\overline{\mathsf{Block}_w^+}(i) = \{j > i \mid (i, j) \notin \mathsf{Block}_w\}$ and $\overline{\mathsf{Block}_w^-}(i) = \{j < i \mid (j, i) \notin \mathsf{Block}_w\}$. We have $j \in \overline{\mathsf{Block}_w^+}(i)$ or $j \in \overline{\mathsf{Block}_w^-}(i)$ if the letter at position $j \neq i$ commutes with the one at position i. The positive and negative signs are used to indicate whether it occurs before or after the letter at position i. In the following, we show that the size of $\overline{\mathsf{Block}_w^+}(i)$ and $\overline{\mathsf{Block}_w^-}(i)$ give us the bound on how long the letter at position i commutes to the right and left, respectively.

Lemma 8. *For all $\mathsf{b} \in \{+, -\}$, $\mathsf{Deg}_w^{\mathsf{b}}(i) = |\overline{\mathsf{Block}_w^{\mathsf{b}}}(i)|$.*

Proof. We will show this for $\mathsf{b} = -$. A similar argument can also be used for $\mathsf{b} = +$. Let $k_1 = \mathsf{Deg}_w^-(i)$ and $k_2 = |\overline{\mathsf{Block}_w^-}(i)|$. If $k_1 < k_2$, then there are at least $k_1 + 1$ many distinct positions in $\overline{\mathsf{Block}}_w^-(i)$, i.e. there are $i_1, \ldots, i_{k_1+1} < i$, such that $(i_1, i), \ldots, (i_{k_1+1}, i) \notin \mathsf{Block}_w$. By Lemma 7, there exists w', such that $w' \sim_I w$ and $(i, i - (k_1 + 1)) \in \mathsf{Corr}_{w,w'}$. This means $\mathsf{Deg}_w^-(i) > k_1$, which contradicts $\mathsf{Deg}_w^-(i) = k_1$.

If $k_1 > k_2$, then $\mathsf{Deg}_w^-(i) > k_2$. There exist a word w' and a position $j \in \mathsf{Pos}(w')$ such that $w \sim_I w'$, $(i, j) \in \mathsf{Corr}_{w,w'}$, and $i - j > k_2$. Consider the set $S = \{i' < i \mid \mathsf{Corr}_{w,w'}(i') > j\}$. We have $|S| = i - j$, and hence $|S| > k_2$. Since there are only k_2 many positions in $\overline{\mathsf{Block}}_w^-(i)$, there is at least one position that is not in $\overline{\mathsf{Block}}_w^-(i)$, but belongs to S. Let i' be such a position. We have $(i', i) \in \mathsf{Block}_w$ and $\mathsf{Corr}_{w,w'}(i') > \mathsf{Corr}_{w,w'}(i)$. This contradicts Lemma 6. We have $k_1 = k_2$ since $k_1 \not< k_2$ and $k_1 \not> k_2$.

One interesting property regarding the cyclic-path-connected automata is that whenever we have a path that goes through a cycle, then every letter on the path does not commute with at least one letter in the cycle. This is always the case since otherwise the cyclic-path will not be connected.

Lemma 9. *Let $\mathcal{A}$ be a cyclic-path-connected automaton, and $p \xrightarrow{w_1} q \xrightarrow{u} q \xrightarrow{w_2} p'$ a cyclic-path over $w = w_1 u w_2$. Let $P_1 = \{1, \ldots, |w_1|\}$, $P_2 = \{|w_1| + 1, \ldots, |w_1 u|\}$, $P_3 = \{|w_1 u| + 1, \ldots, |w_1 u w_2|\} \subseteq \mathsf{Pos}(w)$.*

- *For all $i \in P_1$, there exists $j \in P_2$, such that $(i, j) \in \mathsf{Block}_w$.*
- *For all $j \in P_3$, there exists $i \in P_2$, such that $(i, j) \in \mathsf{Block}_w$.*

Proof. We will show this for the first part. A similar argument can also be used to prove the second one. Let $i \in P_1$, $n = |w_1|$, $P_1' = \{i, i+1, \ldots, n\}$, and $w_1' = w(i)w(i+1)\ldots w(n)$. Since the word $w_1' u$ is produced by a cyclic-path, $w_1' u$ is connected. There exists $j \in P_1' \cup P_2$, such that $(w(i), w(j)) \in D$. If $j \in P_2$, then by definition, $(i, j) \in \mathsf{Block}_w$. If $j \in P_1'$, then by induction hypothesis there exists $j' \in P_2$, such that $(j, j') \in \mathsf{Block}_w$. Since $(i, j) \in \mathsf{Block}_w$, we have $(i, j') \in \mathsf{Block}_w$. $\square$

Let us call a path r in $\mathcal{A}$ *wall* if for every path r' that is extended from r, every letter that is read before r and after r does not commute with each other.

Definition 5. *A path $r = p_0 \xrightarrow{a_1} p_1 \xrightarrow{a_2} \ldots \xrightarrow{a_n} p_n$ over $w = a_1 \ldots a_n$ in $\mathcal{A}$ is called a wall if for every path r' that is extended from r, i.e. $r' = q \xrightarrow{w_1} p_0 \xrightarrow{w} p_n \xrightarrow{w_2} q'$, over $w' = w_1 w w_2$, we have $(i, j) \in \mathsf{Block}_{w'}$ for all $i \in \{1, \ldots, |w_1|\}$, $j \in \{|w_1 w| + 1, \ldots, |w_1 w w_2|\}$.*

Moreover, let $C(\mathcal{A})$ bethe set of simple cycles of $\mathcal{A}$. By simple cycle, we mean a path that does not visit the same state twice except the first and the last state, i.e. $C(\mathcal{A}) = \{p_1 \xrightarrow{a_1} p_2 \xrightarrow{a_2} \ldots \xrightarrow{a_k} p_k \mid p_1 \neq p_2 \ldots \neq p_{k-1} \text{ and } p_1 = p_k\}$. If we have a path of length $|\mathcal{A}|^2 \cdot |C(\mathcal{A})|$, then there exists a simple cycle that is visited at least $n = |\mathcal{A}|$ many times. This is because for every path of length $|\mathcal{A}|$, there exists a state that is visited at least twice.

Proposition 3. *For any automaton $\mathcal{A}$, if r is a path in $\mathcal{A}$ of length $|\mathcal{A}|^2 \cdot |C(\mathcal{A})|$, then there exists $c \in C(\mathcal{A})$ that is visited at least $|\mathcal{A}|$ many times in r.*

We use this proposition to show the following lemma.

Lemma 10. *If $\mathcal{A}$ is a cyclic-path-connected automaton, then every path of length $|\mathcal{A}|^2 \cdot |C(\mathcal{A})|$ is a wall.*

Proof. Suppose r is a path of length $|\mathcal{A}|^2 \cdot |C(\mathcal{A})|$ from p to p'. By Proposition 3, there exists a simple cycle $c \in C(\mathcal{A})$, suppose over u, that is visited at least $n = |\mathcal{A}|$ many times in r. The path r is over the word $w = v_0 u v_1 \ldots u v_n$ for some $v_0, \ldots, v_n \in \Sigma^*$. Let r' be a path extended from r, i.e. $r' = s \xrightarrow{w_1} p \xrightarrow{w} p' \xrightarrow{w_2} s'$, over the word $w' = w_1 w w_2$. Let $i_0 \in \{1, \ldots, |w_1|\}$ and $j_0 \in \{|w_1| + 1, \ldots, |w_1 w w_2|\}$. We will show that $(i_0, j_0) \in \mathsf{Block}_{w'}$. Let $m_k = |w_1 v_0 u \ldots u v_{k-1}|$ and $P_k = \{m_k + 1, \ldots, m_k + |u|\}$ for all $k \in \{1, \ldots, n\}$. Since $\mathcal{A}$ is cyclic-path-connected and we can see r' as $s \xrightarrow{w_1 v_0} q \xrightarrow{u} q \xrightarrow{v_1 u \ldots u v_n w_2} s'$, by the first part of Lemma 9, there exists $i_1 \in P_1$, such that $(i_0, i_1) \in \mathsf{Block}_{w'}$. Moreover, since $s \xrightarrow{w_1 v_0 u \ldots u v_{n-1}} q \xrightarrow{u} q \xrightarrow{v_n w_2} s'$, by the second part of Lemma 9, there exists $j_1 \in P_n$, such that $(j_1, j_0) \in \mathsf{Block}_{w'}$. We will show that $(i_1, j_1) \in \mathsf{Block}_{w'}$.

Since the word u is connected and $w'(i_1), w'(j_1) \in \Sigma_u$, there exists a path from $w'(i_1)$ to $w'(j_1)$ in the dependency graph G_u. There exists such a path of length $m \leq n$ since $|G_u| = |\Sigma_u| \leq n$. Let ℓ be such a path, and $i_2 \in P_2, \ldots, i_m \in P_m$, such that $\ell = w'(i_1) w'(i_2) \ldots w'(i_m)$. Since an edge in the dependency graph represents dependency between letters, we have $(w'(i_1), w'(i_2)), \ldots, (w'(i_{m-1}), w'(i_m)) \in D$. Since $i_1 < \ldots < i_m$, we have $(i_1, i_2), \ldots, (i_{m-1}, i_m) \in \mathsf{Block}_{w'}$. Moreover, since $w'(i_m) = w'(j_1)$ and $i_m \leq j_1$, we also have $(i_m, j_1) \in \mathsf{Block}_{w'}$. Hence $(i_1, j_1) \in \mathsf{Block}_{w'}$, and we have $(i_0, j_0) \in \mathsf{Block}_{w'}$.

This implies that for every finite or infinite path $p_1 a_1 p_2 a_2 \ldots$ over $w = a_1 a_2 \ldots$, in a cyclic-path-connected automaton with n states and m simple cycles, the letter a_i does not commute with a_j for all $j < i - n^2 m$ and $j > i + n^2 m$. This is because for any $i > 0$, the path $p_i a_i \ldots p_{i+n^2m}$ or $p_{i-n^2m} \ldots a_{i-1} p_i$ is a wall in $\mathcal{A}$. Hence there are at most $n^2 m$ many letters to the left or right of a_i that commute with a_i, i.e. $|\mathsf{Block}_w^{\mathsf{b}}(i)| \leq n^2 m$, for any $\mathsf{b} \in \{+, -\}$.

Hence if $\mathcal{A}$ is cyclic-path-connected, then for any word $w \in \mathsf{Tr}(\mathcal{A})$ and position $i \in \mathsf{Pos}(w)$, $\max \{\mathsf{Deg}_w^+(i), \mathsf{Deg}_w^-(i)\} \leq |\mathcal{A}|^2 \cdot |C(\mathcal{A})|$. In other words, the corresponding degree of $\mathsf{Tr}(\mathcal{A})$ is finite. Since $\mathcal{A}$ is cyclic-path-conneted iff the corresponding degree of $\mathsf{Tr}(\mathcal{A})$ is finite, we can refine the characterisation in Theorem 1 into the following theorem.

Theorem 3. *For any two NBA $\mathcal{A}, \mathcal{B}$, in which $\mathcal{A}$ is cyclic-path-connected and $\mathcal{B}$ is complete, then $\mathcal{A} \sqsubseteq^{k, \ldots, k} \mathcal{B}$ for some $k \in \mathbb{N}$ iff there exists a Lipschitz continuous trace preserving function $f : \mathsf{AccRun}(\mathcal{A}) \to \mathsf{AccRun}(\mathcal{B})$.*

$$L(\mathcal{A}) \subseteq [L(\mathcal{B})]_I \overset{\text{Prop. 1}}{\Longleftrightarrow} \exists \text{ trace preserving (TP) } f : \mathsf{AccRun}(\mathcal{A}) \to \mathsf{AccRun}(\mathcal{B})$$

$$\mathcal{A} \sqsubseteq^{\omega,\ldots,\omega} \mathcal{B} \overset{\text{Prop. 2}}{\Longleftarrow} \exists \text{ Continuous TP } f : \mathsf{AccRun}(\mathcal{A}) \to \mathsf{AccRun}(\mathcal{B})$$

$$\mathcal{A} \sqsubseteq^{k,\ldots,k} \mathcal{B} \overset{\text{Lem. 1}}{\Longrightarrow} \exists \text{ Lipschitz continuous TP } f : \mathsf{AccRun}(\mathcal{A}) \to \mathsf{AccRun}(\mathcal{B})$$

$$\overset{\text{Thm. 3}}{\underline{\hspace{4cm}}} \quad +$$
$$\mathcal{A} \text{ cyclic-path-connected, } \mathcal{B} \text{ complete}$$

Fig. 1. Topological characterisation of multi-buffer simulation

6 Conclusion

We have shown that we can lift the characterisation of multi-buffer simulation with unbounded buffers to the one with bounded buffers if the automaton for SPOILER is cyclic-path-connected and the automaton for DUPLICATOR is complete. In this case, multi-buffer simulation with bounded buffers can be characterised by the existence of a Lipschitz continuous function that witnesses trace closure inclusion. We summarise the topological characterisation of multi-buffer simulation in Fig. 1.

References

1. Abdulla, P.A., Bouajjani, A., Holík, L., Kaati, L., Vojnar, T.: Computing simulations over tree automata. In: Ramakrishnan, C.R., Rehof, J. (eds.) TACAS 2008. LNCS, vol. 4963, pp. 93–108. Springer, Heidelberg (2008). doi:10.1007/978-3-540-78800-3_8
2. Clerbout, M., Latteux, M.: Semi-commutations. Inf. Comput. **73**(1), 59–74 (1987)
3. Dill, D.L., Hu, A.J., Wong-Toi, H.: Checking for language inclusion using simulation preorders. In: Larsen, K.G., Skou, A. (eds.) CAV 1991. LNCS, vol. 575, pp. 255–265. Springer, Heidelberg (1992). doi:10.1007/3-540-55179-4_25
4. Etessami, K., Wilke, T., Schuller, R.A.: Fair simulation relations, parity games, and state space reduction for Büchi automata. In: Orejas, F., Spirakis, P.G., Leeuwen, J. (eds.) ICALP 2001. LNCS, vol. 2076, pp. 694–707. Springer, Heidelberg (2001). doi:10.1007/3-540-48224-5_57
5. Finkel, O.: Three applications to rational relations of the high undecidability of the infinite post correspondence problem in a regular ω-language. Int. J. Found. Comput. Sci. **23**(7), 1481–1498 (2012)
6. Fritz, C., Wilke, T.: Simulation relations for alternating Büchi automata. Theor. Comput. Sci. **338**(1), 275–314 (2005)
7. Henzinger, T.A., Kupferman, O., Rajamani, S.K.: Fair simulation. Inf. Comput. **173**(1), 64–81 (2002)
8. Holtmann, M., Kaiser, L., Thomas, W.: Degrees of lookahead in regular infinite games. Log. Methods Comput. Sci. 8(3) (2012)
9. Hutagalung, M., Hundeshagen, N., Kuske, D., Lange, M., Lozes, É.: Multi-buffer simulations for trace language inclusion. In: GandALF 2016, pp. 213–227 (2016)

10. Rozenberg, G., Salomaa, A. (eds.): Handbook of Formal Languages: Vol. 3: Beyond Words. Springer, New York (1977)
11. Sakarovitch, J.: The "last" decision problem for rational trace languages. In: Simon, I. (ed.) LATIN 1992. LNCS, vol. 583, pp. 460–473. Springer, Heidelberg (1992). doi:10.1007/BFb0023848

Distributed Control Synthesis Using Euler's Method

A. Le Coënt[1], J. Alexandre dit Sandretto[4], A. Chapoutot[4], L. Fribourg[2(✉)],
F. De Vuyst[1], and L. Chamoin[3]

[1] CMLA, CNRS, ENS Paris-Saclay, 61 av. du Président Wilson, 94235 Cachan,
Cedex, France
adrien.le-coent@ens-cachan.fr
[2] LSV, CNRS, ENS Paris-Saclay, INRIA, 61 av. du Président Wilson, 94235 Cachan,
Cedex, France
fribourg@lsv.fr
[3] LMT, CNRS, ENS Paris-Saclay,
61 av. du Président Wilson, 94235 Cachan, Cedex, France
[4] U2IS, ENSTA ParisTech, 828 bd des Maréchaux, 91762 Palaiseau, France
{alexandre,chapoutot}@ensta.fr

Abstract. In a previous work, we explained how Euler's method for
computing approximate solutions of systems of ordinary differential
equations can be used to synthesize *safety controllers* for sampled
switched systems. We continue here this line of research by showing how
Euler's method can also be used for synthesizing safety controllers in
a *distributed* manner. The global system is seen as an *interconnection*
of two (or more) sub-systems where, for each component, the sub-state
corresponding to the other component is seen as an "input"; the method
exploits (a variant of) the notions of *incremental input-to-state stability
(δ-ISS)* and *ISS Lyapunov function*. We illustrate this distributed control
synthesis method on a building ventilation example.

1 Introduction

The computation of reachable sets for continuous-time dynamical systems has
been intensively studied during the last decades. Most of the methods to compute
the reachable set start from an *initial value problem* for a system of *ordinary
differential equations* (ODE) defined by

$$\dot{x}(t) = f(t, x(t)) \quad \text{with} \quad x(0) \in X_0 \subset \mathbb{R}^n \quad \text{and} \quad t \in [0, t_{\text{end}}] \ . \tag{1}$$

As an analytical solution of Eq. (1) is usually not computable, numerical
approaches have been considered. A numerical method to solve Eq. (1), when
X_0 is reduced to one value, produces a discretization of time, such that $t_0 \leqslant
\cdots \leqslant t_N = t_{\text{end}}$, and a sequence of states $x_0, \ldots, x_N$ based on an integration
method which starts from an initial value x_0 at time t_0 and a finite time horizon h (the step-size), produces an approximation x_{k+1} at time $t_{k+1} = t_k + h$,
of the exact solution $x(t_{k+1})$, for all $k = 0, \ldots, N - 1$. The simplest numerical

© Springer International Publishing AG 2017
M. Hague and I. Potapov (Eds.): RP 2017, LNCS 10506, pp. 118–131, 2017.
DOI: 10.1007/978-3-319-67089-8_9

method is Euler's method in which $t_{k+1} = t_k + h$ for some step-size h and $x_{k+1} = x_k + hf(t_k, x_k)$; so the derivative of x at time t_k, $f(t_k, x_k)$, is used as an approximation of the derivative on the whole time interval.

The global error $error(t)$ at $t = t_0 + kh$ is equal to $\|x(t) - x_k\|$. In case $n = 1$, if the solution x has a bounded second derivative and f is Lipschitz continuous in its second argument, then it satisfies:

$$error(t) \leq \frac{hM}{2L}(e^{L(t-t_0)} - 1) \tag{2}$$

where M is an upper bound on the second derivative of x on the given interval and L is the Lipschitz constant of f [3].[1]

In [14], we gave an upper bound on the global error $error(t)$, which is more precise than (2). This upper bound makes use of the notion of *One-Sided Lipschitz (OSL)* constant. This notion has been used for the first time by [7] in order to treat "stiff" systems of differential equations for which the explicit Euler method is numerically "unstable" (unless the step size is taken to be extremely small). Unlike Lipschitz constants, OSL constants can be *negative*, which express a form of contractivity of the system dynamics. Even if the OSL constant is positive, it is in practice much lower than the Lipschitz constant [5]. The use of OSL thus allows us to obtain a much more precise upper bound for the global error. We also explained in [14] how such a precise estimation of the global error can be used to synthesize *safety controllers* for a special form hybrid systems, called "sampled switched systems".

In this paper, we explain how such an Euler-based method can be extended to synthesize safety controllers in a *distributed* manner. This allows us to control separately a component using only partial information on the other components. It also allows us to scale up the size of the global systems for which a control can be synthesized. In order to perform such a distributed synthesis, we will see the components of the global systems as being *interconnected* (see, *e.g.*, [18]), and use (a variant of) the notions of *incremental input-to-state stability (δ-ISS)* and *ISS Lyapunov functions* [11] instead of the notion of OSL used in the centralized framework.

The plan of the paper is as follows: In Sect. 2, we recall the results of [14] obtained in the centralized framework; in Sect. 3 we extend these results to the framework of distributed systems; we then apply the distributed synthesis method to a nontrivial example (Sect. 4), and conclude in Sect. 5.

2 Euler's Method Applied to Control Synthesis

In this Section, we recall the results obtained in [14]. We first give results concerning a system governed by a single ODE system (Sect. 2.1), then consider results for a switched system composed of several ODEs (Sect. 2.2).

---

[1] Such a bound has been used in hybridization methods: $error(t) = \frac{E_D}{L}(e^{Lt} - 1)$ [2,4], where E_D gives the maximum difference of the derivatives of the original and approximated systems.

2.1   ODE Systems

We make the following hypothesis:

$(H0)$ f is a locally Lipschitz continuous map.

We make the assumption that the vector field f is such that the solutions of the differential equation (7) are defined. We will denote by $\phi(t; x^0)$ the solution at time t of the system:

$$\dot{x}(t) = f(x(t)),$$
$$x(0) = x^0. \tag{3}$$

Consider a compact and convex set $S \subset \mathbb{R}^n$, called "safety set". We denote by T a compact overapproximation of the image by ϕ of S for $0 \le t \le \tau$, i.e., T is such that

$$T \supseteq \{\phi(t; x^0) \mid 0 \le t \le \tau, x^0 \in S\}.$$

The existence of T is guaranteed by assumption $(H0)$. We know furthermore by $(H0)$ that there exists a constant $L > 0$ such that:

$$\|f(y) - f(x)\| \le L \|y - x\| \quad \forall x, y \in S. \tag{4}$$

Let us define C:

$$C = \sup_{x \in S} L\|f(x)\|. \tag{5}$$

We make the additional hypothesis that the mapping f is one-sided Lipschitz (OSL) [7]. Formally:

$(H1)$ There exists a constant $\lambda \in \mathbb{R}$ such that

$$\langle f(y) - f(x), y - x \rangle \le \lambda \|y - x\|^2 \quad \forall x, y \in T,$$

where $\langle \cdot, \cdot \rangle$ denotes the scalar product of two vectors of $\mathbb{R}^n$.

Remark 1. Constants λ, L and C can be computed using constrained optimization algorithms, namely, the 'sqp' function from GNU Octave [8].

Given an initial point $\tilde{x}^0 \in S$, we define the following "linear approximate solution" $\tilde{\phi}(t; \tilde{x}^0)$ for t on $[0, \tau]$ by:

$$\tilde{\phi}(t; \tilde{x}^0) = \tilde{x}^0 + t f(\tilde{x}^0). \tag{6}$$

We define the closed ball of center $x \in \mathbb{R}^n$ and radius $r > 0$, denoted $B(x, r)$, as the set $\{x' \in \mathbb{R}^n \mid \|x' - x\| \le r\}$.

Given a positive real δ^0, we now define the expression $\delta(t)$ which, as we will see in Theorem 1, represents (an upper bound on) the error associated to $\tilde{\phi}(t; \tilde{x}^0)$ (i.e., $\|\tilde{\phi}(t; \tilde{x}^0) - \phi(t; x^0)\|$).

Definition 1. Let δ^0 be a positive constant. Let us define, for all $0 \le t \le \tau$, $\delta(t)$ as follows:

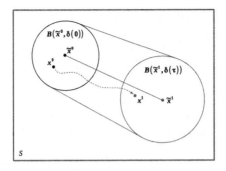

Fig. 1. Illustration of Corollary 1, with $\tilde{x}_1 = \tilde{\phi}(\tau; \tilde{x}^0)$ and $x_1 = \phi(\tau; x^0)$.

– *if $\lambda < 0$:*

$$\delta(t) = \left((\delta^0)^2 e^{\lambda t} + \frac{C^2}{\lambda^2} \left(t^2 + \frac{2t}{\lambda} + \frac{2}{\lambda^2} \left(1 - e^{\lambda t} \right) \right) \right)^{\frac{1}{2}}$$

– *if $\lambda = 0$:*

$$\delta(t) = \left((\delta^0)^2 e^t + C^2 (-t^2 - 2t + 2(e^t - 1)) \right)^{\frac{1}{2}}$$

– *if $\lambda > 0$:*

$$\delta(t) = \left((\delta^0)^2 e^{3\lambda t} + \frac{C^2}{3\lambda^2} \left(-t^2 - \frac{2t}{3\lambda} + \frac{2}{9\lambda^2} \left(e^{3\lambda t} - 1 \right) \right) \right)^{\frac{1}{2}}$$

Note that $\delta(t) = \delta^0$ for $t = 0$. The function $\delta(\cdot)$ depends implicitly on parameter: $\delta^0 \in \mathbb{R}$. In Sect. 2.2, we will use the notation $\delta'(\cdot)$ where the parameter is denoted by $(\delta')^0$.

Theorem 1. *Given an ODE system satisfying (H0-H1), consider a point $\tilde{x}^0$ and a positive real δ^0. We have, for all $x^0 \in B(\tilde{x}^0, \delta^0)$, $t \in [0, \tau]$:*

$$\phi(t; x^0) \in B(\tilde{\phi}(t; \tilde{x}^0), \delta(t)).$$

Corollary 1. *Given an ODE system satisfying (H0-H1), consider a point $\tilde{x}^0 \in S$ and a real $\delta^0 > 0$ such that:*

1. *$B(\tilde{x}^0, \delta^0) \subseteq S$,*
2. *$B(\tilde{\phi}(\tau; \tilde{x}^0), \delta(\tau)) \subseteq S$, and*
3. *$\frac{d^2(\delta(t))}{dt^2} > 0$ for all $t \in [0, \tau]$.*

Then we have, for all $x^0 \in B(\tilde{x}^0, \delta^0)$ and $t \in [0, \tau]$: $\phi(t; x^0) \in S$. See Fig. 1 for an illustration of Corollary 1.

2.2 Sampled Switched Systems

Let us consider the nonlinear switched system

$$\dot{x}(t) = f_{\sigma(t)}(x(t)) \tag{7}$$

defined for all $t \geq 0$, where $x(t) \in \mathbb{R}^n$ is the state of the system, $\sigma(\cdot) : \mathbb{R}^+ \longrightarrow U$ is the switching rule. The finite set $U = \{1, \ldots, N\}$ is the set of switching *modes* of the system. We focus on *sampled switched systems*: given a sampling period $\tau > 0$, switchings will occur at times τ, 2τ, ... The switching rule $\sigma(\cdot)$ is thus constant on the time interval $[(k-1)\tau, k\tau)$ for $k \geq 1$. For all $j \in U$, f_j is a function from $\mathbb{R}^n$ to $\mathbb{R}^n$.

We will denote by $\phi_\sigma(t; x^0)$ the solution at time t of the system:

$$\begin{aligned} \dot{x}(t) &= f_{\sigma(t)}(x(t)), \\ x(0) &= x^0. \end{aligned} \tag{8}$$

Often, we will consider $\phi_\sigma(t; x^0)$ on the interval $0 \leq t < \tau$ for which $\sigma(t)$ is equal to a constant, say $j \in U$. In this case, we will abbreviate $\phi_\sigma(t; x^0)$ as $\phi_j(t; x^0)$. We will also consider $\phi_\sigma(t; x^0)$ on the interval $0 \leq t < k\tau$ where k is a positive integer, and $\sigma(t)$ is equal to a constant, say $j_{k'}$, on each interval $[(k'-1)\tau, k'\tau)$ with $1 \leq k' \leq k$; in this case, we will abbreviate $\phi_\sigma(t; x^0)$ as $\phi_\pi(t; x^0)$, where π is a sequence of k modes (or "pattern") of the form $\pi = j_1 \cdot j_2 \cdots \cdots j_k$.

We will assume that ϕ_σ is *continuous* at time $k\tau$ for all positive integer k. This means that there is no "reset" at time $k'\tau$ $(1 \leq k' \leq k)$; the value of $\phi_\sigma(t, x^0)$ for $t \in [(k'-1)\tau, k\tau]$ corresponds to the solution of $\dot{x}(u) = f_{j_{k'}}(x(u))$ for $u \in [0, \tau]$ with initial value $\phi_\sigma((k'-1)\tau; x^0)$.

More generally, given an initial point $\tilde{x}^0 \in S$ and pattern π of U^k, we can define a "(piecewise linear) approximate solution" $\tilde{\phi}_\pi(t; \tilde{x}^0)$ of ϕ_π at time $t \in [0, k\tau]$ as follows:

- $\tilde{\phi}_\pi(t; \tilde{x}^0) = tf_j(\tilde{x}^0) + \tilde{x}^0$ if $\pi = j \in U$, $k = 1$ and $t \in [0, \tau]$, and
- $\tilde{\phi}_\pi(k\tau + t; \tilde{x}^0) = tf_j(\tilde{z}) + \tilde{z}$ with $\tilde{z} = \tilde{\phi}_{\pi'}((k-1)\tau; \tilde{x}^0)$, if $k \geq 2$, $t \in [0, \tau]$, $\pi = j \cdot \pi'$ for some $j \in U$ and $\pi' \in U^{k-1}$.

We wish to synthesize a safety control σ for ϕ_σ using the approximate functions $\tilde{\phi}_\pi$. Hypotheses (H0) and (H1), as defined in Sect. 2.1, are naturally extended to every mode j of U, as well as definition of T, constants L, C and λ, definitions of $\tilde{\phi}_j$ and δ^0 (see [14]). From a notation point of view, we will assign an index j to symbols $\lambda, L, C, \ldots$ in order to relate them to the dynamics of mode j.

Consider a point $\tilde{x}^0 \in S$, a positive real δ^0 and a pattern π of length k. Let $\pi(k')$ denote the k'-th element (mode) of π for $1 \leq k' \leq k$. Let us abbreviate the k'-th approximate point $\tilde{\phi}_\pi(k'\tau; \tilde{x}^0)$ as $\tilde{x}_\pi^{k'}$ for $k' = 1, ..., k$, and let $\tilde{x}_\pi^{k'} = \tilde{x}^0$ for $k' = 0$. It is easy to show that $\tilde{x}_\pi^{k'}$ can be defined recursively for $k' = 1, ..., k$, by: $\tilde{x}_\pi^{k'} = \tilde{x}_\pi^{k'-1} + \tau f_j(\tilde{x}_\pi^{k'-1})$ with $j = \pi(k')$.

Let us now define the expression $\delta_\pi^{k'}$ as follows: For $k' = 0$: $\delta_\pi^{k'} = \delta^0$, and for $1 \leq k' \leq k$: $\delta_\pi^{k'} = \delta_j'(\tau)$ where $(\delta')^0$ denotes $\delta_\pi^{k'-1}$, and j denotes $\pi(k')$. Likewise, for $0 \leq t \leq k\tau$, let us define the expression $\delta_\pi(t)$ as follows:

- for $t = 0$: $\delta_\pi(t) = \delta^0$,
- for $0 < t \leq k\tau$: $\delta_\pi(t) = \delta_j'(t')$ with $(\delta')^0 = \delta_\pi^\ell$, $j = \pi(\ell)$, $t' = t - \ell\tau$ and $\ell = \lfloor \frac{t}{\tau} \rfloor$.

Note that, for $0 \leq k' \leq k$, we have: $\delta_\pi(k'\tau) = \delta_\pi^{k'}$. We have

Theorem 2. *Given a sampled switched system satisfying (H0-H1), consider a point $\tilde{x}^0 \in S$, a positive real δ^0 and a pattern π of length k such that, for all $1 \leq k' \leq k$:*

1. $B(\tilde{x}_\pi^{k'}, \delta_\pi^{k'}) \subseteq S$ *and*
2. $\frac{d^2(\delta_j'(t))}{dt^2} > 0$ *for all $t \in [0, \tau]$, with $j = \pi(k')$ and $(\delta')^0 = \delta_\pi^{k'-1}$.*

Then we have, for all $x^0 \in B(\tilde{x}^0, \delta^0)$ and $t \in [0, k\tau]$: $\phi_\pi(t; x^0) \in S$.

Remark 2. In Theorem 2, we have supposed that the step size h used in Euler's method was equal to the sampling period τ of the switching system. Actually, in order to have better approximations, it is often convenient to take a *fraction* of τ as for h (e.g., $h = \frac{\tau}{10}$). Such a splitting is called "sub-sampling" in numerical methods.

Consider now a compact set R, called "recurrence set", contained in the safety set $S \subset \mathbb{R}^n$ ($R \subseteq S$). We are interested in the synthesis of a control such that: starting from any initial point $x \in R$, the controlled trajectory always returns to R within a bounded time while never leaving S.

Corollary 2. *Given a switched system satisfying (H0-H1), consider a positive real δ^0 and a finite set of points $\tilde{x}_1, \ldots \tilde{x}_m$ of S such that all the balls $B(\tilde{x}_i, \delta^0)$ cover R and are included into S (i.e., $R \subseteq \bigcup_{i=1}^m B(\tilde{x}_i, \delta^0) \subseteq S$).*

Suppose furthermore that, for all $1 \leq i \leq m$, there exists a pattern π_i of length k_i such that:

1. $B((\tilde{x}_i)_{\pi_i}^{k'}, \delta_{\pi_i}^{k'}) \subseteq S$, *for all $k' = 1, \ldots, k_i - 1$*
2. $B((\tilde{x}_i)_{\pi_i}^{k_i}, \delta_{\pi_i}^{k_i}) \subseteq R$.
3. $\frac{d^2(\delta_j'(t))}{dt^2} > 0$ *with $j = \pi_i(k')$ and $(\delta')^0 = \delta_{\pi_i}^{k'-1}$, for all $k' \in \{1, ..., k_i\}$ and $t \in [0, \tau]$.*

These properties induce a control σ^2 which guarantees

---

[2] Given an initial point $x \in R$, the induced control σ corresponds to a sequence of patterns $\pi_{i_1}, \pi_{i_2}, \ldots$ defined as follows: Since $x \in R$, there exists a a point $\tilde{x}_{i_1}$ with $1 \leq i_1 \leq m$ such that $x \in B(\tilde{x}_{i_1}, \delta^0)$; then using pattern π_{i_1}, one has: $\phi_{\pi_{i_1}}(k_{i_1}\tau; x) \in R$. Let $x' = \phi_{\pi_{i_1}}(k_{i_1}\tau; x)$; there exists a point $\tilde{x}_{i_2}$ with $1 \leq i_2 \leq m$ such that $x' \in B(\tilde{x}_{i_2}, \delta^0)$, etc.

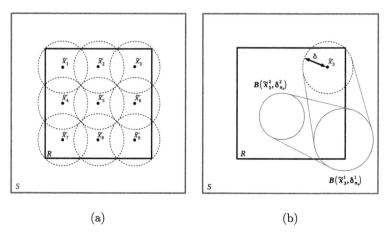

Fig. 2. (a): A set of balls covering R and contained in S. (b): Control of ball $B(\tilde{x}_3, \delta^0)$ with Euler-based method.

- *(safety): if $x \in R$, then $\phi_\sigma(t; x) \in S$ for all $t \geq 0$, and*
- *(recurrence): if $x \in R$ then $\phi_\sigma(k\tau; x) \in R$ for some $k \in \{k_1, \ldots, k_m\}$.*

Corollary 2 gives the theoretical foundations of the following method for synthesizing σ ensuring recurrence in R and safety in S:

- we (pre-)compute λ_j, L_j, C_j for all $j \in U$;
- we find m points $\tilde{x}_1, \ldots \tilde{x}_m$ of S and $\delta^0 > 0$ such that $R \subseteq \bigcup_{i=1}^{m} B(\tilde{x}_i, \delta^0) \subseteq S$;
- we find m patterns π_i $(i = 1, \ldots, m)$ such that conditions 1-2-3 of Corollary 2 are satisfied.

A covering of R with balls as stated in Corollary 2 is illustrated in Fig. 2 (a). The control synthesis method based on Corollary 2 is illustrated in Fig. 2 (b).

For the sake of simplicity, we will suppose in the following that R is a *rectangle*, i.e., the Cartesian product of n closed real intervals, and we will denote its center by c. We will also assume that T is a ball of centre c and radius Δ (i.e., $T = B(c, \Delta)$).

3 Distributed Synthesis

The goal is to split the system into two (or more) sub-systems and synthesize controllers for the sub-systems independently. The allows to break the exponential complexity (curse of dimensionality) of the method w.r.t. the dimension of the system, as well as the dimension of the control input.

We consider the distributed control system

$$\dot{x}_1 = f_{j_1}^1(x_1, x_2) \tag{9}$$
$$\dot{x}_2 = f_{j_2}^2(x_1, x_2) \tag{10}$$

where $x_1 \in \mathbb{R}^{n_1}$ and $x_2 \in \mathbb{R}^{n_2}$, with $n_1 + n_2 = n$. Furthermore, $j_1 \in U_1$ and $j_2 \in U_2$ and $U = U_1 \times U_2$.

Note that the system (9–10) can be seen as the *interconnection* of sub-system (9) where x_2 plays the role of an "input" given by (10), with sub-system (10) where x_1 is an "input" given by (9).

Let: $R = R_1 \times R_2$, $S = S_1 \times S_2$, and $c = (c_1, c_2)^3$. We denote by $L_{j_1}^1$ the Lipschitz constant for sub-system 1 under mode j_1 on S:

$$\|f_{j_1}^1(x_1, x_2) - f_{j_1}^1(y_1, y_2)\| \le L_{j_1}^1 \left\| \begin{pmatrix} x_1 \\ x_2 \end{pmatrix} - \begin{pmatrix} y_1 \\ y_2 \end{pmatrix} \right\|$$

We then introduce the constant:

$$C_{j_1}^1 = \sup_{x_1 \in S_1} L_{j_1}^1 \|f_{j_1}^1(x_1, c_2)\|$$

Similarly, we define the constants for sub-system 2:

$$\|f_{j_2}^2(x_1, x_2) - f_{j_2}^2(y_1, y_2)\| \le L_{j_2}^2 \left\| \begin{pmatrix} x_1 \\ x_2 \end{pmatrix} - \begin{pmatrix} y_1 \\ y_2 \end{pmatrix} \right\|$$

and

$$C_{j_2}^2 = \sup_{x_2 \in S_2} L_{j_2}^2 \|f_{j_2}^2(c_1, x_2)\|$$

Let us now make additional assumptions on the coupled sub-systems, closely related to the notion of (incremental) input-to-state stability.

(H2) For every mode $j_1 \in U_1$, there exists constants $\lambda_{j_1}^1 \in \mathbb{R}$ and $\gamma_{j_1}^1 \in \mathbb{R}_{\ge 0}$ such that $\forall x, x' \in T_1$ and $\forall y, y' \in T_2$, the following expression holds

$$\langle f_{j_1}^1(x, y) - f_{j_1}^1(x', y'), x - x' \rangle \le \lambda_{j_1}^1 \|x - x'\|^2 + \gamma_{j_1}^1 \|x - x'\| \|y - y'\|.$$

(H3) For every mode $j_2 \in U_2$, there exists constants $\lambda_{j_2}^2 \in \mathbb{R}$ and $\gamma_{j_2}^2 \in \mathbb{R}_{\ge 0}$ such that $\forall x, x' \in T_1$ and $\forall y, y' \in T_2$, the following expression holds

$$\langle f_{j_2}^2(x, y) - f_{j_2}^2(x', y'), y - y' \rangle \le \lambda_{j_2}^2 \|y - y'\|^2 + \gamma_{j_2}^2 \|x - x'\| \|y - y'\|.$$

These assumptions express (a variant of) the fact that the function $V(x, x') = \|x - x'\|^2$ is an *ISS-Lyapunov function* (see, e.g., [1,9]). Note that all the constants defined above can be numerically computed using constrained optimization algorithms.

Let us define the distributed Euler scheme:

$$\tilde{x}_1(\tau) = \tilde{x}_1(0) + \tau f_{j_1}^1(\tilde{x}_1(0), c_2) \tag{11}$$
$$\tilde{x}_2(\tau) = \tilde{x}_2(0) + \tau f_{j_2}^2(c_1, \tilde{x}_2(0)) \tag{12}$$

The exact trajectory is now denoted, for all $t \in [0, \tau]$, by $\phi_{(j_1, j_2)}(t; x^0)$ for an initial condition $x^0 = \left(x_1^0 \ x_2^0 \right)^\top$, and when sub-system 1 is in mode $j_1 \in U_1$, and sub-system 2 is in mode $j_2 \in U_2$.

---

[3] So $T = T_1 \times T_2$ with: $T_1 = B(c_1, \Delta)$, $T_2 = B(c_2, \Delta)$.

We define the approximate trajectory computed with the distributed Euler scheme by $\tilde{\phi}^1_{j_1}(t; \tilde{x}^0_1) = \tilde{x}^0_1 + tf^1_{j_1}(\tilde{x}^0_1, c_2)$ for $t \in [0, \tau]$, when sub-system 1 is in mode j_1 and with an initial condition $\tilde{x}^0_1$. Similarly, for sub-system 2, $\tilde{\phi}^2_{j_2}(t; \tilde{x}^0_2) = \tilde{x}^0_2 + tf^2_{j_2}(c_1, \tilde{x}^0_2)$ when sub-system 2 is in mode j_2 and with an initial condition $\tilde{x}^0_2$.

We now give a distributed version of Theorem 1.

Theorem 3. *Given a distributed sampled switched system, a positive real δ^0 and a point $\tilde{x}^0_1 \in S_1$, suppose that sub-system 1 satisfies (H2) and $\tilde{\phi}^1_{j_1}(t; \tilde{x}^0_1)$ belongs to S_1 for all $t \in [0, \tau]$. We have, for all $x^0_1 \in B(\tilde{x}^0_1, \delta^0)$, $x^0_2 \in S_2$, $t \in [0, \tau]$, $j_1 \in U_1$, $j_2 \in U_2$:*

$$\phi_{(j_1, j_2)}(t; x^0)_{|1} \in B(\tilde{\phi}^1_{j_1}(t; \tilde{x}^0_1), \delta_{j_1}(t)).$$

with $x^0 = \begin{pmatrix} x^0_1 & x^0_2 \end{pmatrix}^\top$ and

– if $\lambda^1_{j_1} < 0$,

$$\delta_{j_1}(t) = \left(\frac{(C^1_{j_1})^2}{-(\lambda^1_{j_1})^4} \left(-(\lambda^1_{j_1})^2 t^2 - 2\lambda^1_{j_1} t + 2e^{\lambda^1_{j_1} t} - 2 \right) \right.$$

$$+ \frac{2}{(\lambda^1_{j_1})^2} \left(\frac{C^1_{j_1} \gamma^1_{j_1} \Delta}{-\lambda^1_{j_1}} \left(-\lambda^1_{j_1} t + e^{\lambda^1_{j_1} t} - 1 \right) \right.$$

$$\left. \left. + \lambda^1_{j_1} \left(\frac{(\gamma^1_{j_1})^2 \Delta^2}{-\lambda^1_{j_1}} (e^{\lambda^1_{j_1} t} - 1) + \lambda^1_{j_1} (\delta^0)^2 e^{\lambda^1_{j_1} t} \right) \right) \right)^{1/2} \quad (13)$$

– if $\lambda^1_{j_1} > 0$,

$$\delta_{j_1}(t) = \frac{1}{(3\lambda^1_{j_1})^{3/2}} \left(\frac{C^2_1}{\lambda^1_{j_1}} \left(-9(\lambda^1_{j_1})^2 t^2 - 6\lambda^1_{j_1} t + 2e^{3\lambda^1_{j_1} t} - 2 \right) \right.$$

$$+ 6\lambda^1_{j_1} \left(\frac{C_1 \gamma^1_{j_1} \Delta}{\lambda^1_{j_1}} \left(-3\lambda^1_{j_1} t + e^{3\lambda^1_{j_1} t} - 1 \right) \right.$$

$$\left. \left. + 3\lambda^1_{j_1} \left(\frac{(\gamma^1_{j_1})^2 \Delta^2}{\lambda^1_{j_1}} (e^{3\lambda^1_{j_1} t} - 1) + 3\lambda^1_{j_1} (\delta^0)^2 e^{3\lambda^1_{j_1} t} \right) \right) \right)^{1/2} \quad (14)$$

– if $\lambda^1_{j_1} = 0$,

$$\delta_{j_1}(t) = ((C^1_{j_1})^2 \left(-t^2 - 2t + 2e^t - 2 \right)$$

$$+ (2C^1_{j_1} \gamma^1_{j_1} \Delta \left(-t + e^t - 1 \right)$$

$$+ ((\gamma^1_{j_1})^2 \Delta^2 (e^t - 1) + (\delta^0)^2 e^t)))^{1/2} \quad (15)$$

A similar result can be established for sub-system 2, permitting to perform a distributed control synthesis.

Proof. Consider on $t \in [0, \tau]$ the differential system (9–10) with initial conditions $x_1(0) \in B(\tilde{x}_1(0), \delta^0)$, $x_2(0) \in S_2$, and the system (11–12) with initial conditions $\tilde{x}_1(0) \in S_1$, $\tilde{x}_2(0) \in S_2$. We will abbreviate $\phi_{j_1}(t; x_1(0))$ as x_1, $\phi_{j_2}(t; x_2(0))$ as x_2, and $\tilde{\phi}_{j_1}(t; x_1(0))$ as $\tilde{x}_1$. In order to simplify the notation, we omit the mode j_1 and write $f_{j_1}^1 \equiv f_1$, $L_{j_1}^1 \equiv L_1$, $C_{j_1}^1 \equiv C_1$, $\lambda_{j_1}^1 \equiv \lambda_1$. Since, $\frac{d(x_1 - \tilde{x}_1)}{dt} = f_1(x_1, x_2) - f_1(\tilde{x}_1(0), c_2)$, we have, using the facts $\tilde{x}_1 \in S_1$ and $c_2 \in S_2$:

$$\frac{1}{2}\frac{d(\|x_1 - \tilde{x}_1\|^2)}{dt} = \langle f_1(x_1, x_2) - f_1(\tilde{x}_1(0), c_2), x_1 - \tilde{x}_1 \rangle$$

$$= \langle f_1(x_1, x_2) - f_1(\tilde{x}_1, c_2) + f_1(\tilde{x}_1, c_2) - f_1(\tilde{x}_1(0), c_2), x_1 - \tilde{x}_1 \rangle$$

$$\leq \langle f_1(x_1, x_2) - f_1(\tilde{x}_1, c_2), x_1 - \tilde{x}_1 \rangle + \langle f_1(\tilde{x}_1, c_2) - f_1(\tilde{x}_1(0), c_2), x_1 - \tilde{x}_1 \rangle$$

$$\leq \langle f_1(x_1, x_2) - f_1(\tilde{x}_1, c_2), x_1 - \tilde{x}_1 \rangle + \|f_1(\tilde{x}_1, c_2) - f_1(\tilde{x}_1(0), c_2)\| \|x_1 - \tilde{x}_1\|$$

$$\leq \langle f_1(x_1, x_2) - f_1(\tilde{x}_1, c_2), x_1 - \tilde{x}_1 \rangle + L_1 \left\| \begin{pmatrix} \tilde{x}_1 \\ c_2 \end{pmatrix} - \begin{pmatrix} \tilde{x}_1(0) \\ c_2 \end{pmatrix} \right\| \|x_1 - \tilde{x}_1\|$$

$$\leq \lambda_1 \|x_1 - \tilde{x}_1\|^2 + \gamma_1 \|x_2 - c_2\| \|x_1 - \tilde{x}_1\| + L_1 t \|f_1(\tilde{x}_1(0), c_2)\| \|x_1 - \tilde{x}_1\|$$

$$\leq \lambda_1 \|x_1 - \tilde{x}_1\|^2 + (\gamma_1 \Delta + C_1 t) \|x_1 - \tilde{x}_1\|$$

Using the fact that $\|x_1 - \tilde{x}_1\| \leq \frac{1}{2}(\alpha \|x_1 - \tilde{x}_1\|^2 + \frac{1}{\alpha})$ for any $\alpha > 0$, we can write three formulas following the sign of λ_1.

- if $\lambda_1 < 0$, we can choose $\alpha = \frac{-\lambda_1}{C_1 t + \gamma_1 \Delta}$, and we get the differential inequality:

$$\frac{d(\|x_1 - \tilde{x}_1\|^2)}{dt} \leq \lambda_1 \|x_1 - \tilde{x}_1\|^2 + \frac{C_1^2}{-\lambda_1} t^2 + \frac{2 C_1 \gamma_1 \Delta}{-\lambda_1} t + \frac{\gamma_1^2 \Delta^2}{-\lambda_1}$$

- if $\lambda_1 > 0$, we can choose $\alpha = \frac{\lambda_1}{C_1 t + \gamma_1 \Delta}$, and we get the differential inequality:

$$\frac{d(\|x_1 - \tilde{x}_1\|^2)}{dt} \leq 3\lambda_1 \|x_1 - \tilde{x}_1\|^2 + \frac{C_1^2}{\lambda_1} t^2 + \frac{2 C_1 \gamma_1 \Delta}{\lambda_1} t + \frac{\gamma_1^2 \Delta^2}{\lambda_1}$$

- if $\lambda_1 = 0$, we can choose $\alpha = \frac{1}{C_1 t + \gamma_1 \Delta}$, and we get the differential inequality:

$$\frac{d(\|x_1 - \tilde{x}_1\|^2)}{dt} \leq \|x_1 - \tilde{x}_1\|^2 + C_1^2 t^2 + 2 C_1 \gamma_1 \Delta t + \gamma_1^2 \Delta^2$$

In every case, the differential inequalities can be integrated to obtain the formulas of the theorem.

□

It then follows a distributed version of Corollary 2.

Corollary 3. *Given a positive real δ^0, consider two sets of points $\tilde{x}_1^1, \ldots, \tilde{x}_{m_1}^1$ and $\tilde{x}_1^2, \ldots, \tilde{x}_{m_2}^2$ such that all the balls $B(\tilde{x}_{i_1}^1, \delta^0)$ and $B(\tilde{x}_{i_2}^2, \delta^0)$, for $1 \leq i_1 \leq m_1$ and $1 \leq i_2 \leq m_2$, cover R_1 and R_2. Suppose that there exists patterns $\pi_{i_1}^1$ and $\pi_{i_2}^2$ of length k_{i_1} and k_{i_2} such that:*

1. $B((\tilde{x}_{i_1}^1)_{\pi_{i_1}^1}^{k'}, \delta_{\pi_{i_1}^1}^{k'}) \subseteq S_1$, for all $k' = 1, \ldots, k_{i_1} - 1$

2. $B((\tilde{x}_{i_1}^1)_{\pi_{i_1}^1}^{k_{i_1}}, \delta_{\pi_{i_1}^1}^{k_{i_1}}) \subseteq R_1$.

3. $\frac{d^2(\delta'_{j_1}(t))}{dt^2} > 0$ with $j_1 = \pi_{i_1}^1(k')$ and $(\delta')^0 = \delta_{\pi_{i_1}^1}^{k'-1}$, for all $k' \in \{1, ..., k_{i_1}\}$ and $t \in [0, \tau]$.

1. $B((\tilde{x}_{i_2}^2)_{\pi_{i_2}^2}^{k'}, \delta_{\pi_{i_2}^2}^{k'}) \subseteq S_2$, for all $k' = 1, \ldots, k_{i_2} - 1$

2. $B((\tilde{x}_{i_2}^2)_{\pi_{i_2}^2}^{k_{i_2}}, \delta_{\pi_{i_2}^2}^{k_{i_2}}) \subseteq R_2$.

3. $\frac{d^2(\delta'_{j_2}(t))}{dt^2} > 0$ with $j_2 = \pi_{i_2}^2(k')$ and $(\delta')^0 = \delta_{\pi_{i_2}^2}^{k'-1}$, for all $k' \in \{1, ..., k_{i_2}\}$ and $t \in [0, \tau]$.

The above properties induce a distributed control $\sigma = (\sigma_1, \sigma_2)$ guaranteeing (non simultaneous) recurrence in R and safety in S. I.e.

- *if $x \in R$, then $\phi_\sigma(t; x) \in S$ for all $t \geq 0$*
- *if $x \in R$, then $\phi_\sigma(k_1\tau; x)_{|1} \in R_1$ for some $k_1 \in \{k_{i_1}, \ldots, k_{i_{m_1}}\}$, and symmetrically $\phi_\sigma(k_2\tau; x)_{|2} \in R_2$ for some $k_2 \in \{k_{i_2}, \ldots, k_{i_{m_2}}\}$.*

4 Application

We demonstrate the feasibility of our approach on a (linearized) building ventilation application adapted from [16]. The system is a four-room apartment subject to heat transfer between the rooms, with the external environment and with the underfloor. The dynamics of the system is given by the following equation:

$$\frac{dT_i}{dt} = \sum_{j \in \mathcal{N}^* \setminus \{i\}} a_{ij}(T_j - T_i) + c_i \max\left(0, \frac{V_i - V_i^*}{\bar{V}_i - V_i^*}\right)(T_u - T_i). \qquad (16)$$

The state of the system is given by the temperatures in the rooms T_i, for $i \in \mathcal{N} = \{1, \ldots, 4\}$. Room i is subject to heat exchange with different entities stated by the indexes $\mathcal{N}^* = \{1, 2, 3, 4, u, o, c\}$. The heat transfer between the rooms is given by the coefficients a_{ij} for $i, j \in \mathcal{N}^2$, and the different perturbations are the following:

- The external environment: it has an effect on room i with the coefficient a_{io} and the outside temperature T_o, set to $30°C$.
- The heat transfer through the ceiling: it has an effect on room i with the coefficient a_{ic} and the ceiling temperature T_c, set to $30°C$.
- The heat transfer with the underfloor: it is given by the coefficient a_{iu} and the underfloor temperature T_u, set to $17°C$ (T_u is constant, regulated by a PID controller).

The control V_i, $i \in \mathcal{N}$, is applied through the term $c_i \max\left(0, \frac{V_i - V_i^*}{\bar{V}_i - V_i^*}\right)(T_u - T_i)$. A voltage V_i is applied to force ventilation from the underfloor to room i, and the command of an underfloor fan is subject to a dry friction. Because we work in a switching control framework, V_i can take only discrete values, which removes the problem of dealing with a "max" function in interval analysis. In the experiment, V_1 and V_4 can take the values 0V or 3.5V, and V_2 and V_3 can take the values 0V or 3V. This leads to a system of the form (8) with $\sigma(t) \in U = \{1, \ldots, 16\}$, the 16 switching modes corresponding to the different possible combinations of voltages V_i. The system can be decomposed in sub-systems of the form (9)–(10). The sampling period is $\tau = 30$s. The parameters V_i^*, $\bar{V}_i$, a_{ij}, b_i, c_i are given in [16] and have been identified with a proper identification procedure detailed in [17].

The main difficulty of this example is the large number of modes in the switching system, which induces a combinatorial issue. The centralized controller was obtained with 256 balls in 48 s, the distributed controller was obtained with $16 + 16$ balls in less than a second. In both cases, patterns of length 2 are used. A sub-sampling of $h = \tau/20$ is required to obtain a controller with the centralized approach. For the distributed approach, no sub-sampling is required for the first sub-system, while the second one requires a sub-sampling of $h = \tau/10$. Simulations of the centralized and distributed controllers are given in Fig. 3, where the control objective is to stabilize the temperature in $[20, 22]^4$ while never going out of $[19, 23]^4$ (Tables 1 and 2).

Table 1. Numerical results for centralized four-room example.

	Centralized
R	$[20, 22]^4$
S	$[19, 23]^4$
τ	30
Time subsampling	$\tau/20$
Complete control	Yes
Error parameters	$\max\limits_{j=1,\ldots,16} \lambda_j = -6.30 \times 10^{-3}$ $\max\limits_{j=1,\ldots,16} C_j = 4.18 \times 10^{-6}$
Number of balls/tiles	256
Pattern length	2
CPU time	48 s

Table 2. Numerical results for the distributed four-room example.

	Sub-system 1	Sub-system 2
R	$[20, 22]^2 \times [20, 22]^2$	
S	$[19, 23]^2 \times [19, 23]^2$	
τ	30	
Time subsampling	No	$\tau/10$
Complete control	Yes	Yes
Error parameters	$\max\limits_{j_1=1,\ldots,4} \lambda^1_{j_1} = -1.39 \times 10^{-3}$	$\max\limits_{j_2=1,\ldots,4} \lambda^2_{j_2} = -1.42 \times 10^{-3}$
	$\max\limits_{j_1=1,\ldots,4} \gamma^1_{j_1} = 1.79 \times 10^{-4}$	$\max\limits_{j_2=1,\ldots,4} \gamma^2_{j_2} = 2.47 \times 10^{-4}$
	$\max\limits_{j_1=1,\ldots,4} C^1_{j_1} = 4.15 \times 10^{-4}$	$\max\limits_{j_2=1,\ldots,4} C^2_{j_2} = 5.75 \times 10^{-4}$
Number of balls/tiles	16	16
Pattern length	2	2
CPU time	$< 1\,\text{s}$	$< 1\,\text{s}$

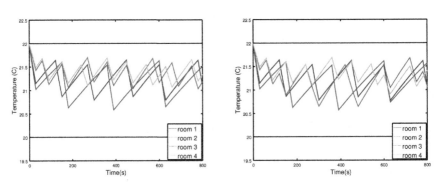

Fig. 3. Simulation of the centralized (left) and distributed (right) controllers from the initial condition $(22, 22, 22, 22)$.

5   Final Remarks and Future Work

We have given a new distributed control synthesis method based on Euler's method. The method makes use of the notions of δ-ISS-stability and ISS Lyapunov functions. From a certain point of view, this method is along the lines of [6,12] which are inspired by small-gain theorems of control theory (see, *e.g.*, [10]). In the future, we plan to apply our distributed Euler-based method to significant examples such as the 11-room example treated in [13,15].

References

1. Angeli, D.: A Lyapunov approach to incremental stability. In: Proceeding of IEEE Conference on Decision and Control, vol. 3, pp. 2947–2952 (2000)
2. Asarin, E., Dang, T., Girard, A.: Hybridization methods for the analysis of nonlinear systems. Acta Inform. **43**(7), 451–476 (2007)
3. Atkinson, K.E.: An Introduction to Numerical Analysis. Wiley, Hoboken (2008)
4. Chen, X., Sankaranarayanan, S.: Decomposed reachability analysis for nonlinear systems. In: Proceeding of IEEE Real-Time Systems Symposium, pp. 13–24 (2016)
5. Dahlquist, G.: Error analysis for a class of methods for stiff non-linear initial value problems. In: Watson, G.A. (ed.) Numerical Analysis. LNM, vol. 506, pp. 60–72. Springer, Heidelberg (1976). doi:10.1007/BFb0080115
6. Dallal, E., Tabuada, P.: On compositional symbolic controller synthesis inspired by small-gain theorems. In: Proceeding of IEEE Conference on Decision and Control, pp. 6133–6138 (2015)
7. Donchev, T., Farkhi, E.: Stability and euler approximation of one-sided lipschitz differential inclusions. SIAM J. Control Optim. **36**(2), 780–796 (1998)
8. Eaton, J.W., Bateman, D., Hauberg, S.: Gnu Octave. Network theory Ltd., London (1997)
9. Hespanha, J.P., Liberzon, D., Teel, A.R.: Lyapunov conditions for input-to-state stability of impulsive systems. Automatica **44**(11), 2735–2744 (2008)
10. Jiang, Z.-P., Teel, A.R., Praly, L.: Small-gain theorem for ISS systems and applications. Math. Control Sig. Syst. **7**(2), 95–120 (1994)
11. Jiang, Z.-P., Mareels, I.M.Y., Wang, Y.: A Lyapunov formulation of the nonlinear small-gain theorem for interconnected iss systems. Automatica **32**(8), 1211–1215 (1996)
12. Kim, E.S., Arcak, M., Seshia, S.A.: Compositional controller synthesis for vehicular traffic networks. In: Proceeding of IEEE Annual Conference on Decision and Control, pp. 6165–6171 (2015)
13. Larsen, K.G., Mikučionis, M., Muniz, M., Srba, J., Taankvist, J.H.: Online and compositional learning of controllers with application to floor heating. In: Proceeding of International Conference Tools and Algorithms for Construction and Analysis of Systems (2016)
14. Le Coënt, A., De Vuyst, F., Chamoin, L., Fribourg, L.: Control synthesis of nonlinear sampled switched systems using Euler's method. In: Proceeding of International Workshop on Symbolic and Numerical Methods for Reachability Analysis of EPTCS, vol. 247, pp. 18–33. Open Publishing Association (2017)
15. Le Coënt, A., Fribourg, L., Markey, N., De Vuyst, F., Chamoin, L.: Distributed synthesis of state-dependent switching control. In: Larsen, K.G., Potapov, I., Srba, J. (eds.) RP 2016. LNCS, vol. 9899, pp. 119–133. Springer, Cham (2016). doi:10.1007/978-3-319-45994-3_9
16. Meyer, P.-J.: Invariance and symbolic control of cooperative systems for temperature regulation in intelligent buildings. Université Grenoble Alpes, Theses (2015)
17. Meyer, P.-J., Nazarpour, H., Girard, A., Witrant, E.: Experimental implementation of UFAD regulation based on robust controlled invariance. In: Proceeding of European Control Conference, pp. 1468–1473 (2014)
18. Yang, G., Liberzon, D.: A lyapunov-based small-gain theorem for interconnected switched systems. Syst. Control Lett. **78**, 47–54 (2015)

Reachability Problem for Polynomial Iteration
Is **PSPACE**-complete

Reino Niskanen[⊠]

Department of Computer Science, University of Liverpool, Liverpool, UK
r.niskanen@liverpool.ac.uk

Abstract. In the reachability problem for polynomial iteration, we are given a set of polynomials over integers and we are asked whether a particular integer can be reached by a non-deterministic application of polynomials. This model can be seen as a generalisation of vector addition systems. Our main result is that the problem is PSPACE-complete for single variable polynomials. On the other hand, the problem is undecidable for multidimensional polynomials, already starting with three dimensions.

Keywords: Reachability problem · Polynomial iteration · Decidability

1 Introduction

In this paper, we consider the reachability problem for polynomial iteration. That is, we are given a set of integer valued polynomials $\{p_1(x), p_2(x), \ldots, p_n(x)\} \subseteq \mathbb{Z}[x]$, two integers x_0 and x_f, and asked whether there exists a finite sequence of polynomials $p_{i_1}(x), p_{i_2}(x), \ldots, p_{i_j}(x)$ that maps x_0 to x_f, i.e., whether

$$p_{i_j}(p_{i_{j-1}}(\cdots p_{i_2}(p_{i_1}(x_0))\cdots)) = x_f.$$

The problem can be seen as a special case of *polynomial register machines* of [6], where the machine has a single state. In [6], it was proved that the reachability problem is PSPACE-complete. We show that the reachability problem for polynomial iteration has the same complexity. The upper bound follows naturally from [6] and we highlight authors' observations regarding this surprising complexity. First observation is that the reachability set is not semi-linear which can be seen by considering the polynomial $p(x) = x^2$ and its reachability set, which is illustrated in Fig. 1. The second observation is that the representation of evaluations of x grows exponentially with the number of times a polynomial is applied.

To prove the lower bound, we need to modify the proof of PSPACE-hardness for register machines with polynomial updates to remove the need for the state structure of the machine. To this end, we follow the proof of [6] and reduce the reachability problem for linear-bounded automata to polynomial iteration. Linear-bounded automata were studied in [12,13], where the authors showed

© Springer International Publishing AG 2017
M. Hague and I. Potapov (Eds.): RP 2017, LNCS 10506, pp. 132–143, 2017.
DOI: 10.1007/978-3-319-67089-8_10

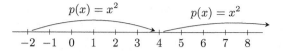

Fig. 1. Iterating -2 with polynomial $p(x) = x^2$ two times.

that the linear-bounded automata accept exactly context-sensitive languages. A linear-bounded automaton is a Turing machine with a finite tape whose length is bounded by a linear function of the length of the input. The reachability problem for the linear-bounded automaton is to decide whether starting from the initial state and the read/write head in the leftmost cell of the empty tape, the machine can reach a final state with the empty tape. The problem is a well-known PSPACE-complete problem. We use a similar encoding to the encoding used in [6], where the tape content of a linear-bounded automaton was encoded as a solution to a system of linear congruences and the state structure was encoded as a state structure of a polynomial register machine. Unlike Finkel's, Göller's and Haase's encoding, we will also encode the state structure of the linear-bounded automaton as a solution to additional linear congruences making our automaton stateless.

We also consider iterating multidimensional polynomials and show that the reachability problem is undecidable for three-dimensional polynomials. The result is not surprising as the reachability problem for register machines with two-dimensional affine updates is undecidable [15]. Unfortunately, we are not able to obtain as strong result for polynomial iteration as, in our construction, simulating the state structure requires an additional dimension and polynomials of higher degree than one.

The models similar to our polynomial iteration have been studied before. In [3], polynomial iteration in $\mathbb{Q}$ was studied and the reachability problem was proved to be decidable using p-adic norms. Polynomials over $\mathbb{Q}$ are significantly harder to analyze than polynomials over $\mathbb{Z}$, as in a finite interval $[a, b]$, there might be infinite number of reachable values.

Multidimensional linear polynomial iteration has been considered from a different aspect. The vector reachability problem for d-dimensional matrices over $\mathbb{F}$, where $\mathbb{F} = \mathbb{Z}, \mathbb{Q}, \mathbb{C}, \ldots$, studies whether for given two vectors $\mathbf{x}_0, \mathbf{x}_f$ and a set of matrices $\{M_1, \ldots M_k\} \subseteq \mathbb{F}^{d \times d}$, there exists a finite sequence of matrices such that $M_{i_1} \cdots M_{i_j} \mathbf{x}_0 = \mathbf{x}_f$. Since transforming a vector by a matrix can be expressed as a system of linear equations, the multidimensional linear polynomial iteration can be seen as a vector reachability problem. The main difference from our consideration is that we consider only polynomials of the form $p(x_1, \ldots, x_d) = (p_1(x_1), \ldots, p_d(x_d))$ for some univariate polynomials $p_i(x)$, while the polynomials in the vector reachability problem are of the form $p(x_1, \ldots, x_d) = (a_{11}x_1 + \ldots + a_{1d}x_d, \ldots, a_{d1}x_1 + \ldots + a_{dd}x_d)$. The vector reachability problem has been proven to be undecidable for six 3-dimensional integer matrices in [7] and for two 11-dimensional integer matrices in [8].

In [1], the authors studied reachability of a point in $\mathbb{Q}^2$ by two-dimensional affine transformations. They proved that the problem is undecidable already for five such affine polynomials. The affine transformations used are of the form

$$p(x, y) = (q_1 x + q_2 y + q_3, q_4 x + q_5 y + q_6).$$

The above mentioned undecidability results relied on the undecidability of the Post correspondence problem with seven pairs of words and having particular structure known as Claus instances [4]. The state-of-art bound on number of pairs of words is five [14], which could result in lower bounds on number of matrices and linear transformations as well.

The polynomial iteration can be also considered as piecewise maps. That is, a polynomial $p(x)$ is applicable only when $x \in [a, b)$ for some $a, b \in \mathbb{Z} \cup \{\pm\infty\}$. Piecewise maps and related reachability problems have been studied extensively [2,9,10]. The problem is undecidable for two-dimensional piecewise affine maps. The decidability of the reachability problem for one-dimensional piecewise affine map is an open problem even when there are only two intervals. On the other hand, for more general updates the problem is undecidable. For example if the updates are based on the elementary functions $\{x^2, x^3, \sqrt{x}, \sqrt[3]{x}, 2x, x + 1, x - 1\}$ or on rational functions of the form $p(x) = \frac{ax^2 + bx + c}{dx + e}$, where the coefficients are rational numbers [11], then the problem is undecidable.

This paper is organized as follows. In the next section, we introduce basic definitions and models used in the paper. In Sect. 3, we prove our main result that the reachability problem for polynomial iteration is PSPACE-complete. We also consider the multidimensional case and prove undecidability for three-dimensional polynomials.

2   Preliminaries

In this section we present basic definitions used throughout the paper. The sets of integers and rational numbers are denoted by $\mathbb{Z}$ and $\mathbb{Q}$, respectively. The integers are assumed to be encoded in binary. By $\mathbb{Z}[x]$ we denote the ring of polynomials with integer variable x. A polynomial $p(x) \in \mathbb{Z}[x]$ is $p(x) = a_n x^n + \ldots + a_1 x + a_0$, where $a_i \in \mathbb{Z}$ and $n \geq 0$. We represent polynomials in sparse encoding by a sequence of pairs $(i, a_i)_{i \in I}$, where $I = \{i \in \{0, \ldots, n\} \mid a_i \neq 0\}$. Deciding whether for a given $y \in \mathbb{Z}$, the polynomial $p(y)$ evaluates to a positive number can be done in polynomial time [5].

In our encoding, we use the Chinese remainder theorem to find the unique solution to a system of linear congruences. That is, for given pairwise co-prime positive integers $n_1, \ldots, n_k$ and $b_1, \ldots, b_k \in \mathbb{Z}$, the system of linear congruences $x \equiv b_i \mod n_i$ for $i = 1, \ldots, k$ has a unique solution modulo $n_1 \cdots n_k$. Recall that a residue class b modulo n is the set of integers $\{\ldots, b - n, b, b + n, \ldots\}$.

A *polynomial register machine* (PRM) is a tuple $\mathcal{R} = (S, \Delta)$, where S is a finite set of states, $\Delta \subseteq S \times \mathbb{Z}[x] \times S$ is the set of transitions labelled with update polynomials. A transition $(s, p(x), s')$ is often written as $s \xrightarrow{p(x)} s'$. A *configuration* c of $\mathcal{R}$ is a tuple $[s, z] \in S \times \mathbb{Z}$. A configuration $[s, z]$ is said to yield a configuration $[s', y]$ if there is a transition $(s, p(x), s') \in \Delta$ such that $p(z) = y$. This is denoted by $[s, z] \rightarrow_{\mathcal{R}} [s', y]$. The reflexive and transitive closure of $\rightarrow_{\mathcal{R}}$ is denoted by $\rightarrow_{\mathcal{R}}^*$. The *reachability problem* is to decide, given two configurations $[s_0, x_0]$ and $[s_f, x_f]$, does $[s_0, x_0] \rightarrow_{\mathcal{R}}^* [s_f, x_f]$ hold? It is easy to reduce the general reachability problem to $[s_0, 0] \rightarrow_{\mathcal{R}'}^* [s_f, 0]$ for some $\mathcal{R}'$. Note, that when considering d-dimensional polynomial updates, the updates are applied componentwise, i.e., $p(x_1, \ldots, x_d) = (p_1(x_1), \ldots, p_d(x_d))$, where $p_i(x) \in \mathbb{Z}[x]$.

A *linear-bounded automaton* (LBA) is a Turing machine with a tape bounded by a linear function of the length of the input. Equivalently, LBA can be defined as a Turing machine with a finite tape. We denote an LBA $\mathcal{M}$ by a tuple (Q, Γ, δ), where Q is a finite set of states, $\Gamma = \{\triangleright, \triangleleft, 0, 1\}$ is a finite tape alphabet, containing two special symbols $\triangleright$ and $\triangleleft$, which mark the left and right borders of the tape. The transition function δ is a mapping from $Q \times \Gamma$ to $Q \times \Gamma \times \{L, R\}$, where L and R tell the read/write head to move left or right, respectively. The automaton respects the boundary symbols, that is, $\delta(q_1, \triangleleft) = (q_2, \triangleleft, L)$ and $\delta(q_3, \triangleright) = (q_4, \triangleright, R)$ for any states $q_1, q_3 \in Q$ and where $q_2, q_4 \in Q$. A configuration is a triple $[q, i, \triangleright w \triangleleft]$, where $w \in \{0, 1\}^n$ and $i = 0, \ldots, n + 1$. Intuitively, in the configuration the automaton is in state q, the read/write head is in the ith cell and w is written on the tape. Let $\rightarrow_{\mathcal{M}}^*$ be the reflexive and transitive closure of the transition relation $\rightarrow_{\mathcal{M}}$ defined in the usual way. The reachability problem for a given LBA is to decide whether $[q_0, 0, \triangleright 0^n \triangleleft] \rightarrow_{\mathcal{M}}^* [q_f, 0, \triangleright 0^n \triangleleft]$ holds and is a well-known PSPACE-complete problem. Without loss of generality, we can assume that q_f appears only in the configuration $[q_f, 0, \triangleright 0^n \triangleleft]$. Furthermore, we can enumerate the states such that q_0 is the first state and q_f is the last state, i.e., $q_f = q_{|Q|-1}$. By $w[i]$ we denote the ith letter of w.

Finally, we define the main decision problem of the paper. Given a finite set of polynomials $\mathcal{P} = \{p_1(x), \ldots, p_n(x)\} \subseteq \mathbb{Z}[x]$ and an initial integer x_0, we iterate x_0 by non-deterministically applying polynomials from $\mathcal{P}$ to it. We are interested whether when iterating x_0 in such way the result is 0 or not. This model can be seen as a PRM where $|S| = 1$ and self-loops are labelled with $p_i(x)$.

3   Iterating Polynomials

In this section we prove that the reachability problem for iterating polynomials is PSPACE-complete. The proof of lower bound is similar to the proof of PSPACE-hardness of the reachability problem for polynomial register machines. Both proofs reduce from the reachability problem for LBA. Let us fix an LBA $\mathcal{M}$ with tape of n symbols for the remainder of the section. The main difference of the proofs is that in [6], the states of PRM contain the information on the state of $\mathcal{M}$, position of the read/write head and the letter that the head is currently reading, while the tape content was encoded as an integer and modified by the transitions according to the instructions of $\mathcal{M}$. In our proof, the whole configuration of $\mathcal{M}$ is encoded as an integer and updated according to the instructions of $\mathcal{M}$.

First, let us recall some definitions from [6]. Let p_i denote the $(i+3)$-th prime number, that is, $p_1 = 7, p_2 = 11, \ldots$ and let P be the product of m such primes, $P = \prod_{i=1}^{m} p_i$, where $m = n + n \cdot |Q|$. The main idea of the encoding is to consider the integer line $\mathbb{Z}$ modulo P and integers as the corresponding residue classes. We are interested in the residue classes that satisfy linear equations modulo p_i for different p_i. First n primes will correspond to each cell of the tape and the next $n \cdot |Q|$ primes will correspond to the head being in a particular state in a particular cell. Note, that for the sake of simplicity, we omit the border symbols of the tape and the behaviour of the head on them. In fact, it is quite easy to deal with them as, among other information, we also encode the position of the head into our integer. Then, it is easy to hard-code the behaviour of $\mathcal{M}$ on the border symbols into corresponding polynomials.

We are not interested in all residue classes modulo P and only a tiny fraction of residue classes is used to store information. A residue class r is of interest to us if for every $1 \leq i \leq m$ there is some $b_i \in \{0, 1, 2\}$ such that $r = b_i \mod p_i$. We call such residue class *sane* and denote the set of all sane residue classes by S. A configuration $[q_j, i, w]$, where $i = \{1, \ldots, n\}$ and $w \in \{0, 1\}^n$, corresponds to a residue class r satisfying the system of congruence equations

$$
\begin{aligned}
r &\equiv w[1] \mod p_1, \\
r &\equiv w[2] \mod p_2, \\
&\vdots \\
r &\equiv w[n] \mod p_n, \\
r &\equiv 1 \mod p_\ell \text{ if } \ell = n + j + (i-1)|Q|, \\
r &\equiv 0 \mod p_\ell \text{ if } \ell > n \text{ and } \ell \neq n + j + (i-1)|Q|.
\end{aligned}
\tag{1}
$$

We illustrate how a configuration $[q_3, 2, 1001 \cdots 1]$ of an LBA corresponds to the residue class r satisfying the system of linear Eq. (1) in Fig. 2.

To simulate a move $\delta(q_j, a) = (q_k, a', L)$, we need to check that the current residue class r satisfies congruence equations

$$
r \equiv 1 \mod p_{n+j+(i-1)|Q|} \qquad \text{and} \qquad r \equiv a \mod p_i
$$

for some $i \in \{1, \ldots, n\}$ and then move to a residue class r' satisfying congruence equations

$$
\begin{aligned}
r' &\equiv 0 \mod p_{n+j+(i-1)|Q|}, \\
r' &\equiv 1 \mod p_{n+k+(i-2)|Q|}, \\
r' &\equiv a' \mod p_i, \\
r' &\equiv r \mod p_\ell \text{ for all} \\
&\quad \ell \in \{1, \ldots, n + n \cdot |Q|\} \setminus \{i, n+j+(i-1)|Q|, n+k+(i-2)|Q|\}.
\end{aligned}
$$

That is, first we need to check that the current residue class r corresponds to a configuration $[q_j, i, w]$, where $w[i] = a$. Then, we move to the residue class r'

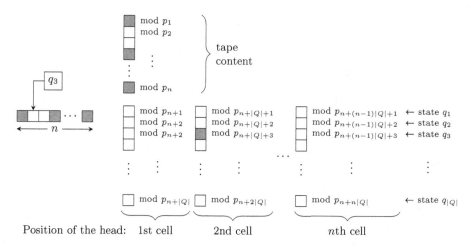

Fig. 2. An illustration how configuration $[q_3, 2, 1001 \cdots 1]$ of an LBA (left) is encoded as residue class r satisfying a system of linear equations. Here, symbols 0 and 1 are represented by a white and gray squares, respectively. A gray square in the ith cell column and the jth state row represents the head being in the ith cell in state q_j.

corresponding to the configuration $[q_k, i - 1, w']$, where $w'[i] = a'$ and $w'[\ell] = w[\ell]$, for all $\ell = \{1, \ldots, n\} \setminus \{i\}$.

To this end, we need to *locally* modify the residue classes. That is, we need to have a polynomial $p(x)$ such that $p(r) = r'$. There are three mappings that are defined for each index $i \in \{1, \ldots, m\}$, $\mathrm{FLIP}_i, \mathrm{EQZERO}_i, \mathrm{EQONE}_i : S \to S$.

For the mapping $\mathrm{FLIP}_i(r)$ there are three cases depending on whether $r \equiv 0, 1, 2 \mod p_i$:

if $r \equiv 0 \mod p_i$:   if $r \equiv 1 \mod p_i$:   if $r \equiv 2 \mod p_i$:

$$\mathrm{FLIP}_i(r) \equiv \begin{cases} 1 & \mod p_i \\ r & \mod p_j \end{cases} \quad \mathrm{FLIP}_i(r) \equiv \begin{cases} 0 & \mod p_i \\ r & \mod p_j \end{cases} \quad \mathrm{FLIP}_i(r) \equiv \begin{cases} 2 & \mod p_i \\ r & \mod p_j. \end{cases}$$

Similarly, for the remaining two mappings, there are three cases depending on whether $r \equiv 0, 1, 2 \mod p_i$.

if $r \equiv 0 \mod p_i$:   if $r \equiv 1, 2 \mod p_i$:

$$\mathrm{EQZERO}_i(r) \equiv \begin{cases} 0 & \mod p_i \\ r & \mod p_j \end{cases} \qquad \mathrm{EQZERO}_i(r) \equiv \begin{cases} 2 & \mod p_i \\ r & \mod p_j \end{cases}$$

if $r \equiv 1 \mod p_i$:   if $r \equiv 0, 2 \mod p_i$:

$$\mathrm{EQONE}_i(r) \equiv \begin{cases} 1 & \mod p_i \\ r & \mod p_j \end{cases} \qquad \mathrm{EQZERO}_i(r) \equiv \begin{cases} 2 & \mod p_i \\ r & \mod p_j. \end{cases}$$

The move $\delta(q_j, 0) = (q_k, 0, L)$ of LBA $\mathcal{M}$ when the head is in ith position is now realized by

$$\text{FLIP}_{n+k+(i-2)|Q|} \circ \text{FLIP}_{n+j+(i-1)|Q|} \circ \text{EQZERO}_i \circ \text{EQONE}_{n+j+(i-1)|Q|}.$$

In Fig. 3 we illustrate how moves $\delta(q_j, 0) = (q_k, 0, L)$ and $\delta(q_j, 1) = (q_k, 0, R)$ of LBA $\mathcal{M}$ are realized for the configuration $[q, i, w]$. Note, that we do not assume that $q = q_j$ or that $w[i] = 0$ for the first move or $w[i] = 1$ for the second move. Moves EQZERO_ℓ and EQONE_ℓ verify that the bit encoded in the residue class modulo p_ℓ is 0 or 1, respectively.

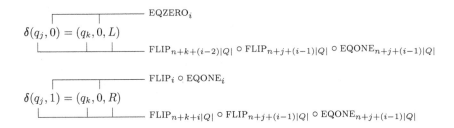

Fig. 3. An illustration of mappings corresponding to moves of LBA.

The crucial ingredient for the simulation is that the functions FLIP_i, EQZERO_i and EQONE_i can be realized by polynomials with coefficients in $\{0, \ldots, P-1\}$. We present the lemma of [6].

Lemma 1. *For any $1 \leq i \leq m$ and any of $\text{FLIP}_i, \text{EQZERO}_i, \text{EQONE}_i : S \to S$, there is a a quadratic polynomial with coefficients from $\{0, \ldots, P-1\}$ that realizes the respective function.*

Proof. First, we show the polynomials corresponding to the mappings FLIP_i, EQZERO_i and EQONE_i that map the values correctly when considering only $\mathbb{Z}/p_i\mathbb{Z}$. Then, we mention how to modify them to also map the values correctly for all $\mathbb{Z}/p_j\mathbb{Z}$ where $j \neq i$.

It is easy to verify that the polynomials

$$p_{eqzero}(x) = -x^2 + 3x, \; p_{eqone}(x) = x^2 - 2x + 2 \text{ and}$$
$$p_{flip}(x) = 3 \cdot 2^{-1}x^2 - 5 \cdot 2^{-1}x + 1$$

realize the respective mappings. Note that since $p_i \geq 7$, 2 has a multiplicative inverse. For example, let $p_i = 11$, then $2^{-1} = 6$ and

Although these polynomials realize the conditions of FLIP_i, EQZERO_i and EQONE_i for i, they (generally) do not realize the conditions when $j \neq i$. That is, $p_{eqzero}(x) \neq x$ when considering the polynomials in $\mathbb{Z}/p_j\mathbb{Z}$. To illustrate this, consider $p_{eqzero}(1)$ as above, but now with respect to $p_j = 7$. By the definition

x	$p_{eqzero}(x)$	$p_{eqone}(x)$	$p_{flip}(x)$
0	$-0^2 + 3 \cdot 0 \equiv \mathbf{0}$	$0^2 - 2 \cdot 0 + 2 \equiv \mathbf{2}$	$3 \cdot 6 \cdot 0^2 - 5 \cdot 6 \cdot 0 + 1 \equiv \mathbf{1}$
1	$-1^2 + 3 \cdot 1 \equiv \mathbf{2}$	$1^2 - 2 \cdot 1 + 2 \equiv \mathbf{1}$	$3 \cdot 6 \cdot 1^2 - 5 \cdot 6 \cdot 1 + 1 = -11 \equiv \mathbf{0}$
2	$-2^2 + 3 \cdot 2 \equiv \mathbf{2}$	$2^2 - 2 \cdot 2 + 2 \equiv \mathbf{2}$	$3 \cdot 6 \cdot 2^2 - 5 \cdot 6 \cdot 2 + 1 = 13 \equiv \mathbf{2}$

of EQZERO$_i$, it should remain unchanged, that is $p_{eqzero}(1) = 1$ with respect to p_j. This is not the case, as 1 and 2 are different residue classes. To obtain polynomials corresponding to FLIP$_i$, EQZERO$_i$ and EQONE$_i$, we consider polynomials $p_{eqzero}(x)$, $p_{eqone}(x)$ and $p_{flip}(x)$ as $a_2 x_2 + a_1 x + a_0$ and construct a system of congruences for each $\ell = \{0, 1, 2\}$:

$$x \equiv a_\ell \mod p_i$$
$$x \equiv b_\ell \mod p_j \text{ for each } j \in \{1, \ldots, m\} \setminus \{i\},$$

where $b_1 = 1$ and $b_0 = b_2 = 0$. By applying the Chinese remainder theorem, we obtain the unique solution for each coefficient and obtain the polynomials $p_{eqzero,i}(x)$, $p_{eqone,i}(x)$ and $p_{flip,i}(x)$ by replacing the original coefficients with these unique solutions. $\square$

Now, for each $i \in \{1, \ldots, n\}$ and each transition $\delta(q_j, a) = (q_k, a', D)$, where $a, a' \in \{0, 1\}$ and $D = \{L, R\}$, there exists a polynomial of at most degree 32 realizing this transition by Lemma 1. These polynomials are exactly our set of polynomials $\mathcal{P}$. Note, that our simulation is slightly different from [6] as there, in each step, the PRM guessed (and verified) the content of the cell where the head moves in the successive configuration and only correct moves are available due to the state structure. In our model, as there is no state structure, each time a move is simulated, we have to verify that indeed both the state and current cell are correct. The initial value x_0 satisfies

$$x_0 \equiv 1 \mod p_{n+1} \quad \text{and} \quad x_0 \equiv 0 \mod p_\ell \text{ if } \ell \neq n + 1.$$

Main idea is still the same, if $\mathcal{M}$ is simulated incorrectly, the value x becomes 2 modulo some prime p_ℓ and will remain 2 forever.

By induction on the length of the run of LBA $\mathcal{M}$, it is easy to see that $[q_1, 0, \triangleright 0^n \triangleleft] \to^* [q_f, 0, \triangleright 0^n \triangleleft]$ in $\mathcal{M}$ if and only if a residue class r, such that

$$r \equiv 1 \mod p_{n+|Q|-1} \quad \text{and} \quad r \equiv 0 \mod p_\ell \text{ if } \ell \neq n + |Q| - 1,$$

is reachable from x_0 by applying polynomials from $\mathcal{P}$. To reach 0, we need three additional polynomials: one polynomial to move to a residue class r' such that $r' \equiv 0 \mod p_\ell$ for all $1 \leq \ell \leq m$, and two polynomials to move from the *integer* r' to 0. The first polynomial is $p_{flip,n+|Q|-1}(p_{eqone,n+|Q|-1}(x))$ as we assumed that the final state appears only in the configuration $[q_{|Q|-1}, 0, \triangleright 0^n \triangleleft]$. The latter polynomials are $p_+(x) = x + P$ and $p_-(x) = x - P$.

We have proved the following lemma:

Lemma 2. *The reachability problem for polynomial iteration is* PSPACE*-hard for polynomials with integer coefficients.*

Example 3. We illustrate the simulation of an LBA with polynomials. Let $\mathcal{M}$ be an LBA with a single state, a tape with two cells and a move $\delta(q_1, 0) = (q_1, 1, R)$. For the sake of readability, we present all the integers modulo $P = 7 \cdot 11 \cdot 13 \cdot 17 = 17017$. The integers r and s representing configurations $[q_1, 1, 00]$ and $[q_1, 2, 10]$ can be solved from the system of congruences

$$
\begin{aligned}
r &\equiv 0 \quad \text{mod } 7, & s &\equiv 1 \quad \text{mod } 7 \\
r &\equiv 0 \quad \text{mod } 11, & s &\equiv 0 \quad \text{mod } 11, \\
r &\equiv 1 \quad \text{mod } 13, & s &\equiv 0 \quad \text{mod } 13, \\
r &\equiv 0 \quad \text{mod } 17, & s &\equiv 1 \quad \text{mod } 17.
\end{aligned}
$$

That is, $r = 3927$ and $s = 715$. The move $\delta(q_1, 0) = (q_1, 1, R)$ is realized by $\text{FLIP}_1 \circ \text{EQZERO}_1 \circ \text{FLIP}_4 \circ \text{FLIP}_3 \circ \text{EQONE}_3$. By Lemma 1, EQONE_3 is realized by a quadratic polynomial $a_2' x^2 + a_1' x + a_0'$ with coefficients satisfying the congruences

$$
\begin{aligned}
a_2' &\equiv 0 \quad \text{mod } 7, & a_1' &\equiv 1 \quad \text{mod } 7, & a_0' &\equiv 0 \quad \text{mod } 7, \\
a_2' &\equiv 0 \quad \text{mod } 11, & a_1' &\equiv 1 \quad \text{mod } 11, & a_0' &\equiv 0 \quad \text{mod } 11, \\
a_2' &\equiv 1 \quad \text{mod } 13, & a_1' &\equiv -2 \quad \text{mod } 13, & a_0' &\equiv 2 \quad \text{mod } 13, \\
a_2' &\equiv 0 \quad \text{mod } 17, & a_1' &\equiv 1 \quad \text{mod } 17, & a_0' &\equiv 0 \quad \text{mod } 17.
\end{aligned}
$$

Solving these systems, we see that $p_{eqone,3}(x) = 3927x^2 + 5237x + 7854$. The other polynomials are solved from similar systems of congruences.

$$
\begin{aligned}
p_{flip,3} &= 14399x^2 + 11782x + 3927, \\
p_{flip,4} &= 12012x^2 + 6007x + 8008, \\
p_{eqzero,1} &= 7293x^2 + 2432x, \\
p_{flip,1} &= 14586x^2 + x + 9724.
\end{aligned}
$$

Finally, the composition of the polynomials is $p(x) = 11968x^4 + 8041x^3 + 9207x^2 + 11056x + 8569$. It can be easily verified that $p(x)$ simulates the move $\delta(q_1, 0) = (q_1, 1, R)$ from the configuration $[q_1, 1, 00]$ correctly, i.e., $p(r) = s$.

To prove that the reachability problem is PSPACE-complete, it remains to prove that the problem can be solved in PSPACE.

Lemma 4. *The reachability problem for polynomial iteration is* PSPACE *for polynomials with integer coefficients.*

Proof. Consider the set $\mathcal{P}$ as a PRM with a single state and where the transitions are labelled by the polynomials of $\mathcal{P}$. The reachability problem for PRM can be solved in PSPACE and thus also the reachability problem for polynomial iteration is in PSPACE. □

We highlight some crucial observations from the proof that the reachability problem for PRM is in PSPACE of [6]. Firstly, most of the polynomials have monotonic behaviour when integers with large absolute values are evaluated, and this bound is of polynomial size. Secondly, the only polynomials that do not have monotonic behaviour are of the form $\pm x + b$ for some $b \in \mathbb{Z}$. They can be simulated by a one-dimensional vector addition system with states extracted from the given PRM.

Combining Lemmas 2 and 4, we have our main result.

Theorem 5. *The reachability problem for polynomial iteration is* PSPACE-*complete for polynomials with integer coefficients.*

Next, we extend the previous results by considering polynomials over the field $\mathbb{Q}$. Additionally, we modify the polynomials to ensure that the image is always in $[0, 1]$.

Let $p(x)$ be a polynomial from our set $\mathcal{P}$. Then, the corresponding set of rational polynomials $\mathcal{Q}$ has a polynomial $p'(x) = \frac{1}{p(\frac{1}{x})}$. It is easy to see that in fact p' is of the form $\frac{r(x)}{q(x)}$ for some $r(x), q(x) \in \mathbb{Z}[x]$. We can inherit the lower bound for the reachability for rational polynomials from Lemma 2.

Corollary 6. *The reachability problem for polynomial iteration is* PSPACE-*hard, when the polynomials are of form $\frac{r(x)}{q(x)} : [0, 1] \to [0, 1]$ over polynomial ring $\mathbb{Q}[x]$.*

Finally, we prove that the reachability problem for multidimensional polynomial iteration is undecidable. We construct a three-dimensional polynomials that simulate a two-dimensional PRM with affine updates with undecidable reachability problem [15].

Theorem 7. *The reachability problem for multidimensional polynomial iteration is undecidable already for three-dimensional polynomials.*

Proof. Let $\mathcal{M}$ be a two-dimensional PRM with affine updates and n states. Let $Q = \{q_1, \ldots, q_n\}$ be its states and Δ the set of transitions. Without loss of generality, we can assume that q_1 is the initial state and q_n is the final state. We construct a three-dimensional set of polynomials $\mathcal{P}$ such that the first two dimensions are updated as in $\mathcal{M}$ and the third dimension is used to simulate the state transition of $\mathcal{M}$. As in the beginning of the section, let p_i be the $(i+3)$-th prime number and P be the product of n primes $P = \prod_{i=1}^{n} p_i$. Intuitively, we will encode current state q_j into a residue class r satisfying $r \equiv 1 \mod p_j$ and $r \equiv 0 \mod p_\ell$ if $\ell \neq j$. Then a transition $q_j \to q_k$ is simulated by a polynomial corresponding to $\text{FLIP}_k \circ \text{FLIP}_j \circ \text{EQONE}_j$. By Lemma 1, such polynomials exist. More formally, for each transition $(q_j, (p_1(x), p_2(x)), q_k) \in \Delta$ the polynomial $(p_1(x), p_2(x), p_{flip,k}(p_{flip,j}(p_{eqone,j}(x))))$ is added to $\mathcal{P}$.

It is easy to see that $[q_1, (x_0, y_0)] \to^*_{\mathcal{M}} [q_n, (x_f, y_f)]$ if and only if (x_f, y_f, r_f) is reachable from (x_0, y_0, r_0), where r_0 is the residue class satisfying $r_0 \equiv 1 \mod p_1$ and $r_0 \equiv 0 \mod p_\ell$ if $\ell > 1$ and r_1 satisfies $r_f \equiv 1 \mod p_n$ and $r_f \equiv 0 \mod p_\ell$

if $\ell < n$. We add polynomials $p_-(x, y, z) = (x, y, z - P)$, $p_+(x, y, z) = (x, y, z + P)$ and $p(x, y, z) = (x, y, p_{flip,n}(p_{eqone,n}(z)))$ to $\mathcal{P}$ to reach $(0, 0, 0)$.

The reachability problem for two-dimensional PRM with affine updates is undecidable [15] and hence so is the reachability for three-dimensional polynomial iteration.   □

4   Conclusion

In this paper, we considered the reachability problem for polynomial iteration. We showed that for one-dimensional polynomials, the problem is PSPACE-complete and for three-dimensional polynomials it is undecidable. The remaining case of two-dimensional polynomials remains open.

It would be interesting to see how the techniques of the proof can be applied to polynomials over rational numbers. Corollary 6 provides a lower bound for polynomials in the interval $[0, 1]$ but the upper bound is not clear as there are infinite number of rational numbers in the interval. It is possible that p-adic norms used in similar settings in [3] can be useful to provide an upper bound, or at the very least, to prove decidability.

References

1. Bell, P., Potapov, I.: On undecidability bounds for matrix decision problems. Theor. Comput. Sci. **391**(1–2), 3–13 (2008). http://dx.doi.org/10.1016/j.tcs.2007.10.025
2. Ben-Amram, A.M.: Mortality of iterated piecewise affine functions over the integers: decidability and complexity. Computability **4**(1), 19–56 (2015). https://doi.org/10.3233/COM-150032
3. Bournez, O., Kurganskyy, O., Potapov, I.: Reachability problems for one-dimensional piecewise affine maps. Manuscript (2017)
4. Claus, V.: Some remarks on PCP(k) and related problems. Bull. EATCS **12**, 54–61 (1980)
5. Cucker, F., Koiran, P., Smale, S.: A polynomial time algorithm for diophantine equations in one variable. J. Symb. Comput. **27**(1), 21–29 (1999). https://doi.org/10.1006/jsco.1998.0242
6. Finkel, A., Göller, S., Haase, C.: Reachability in register machines with polynomial updates. In: Chatterjee, K., Sgall, J. (eds.) MFCS 2013. LNCS, vol. 8087, pp. 409–420. Springer, Heidelberg (2013). doi:10.1007/978-3-642-40313-2_37
7. Halava, V., Harju, T., Hirvensalo, M.: Undecidability bounds for integer matrices using Claus instances. Int. J. Found. Comput. Sci. **18**(5), 931–948 (2007). http://doi.org/10.1142/s0129054107005066
8. Halava, V., Hirvensalo, M.: Improved matrix pair undecidability results. Acta Inf. **44**(3), 191–205 (2007). http://dx.doi.org/10.1007/s00236-007-0047-y
9. Koiran, P., Cosnard, M., Garzon, M.H.: Computability with low-dimensional dynamical systems. Theor. Comput. Sci. **132**(2), 113–128 (1994). http://doi.org/10.1016/0304-3975(94)90229-1
10. Kurganskyy, O., Potapov, I.: Reachability problems for PAMs. In: Freivalds, R.M., Engels, G., Catania, B. (eds.) SOFSEM 2016. LNCS, vol. 9587, pp. 356–368. Springer, Heidelberg (2016). doi:10.1007/978-3-662-49192-8_29

11. Kurganskyy, O., Potapov, I., Sancho-Caparrini, F.: Reachability problems in low-dimensional iterative maps. Int. J. Found. Comput. Sci. **19**(4), 935–951 (2008). https://doi.org/10.1142/S0129054108006054

12. Kuroda, S.Y.: Classes of languages and linear-bounded automata. Inf. Control **7**(2), 207–223 (1964). http://doi.org/10.1016/s0019-9958(64)90120-2

13. Landweber, P.S.: Three theorems on phrase structure grammars of type 1. Inf. Control **6**(2), 131–136 (1963). http://doi.org/10.1016/s0019-9958(63)90169-4

14. Neary, T.: Undecidability in binary tag systems and the post correspondence problem for five pairs of words. In: STACS 2015. LIPIcs, pp. 649–661 (2015). http://doi.org/10.4230/LIPIcs.STACS.2015.649

15. Reichert, J.: Reachability Games with Counters: Decidability and Algorithms. Doctoral thesis, Laboratoire Spécification et Vérification, ENS Cachan, France (2015)

Probabilistic Timed Automata
with Clock-Dependent Probabilities

Jeremy Sproston[(✉)]

Dipartimento di Informatica, University of Turin, Turin, Italy
sproston@di.unito.it

Abstract. Probabilistic timed automata are classical timed automata extended with discrete probability distributions over edges. We introduce clock-dependent probabilistic timed automata, a variant of probabilistic timed automata in which transition probabilities can depend linearly on clock values. Clock-dependent probabilistic timed automata allow the modelling of a continuous relationship between time passage and the likelihood of system events. We show that the problem of deciding whether the maximum probability of reaching a certain location is above a threshold is undecidable for clock-dependent probabilistic timed automata. On the other hand, we show that the maximum and minimum probability of reaching a certain location in clock-dependent probabilistic timed automata can be approximated using a region-graph-based approach.

1 Introduction

Reactive systems are increasingly required to satisfy a combination of qualitative criteria (such as safety and liveness) and quantitative criteria (such as timeliness, reliability and performance). This trend has led to the development of techniques and tools for the formal verification of both qualitative and quantitative properties. In this paper, we consider a formalism for real-time systems that exhibit randomised behaviour, namely probabilistic timed automata (PTA) [10,17]. PTAs extend classical Alur-Dill timed automata [4] with discrete probabilistic branching over automata edges; alternatively a PTA can be viewed as a Markov decision process [20] or a Segala probabilistic automaton [21] extended with timed-automata-like clock variables and constraints over those clocks. PTAs have been used previously to model case studies including randomised protocols and scheduling problems with uncertainty [16,19], some of which have become standard benchmarks in the field of probabilistic model checking.

We recall briefly the behaviour of a PTA: as time passes, the model stays within a particular discrete state, and the values of its clocks increase at the same rate; at a certain point in time, the model can leave the discrete state if the current values of the clocks satisfy a constraint (called a guard) labelling one of the probability distributions over edges leaving the state; then a probabilistic choice as to which discrete state to then visit is made according to the chosen edge distribution. In the standard presentation of PTAs, any dependencies between time and probabilities over edges must be defined by utilising multiple

© Springer International Publishing AG 2017
M. Hague and I. Potapov (Eds.): RP 2017, LNCS 10506, pp. 144–159, 2017.
DOI: 10.1007/978-3-319-67089-8_11

distributions enabled with different sets of clock values. For example, to model the fact that a packet loss is more likely as time passes, we can use clock x to measure time, and two distributions μ_1 and μ_2 assigning probability λ_1 and λ_2 (for $\lambda_1 < \lambda_2$), respectively, to taking edges leading to a discrete state corresponding to packet loss, where the guard of μ_1 is $x \leq c$ and the guard of μ_2 is $x > c$, for some constant $c \in \mathbb{N}$. Hence, when the value of clock x is not more than c, a packet loss occurs with probability λ_1, otherwise it occurs with probability λ_2. A more direct way of expressing the relationship between time and probability would be letting the probability of making a transition to a discrete state representing packet loss be dependent on the value of the clock, i.e., let the value of this probability be equal to $f(x)$, where f is an increasing function from the values of x to probabilities. We note that such a kind of dependence of discrete branching probabilities on values of continuous variables is standard in the field of stochastic hybrid systems, for example in [1].

In this paper we consider such a formalism based on PTAs, in which all probabilities used by edge distributions can be expressed as functions of values of the clocks used by the model: the resulting formalism is called *clock-dependent probabilistic timed automata* (cdPTA). We focus on a simple class of functions from clock values to probabilities, namely those that can be expressed as sums of continuous piecewise linear functions, and consider a basic problem in the context of probabilistic model checking, namely probabilistic reachability: determine whether the maximum (respectively, minimum) probability of reaching a certain set of locations from the initial state is above (respectively, below) a threshold. After introducing cdPTAs (in Sect. 2), our first result (in Sect. 3) is that the probabilistic reachability problem is undecidable for cdPTA with a least three clocks. This result is inspired from recent related work on stochastic timed Markov decision processes [2]. Furthermore, we give an example of cdPTA with one clock for which the maximal probability of reaching a certain location involves a particular edge being taken when the clock has an irrational value. This suggests that classical techniques for partitioning the state space into a finite number of equivalence classes on the basis of a fixed, rational-numbered time granularity, such as the region graph [4] or the corner-point abstraction [8], cannot be applied directly to the case of cdPTA to obtain optimal reachability probabilities, because they rely on the fact that optimal choices can be made either at or arbitrarily closely to clock values that are multiples of the chosen rational-numbered time granularity. In Sect. 4, we present a conservative approximation method for cdPTA, i.e., maximum (respectively, minimum) probabilities are bounded from above (respectively, from below) in the approximation. This method is based on the region graph but uses concepts from the corner-point abstraction to define transition distributions. We show that successive refinement of the approximation, obtained by increasing the time granularity by a constant factor, does not lead to a more conservative approximation: in practice, in many cases such a refinement can lead to a substantial improvement in the computed probabilities, which we show using a small example.

2   Clock-Dependent Probabilistic Timed Automata

Preliminaries. We use $\mathbb{R}_{\geq 0}$ to denote the set of non-negative real numbers, $\mathbb{Q}$ to denote the set of rational numbers and $\mathbb{N}$ to denote the set of natural numbers. A (discrete) probability *distribution* over a countable set Q is a function $\mu : Q \to [0,1]$ such that $\sum_{q \in Q} \mu(q) = 1$. For a function $\mu : Q \to \mathbb{R}_{\geq 0}$ we define $\mathsf{support}(\mu) = \{q \in Q : \mu(q) > 0\}$. Then for an uncountable set Q we define $\mathsf{Dist}(Q)$ to be the set of functions $\mu : Q \to [0,1]$, such that $\mathsf{support}(\mu)$ is a countable set and μ restricted to $\mathsf{support}(\mu)$ is a (discrete) probability distribution. Given $q \in Q$, we use $\{q \mapsto 1\}$ to denote the distribution that assigns probability 1 to the single element q.

A *probabilistic transition system* (PTS) $\mathcal{T} = (S, \overline{s}, Act, \Delta)$ comprises the following components: a set S of *states* with an *initial state* $\overline{s} \in S$, a set Act of *actions*, and a *probabilistic transition relation* $\Delta \subseteq S \times Act \times \mathsf{Dist}(S)$. The sets of states, actions and the probabilistic transition relation can be uncountable. Transitions from state to state of a PTS are performed in two steps: if the current state is s, the first step concerns a nondeterministic selection of a probabilistic transition $(s, a, \mu) \in \Delta$; the second step comprises a probabilistic choice, made according to the distribution μ, as to which state to make the transition (that is, a transition to a state $s' \in S$ is made with probability $\mu(s')$). We denote such a completed transition by $s \xrightarrow{a,\mu} s'$. We assume that for each state $s \in S$ there exists some $(s, a, \mu) \in \Delta$.

An *infinite run* of the PTS $\mathcal{T}$ is an infinite sequence of consecutive transitions $r = s_0 \xrightarrow{a_0,\mu_0} s_1 \xrightarrow{a_1,\mu_1} \cdots$ (i.e., the target state of one transition is the source state of the next). Similarly, a *finite run* of $\mathcal{T}$ is a finite sequence of consecutive transitions $r = s_0 \xrightarrow{a_0,\mu_0} s_1 \xrightarrow{a_1,\mu_1} \cdots \xrightarrow{a_{n-1},\mu_{n-1}} s_n$. We use $InfRuns^{\mathcal{T}}$ to denote the set of infinite runs of $\mathcal{T}$, and $FinRuns^{\mathcal{T}}$ the set of finite runs of $\mathcal{T}$. If r is a finite run, we denote by $last(r)$ the last state of r. For any infinite run r and $i \in \mathbb{N}$, let $r(i) = s_i$ be the $(i+1)$th state along r. Let $InfRuns^{\mathcal{T}}(s)$ refer to the set of infinite runs of $\mathcal{T}$ commencing in state $s \in S$.

A *strategy* of a PTS $\mathcal{T}$ is a function σ mapping every finite run $r \in FinRuns^{\mathcal{T}}$ to a distribution in $\mathsf{Dist}(\Delta)$ such that $(s, a, \mu) \in \mathsf{support}(\sigma(r))$ implies that $s = last(r)$. From [11, Lemma 4.10], without loss of generality we can assume henceforth that strategies map to distributions assigning positive probability to finite sets of elements, i.e., strategies σ for which $|\mathsf{support}(\sigma(r))|$ is finite for all $r \in FinRuns^{\mathcal{T}}$. For any strategy σ, let $InfRuns^{\sigma}$ denote the set of infinite runs resulting from the choices of σ. For a state $s \in S$, let $InfRuns^{\sigma}(s) = InfRuns^{\sigma} \cap InfRuns^{\mathcal{T}}(s)$. Given a strategy σ and a state $s \in S$, we define the probability measure $\Pr_{\overline{s}}^{\sigma}$ over $InfRuns^{\sigma}(s)$ in the standard way [14].

Given a set $S_F \subseteq S$, define $\Diamond S_F = \{r \in InfRuns^{\mathcal{T}} : \exists i \in \mathbb{N} \text{ s.t. } r(i) \in S_F\}$ to be the set of infinite runs of $\mathcal{T}$ such that some state of S_F is visited along the run. Given a set $\Sigma' \subseteq \Sigma$ of strategies, we define the *maximum value over Σ'* with respect to S_F as $\mathbb{P}_{\mathcal{T},\Sigma'}^{\max}(S_F) = \sup_{\sigma \in \Sigma'} \Pr_{\overline{s}}^{\sigma}(\Diamond S_F)$. Similarly, the *minimum value over Σ'* with respect to S_F is defined as $\mathbb{P}_{\mathcal{T},\Sigma'}^{\min}(S_F) = \inf_{\sigma \in \Sigma'} \Pr_{\overline{s}}^{\sigma}(\Diamond S_F)$. The *maximal reachability problem* for $\mathcal{T}$, $S_F \subseteq S$, $\Sigma' \subseteq \Sigma$, $\trianglerighteq \in \{\geq, >\}$ and

$\lambda \in [0,1]$ is to decide whether $\mathbb{P}^{\max}_{\mathcal{T},\Sigma'}(S_F) \trianglerighteq \lambda$. Similarly, the *minimal reachability problem* for $\mathcal{T}$, $S_F \subseteq S$, $\Sigma' \subseteq \Sigma$, $\trianglelefteq \in \{\leq, <\}$ and $\lambda \in [0,1]$ is to decide whether $\mathbb{P}^{\min}_{\mathcal{T},\Sigma'}(S_F) \trianglelefteq \lambda$.

Clock-Dependent Probabilistic Timed Automata. Let $\mathcal{X}$ be a finite set of real-valued variables called *clocks*, the values of which increase at the same rate as real-time and which can be reset to 0. A function $v : \mathcal{X} \to \mathbb{R}_{\geq 0}$ is referred to as a *clock valuation* and the set of all clock valuations is denoted by $\mathbb{R}^{\mathcal{X}}_{\geq 0}$. For $v \in \mathbb{R}^{\mathcal{X}}_{\geq 0}$, $t \in \mathbb{R}_{\geq 0}$ and $X \subseteq \mathcal{X}$, we use $v+t$ to denote the clock valuation that increments all clock values in v by t, and $v[X{:=}0]$ to denote the clock valuation in which clocks in X are reset to 0.

For a set Q, a *distribution template* $\mathfrak{d} : \mathbb{R}^{\mathcal{X}}_{\geq 0} \to \mathsf{Dist}(Q)$ gives a distribution over Q for each clock valuation. In the following, we use notation $\mathfrak{d}[v]$, rather than $\mathfrak{d}(v)$, to denote the distribution corresponding to distribution template $\mathfrak{d}$ and clock valuation v. Let $\mathfrak{Dist}(Q)$ be the set of distribution templates over Q.

The set $CC(\mathcal{X})$ of *clock constraints* over $\mathcal{X}$ is defined as the set of conjunctions over atomic formulae of the form $x \sim c$, where $x \in \mathcal{X}$, $\sim \in \{<, \leq, \geq, >\}$, and $c \in \mathbb{N}$. A clock valuation v satisfies a clock constraint ψ, denoted by $v \models \psi$, if ψ resolves to **true** when substituting each occurrence of clock x with $v(x)$.

A *clock-dependent probabilistic timed automaton* (cdPTA) $\mathcal{P} = (L, \bar{l}, \mathcal{X}, inv, prob)$ comprises the following components: a finite set L of *locations* with an *initial location* $\bar{l} \in L$; a finite set $\mathcal{X}$ of clocks; a function $inv : L \to CC(\mathcal{X})$ associating an *invariant condition* with each location; a set $prob \subseteq L \times CC(\mathcal{X}) \times \mathfrak{Dist}(2^{\mathcal{X}} \times L)$ of *probabilistic edges*. A probabilistic edge $(l, g, \mathfrak{p}) \in prob$ comprises: (1) a source location l; (2) a clock constraint g, called a *guard*; and (3) a distribution template $\mathfrak{p}$ with respect to pairs of the form $(X, l') \in 2^{\mathcal{X}} \times L$ (i.e., pairs consisting of a set X of clocks to be reset and a target location l').

The behaviour of a cdPTA takes a similar form to that of a standard probabilistic timed automaton [10,17]: in any location time can advance as long as the invariant holds, and the choice as to how much time elapses is made nondeterministically; a probabilistic edge can be taken if its guard is satisfied by the current values of the clocks and, again, the choice as to which probabilistic edge to take is made nondeterministically; for a taken probabilistic edge, the choice of which clocks to reset and which target location to make the transition to is *probabilistic*. The key difference with cdPTAs is that the distribution used to make this probabilistic choice depends on the probabilistic edge taken *and* on the current clock valuation.

Example 1. In Fig. 1 we give an example of a cdPTA modelling a simple robot that must reach a certain geographical area and then carry out a particular task. The usual conventions for the graphical representation of timed automata are used in the figure. Black squares denote the distributions of probabilistic edges, and expressions on probabilities used by distribution templates are written with a grey background on their outgoing arcs. The robot can be in one of four

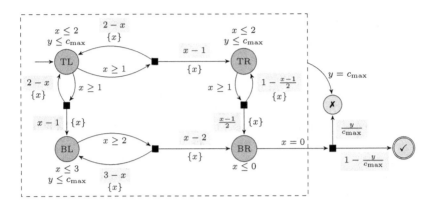

Fig. 1. A cdPTA modelling a simple robot example.

geographical areas, which can be thought of as cells in a 2×2 grid, each of which corresponds to a cdPTA location. The robot begins in the top-left cell (corresponding to location TL), and its objective is to reach the bottom-right cell (location BR). The robot can move either to the top-right cell (location TR), or to the bottom-left cell (location BL), then to the bottom-right cell. In each cell, the robot must wait a certain amount of time (1 time units in the top cells and 2 time units in the bottom-left cell) before attempting to leave the cell (for example, to recharge solar batteries), after which it can spend at most 1 time unit attempting to leave the cell. With a certain probability, the attempt to leave the cell will fail, and the robot must wait before trying to leave the cell again; the more time is dedicated to leaving the cell, the more likely the robot will succeed. Although passing through the top-right cell is not slower than passing through the bottom-left cell, the probability of leaving the cell successfully increases at a slower rate than in other cells (representing, for example, terrain in which the robot finds it difficult to navigate). On arrival in the bottom-right cell, the robot successfully carries out its task with a probability that is inversely proportional to the total time elapsed (for example, the robot could be transporting medical supplies, the efficacy of which may be inversely proportional to the time elapsed). The clock x is used to represent the amount of time used by the robot in its attempt to move from cell to cell, whereas the clock y represents the total amount of time since the start of the robot's mission. If the clock y reaches its maximum amount $c_{\max}$, then the mission fails (as denoted by the edge to the location denoted by ✗, which is available in locations TL, TR, BL and BR, as indicated by the dashed box). The objective of the robot's controller is to maximise the probability of reaching the location denoted by ✓. Note that there is a trade-off between dedicating more time to movement between the cells, which increases the probability of successful navigation and therefore progress towards the target point, and spending less time on the overall mission, which increases the probability of carrying out the required task at the target point. □

A *state* of a cdPTA is a pair comprising a location and a clock valuation satisfying the location's invariant condition, i.e., $(l, v) \in L \times \mathbb{R}^{\mathcal{X}}_{\geq 0}$ such that $v \models inv(l)$. In any state (l, v), either a certain amount of time $\delta \in \mathbb{R}_{>0}$ elapses, or a probabilistic edge is traversed. If time elapses, then the choice of δ requires that the invariant $inv(l)$ remains continuously satisfied while time passes. The resulting state after this transition is $(l, v+\delta)$. A probabilistic edge $(l', g, \mathfrak{p}) \in prob$ can be chosen from (l, v) if $l = l'$ and it is *enabled*, i.e., the clock constraint g is satisfied by v. Once a probabilistic edge $(l, g, \mathfrak{p})$ is chosen, a set of clocks to reset and a successor location are selected at random, according to the distribution $\mathfrak{p}[v]$.

We make a number of assumptions concerning the cdPTA models considered. Firstly, we restrict our attention to cdPTAs for which it is always possible to take a probabilistic edge, either immediately or after letting time elapse. This condition holds generally for PTA models in practice [16]. A sufficient syntactic condition for this property has been presented formally in [12]. Secondly, we consider cdPTAs that feature invariant conditions that prevent clock values from exceeding some bound: formally, for each location $l \in L$, we have that $inv(l)$ contains a constraint of the form $x \leq c$ or $x < c$ for each clock $x \in \mathcal{X}$. Thirdly, we assume that all possible target states of probabilistic edges satisfy their invariants: for all probabilistic edges $(l, g, \mathfrak{p}) \in prob$, for all clock valuations $v \in \mathbb{R}^{\mathcal{X}}_{\geq 0}$ such that $v \models g$, and for all $(X, l') \in 2^{\mathcal{X}} \times L$, we have that $\mathfrak{p}[v](X, l') > 0$ implies $v[X := 0] \models inv(l')$. Finally, we assume that any clock valuation that satisfies the guard of a probabilistic edge also satisfies the invariant of the source location: this can be achieved, without changing the underlying semantic PTS, by replacing each probabilistic edge $(l, g, \mathfrak{p}) \in prob$ by $(l, g \wedge inv(l), \mathfrak{p})$.

Let $\mathbf{0} \in \mathbb{R}^{\mathcal{X}}_{\geq 0}$ be the clock valuation which assigns 0 to all clocks in $\mathcal{X}$. The semantics of the cdPTA $\mathcal{P} = (L, \bar{l}, \mathcal{X}, inv, prob)$ is the PTS $[\![\mathcal{P}]\!] = (S, \bar{s}, Act, \Delta)$ where:

- $S = \{(l, v) : l \in L \text{ and } v \in \mathbb{R}^{\mathcal{X}}_{\geq 0} \text{ s.t. } v \models inv(l)\}$ and $\bar{s} = \{(\bar{l}, \mathbf{0})\}$;
- $Act = \mathbb{R}_{\geq 0} \cup prob$;
- $\Delta = \vec{\Delta} \cup \widehat{\Delta}$, where $\vec{\Delta} \subseteq S \times \mathbb{R}_{\geq 0} \times \text{Dist}(S)$ and $\widehat{\Delta} \subseteq S \times prob \times \text{Dist}(S)$ such that:
  - $\vec{\Delta}$ is the smallest set such that $((l, v), \delta, \{(l, v + \delta) \mapsto 1\}) \in \vec{\Delta}$ if there exists $\delta \in \mathbb{R}_{\geq 0}$ such that $v + \delta' \models inv(l)$ for all $0 \leq \delta' \leq \delta$;
  - $\widehat{\Delta}$ is the smallest set such that $((l, v), (l, g, \mathfrak{p}), \mu) \in \widehat{\Delta}$ if
    1. $v \models g$;
    2. for any $(l', v') \in S$, we have $\mu(l', v') = \sum_{X \in \text{Reset}(v, v')} \mathfrak{p}[v](X, l')$, where $\text{Reset}(v, v') = \{X \subseteq \mathcal{X} \mid v[X := 0] = v'\}$.

When considering maximum and minimum values for cdPTAs, we henceforth consider strategies that alternate between transitions from $\vec{\Delta}$ (time elapse transitions) and transitions from $\widehat{\Delta}$ (probabilistic edge transitions). Formally, a *cdPTA strategy* σ is a strategy such that, for a finite run $r \in FinRuns^{[\![\mathcal{P}]\!]}$ that has $s \xrightarrow{a, \mu} s'$ as its final transition, either $(s, a, \mu) \in \vec{\Delta}$ and $\text{support}(\sigma(r)) \in \widehat{\Delta}$, or $(s, a, \mu) \in \widehat{\Delta}$ and $\text{support}(\sigma(r)) \in \vec{\Delta}$. We write Σ for the set of cdPTA strategies

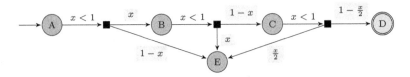

Fig. 2. A one-clock cdPTA for which the maximum probability is attained by a time delay corresponding to an irrational number.

of $[\![\mathcal{P}]\!]$. Given a set $F \subseteq L$ of locations, subsequently called *target locations*, we let $S_F = \{(l,v) \in S : l \in F\}$. Let $\unrhd \in \{\geq, >\}$, $\unlhd \in \{\leq, <\}$ and $\lambda \in [0,1]$: then the maximal (respectively, minimal) reachability problem for cdPTA is to decide whether $\mathbb{P}^{\max}_{[\![\mathcal{P}]\!],\Sigma}(S_F) \unrhd \lambda$ (respectively, $\mathbb{P}^{\min}_{[\![\mathcal{P}]\!],\Sigma}(S_F) \unlhd \lambda$).

Piecewise Linear Clock Dependencies. In this paper, we concentrate on a particular subclass of distribution templates based on continuous piecewise linear functions. Let $x \in \mathcal{X}$ be a clock and $p = (l,g,\mathfrak{p}) \in prob$ be a probabilistic edge. Let I^p_x be the interval containing the values of x of clock valuations that satisfy g: formally $I^p_x = \{v(x) \in \mathbb{R}_{\geq 0} : v \in \mathbb{R}^{\mathcal{X}}_{\geq 0} \text{ s.t. } v \models g\}$. For example, for $g = (x \geq 3) \wedge (x < 5) \wedge (y \leq 8)$, we have $I^p_x = [3,5)$ and $I^p_y = [0,8]$. We equip each probabilistic edge $p = (l,g,\mathfrak{p}) \in prob$ and $e = (X,l') \in 2^{\mathcal{X}} \times L$ with a continuous piecewise linear function $f^{p,e}_x$ with domain I^p_x for each clock $x \in \mathcal{X}$. Formally, we consider a partition $\mathcal{I}^{p,e}_x$ of I^p_x (i.e., $\bigcup_{I \in \mathcal{I}^{p,e}_x} I = I^p_x$ and $I \cap I' = \emptyset$ for each $I, I' \in \mathcal{I}^{p,e}_x$ such that $I \neq I'$), and sets $\{c^{p,e}_{x,I}\}_{I \in \mathcal{I}^{p,e}_x}$ and $\{d^{p,e}_{x,I}\}_{I \in \mathcal{I}^{p,e}_x}$ of constants in $\mathbb{Q}$ such that: (a) for every $I \in \mathcal{I}^{p,e}_x$ and $\gamma \in I$, we have $f^{p,e}_x(\gamma) = c^{p,e}_{x,I} + d^{p,e}_{x,I} \cdot \gamma$; (b) $f^{p,e}_x$ is continuous (i.e., for each $\gamma \in I^p_x$, we have $\lim_{\zeta \to \gamma} f^{p,e}_x(\zeta) = f^{p,e}_x(\gamma)$). We make the following assumptions for each probabilistic edge $p \in prob$: (1) all endpoints of intervals in $\mathcal{I}^{p,e}_x$ are natural numbers, for all clocks $x \in \mathcal{X}$ and $e \in 2^{\mathcal{X}} \times L$; (2) $\sum_{x \in \mathcal{X}} f^{p,e}_x(v(x)) \in [0,1]$ for each $e \in 2^{\mathcal{X}} \times L$ and $v \in \mathbb{R}^{\mathcal{X}}_{\geq 0}$ such that $v \models g$; (3) $\sum_{e \in 2^{\mathcal{X}} \times L} \sum_{x \in \mathcal{X}} f^{p,e}_x(v(x)) = 1$ for each $v \in \mathbb{R}^{\mathcal{X}}_{\geq 0}$ such that $v \models g$. Then the probabilistic edge p is *piecewise linear* if, for each $e \in 2^{\mathcal{X}} \times L$ and each $v \in \mathbb{R}^{\mathcal{X}}_{\geq 0}$ such that $v \models g$, we have $\mathfrak{p}[v](e) = \sum_{x \in \mathcal{X}} f^{p,e}_x(v(x))$. We assume henceforth that all probabilistic edges of cdPTAs are piecewise linear.

Example 2. Standard methods for the analysis of timed automata typically consist of a finite-state system that represents faithfully the original model. In particular, the region graph [4] and the corner-point abstraction [8] both involve the division of the state space according to a fixed, rational-numbered granularity. The example of a one-clock cdPTA $\mathcal{P}$ of Fig. 2 shows that such an approach cannot be used for the exact computation of optimal reachability probabilities in cdPTAs, because optimality may be attained when the clock has an irrational value. For an example of the formal description of a piecewise linear probabilistic edge, consider the probabilistic edge from location C, which we denote by p_C: then we have $\mathcal{I}^{p_C,(\emptyset,D)}_x = \mathcal{I}^{p_C,(\emptyset,E)}_x = \{[0,1)\}$, with $c^{p_C,(\emptyset,D)}_{x,[0,1)} = 1$, $d^{p_C,(\emptyset,D)}_{x,[0,1)} = -\frac{1}{2}$, $c^{p_C,(\emptyset,E)}_{x,[0,1)} = 0$, and $d^{p_C,(\emptyset,E)}_{x,[0,1)} = \frac{1}{2}$. Now consider the maximum probability of reaching location D (that is, $\mathbb{P}^{\max}_{[\![\mathcal{P}]\!],\Sigma}(S_{\{D\}})$). Intuitively, the longer the cdPTA remains in location A, the lower the probability of making a transition to location E from A, but the higher the probability of making a transition to E from B and C. Note that, after A is left, the choice resulting in the maximum probability of reaching D is to take the outgoing transitions from B and C as soon as possible (delaying in B and C will increase the value of x, therefore increasing the probability of making a transition to E). Denoting by δ the amount of time elapsed in A, the maximum probability of reaching D is equal to $\delta(1-\delta)(1-\frac{\delta}{2})$, which (within the interval $[0,1)$) reaches its maximum at $1 - \frac{\sqrt{3}}{3}$. Hence, this example indicates that abstractions based on the optimality of choices made at (or arbitrarily close to) rational-numbered clock values (such as the region graph or corner-point abstraction) do not yield exact analysis methods for cdPTAs. □

3   Undecidability of Maximal Reachability of cdPTAs

Theorem 1. *The maximal reachability problem is undecidable for cdPTAs with at least 3 clocks.*

Proof (sketch). We proceed by reducing the non-halting problem for two-counter machines to the maximal reachability problem for cdPTAs. The reduction has close similarities to a reduction presented in [2].

A two-counter machine $\mathcal{M} = (\mathcal{L}, \mathcal{C})$ comprises a set $\mathcal{L} = \{\ell_1, ..., \ell_n\}$ of instructions and a set $\mathcal{C} = \{c_1, c_2\}$ of counters. The instructions are of the following form (for $1 \leq i, j, k \leq n$ and $l \in \{1, 2\}$):

1. $\ell_i : c_l := c_l + 1$; goto ℓ_j (increment c_l);
2. $\ell_i : c_l := c_l - 1$; goto ℓ_j (decrement c_l);
3. $\ell_i :$ if $(c_l > 0)$ them goto ℓ_j else goto ℓ_k (zero check c_l);
4. $\ell_n :$ HALT (halting instruction).

A configuration (ℓ, v_1, v_2) of a two-counter machine comprises an instruction ℓ and values v_1 and v_2 of counters c_1 and c_2, respectively. A run of a two-counter machine consists of a finite or infinite sequence of configurations, starting from configuration $(\ell_1, 0, 0)$, and where subsequent configurations are successively generated by following the rule specified in the associated configuration. A run is finite if and only if the final instruction visited along the run is ℓ_n (the halting instruction). The halting problem for two-counter machines concerns determining whether the unique run of the two-counter machine is finite, and is undecidable [18]; hence the non-halting problem (determining whether the unique run of the two-counter machine is infinite) is also undecidable.

Consider a two-counter machine $\mathcal{M}$. We reduce the non-halting problem for $\mathcal{M}$ to the maximal reachability problem in the following way. We construct a cdPTA $\mathcal{P}_{\mathcal{M}}$ with three clocks $\{x_1, x_2, x_3\}$ by considering modules for each form that the instructions of a two-counter machine can take. On entry to each module, we have that $x_1 = \frac{1}{2^{c_1}}$, $x_2 = \frac{1}{2^{c_2}}$ and $x_3 = 0$. The module for simulating an increment instruction is shown in Fig. 3. In location ℓ_i, there is a delay of

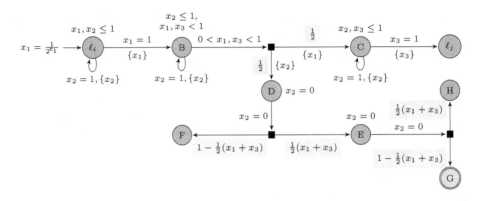

Fig. 3. The cdPTA module for simulating an increment instruction for counter c_1.

$1 - \frac{1}{2^{c_1}}$, and hence the values of the clocks on entry to location B are $x_1 = 0$, $x_2 = \frac{1}{2^{c_2}} + 1 - \frac{1}{2^{c_1}}$ mod 1 and $x_3 = 1 - \frac{1}{2^{c_1}}$. A nondeterministic choice is then made concerning the amount of time that elapses in location B: note that this amount must be in the interval $(0, \frac{1}{2^{c_1}})$. In order to correctly simulate the increment of counter c_1, the choice of delay in location B should be equal to $\frac{1}{2^{c_1+1}}$. On leaving location B, a probabilistic choice is made: the rightward outcome corresponds to continuing the simulation of the two-counter machine, whereas the downward outcome corresponds to checking that the delay in location B was correctly $\frac{1}{2^{c_1+1}}$. We write the delay in location B as $\frac{1}{2^{c_1+1}} + \epsilon$, where $-\frac{1}{2^{c_1+1}} < \epsilon < \frac{1}{2^{c_1+1}}$: hence, for a correct simulation of the increment of c_1, we require that $\epsilon = 0$.

Consider the case in which the downward outcome (from the outgoing probabilistic edge of location B) is taken: then the cdPTA fragment from location D has the role of checking whether $\epsilon = 0$. Note that, after entering location D, no time elapses in locations D and E (as enforced by the reset of x_2 to zero and the invariant condition $x_2 = 0$), and hence both clocks x_1 and x_3 retain the same values that they had when location B was left. We show that the probability of reaching the target location G from location D is $\frac{1}{4} - \epsilon^2$, and hence equal to $\frac{1}{4}$ if and only if $\epsilon = 0$. To see that the probability of reaching G from D is $\frac{1}{4} - \epsilon^2$, observe that the probability is equal to $\frac{1}{2}(x_1 + x_3) = \frac{1}{2}(\frac{1}{2^{c_1+1}} + \epsilon + (1 - \frac{1}{2^{c_1+1}}) + \epsilon) = \frac{1}{2} + \epsilon$ multiplied by $1 - \frac{1}{2}(x_1 + x_3) = \frac{1}{2} - \epsilon$, i.e., equal to $\frac{1}{4} - \epsilon^2$. Hence the probability of reaching location G from location D is equal to $\frac{1}{4}$ if and only if $\epsilon = 0$ (otherwise, the probability is less than $\frac{1}{4}$).

The module for simulating a decrement instruction is shown in Fig. 4. In a similar manner to the cdPTA fragment in Fig. 3 for the simulation of an increment instruction, the only nondeterministic choice made is with regard to the amount of time spent in location ℓ_i, which is denoted by δ. For the correct simulation of the decrement instruction, δ should equal $1 - \frac{1}{2^{c_1-1}}$. The rightward outcome is taken from the probabilistic edge leaving location ℓ_i corresponds to the continuation of the simulation of the two-counter machine: hence, on entry

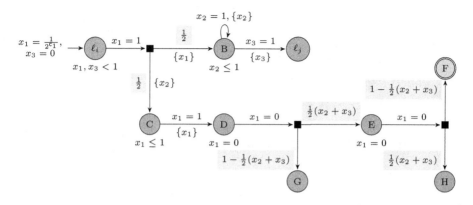

Fig. 4. The cdPTA module for simulating a decrement instruction for counter c_1.

to location B, we have $x_1 = 0$, $x_2 = \frac{1}{2^{c_2}} + \delta$ and $x_3 = \delta$; then, on entry to location ℓ_j, we have $x_1 = \delta$, $x_2 = \frac{1}{2^{c_2}}$ and $x_3 = 0$.

Let $\delta = 1 - \frac{1}{2^{c_1 - 1}} + \epsilon$. For the correct simulation of the decrement instruction, we require that $\epsilon = 0$. The downward outcome from the probabilistic edge leaving location ℓ_i corresponds to checking that $\epsilon = 0$, and takes a similar form to the analogous downward edge of the cdPTA fragment for the increment instruction, as shown in Fig. 3. Note that, on entry to location C, we have that $x_1 = 1 - \frac{1}{2^{c_1}} + \epsilon$, $x_2 = 0$ and $x_3 = 1 - \frac{1}{2^{c_1 - 1}} + \epsilon$. Then, on entry to location D, we have that $x_1 = 0$, $x_2 = \frac{1}{2^{c_1}} - \epsilon$ and $x_3 = 1 - \frac{1}{2^{c_1}}$. As no time elapses in locations D and E, we have that target location F is then reached with probability $\frac{1}{2}(x_2 + x_3) = \frac{1}{2}(\frac{1}{2^{c_1}} - \epsilon + 1 - \frac{1}{2^{c_1}}) = \frac{1}{2} + \frac{\epsilon}{2}$ multiplied by the probability $1 - \frac{1}{2}(x_2 + x_3) = \frac{1}{2} - \frac{\epsilon}{2}$, which equals $\frac{1}{4} - \frac{\epsilon^2}{4}$. Hence we conclude that the probability of reaching location F from location C is equal to $\frac{1}{4}$ if and only if $\epsilon = 0$.

Finally, the module for a zero test instruction ℓ_i : if $(c_1 > 0)$ then goto ℓ_j else goto ℓ_k is shown in Fig. 5. The module is almost identical to that of [3], and we present it here only for completeness. After entry to location ℓ_i, two probabilistic edges are enabled: the rightward one is taken if $c_1 = 0$ (i.e., if $x_1 = \frac{1}{2^0} = 1$), whereas the leftward one is taken otherwise. Both probabilistic edges involve an outcome leading to a target location with probability $\frac{1}{4}$: if this outcome is not taken, the cdPTA fragment then proceeds to location ℓ_j or ℓ_j, depending on which probabilistic edge was taken.

Given the construction of a cdPTA simulating the two-counter machine using the modules described above, we can now proceed to show Theorem 1. The reasoning is the same as that of Lemma 5 of [2]. If the two-counter machine halts in k steps, and the strategy of the cdPTA correctly simulates the two-counter machine the probability of reaching a target location will be $\frac{1}{2} \cdot \frac{1}{4} + (\frac{1}{2})^2 \cdot \frac{1}{4} + ... + (\frac{1}{2})^k \cdot \frac{1}{4} < \frac{1}{4}$. If the two-counter machine halts in k steps, and the strategy of the cdPTA does not correctly simulate the two-counter machine, then this means that the probability of reaching a target location is strictly less than that corresponding to correct simulation, given that deviation from simulation of a certain step

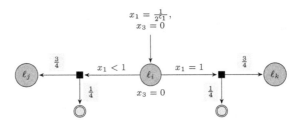

Fig. 5. The cdPTA module for simulating a zero-test instruction for counter c_1.

corresponds to reaching the target locations with probability strictly less than $\frac{1}{4}$ in that step. Now consider the case in which the two-counter machine does not halt: in this case, faithful simulation in the cdPTA corresponds to reaching target locations with probability $\sum_{i=1}^{\infty}(\frac{1}{2})^i \cdot \frac{1}{4} = \frac{1}{4}$, whereas unfaithful simulation in the cdPTA corresponds to reaching the target locations with probability $\sum_{i=1}^{\infty}(\frac{1}{2})^i \cdot \gamma_i$ where $\gamma_i \leq \frac{1}{4}$ for all $i \in \mathbb{N}$ and $\gamma_j < \frac{1}{4}$ for at least one $j \in \mathbb{N}$, and hence $\sum_{i=1}^{\infty}(\frac{1}{2})^i \cdot \gamma_i < \frac{1}{4}$. Therefore the two-counter machine does not halt if and only if there exists a strategy in the constructed cdPTA that reaches the target locations with probability at least $\frac{1}{4}$, concluding the proof of Theorem 1.   □

4   Approximation of Reachability Probabilities

We now consider the approximation of maximal and minimal reachability probabilities of cdPTAs. Our approach is to utilise concepts from the corner-point abstraction [8]. However, while the standard corner-point abstraction is a finite-state system that extends the classical region graph by encoding corner points within states, the states of our finite-state system correspond to regions, and we use corners of regions only to define available distributions. Furthermore, in contrast to the widespread use of the corner-point abstraction in the context of weighted (or priced) timed automata (see [7] for a survey), and in line with the undecidability results presented in Sect. 3, our variant of the corner-point abstraction does not result in a finite-state system that can be used to obtain a quantitative measure that is arbitrarily close to the actual one: in the context of cdPTAs, we will present a method that approximates maximal and minimal reachability properties, and show that successive refinement of regions leads to a more accurate approximation.

First we define regions and corner points. Let $\mathcal{P} = (L, \bar{l}, \mathcal{X}, inv, prob)$ be a cdPTA, which we assume to be fixed throughout this section, and let $M \in \mathbb{N}$ denote the upper bound on clocks in $\mathcal{P}$. We choose $k \in \mathbb{N}$, which we will refer to as the *(time) granularity*, and let $[k] = \{\frac{c}{k} : c \in \mathbb{N}\}$ be the set of multiples of $\frac{1}{k}$. A *k-region* $(h, [X_0, ..., X_n])$ over $\mathcal{X}$ comprises:

1. a function $h : \mathcal{X} \rightarrow ([k] \cap [0, M])$ assigning a multiple of $\frac{1}{k}$ no greater than M to each clock and

2. a partition $[X_0, ..., X_n]$ of $\mathcal{X}$, where $X_i \neq \emptyset$ for all $1 \leq i \leq n$ and $h(x) = M$ implies $x \in X_0$ for all $x \in \mathcal{X}$.

Given clock valuation $v \in \mathbb{R}_{\geq 0}^{\mathcal{X}}$ and granularity k, the k-region $R = (h, [X_0, ..., X_n])$ containing v (written $v \in R$) satisfies the following conditions:

1. $\lfloor k \cdot v(x) \rfloor = k \cdot h(x)$ for all clocks $x \in \mathcal{X}$;
2. $v(x) = h(x)$ for all clocks $x \in X_0$;
3. $k \cdot v(x) - \lfloor k \cdot v(x) \rfloor \leq k \cdot v(y) - \lfloor k \cdot v(y) \rfloor$ if and only if $x \in X_i$ and $y \in X_j$ with $i \leq j$, for all clocks $x, y \in \mathcal{X}$.

Note that, rather than considering regions delimited by valuations corresponding to natural numbers, in our definition regions are delimited by valuations corresponding to multiples of $\frac{1}{k}$. We use Regs_k to denote the set of k-regions. For $R, R' \in \mathsf{Regs}_k$ and clock constraint $\psi \in CC(\mathcal{X})$, we say that R' is a ψ-satisfying time successor of R if there exist $v \in R$ and $\delta \in \mathbb{R}_{\geq 0}$ such that $(v+\delta) \in R'$ and $(v+\delta') \models \psi$ for all $0 \leq \delta' \leq \delta$. For a given k-region $R \in \mathsf{Regs}_k$, we let $R[X := 0]$ be the k-region that corresponds to resetting clocks in X to 0 from clock valuations in R (that is, $R[X := 0]$ contains valuations $v[X := 0]$ for $v \in R$). We use R_0 to denote the k-region that contains the valuation $\mathbf{0}$.

A *corner point* $\alpha = \langle a_i \rangle_{0 \leq i \leq n} \in ([k] \cap [0, M])^n$ of k-region $(h, [X_0, ..., X_n])$ is defined by:

$$a_i(x) = \begin{cases} h(x) & \text{if } x \in X_j \text{ with } j \leq i \\ h(x) + \frac{1}{k} & \text{if } x \in X_j \text{ with } j > i . \end{cases}$$

Note that a k-region $(h, [X_0, ..., X_n])$ is associated with $n+1$ corner points. Let $\mathsf{CP}(R)$ be the set of corner points of k-region R. Given granularity k, we let $\mathsf{CornerPoints}_k$ be the set of all corner points.

Next we define the *clock-dependent region graph with granularity k* as the finite-state PTS $\mathcal{A}_k = (\mathsf{S}_k, \bar{\mathsf{s}}, \mathsf{Act}_k, \Gamma_k)$, where $\mathsf{S}_k = L \times \mathsf{Regs}_k$, $\bar{\mathsf{s}} = (\bar{l}, R_0)$, $\mathsf{Act}_k = \{\tau\} \cup (\mathsf{CornerPoints}_k \times prob)$, and $\Gamma_k = \overrightarrow{\Gamma_k} \cup \widehat{\Gamma_k}$ where $\overrightarrow{\Gamma_k} \subseteq \mathsf{S}_k \times \{\tau\} \times \mathsf{Dist}(\mathsf{S}_k)$ and $\widehat{\Gamma_k} \subseteq \mathsf{S}_k \times \mathsf{CornerPoints}_k \times prob \times \mathsf{Dist}(\mathsf{S}_k)$ such that:

- $\overrightarrow{\Gamma_k}$ is the smallest set of transitions such that $((l, R), \tau, \{(l, R') \mapsto 1\}) \in \overrightarrow{\Gamma_k}$ if (l, R') is an $inv(l)$-satisfying time successor of (l, R);
- $\widehat{\Gamma_k}$ is the smallest set such that $((l, R), (\alpha, (l, g, \mathsf{p})), \nu) \in \widehat{\Gamma_k}$ if:
  1. $R \models g$;
  2. $\alpha \in \mathsf{CP}(R)$;
  3. for any $(l', R') \in \mathsf{S}_k$, we have that $\nu(l', R') = \sum_{X \in \mathsf{Reset}(R,R')} \mathsf{p}[\alpha](X, l')$, where $\mathsf{Reset}(R, R') = \{X \subseteq \mathcal{X} \mid R[X := 0] = R'\}$.

Hence the clock-dependent region graph of a cdPTA encodes corner points within (probabilistic-edge-based) transitions, in contrast to the corner-point abstraction, which encodes corner points within states. In fact, a literal application of the standard corner-point abstraction, as presented in [7], does not result in a conservative approximation, which we now explain with reference to Example 2.

Example 2 (continued). Recall that the states of the corner-point abstraction comprise a location, a region and a corner point of the region, and transitions maintain consistency between corner points of the source and target states. For example, for the cdPTA of Fig. 2, consider the state $(A, 0 < x < 1, x = 1)$, where $0 < x < 1$ is used to refer to the state's region component and $x = 1$ is used to refer to the state's corner point. Then the probabilistic edge leaving location A is enabled (because the state represents the situation in which clock x is in the interval $(0, 1)$ and arbitrarily close to 1). Standard intuition on the corner-point abstraction (adapted from weights in [7] to probabilities in distribution templates in this paper) specifies that, when considering probabilities of outgoing probabilistic edges, the state $(A, 0 < x < 1, x = 1)$ should be associated with probabilities for which $x = 1$. Hence the probability of making a transition to location B is 1, and the target corner-point-abstraction state is $(B, 0 < x < 1, x = 1)$. However, now consider the probabilistic edge leaving location B: in this case, given that the corner point under consideration is $x = 1$, the probability of making a transition to location C is 0, and hence the target location D is reachable with probability 0. Furthermore, consider the state $(A, 0 < x < 1, x = 0)$: in this case, if the probabilistic edge leaving location A is taken, then location B is reached with probability 0, and hence location D is again reachable with probability 0. We can conclude that such a direct application of the corner-point abstraction to cdPTA is not a conservative approximation of the cdPTA, because the maximum reachability probability in the corner-point abstraction is 0, i.e., less than the maximum reachability probability of the cdPTA (which we recall is $1 - \frac{\sqrt{3}}{3}$). Instead, in our definition of the clock-dependent region graph, we allow "inconsistent" corner points to be used in successive transitions: for example, from location A, the outgoing probabilistic edge can be taken using the value of x corresponding to the corner point $x = 1$; then, from locations B and C, the outgoing probabilistic edge can be taken using corner point $x = 0$. Hence maximum probability of reaching the target location D, with $k = 1$, is 1.   □

Analogously to the case of cdPTA strategies, we consider strategies of clock-dependent region graphs that alternate between transitions from $\overrightarrow{\Gamma_k}$ (time elapse transitions) and transitions from $\widehat{\Gamma_k}$ (probabilistic edge transitions). Formally, a *region graph strategy* σ is a strategy of $\mathcal{A}_k$ such that, for a finite run $r \in FinRuns^{\mathcal{A}_k}$ that has $(l, R) \xrightarrow{a, \nu} (l', R')$ as its final transition, either $((l, R), a, \nu) \in \overrightarrow{\Gamma_k}$ and $\mathsf{support}(\sigma(r)) \in \widehat{\Gamma_k}$, or $((l, R), a, \nu) \in \widehat{\Gamma_k}$ and $\mathsf{support}(\sigma(r)) \in \overrightarrow{\Gamma_k}$. We write $\mathbf{\Pi}_k$ for the set of region graph strategies of $\mathcal{A}_k$.

Let $F \subseteq L$ be the set of target locations, which we assume to be fixed in the following. Recall that $S_F = \{(l, v) \in L \times \mathbb{R}^{\mathcal{X}}_{\geq 0} : l \in F\}$ and let $\mathsf{Regs}^F_k = \{(l, R) \in S_k : l \in F\}$. The following result specifies that the maximum (minimum) probability for reaching target locations from the initial state of a cdPTA is bounded from above (from below, respectively) by the corresponding maximum (minimum, respectively) probability in the clock-dependent region graph with granularity k. Similarly, the maximum (minimum) probability computed in the region graph of granularity k is an upper (lower, respectively) bound on the maximum (minimum, respectively) probability computed in the

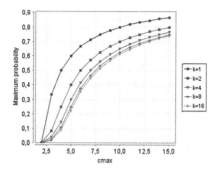

Fig. 6. Maximum probability of reaching location ✓ in the cdPTA of Fig. 1.

region graph of granularity $2k$ (we note that this result can be adapted to hold for granularity ck rather than $2k$, for any $c \in \mathbb{N} \setminus \{0, 1\}$). The proof of the proposition can be found in [22].

Proposition 1

1. $\mathbb{P}^{\max}_{[\mathcal{P}], \Sigma}(S_F) \leq \mathbb{P}^{\max}_{\mathcal{A}_k, \Pi_k}(\text{Regs}^F_k)$, $\mathbb{P}^{\min}_{[\mathcal{P}], \Sigma}(S_F) \geq \mathbb{P}^{\min}_{\mathcal{A}_k, \Pi_k}(\text{Regs}^F_k)$.
2. $\mathbb{P}^{\max}_{\mathcal{A}_{2k}, \Pi_{2k}}(\text{Regs}^F_{2k}) \leq \mathbb{P}^{\max}_{\mathcal{A}_k, \Pi_k}(\text{Regs}^F_k)$, $\mathbb{P}^{\min}_{\mathcal{A}_{2k}, \Pi_{2k}}(\text{Regs}^F_{2k}) \geq \mathbb{P}^{\min}_{\mathcal{A}_k, \Pi_k}(\text{Regs}^F_k)$.

Example 2 (continued). We give the intuition underlying Proposition 1 using Example 2 (Fig. 2), considering the maximum probability of reaching the target location D. When $k = 1$, as described above, the maximum probability of reaching D is 1. Instead, for $k = 2$, the maximum probability of reaching location D corresponds to taking the probabilistic edge from location A for the corner point $x = \frac{1}{2}$ corresponding to the 2-region $0 < x < \frac{1}{2}$ and the probabilistic edges from locations B and C for corner point $x = 0$, again for the 2-region $0 < x < \frac{1}{2}$ i.e., the probability is $\frac{1}{2}$. With granularity $k = 4$, the maximum probability of reaching location D is 0.328125, obtained by taking the probabilistic edge from A for the corner point $x = \frac{1}{2}$, and the probabilistic edges from B and C for corner point $x = \frac{1}{4}$, where the 4-region used in all cases is $\frac{1}{4} < x < \frac{1}{2}$. □

Example 1 (continued). In Fig. 6 we plot the values of the maximum probability of reaching location ✓ in the example of Fig. 1 for various values of $c_{\max}$ and k, obtained by encoding the clock-dependent region graph as a finite-state PTS and using PRISM [15]. For this example, the difference between the probabilities obtained from low values of k is substantial. We note that the number of states of the largest instance that we considered here (for $k = 16$ and $c_{\max} = 15$) was 140174. □

5   Conclusion

In this paper we presented cdPTAs, an extension of PTAs in which probabilities can depend on the values of clocks. We have shown that a basic probabilistic model checking problem, maximal reachability, is undecidable for cdPTAs with at least three clocks. One direction of future research could be attempting to improve these results by considering cdPTAs with one or two clocks, or identifying other kinds of subclass of cdPTAs for which for which probabilistic reachability is decidable: for example, we conjecture decidability can be obtained for cdPTAs in which all clock variables are reset after utilising a probabilistic edge that depends non-trivially on clock values. Furthermore, we conjecture that qualitative reachability problems (whether there exists a strategy such that the target locations are reached with probability strictly greater than 0, or equal to 1) are decidable (and in exponential time) for cdPTAs for which the piecewise linear functions are bounded away from 0 by a region graph construction. The case of piecewise linear functions that can approach arbitrarily closely to 0 requires more care (because non-forgetful cycles, in the terminology of [5], can lead to convergence of a probability used along a cdPTA path to 0). We also presented a conservative overapproximation method for cdPTAs. At present this method gives no guarantees on the distance of the obtained bounds to the actual optimal probability: future work could address this issue, by extending the region graph construction from a PTS to a stochastic game (to provide upper and lower bounds on the maximum/minimum probability in the manner of [13]), or by considering approximate relations (by generalising the results of [6,9] from Markov chains to PTSs).

Acknowledgments. The inspiration for cdPTA arose from a discussion with Patricia Bouyer on the corner-point abstraction. Thanks also to Holger Hermanns, who expressed interest in a cdPTA-like formalism in a talk at Dagstuhl Seminar 14441.

References

1. Abate, A., Katoen, J., Lygeros, J., Prandini, M.: Approximate model checking of stochastic hybrid systems. Eur. J. Control **16**(6), 624–641 (2010)
2. Akshay, S., Bouyer, P., Krishna, S.N., Manasa, L., Trivedi, A.: Stochastic timed games revisited. In: Proceedings of the 41st International Symposium on Mathematical Foundations of Computer Science (MFCS 2016). LIPIcs, vol. 58, pp. 8:1–8:14. Leibniz-Zentrum für Informatik (2016)
3. Akshay, S., Bouyer, P., Krishna, S.N., Manasa, L., Trivedi, A.: Stochastic timed games revisited. CoRR, abs/1607.05671 (2016)
4. Alur, R., Dill, D.L.: A theory of timed automata. Theoret. Comput. Sci. **126**(2), 183–235 (1994)
5. Basset, N., Asarin, E.: Thin and thick timed regular languages. In: Fahrenberg, U., Tripakis, S. (eds.) FORMATS 2011. LNCS, vol. 6919, pp. 113–128. Springer, Heidelberg (2011). doi:10.1007/978-3-642-24310-3_9
6. Bian, G., Abate, A.: On the relationship between bisimulation and trace equivalence in an approximate probabilistic context. In: Esparza, J., Murawski, A.S. (eds.) FoSSaCS 2017. LNCS, vol. 10203, pp. 321–337. Springer, Heidelberg (2017). doi:10.1007/978-3-662-54458-7_19
7. Bouyer, P.: On the optimal reachability problem in weighted timed automata and games. In: Proceedings of the 7th Workshop on Non-Classical Models of Automata and Applications (NCMA 2015). books@ocg.at, vol. 318, pp. 11–36. Austrian Computer Society (2015)

8. Bouyer, P., Brinksma, E., Larsen, K.G.: Optimal infinite scheduling for multi-priced timed automata. Formal Methods Syst. Des. **32**(1), 2–23 (2008)
9. D'Innocenzo, A., Abate, A., Katoen, J.: Robust PCTL model checking. In: Proceedings of the 15th ACM International Conference on Hybrid Systems: Computation and Control (HSCC 2012), pp. 275–286. ACM (2012)
10. Gregersen, H., Jensen, H.E.: Formal design of reliable real time systems. Master's thesis, Department of Mathematics and Computer Science, Aalborg University (1995)
11. Hahn, E.M.: Model checking stochastic hybrid systems. Ph.D. thesis, Universität des Saarlandes (2013)
12. Jurdziński, M., Laroussinie, F., Sproston, J.: Model checking probabilistic timed automata with one or two clocks. Log. Methods Comput. Sci. **4**(3), 1–28 (2008)
13. Kattenbelt, M., Kwiatkowska, M., Norman, G., Parker, D.: A game-based abstraction-refinement framework for Markov decision processes. Formal Methods Syst. Des. **36**(3), 246–280 (2010)
14. Kemeny, J.G., Snell, J.L., Knapp, A.W.: Denumerable Markov Chains. Graduate Texts in Mathematics, 2nd edn. Springer, New York (1976)
15. Kwiatkowska, M., Norman, G., Parker, D.: PRISM 4.0: verification of probabilistic real-time systems. In: Gopalakrishnan, G., Qadeer, S. (eds.) CAV 2011. LNCS, vol. 6806, pp. 585–591. Springer, Heidelberg (2011). doi:10.1007/978-3-642-22110-1_47
16. Kwiatkowska, M., Norman, G., Parker, D., Sproston, J.: Performance analysis of probabilistic timed automata using digital clocks. Formal Methods Syst. Des. **29**, 33–78 (2006)
17. Kwiatkowska, M., Norman, G., Segala, R., Sproston, J.: Automatic verification of real-time systems with discrete probability distributions. Theoret. Comput. Sci. **286**, 101–150 (2002)
18. Minsky, M.: Computation: Finite and Infinite Machines. Prentice Hall International, Upper Saddle River (1967)
19. Norman, G., Parker, D., Sproston, J.: Model checking for probabilistic timed automata. Formal Methods Syst. Des. **43**(2), 164–190 (2013)
20. Puterman, M.L.: Markov Decision Processes. Wiley, Hoboken (1994)
21. Segala, R.: Modeling and verification of randomized distributed real-time systems. Ph.D. thesis, Massachusetts Institute of Technology (1995)
22. Sproston, J.: Probabilistic timed automata with clock-dependent probabilities. CoRR (2017)

Stubborn Sets with Frozen Actions

Antti Valmari[(✉)]

Mathematics, Tampere University of Technology,
P.O. Box 553, 33101 Tampere, Finland
`antti.valmari@tut.fi`

Abstract. Most ample, persistent, and stubborn set methods use some special condition for ensuring that the analysis is not terminated prematurely. In the case of stubborn set methods for safety properties, implementation of the condition is usually based on recognizing the terminal strong components of the reduced state space and, if necessary, expanding the stubborn sets used in their roots. In an earlier study it was pointed out that if the system may execute a cycle consisting of only invisible actions and that cycle is concurrent with the rest of the system in a non-obvious way, then the method may be fooled to construct all states of the full parallel composition. This problem is solved in this study by a method that is based on "freezing" the actions in the cycle.

Keywords: Partial-order methods · Stubborn sets · Safety properties · Ignoring problem

1 Introduction

Ample set [1,8,9], persistent set [5,6], and stubborn set [12,15] methods, or *aps* set methods in brief, alleviate state explosion by only firing a subset of enabled actions in each constructed state. Statically available information on generalized concurrency and causal dependency between actions is exploited to choose the subsets so that correct answers to analysis questions are obtained. Also the class of analysis questions affects the choice of the subsets. In general, the smaller is the class, the weaker conditions the subsets must satisfy, the better are the chances of finding legal subsets with only few enabled actions, and the better are the reduction results. In this study we focus on *safety properties*, that is, properties whose counter-examples are finite sequences of actions.

Ample, persistent, and stubborn sets are based on the same overall idea, but differ significantly at a more detailed level. They also differ in the mathematical language used to develop the methods and prove them correct. The differences are discussed extensively in [17].

Excluding the earliest publications, aps set methods are usually described using abstract conditions. Theorems on the correctness of the methods rely on these conditions, instead of information about how the sets are actually constructed. Then zero or more algorithms are described and proven correct that

© Springer International Publishing AG 2017
M. Hague and I. Potapov (Eds.): RP 2017, LNCS 10506, pp. 160–175, 2017.
DOI: 10.1007/978-3-319-67089-8_12

yield sets that obey the conditions in question. Usually more than one set satisfies the conditions. In particular, usually the set of all (enabled) actions satisfies them. To obtain good reduction results, the algorithms prefer sets with few enabled actions.

As illustrated in [17], in most cases, ample and persistent set conditions are more straightforward and perhaps easier to understand but have less potential for state space reduction than stubborn set conditions. In most cases, ample and persistent set algorithms are simpler than stubborn set algorithms but take more enabled actions to the sets. An important difference is that ample and persistent sets were defined as sets of enabled actions, while stubborn sets may also contain disabled actions. This implies, among other things, that condition 1 of Theorem 1 of the present study cannot be expressed naturally in ample and persistent set terminology. Indeed, the algorithm described after the theorem has only been used with stubborn sets. A similar comment holds on the condition **V** in Sect. 2, which is provably better than the corresponding ample set condition [17].

Almost all aps set methods need a condition to solve the *ignoring problem* illustrated in Sect. 2. The best conditions that are known to solve the ignoring problem in the case of safety properties are implemented based on recognizing the terminal strong components of the reduced state space [13, 14]. Recently, there has been significant advances in them [16, 17, 19]. Perhaps ironically, when writing [20], it turned out that excluding a somewhat pathological situation, the condition is not needed in the end, and in the pathological situation, even its recently improved forms suffer from a problem. The goal of this study is to first illustrate this background and then solve the remaining problem.

Ample and persistent set methods do not use terminal strong component conditions, probably because of the following reason. A well-known example (e.g., [17, Fig. 5]) demonstrates that terminal strong component conditions do not necessarily suffice for infinite counter-examples. As a consequence, when the goal is to preserve also so-called *liveness properties*, a stricter condition called the *cycle condition* is usually used. It has been described in [1] and elsewhere, together with a concrete implementation. The cycle condition does not make the terminal strong component conditions useless, because it is much stronger than the latter and thus has less potential for good reduction results. Furthermore, a drawback has been found in its most widely known implementation; please see [2] and, for instance, [17].

Section 2 explains the intuition behind stubborn sets in general. Terminal strong component conditions, including recent developments and the remaining problem, are illustrated in Sect. 3. The remaining problem can be solved with a new method of frozen actions that is described in Sect. 4 and proven correct in Sect. 5. The correctness proof assumes that actions are deterministic. Fortunately, Sect. 6 demonstrates that for the usual way of computing stubborn sets, the assumption is not needed in the end. Section 7 concludes this study.

2   Stubborn Sets and (In)visible Actions

We use the obvious arrow notation for occurrences of actions and finite sequences of actions. In Sect. 5 we will assume that actions are deterministic, that is, if $s -a\to s_1$ and $s -a\to s_2$, then $s_1 = s_2$. Let $\mathsf{en}(s)$ denote the set of actions that are enabled at s. The stubborn set used at s is denoted with $\mathsf{stubb}(s)$. The *reduced state space* is the triple $(S_r, \Delta_r, \hat{s})$, where $\hat{s}$ is the initial state, and S_r and Δ_r are the smallest sets such that $\hat{s} \in S_r$ and whenever $s \in S_r$, $s -a\to s'$ and $a \in \mathsf{stubb}(s)$, we have $s' \in S_r$ and $(s, a, s') \in \Delta_r$. The full (that is, ordinary) state space $(S, \Delta, \hat{s})$ is obtained by always letting $\mathsf{stubb}(s)$ be the set of all actions. Obviously $S_r \subseteq S$ and $\Delta_r \subseteq \Delta$. By an *r-state*, *r-path*, and so on we mean a state, path, and so on in the reduced state space.

All ample, persistent, and stubborn set methods have a condition that "keeps the system running" in a sense illustrated soon, and one or two conditions that describe how generalized concurrency and dependency relations are exploited. In the case of stubborn sets on nondeterministic actions, the following triple can be used.

D0. If $\mathsf{en}(s_0) \neq \emptyset$, then $\mathsf{stubb}(s_0) \cap \mathsf{en}(s_0) \neq \emptyset$.
D1. If $a \in \mathsf{stubb}(s_0)$, $s_0 -a_1 \cdots a_n a\to s'_n$, and $a_1, \ldots, a_n$ are not in $\mathsf{stubb}(s_0)$, then $s_0 -a a_1 \cdots a_n\to s'_n$.
D2. If $a \in \mathsf{stubb}(s_0)$, $s_0 -a_1 \cdots a_n\to s_n$, $a_1, \ldots, a_n$ are not in $\mathsf{stubb}(s_0)$, and $s_0 -a\to s'_0$, then there is s'_n such that $s'_0 -a_1 \cdots a_n\to s'_n$ and $s_n -a\to s'_n$.

With deterministic actions, the part "$s'_0 -a_1 \cdots a_n\to s'_n$" is unnecessary in **D2**, because it can be derived from $s_n -a\to s'_n$, **D1**, and the determinism of actions.

Before discussing the consequences of these conditions, let us briefly show one possible way of computing sets that satisfy them. The ideas are not strictly tied to any particular formalism, but, to avoid being too abstract, it is useful to choose some formalism. We consider systems of the form $(L_1 \| \cdots \| L_N) \setminus H$, where $L_1, \ldots, L_N$ are labelled transition systems (LTSs). An LTS is a rooted edge-labelled directed graph with a set called the *alphabet*. The labels of the edges must belong to the alphabet. The elements of the alphabet are called *actions*. The states of the system are of the form $s = (s_1, \ldots, s_N)$. The system executes an action a such that every L_i that has a in its alphabet executes a, and the remaining L_i stand still. An action is *invisible* if and only if it is of the form τ_i or it belongs to H (this is the purpose of H), and *visible* otherwise. Figure 2 shows an example of a system of this form.

Compared to familiar process-algebraic notation, we do not use the special invisible action symbol τ as such, but may use it with a subscript that refers to the component who executes it. The symbols $\|$ and $\setminus$ have the same meaning as in process algebras, except that $\setminus$ only declares actions invisible instead of converting them to τ. For more details on this formalism, please see [14,16,19].

By $\mathsf{en}_i(s_i)$ we mean the actions that L_i is ready to execute when it is in its local state s_i. That is, $\mathsf{en}_i(s_i)$ is the set of the labels of the edges of L_i whose tail is s_i. The proof of the following theorem can be found in [19]. The key idea is that in case 1, L_i keeps a disabled until an element of $\mathsf{stubb}(s)$ occurs, and in case 2, a is concurrent with all actions that are not in $\mathsf{stubb}(s)$.

Theorem 1. *Assume that the following hold for $s = (s_1, \ldots, s_N)$ and for every $a \in \mathsf{stubb}(s)$:*

1. *If $a \notin \mathsf{en}(s)$, then there is i such that $1 \leq i \leq N$, a is in the alphabet of L_i, and $a \notin \mathsf{en}_i(s_i) \subseteq \mathsf{stubb}(s)$.*
2. *If $a \in \mathsf{en}(s)$, then for every i such that $1 \leq i \leq N$ and a is in the alphabet of L_i we have $\mathsf{en}_i(s_i) \subseteq \mathsf{stubb}(s)$.*

*Then $\mathsf{stubb}(s)$ satisfies **D1** and **D2**.*

Cases 1 and 2 can be interpreted as spanning rules of the form $a \leadsto_s b$, meaning that if $a \in \mathsf{stubb}(s)$, then also b must be in $\mathsf{stubb}(s)$ (but not necessarily vice versa). In case 1, there may be more than one i that satisfies the condition. To avoid ambiguity, we artificially assume that the smallest one is chosen. Whether or not $a \leadsto_s b$ may depend on the state s.

If there are no enabled actions, then any set of actions trivially satisfies **D0**, **D1**, and **D2**. Otherwise, any set that contains an enabled action and is closed with respect to the $\leadsto_s$-relation satisfies them. Good such sets can be found efficiently using Tarjan's strong component algorithm [11], as has been explained in [17,19] and elsewhere. A good practical improvement to Tarjan's algorithm has been presented in [3]. It was re-invented and slightly modified in [4].

It is now the time to start discussing the consequencies of **D0**, **D1**, and **D2**. For the sake of illustration, assume that the goal is to verify that the system cannot reach a state after which action b can never occur. Assume that $s_0 -b_1 \to s_1 -b_2 \to \cdots -b_m \to s_m$ is a counter-example to this property, where s_0 is the initial state of the system. If $b_1 \in \mathsf{stubb}(s_0)$, then the transition $s_0 -b_1 \to s_1$ is in the reduced state space, that is, an r-transition. So the problem becomes the problem of finding a counter-example for s_1. More generally, if any of $b_1, \ldots, b_m$ is in $\mathsf{stubb}(s_0)$, then let b_i be the first one. **D1** yields s_0' and s_i such that $s_0 -b_i \to s_0' -b_1 \cdots b_{i-1} \to s_i -b_{i+1} \cdots b_m \to s_m$, transforming the problem to finding a counter-example for s_0'.

The case remains where none of $b_1, \ldots, b_m$ is in $\mathsf{stubb}(s_0)$. If $\mathsf{en}(s_0) = \emptyset$ (implying $m = 0$), then s_0 is an r-state after which b can never occur. So a counter-example has been found. Otherwise **D0** implies that $\mathsf{stubb}(s_0)$ contains an enabled action a. So for some s_0', $s_0 -a \to s_0'$ in the reduced state space. By **D2**, there is s_m' such that $s_m -a \to s_m'$ and $s_0' -b_1 \cdots b_m \to s_m'$. Because $s_m -a \to s_m'$ and b can never occur after s_m, b can never occur after s_m'. Again, the problem has been moved to s_0'.

In this example, **D0** "kept the system running" by ensuring that whenever **D1** does not apply and the goal has not yet been reached, **D2** does apply. Unfortunately, this does not suffice for guaranteeing that the reduced state space contains a counter-example if the full state space does. Consider $\circlearrowleft \tau_1 \| \circlearrowleft \xrightarrow{b} \circ$. Let $\hat{s}$ denote its initial state. Firing b once disables b forever and is thus a counter-example. The choice $\mathsf{stubb}(\hat{s}) = \{\tau_1\}$ satisfies **D0**, **D1**, and **D2**. It constructs the r-transition $\hat{s} - \tau_1 \rightarrow \hat{s}$, after which all encountered states have been investigated and the analysis stops. So b was never fired and no counter-example was found.

In terms of **D0**, **D1**, and **D2**, the problem is that an application of **D2** does not necessarily make any progress towards completing a counter-example: the path $s'_0 - b_1 \cdots b_{i-1} b_{i+1} \cdots b_m \rightarrow s_m$ yielded by **D1** is shorter than the original counter-example, but the path $s'_0 - b_1 \cdots b_m \rightarrow s'_m$ yielded by **D2** is not. That the analysis terminates without completing any existing counter-example is called *the ignoring problem* in the literature. In this example, b was ignored.

With many properties, it suffices to observe a subset of actions. For instance, when checking mutual exclusion between two clients, the only important thing is the projection of the execution on the actions $enter_1$, $enter_2$, $leave_1$, and $leave_2$. The location of $request\_access_1$ and $request\_access_2$ does not matter. We follow process algebra parlance and call this kind of projections *traces*. This notion is not the same as Mazurkiewicz traces [7].

To take this into account in stubborn, ample, and persistent set methods, the distinction between *visible* and *invisible* actions has been introduced. When applying the methods to process algebras, the distinction is already there to start with. In other applications, an action is declared invisible if and only if it is known that it need not be observed. This formulation allows the use of the methods even if, as is sometimes the case, for some actions, it is difficult to find out whether observing them is important.

Let V denote the set of visible actions. We discuss the following condition.

V If $stubb(s_0)$ contains an enabled visible action, then $V \subseteq stubb(s_0)$.

If the a in **D1** is invisible, then the trace of $a_1 \cdots a_n a$ (that is, the projection of $a_1 \cdots a_n a$ on V) is the same as the trace of $aa_1 \cdots a_n$, so the trace is preserved. The same holds with **D2**, $a_1 \cdots a_n$, and $aa_1 \cdots a_n$. If the a in **D1** is visible, then $a_1, \ldots, a_n$ are invisible, because then a is an enabled action in $stubb(s_0) \cap V$, so all visible actions are in $stubb(s_0)$ by **V**, but $a_1, \ldots, a_n$ are not in $stubb(s_0)$ by **D1**. Similar reasoning applies when the a in **D2** is visible. So **V** guarantees that when applying **D1** or **D2**, the traces are not broken.

V can be taken into account in the construction of stubborn sets by extending the $\leadsto_s$-relation with $a \leadsto_s b$ for every enabled visible a and every visible b. (Please see [17] for why **V** has potential for better reduction results than the corresponding condition **C2** in ample set theory.)

3   Terminal Strong Component Conditions

When counter-examples are finite, the ignoring problem can be solved with a *terminal strong component condition*. The reduced state space is constructed in depth-first order and its terminal strong components are recognized on-the-fly. This can be done efficiently with Tarjan's algorithm [3,4,11], as is described in [17] and elsewhere.

The *root* of a strong component is the state in it that the depth-first search finds first (and therefore backtracks from last). Each time when the construction

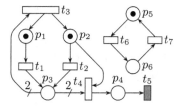

Fig. 1. Illustrating the non-optimality of **Sen** and **SV**.

is about to backtrack from a root of a terminal strong component, it checks that the stubborn sets used in the component together contain "sufficiently many" actions. Different terminal strong component conditions use different notions of "sufficiently many". If necessary, the stubborn set used at the root is expanded, that is, actions are added to it such that also the result is stubborn. Expanding the stubborn set of the root does not conflict with Tarjan's algorithm. Unless the analysis is terminated earlier because of finding a counter-example, eventually every terminal strong component covers "sufficiently many" actions. At that point, for every r-state s, either a state where **D1** applies is r-reachable from s, or it is known that s does not have any counter-example.

The first two terminal strong component conditions were the following.

Sen. For every $a \in \mathsf{en}(s_0)$ there is s_a such that $a \in \mathsf{stubb}(s_a)$ and s_a is r-reachable from s_0 [13,14].

SV. For every $a \in V$ there is s_a such that $a \in \mathsf{stubb}(s_a)$ and s_a is r-reachable from s_0 [14].

Among other things, **Sen** suffices for checking whether the system can reach a state after which b can never occur. Together with **V** it preserves the process-algebraic trace equivalence. Surprisingly, they also preserve the fair testing equivalence of [10,21], although it appears to be of branching time nature and is strong enough for processing a meaningful fairness assumption [19]. These two process-algebraic equivalences are also preserved by **SV** and **V**.

Applying **Sen** to an r-deadlock state s_0 implies $\mathsf{en}(s_0) = \emptyset$, that is, s_0 is a deadlock also in the full state space. This is because otherwise s_0 must either have an a-transition (if $s_a = s_0$) or a transition towards the state s_a (if $s_a \neq s_0$). So **Sen** implies **D0**. Applying **SV** to an r-deadlock state s_0 yields that no visible action can be enabled in the future, because then $V \subseteq \mathsf{stubb}(s_0)$, so each execution leading to an occurrence of a visible action must contain, by **D1**, an element of $\mathsf{stubb}(s_0) \cap \mathsf{en}(s_0)$. **D0** does not necessarily follow, but where it does not, the only trace of the state is the empty trace that it trivially also has in the reduced state space. In conclusion, **Sen** and **SV** "keep the system running" to the necessary extent, and **D0** need not be (explicitly) required.

It has been known for a long time that both **Sen** and **SV** are not optimal, at least with the implementation described above. In [18], this was illustrated with Fig. 1. In it, t_5 is the only visible Petri net transition, and t_4 is permanently disabled in a non-trivial way. The stubborn set method first constructs the cycle

$\hat{M} -t_1t_2t_3\rightarrow \hat{M}$. Then **Sen** forces it to expand $\mathsf{stubb}(\hat{M})$ with t_6, although t_6 is clearly irrelevant for checking whether t_5 can ever occur. On the other hand, **SV** allows to forget about t_6. Unfortunately, it requires $t_5 \in \mathsf{stubb}(M)$ for some M in the cycle. Therefore, the implementation expands $\mathsf{stubb}(\hat{M})$ by adding t_2, t_4, and t_5 to it, although t_2 already occurs elsewhere in the cycle.

This problem was solved in [17] with a new condition. In the root r of each terminal strong component, a set $\mathcal{V}(r)$ of actions is computed so that $V \subseteq \mathcal{V}(r)$ and the following holds:

Dd. If $a \in \mathcal{V}(r)$, $r -a_1\cdots a_n\rightarrow s_n$, $a_1,\ldots,a_n$ are not in $\mathcal{V}(r)$, and $\neg(r -a\rightarrow)$, then $\neg(s_n -a\rightarrow)$.

That is, if an element of $\mathcal{V}(r)$ is disabled in r, then it remains disabled at least until an occurrence of an element of $\mathcal{V}(r)$. The set $\mathcal{V}(r)$ can be computed using similar techniques as when ensuring **D1**, **D2**, and **V**.

Then it is checked that each element of $\mathcal{V}(r)\cap \mathsf{en}(r)$ occurs somewhere in the component. If necessary, $\mathsf{stubb}(r)$ is expanded with at least one missing element of $\mathcal{V}(r) \cap \mathsf{en}(r)$ and whatever else is needed to maintain **D1**, **D2**, and **V**. In Fig. 1, $\mathcal{V}(\hat{M}) = \{t_1,t_2,t_4,t_5\}$ and $\mathcal{V}(\hat{M})\cap \mathsf{en}(\hat{M}) = \{t_1,t_2\}$. Because both t_1 and t_2 occur in the cycle $\hat{M} -t_1t_2t_3\rightarrow \hat{M}$, $\mathsf{stubb}(\hat{M})$ need not be expanded.

This implements the following abstract condition:

S. There are r and $\mathcal{V}(r)$ such that r is r-reachable from s_0, $V \subseteq \mathcal{V}(r)$, $\mathcal{V}(r)$ satisfies **Dd**, and for every $a \in \mathcal{V}(r) \cap \mathsf{en}(r)$ there is s_a such that it is r-reachable from r and $a \in \mathsf{stubb}(s_a)$.

Theorem 2. *If every r-state satisfies* **D1**, **D2**, **V**, *and* **S**, *then the reduced and full state space have the same traces.*

Proof. Any trace of the reduced state space is also a trace of the full state space, because every r-path is also a path in the full state space by $S_r \subseteq S$ and $\Delta_r \subseteq \Delta$.

To prove the opposite direction, consider a path $s_0 -b_1\cdots b_m\rightarrow$ in the full state space such that s_0 is an r-state. If none of $b_1,\ldots,b_m$ is visible, then the trace of $s_0 -b_1\cdots b_m\rightarrow$ is the empty sequence. It is yielded by the trivial r-path that consists of just s_0.

Otherwise there is some $1 \le v \le m$ such that $b_v \in V$. By **S**, there is an r-path $s_0' -c_1\rightarrow s_1' -c_2\rightarrow \cdots -c_h\rightarrow s_h'$ such that $s_0' = s_0$ and s_h' plays the role of r in **S**. Let j be the smallest such that $j = h$ or $\{b_1,\ldots,b_m\} \cap \mathsf{stubb}(s_j') \ne \emptyset$. By applying **D2** j times we get $s_0 -c_1\cdots c_j\rightarrow s_j' -b_1\cdots b_m\rightarrow$. For $1 \le k \le j$, c_k is invisible, because otherwise **V** would imply $b_v \in \mathsf{stubb}(s_{k-1}')$, contradicting the choice of j. Therefore, $c_1\cdots c_jb_1\cdots b_m$ has the same trace as $b_1\cdots b_m$.

If $\{b_1,\ldots,b_m\} \cap \mathsf{stubb}(s_j') \ne \emptyset$, then let ι be the smallest such that $b_\iota \in \{b_1,\ldots,b_m\}\cap\mathsf{stubb}(s_j')$. By **D1** there is s'' such that $s_j' -b_\iota\rightarrow s''$ is an r-transition and $s'' -b_1\cdots b_{\iota-1}b_{\iota+1}\cdots b_m\rightarrow$. By **V**, $b_\iota b_1\cdots b_{\iota-1}b_{\iota+1}\cdots b_m$ has the same trace as $b_1\cdots b_m$. By induction, there is an r-path $s'' -\sigma\rightarrow$ that has the same trace as $b_1\cdots b_{\iota-1}b_{\iota+1}\cdots b_m$. Now $s_0 -c_1\cdots c_j\rightarrow s_j' -b_\iota\rightarrow s'' -\sigma\rightarrow$ is an r-path that has the same trace as $s_0 -b_1\cdots b_m\rightarrow$.

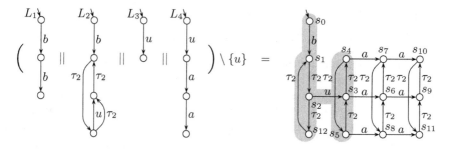

Fig. 2. A system with $V = \{a, b\}$ where after s_3, every state has an invisible transition

Otherwise $j = h$ and we have $s'_h -b_1 \cdots b_m \rightarrow$. Because $b_v \in V \subseteq \mathcal{V}(s'_h)$, there is a smallest ι such that $b_\iota \in \mathcal{V}(s'_h)$. **Dd** yields $b_\iota \in \mathsf{en}(s'_h)$. **S** implies the existence of s_{b_ι} such that $b_\iota \in \mathsf{stubb}(s_{b_\iota})$ and there is an r-path from s'_h to s_{b_ι}. The proof continues by applying **D2** along this path until a state z with $\{b_1, \ldots, b_m\} \cap \mathsf{stubb}(z) \neq \emptyset$ is reached and then applying **D1** and induction, similarly to the above.   □

Figure 2 [20] illustrates a problem with the method in Theorem 2. In it, the actions u and τ_2 are invisible. Originally only b is enabled, then only τ_2, and then only u and τ_2. After firing u, the τ_2-cycle of L_2 and the aa-sequence of L_4 are in parallel, and b and u are permanently disabled.

Assume that in s_3, the construction of stubborn sets is started with a. Because a is enabled and visible, **V** forces to also take b into $\mathsf{stubb}(s_3)$, if a is taken. However, b is disabled because of L_2. If the stubborn set construction algorithm is good enough, it detects that b is permanently disabled, chooses $\mathsf{stubb}(s_3) = \{a, b\}$, and only fires a in s_3. However, detecting that an action is permanently disabled is **PSPACE**-hard in general. So it is not realistic to assume that a stubborn set construction algorithm can always detect that an action is permanently disabled. For the sake of an example, we assume that the algorithm in [19] is used without any advanced features. It fails to detect that b is permanently disabled.

Because b is disabled by L_2 and only by it, the algorithm in [19] focuses on what L_2 can do next, that is, τ_2. Because τ_2 is enabled, invisible, not synchronized to by any other component, and its start state has no other outgoing transitions, $\{\tau_2\}$ qualifies as $\mathsf{stubb}(s_3)$. Because $\{\tau_2\}$ has fewer enabled actions than $\{a, b, \tau_2\}$, the algorithm chooses $\mathsf{stubb}(s_3) = \{\tau_2\}$. So the method constructs the r-transition $s_3 -\tau_2 \rightarrow s_4$. In the resulting state s_4 the situation is similar to s_3, so the r-transition $s_4 -\tau_2 \rightarrow s_5$ is constructed.

The situation is only slightly more complicated in s_5. Because u is an alternative for τ_2, the algorithm takes also u into $\mathsf{stubb}(s_5)$. The algorithm detects that u is disabled by L_3 which is in a deadlock, so it does not continue analysis further from u. So the method constructs (only) the r-transition $s_5 -\tau_2 \rightarrow s_3$. In conclusion, the cycle $s_3 -\tau_2 \rightarrow s_4 -\tau_2 \rightarrow s_5 -\tau_2 \rightarrow s_3$ is constructed.

At this point the method computes $V(s_3) = \{a, b, \tau_2\}$, to satisfy **S**. We have $V(s_3) \cap \text{en}(s_3) = \{a, \tau_2\}$, but τ_2 already occurs in the cycle. So the method constructs $s_3 -a\rightarrow s_6$.

The same behaviour repeats in s_6 and finally in s_9 (except that a is found disabled in s_9). The method constructed all states of the full state space, although the τ_2-cycle and aa-sequence are in parallel.

We say that a state is *stable* if and only if it cannot execute any invisible action. In the next section we will present a novel idea that solves the problem that was illustrated above. Before that, let us point out that the problem arose in a situation where from s_3 on, no stable state was reachable. We will soon prove that this was not a coincidence. Before that, let us replace **D0** by a condition that exploits the fact that when verifying safety properties, if it is certain that no visible action can become enabled after a state, then it is not necessary to continue the analysis from that state even if it has enabled actions.

D0V. If $\text{en}(s_0) \neq \emptyset$, then either $\text{stubb}(s_0) \cap \text{en}(s_0) \neq \emptyset$ or $V \subseteq \text{stubb}(s_0)$.

The following theorem is from [16, 20].

Theorem 3. *Assume that s_0 is an r-state and $s_0 -b_1 \cdots b_m\rightarrow s_m$ such that s_m is stable and at least one of $b_1, \ldots, b_m$ is visible. If **D0V**, **D1**, **D2**, and **V** are obeyed, then there is an r-path of length at most m such that it starts at s_0 and has the same trace as $b_1 \cdots b_m$.*

Proof. Let b_v be visible. Because it exists, also b_1 exists. So $s_0 -b_1\rightarrow$. Assume that none of $b_1, \ldots, b_m$ is in $\text{stubb}(s_0)$. Then $b_v \notin \text{stubb}(s_0)$, and **D0V** implies that $\text{stubb}(s_0)$ contains some enabled action a. By **D2**, $s_m -a\rightarrow$. Because s_m is stable, $a \in V$. So **V** implies that $V \subseteq \text{stubb}(s_0)$, a contradiction with $b_v \notin \text{stubb}(s_0)$. So at least one of $b_1, \ldots, b_m$ is in $\text{stubb}(s_0)$. Application of first **D1** and then induction yields the claim.   □

This means that every trace leading to a stable state is preserved, even if the simple condition **D0V** is used instead of **S**. That is, if the system has the property that from every reachable state, a stable state is reachable, then the condition **S** is not needed. Furthermore, thanks to the following theorem, the user need not know in advance that the system has this property.

Theorem 4. *Assume that s_0 is an r-state and has the trace σ in the full but not in the reduced state space. If **D0V**, **D1**, **D2**, and **V** are obeyed, then some prefix of σ that s_0 has in the reduced state space leads to an r-state after which all r-states are r-unstable and have no visible output r-transitions.*

Proof. Assume that σ arises from $s_0 -b_1 \cdots b_m\rightarrow$. Let $s'_0 = s_0$ and let us choose the states s'_1, s'_2, ... as follows. If $b_j \in \text{stubb}(s'_{i-1})$ for some $1 \leq j \leq m$, then let k be the smallest such j and let $s'_{i-1} -b_k\rightarrow s'_i$ be the r-transition yielded by **D1**. We say that the application of **D1** *consumes* b_k. Otherwise, if s'_{i-1} is not in a terminal strong component, choose $s'_{i-1} -a\rightarrow s'_i$ such that $a \in \text{en}(s'_{i-1}) \cap \text{stubb}(s'_{i-1})$ and s'_i is closer to a terminal strong component than

s'_{i-1}, and apply **D2**. Applications of **D2** consume nothing from $b_1 \cdots b_m$. Because **D1** can be applied at most $m-1$ times, this procedure eventually leads to a terminal strong component C. Then traverse around C applying **D1** and **D2** until **D1** can no longer be applied.

Let $c_1 \cdots c_k$ be the remaining part of $b_1 \cdots b_m$, and let s be any state in C. **D2** yields $s -c_1 \cdots c_k \rightarrow$ in the full state space. Because σ was not fully consumed, some c_v is visible. We have $\mathsf{stubb}(s) \cap \mathsf{en}(s) \cap V = \emptyset$, because otherwise **V** would make **D1** applicable, because of c_v. For the same reason, $V \not\subseteq \mathsf{stubb}(s)$. So **D0V** implies that C is not an r-deadlock. □

This means that if the reduced state space obeys **D0V**, **D1**, **D2**, and **V**, then either the traces are preserved or the reduced state space exhibits pathological behaviour: it contains a state from which neither termination nor any visible activity is reachable. This pathological property can be detected from the reduced state space with well-known linear-time algorithms, by performing a graph search using the edges in reverse and using the deadlocks and tail states of visible transitions as the starting points. That the reduced state space has this property does not prove that also the original system does. However, by Theorem 3, it does prove that the original system cannot reach a stable state from the states in question. If this is considered as sufficient reason for declaring the original system incorrect, then the easily implementable conditions **D0V**, **D1**, **D2**, and **V** suffice.

If we want to preserve the traces even when we already know that the system can no longer reach a stable state, we run the risk of the problem that was illustrated with Fig. 2. The next section solves this problem.

4   Frozen Actions

In this section we solve the performance problem pointed out in the previous section with the new notion of *frozen actions*. The idea resembles the frozen actions in [16], but also has important differences. In [16], the goal was to improve the performance when preserving divergence traces.

Figure 3 shows how frozen actions are used during the construction of the reduced state space. The algorithm is based on the well-known recursive method for constructing $(S_r, \Delta_r, \hat{s})$ in depth-first order. It is initially called with $\mathrm{DFS}(\hat{s}, \emptyset)$. Like in the previous section, Tarjan's algorithm [3,4,11] is applied on top of the depth-first search, to recognize terminal strong components. In the figure, $\mathsf{stubb}(S') = \bigcup_{s' \in S'} \mathsf{stubb}(s')$ and $\mathcal{R}_r(s) = \{s' \mid s' \text{ is r-reachable from } s\}$.

The parameter *old_frozen* and variable *new_frozen* are pointers to or index numbers of sets of actions. The computation of stubborn sets behaves as if frozen actions did not exist. This implies that frozen actions never enter the set *more_stubborn* computed on line 5 and are thus never fired. When line 5 is re-executed, the computation does not return the stubborn set in full, but only the expansion to the previous stubborn set. The previous stubborn set consists of the originally computed stubborn set and its already returned expansions.

$$\mathrm{DFS}(s, \textit{old\_frozen})$$

1 $S_r := S_r \cup \{s\}$
2 $\textit{new\_frozen} := \textit{old\_frozen}$
3 $done := $ false
4 **while** $\neg done$ **do**
5      $\textit{more_stubborn} := $ compute or expand $\mathsf{stubb}(s, \textit{new\_frozen})$
6   **for** $a \in \textit{more\_stubborn} \cap \mathsf{en}(s)$ **do**
7   **for** s' such that $s -a\rightarrow s'$ **do**
8              $\Delta_r := \Delta_r \cup \{(s, a, s')\}$
9   **if** $s' \notin S_r$ **then** $\mathrm{DFS}(s', \textit{new\_frozen})$
10   **if** $\textit{more\_stubborn} \cap \mathsf{en}(s) = \emptyset$
11         $\vee$ s is not a root of a terminal strong component of $(S_r, \Delta_r, \hat{s})$
12         $\vee$ $\exists s' \in \mathcal{R}_r(s) : \mathsf{stubb}(s') \cap V \cap \mathsf{en}(s') \neq \emptyset$
13   **then** $done := $ true
14   **else** $\textit{new\_frozen} := \textit{new\_frozen} \cup \mathsf{stubb}(\mathcal{R}_r(s))$

Fig. 3. Implementation of **S** with frozen actions

When an r-state s is entered, the algorithm enters the **while**-loop. It computes a stubborn set avoiding the elements of *new_frozen*. The algorithm executes all enabled actions in the stubborn set in all possible ways, storing the resulting r-transitions and entering those of the resulting r-states that have not yet been entered. In later iterations of the **while**-loop, this is done to the current expansion of the stubborn set, not to the stubborn set as a whole.

After having processed the stubborn set or expansion, the algorithm backtracks if it contained no enabled actions; s is currently not the root of a terminal strong component of the reduced state space; or a visible action occurs in the terminal strong component whose root s is. Otherwise, the algorithm *freezes* all actions in all stubborn sets of the component and computes an expansion to the stubborn set or previous expansion. All enabled actions in the original stubborn set and previous expansions are now frozen, so line 5 gives a new result. Each iteration of the **while**-loop other than the last freezes at least one enabled action, so the loop terminates.

Consider again Fig. 2. We already saw that the algorithm constructs the cycle $s_3 -\tau_2\rightarrow s_4 -\tau_2\rightarrow s_5 -\tau_2\rightarrow s_3$. When it has done so and is about to backtrack from s_3, it freezes u and τ_2, and computes an expansion to the stubborn set. This computation returns $\{a, b\}$, because τ_2 is frozen and a non-frozen enabled action must be returned if possible. So the algorithm executes $s_3 -a\rightarrow s_6$. In s_6 it again only executes a, for the same reason. In the next state s_9 it executes nothing.

The example also illustrates that freezing an action prematurely may cause an erroneous result. If τ_2 is frozen already in the initial state, the trace ba is lost.

5   Correctness

In this section we assume that actions are deterministic, that is, if $s -a\rightarrow s_1$ and $s -a\rightarrow s_2$, then $s_1 = s_2$. To prove the correctness of the method in the previous section, we re-develop **D1**, **D2**, and **Dd** in the presence of frozen actions. The set of actions that are frozen in s is denoted with $\mathcal{F}(s)$. More precisely, s was constructed by some call DFS(s, *old_frozen*), and $\mathcal{F}(s)$ is the value of *old_frozen*.

D1F. If $a \in \text{stubb}(s_0) \setminus \mathcal{F}(s_0)$, $s_0 -a_1 \cdots a_n a\rightarrow s'_n$, and $a_1,\ldots,a_n$ are not in $\text{stubb}(s_0) \cup \mathcal{F}(s_0)$, then $s_0 -aa_1 \cdots a_n\rightarrow s'_n$.

D2F. If $a \in \text{stubb}(s_0) \setminus \mathcal{F}(s_0)$, $s_0 -a_1 \cdots a_n\rightarrow s_n$, $a_1,\ldots,a_n$ are not in $\text{stubb}(s_0) \cup \mathcal{F}(s_0)$, and $s_0 -a\rightarrow s'_0$, then there is s'_n such that $s'_0 -a_1 \cdots a_n\rightarrow s'_n$ and $s_n -a\rightarrow s'_n$.

DdF. If $a \in \mathcal{V}(r) \setminus \mathcal{F}(s_0)$, $r -a_1 \cdots a_n\rightarrow s_n$, $a_1,\ldots,a_n$ are not in $\mathcal{V}(r) \cup \mathcal{F}(s_0)$, and $\neg(r -a\rightarrow)$, then $\neg(s_n -a\rightarrow)$.

We have to prove that the full and reduced state spaces have the same traces. One direction remains trivial: every r-trace is a trace of the system because we still have $S_r \subseteq S$ and $\Delta_r \subseteq \Delta$.

To prove the other direction, consider a path $s_0 -b_1 \cdots b_m\rightarrow s_m$ such that $s_0 \in S_r$ and none of $b_1,\ldots,b_m$ is in $\mathcal{F}(s_0)$. The initial call DFS($\hat{s}, \emptyset$) makes the parameter *old_frozen* empty, justifying the assumption that none of $b_1, \ldots, b_m$ is in $\mathcal{F}(s_0)$. We will soon show that the assumption is justified also when the set of frozen actions is not empty.

Because none of $b_1,\ldots,b_m$ is in $\mathcal{F}(s_0)$, **D1F**, **D2F**, and **DdF** work like **D1**, **D2**, and **Dd** did in Sects. 2 and 3. **V** has not changed, so it works in the good old way. **S** has changed only by using **DdF** instead of **Dd**. What is different from Sects. 2 and 3 is that when **D1F** or **D2F** yields an r-transition $s_0 -a\rightarrow s'_0$, we may have $\mathcal{F}(s'_0) \neq \mathcal{F}(s_0)$. To cope with this, we will use the following lemma.

Lemma 5. *For each r-state s_0, if $s_0 -b_1 \cdots b_m\rightarrow$ and $c_1 \cdots c_n$ is the result of the removal of all elements of $\mathcal{F}(s_0)$ from $b_1 \cdots b_m$, then $s_0 -c_1 \cdots c_n\rightarrow$.*

Proof. The r-state s_0 was originally found via some r-path $\hat{s} = z_0 -d_1 \cdots d_k\rightarrow z_k = s_0$, where always on line 9, $z_i \notin S_r$ held. We use induction along this r-path. Because *old_frozen* $\subseteq$ *new_frozen* in the algorithm, $\emptyset = \mathcal{F}(z_0) \subseteq \mathcal{F}(z_1) \subseteq \cdots \subseteq \mathcal{F}(z_k)$.

The base case has $\mathcal{F}(z_0) = \emptyset$, so the claim holds with $c_1 \cdots c_n = b_1 \cdots b_m$.

If $z_i -b_1 \cdots b_m\rightarrow$, then $z_{i-1} -d_i b_1 \cdots b_m\rightarrow$. Because $z_{i-1} -d_i\rightarrow z_i$ was constructed, $d_i \notin \mathcal{F}(z_{i-1})$. By the induction assumption, $z_{i-1} -d_i e_1 \cdots e_\ell\rightarrow$, where $e_1 \cdots e_\ell$ is the result of the removal of all elements of $\mathcal{F}(z_{i-1})$ from $b_1 \cdots b_m$. Because actions are deterministic, we have $z_i -e_1 \cdots e_\ell\rightarrow$.

If $\mathcal{F}(z_i) = \mathcal{F}(z_{i-1})$, then $c_1 \cdots c_n = e_1 \cdots e_\ell$, and we have the claim. Otherwise $\mathcal{F}(z_i)$ contains extra actions that were added during one or more iterations of the **while**-loop in Fig. 3. At that time, z_{i-1} was the root of a terminal strong component. If $e_i \in \mathcal{F}(z_i) \setminus \mathcal{F}(z_{i-1})$, then e_i was added to *new_frozen* by line 14. This means that the component contains a state z' such that $e_i \in \text{stubb}(z')$.

By the definition of strong component, there is an r-path from z_{i-1} to z' and back. We apply **D1F** and **D2F** along this r-path. **D1F** can be applied at least in z', so at least one element of $\mathcal{F}(z_i) \setminus \mathcal{F}(z_{i-1})$ is consumed. The action d_i is not consumed, because we are now discussing events that took place before firing $z_{i-1} -d_i\rightarrow z_i$. This reasoning can be repeated until $z_{i-1} -d_i c_1 \cdots c_n\rightarrow$ is obtained. □

As a consequence, each time when an application of **D1F** or **D2F** takes the reasoning to an r-state, the frozen actions of that state can be removed from the sequence. This implies that the above assumption is justified, and correctness follows analogously to Sects. 2 and 3.

6 Nondeterministic Actions

In this section we present a construction via which a system of LTSs with nondeterministic actions can be converted to an equivalent system of LTSs with deterministic actions. The construction is *transparent* in the sense that stubborn sets of the original system that are obtained using Theorem 1 correspond to stubborn sets of the deterministic system. This means that the construction need not be implemented. Its existence suffices for dropping the assumption of determinism. In conclusion, if stubborn sets are computed using Theorem 1, then the algorithm in Fig. 3 also applies with nondeterministic actions.

Intuitively, the system executes deterministic *verbose actions*, and actions in the original sense are abstractions of verbose actions. So the original system is an abstraction of a deterministic system, although the original notion of actions conceals this fact.

Let L be an LTS and a an action. The *a-width* of L, denoted with $w(L, a)$, is the maximum i such that some state of L has precisely i outgoing transitions labelled with a. If $w(L, a) = 0$, then (and only then) L has no a-transitions.

We still consider systems of the form $(L_1 \| \cdots \| L_N) \setminus H$. For $1 \leq i \leq N$, let $L_i = (S_i, \Sigma_i, \Delta_i, \hat{s}_i)$, where S_i is the set of the states of L_i, $\hat{s}_i$ is the initial state of L_i (so $\hat{s}_i \in S_i$), Σ_i is the alphabet of L_i, and Δ_i is the set of the transitions of L_i (so $\Delta_i \subseteq S_i \times \Sigma_i \times S_i$). For each a in $\Sigma_1 \cup \cdots \cup \Sigma_N$, let $\mathsf{Vb}(a)$ (called the *verbose set of* a) be the set of the vectors $(a; j_1, \ldots, j_N)$, where $j_i = 0$ if $a \notin \Sigma_i$, and $j_i \in \{1, \ldots, w(L_i, a)\}$ if $a \in \Sigma_i$. If some L_i has a in its alphabet but has no a-transitions, then $\mathsf{Vb}(a) = \emptyset$.

Each L_i is replaced by $L'_i = (S_i, \Sigma'_i, \Delta'_i, \hat{s}_i)$, where $\Sigma'_i = \bigcup_{a \in \Sigma_i} \mathsf{Vb}(a)$ (that is, the actions are replaced by the verbose actions) and Δ'_i is obtained as follows. Let $(s, a, s') \in \Delta_i$. We artificially give each a-labelled outgoing transition of s a distinct number starting from 1. Let the number of (s, a, s') be k. Then Δ'_i contains the transition $(s, (a; j_1, \ldots, j_N), s')$ for each $(a; j_1, \ldots, j_N) \in \mathsf{Vb}(a)$ such that $j_i = k$. That is, the kth outgoing a-transition of s is replaced by $|\mathsf{Vb}(a)|/w(L_i, a)$ transitions, one for each possible way of synchronizing with a-transitions of the other component LTSs. Finally, an operator is added on top of $L_1 \| \cdots \| L_N$ that maps each $(a; j_1, \ldots, j_N)$ to a.

The nondeterminism of the original action a of L_i is resolved by the component j_i of $(a; j_1, \ldots, j_N)$. It is straightforward to check that the construction yields the same (full) LTS as the original system. This is because the only thing that has happened is that the names of actions have been extended, for $1 \leq i \leq N$, with information about which alternative L_i chose from among the possible ways of executing the action.

It remains to be shown that the construction is transparent regarding stubborn set computation. We assume that $\mathsf{stubb}(s)$ is computed as suggested by Theorem 1 using original actions, and show that $\mathsf{stubb}'(s) = \bigcup\limits_{a \in \mathsf{stubb}(s)} \mathsf{Vb}(a)$ is stubborn in terms of verbose actions. Analogously to $\mathsf{en}_i(s_i)$, let $\mathsf{en}'_i(s_i)$ denote the set of the labels of the outgoing transitions of s_i in L'_i. We first point out that if $(a; j_1, \ldots, j_N) \in \mathsf{en}'_i(s_i)$, then $a \in \mathsf{en}_i(s_i)$. (The reverse does not necessarily hold, but it will not be needed.) Therefore, if $\mathsf{en}_i(s_i) \subseteq \mathsf{stubb}(s)$, then $\mathsf{en}'_i(s_i) \subseteq \mathsf{stubb}'(s)$.

If a is disabled, then case 1 of Theorem 1 yields some i such that L_i disables a and $\mathsf{en}_i(s_i) \subseteq \mathsf{stubb}(s)$. The corresponding L'_i disables every member of $\mathsf{Vb}(a)$. So case 1 holds also with verbose actions. If a is enabled, then by case 2 of Theorem 1, $\mathsf{en}_i(s_i) \subseteq \mathsf{stubb}(s)$ holds for every $1 \leq i \leq N$ such that $a \in \Sigma_i$. Therefore, for each $(a; j_1, \ldots, j_N) \in \mathsf{Vb}(a)$, $\mathsf{en}'_i(s_i) \subseteq \mathsf{stubb}'(s)$ holds for every $1 \leq i \leq N$ such that $(a; j_1, \ldots, j_N) \in \Sigma'_i$. If $(a; j_1, \ldots, j_N)$ is enabled, this directly matches case 2. If $(a; j_1, \ldots, j_N)$ is disabled, then some L'_i disables it, and case 1 holds with that i.

7   Conclusions

We discussed the motivation behind and recent developments in terminal strong component conditions that are used to solve the ignoring problem in the use of stubborn set methods for checking safety properties. We have pointed out that the earlier conditions may be fooled to compute all states of the full parallel composition. Now we developed a new freezing technique that solves this problem. At the time of writing, the new method has not been implemented and experimented with.

Trace-preserving stubborn set methods tend to also preserve [16,19] a certain non-standard but useful notion of fairness [10,21]. This probably makes the results in this study applicable also beyond safety properties.

Until now, stubborn set methods for process algebras have used nondeterministic actions. In the present study, the proof of Lemma 5 relied on the assumption that actions are deterministic. The assumption was dropped in Sect. 6 for the typical way of computing stubborn sets of systems with nondeterministic actions, that is, using Theorem 1. This works, but is not as elegant as one might wish. It requires checking the validity of stubborn set algorithms that go beyond Theorem 1. It would be nicer, if the inherent hidden determinism could be captured into some abstract condition similar to **D1** and **D2**.

Because **D0V**, **D1**, **D2**, and **V** are strictly weaker than or the same as the corresponding conditions in ample and persistent set methods, the discussion towards the end of Sect. 3 applies to aps set methods in general. It is likely that also the problem illustrated with Fig. 2 affects aps set methods in general. The message is that, when verifying safety properties, for many systems, nothing needs to be done to solve the ignoring problem; and for the remaining systems, the ignoring problem is nastier than has been thought. This nasty part has not been detected until recently, because the domain where nothing needs to be done is rather wide (although also this has not been known until recently).

Originally, ample set methods focused on verifying both safety and liveness properties. A well-known example presented in [17] and elsewhere demonstrates that terminal strong component conditions do not suffice for that purpose. Instead, the standard solution has been to construct the reduced state space in depth-first order and, whenever firing an action in the aps set leads to a state in the depth-first stack, the aps set must contain all enabled actions (please see, e.g., [1]). A performance problem with this solution was pointed out in [2]. In [17] it was demonstrated that with two cyclic non-interacting processes, the solution may lead to the construction of all reachable states. That is, analogously to the failure of terminal strong component conditions that motivated the present study, also this solution may fail totally, this time in a situation that should have been easy.

The message is that standard solutions should not be taken for granted, although they are now more than 20 years old. More research on these conditions is still needed.

Acknowledgements. We thank the anonymous reviewers for their comments.

References

1. Clarke, E.M., Grumberg, O., Peled, D.A.: Model Checking, p. 314. MIT Press, Cambridge (1999)
2. Evangelista, S., Pajault, C.: Solving the ignoring problem for partial order reduction. Softw. Tools Technol. Transf. **12**(2), 155–170 (2010)
3. Eve, J., Kurki-Suonio, R.: On computing the transitive closure of a relation. Acta Informatica **8**(4), 303–314 (1977)
4. Gabow, H.N.: Path-based depth-first search for strong and biconnected components. Inf. Process. Lett. **74**(3–4), 107–114 (2000)
5. Godefroid, P.: Using partial orders to improve automatic verification methods. In: Clarke, E.M., Kurshan, R.P. (eds.) CAV 1990. LNCS, vol. 531, pp. 176–185. Springer, Heidelberg (1991). doi:10.1007/BFb0023731
6. Godefroid, P. (ed.): Partial-Order Methods for the Verification of Concurrent Systems. LNCS, vol. 1032. Springer, Heidelberg (1996)
7. Mazurkiewicz, A.: Trace theory. In: Brauer, W., Reisig, W., Rozenberg, G. (eds.) ACPN 1986. LNCS, vol. 255, pp. 278–324. Springer, Heidelberg (1987). doi:10.1007/3-540-17906-2_30
8. Peled, D.: All from one, one for all: on model checking using representatives. In: Courcoubetis, C. (ed.) CAV 1993. LNCS, vol. 697, pp. 409–423. Springer, Heidelberg (1993). doi:10.1007/3-540-56922-7_34

9. Peled, D.: Partial order reduction: linear and branching temporal logics and process algebras. In: Peled, D.A., Pratt, V.R., Holzmann, G.J. (eds.) Partial Order Methods in Verification: DIMACS Workshop. DIMACS Series in Discrete Mathematics and Theoretical Computer Science, vol. 29, pp. 233–257. American Mathematical Society (1997)

10. Rensink, A., Vogler, W.: Fair testing. Inf. Comput. **205**(2), 125–198 (2007)

11. Tarjan, R.E.: Depth-first search and linear graph algorithms. SIAM J. Comput. **1**(2), 146–160 (1972)

12. Valmari, A.: Error detection by reduced reachability graph generation. In: Proceedings of the 9th European Workshop on Application and Theory of Petri Nets, pp. 95–122 (1988)

13. Valmari, A.: Stubborn sets for reduced state space generation. In: Rozenberg, G. (ed.) ICATPN 1989. LNCS, vol. 483, pp. 491–515. Springer, Heidelberg (1991). doi:10.1007/3-540-53863-1_36

14. Valmari, A.: Stubborn set methods for process algebras. In: Peled, D.A., Pratt, V.R., Holzmann, G.J. (eds.) Partial Order Methods in Verification: DIMACS Workshop. DIMACS Series in Discrete Mathematics and Theoretical Computer Science, vol. 29, pp. 213–231. American Mathematical Society (1997)

15. Valmari, A.: The state explosion problem. In: Reisig, W., Rozenberg, G. (eds.) ACPN 1996. LNCS, vol. 1491, pp. 429–528. Springer, Heidelberg (1998). doi:10.1007/3-540-65306-6_21

16. Valmari, A.: More stubborn set methods for process algebras. In: Gibson-Robinson, T., Hopcroft, P., Lazić, R. (eds.) Concurrency, Security, and Puzzles: Essays Dedicated to Andrew William Roscoe on the Occasion of His 60th Birthday. LNCS, vol. 10160, pp. 246–271. Springer, Cham (2017). doi:10.1007/978-3-319-51046-0_13

17. Valmari, A., Hansen, H.: Stubborn set intuition explained. In: Cabac, L., Kristensen, L.M., Rölke, H. (eds.) Proceedings of the International Workshop on Petri Nets and Software Engineering 2016. CEUR Workshop Proceedings, vol. 1591, pp. 213–232 (2016)

18. Valmari, A., Hansen, H.: Stubborn set intuition explained. In: Transactions on Petri Nets and Other Models of Concurrency. LNCS (accepted for publication). An extended version of [17]

19. Valmari, A., Vogler, W.: Fair testing and stubborn sets. In: Bošnački, D., Wijs, A. (eds.) SPIN 2016. LNCS, vol. 9641, pp. 225–243. Springer, Cham (2016). doi:10.1007/978-3-319-32582-8_16

20. Valmari, A., Vogler, W.: Fair testing and stubborn sets (submitted for publication). An extended journal version of [19]

21. Vogler, W. (ed.): Modular Construction and Partial Order Semantics of Petri Nets. LNCS, vol. 625. Springer, Heidelberg (1992)

Parameterized Graph Connectivity and Polynomial-Time Sub-Linear-Space Short Reductions
(Preliminary Report)

Tomoyuki Yamakami[✉]

Faculty of Engineering, University of Fukui, 3-9-1 Bunkyo, Fukui 910-8507, Japan
TomoyukiYamakami@gmail.com

Abstract. We are focused on the solvability/insolvability of the directed *s-t* connectivity problem (DSTCON) parameterized by suitable size parameters $m(x)$ on multi-tape deterministic Turing machines working on instances x to DSTCON by consuming simultaneously polynomial time and sub-linear space, where the informal term "sub-linear" refers to a function of the form $m(x)^\varepsilon \ell(|x|)$ on instances x for a certain absolute constant $\varepsilon \in (0, 1)$ and a certain polylogarithmic function $\ell(n)$. As natural size parameters, we take the numbers $m_{ver}(x)$ of vertices and of edges $m_{edg}(x)$ of a graph cited in x. Parameterized problems solvable simultaneously in polynomial time using sub-linear space form a complexity class PsubLIN and it is unknown whether DSTCON parameterized by m_{ver} belongs to PsubLIN. Toward this open question, we wish to investigate the relative complexity of DSTCON and its natural variants and classify them according to a restricted form of many-one and Turing reductions, known as "short reductions," which preserve the polynomial-time sub-linear-space complexity. As variants of DSTCON, we consider the breadth-first search problem, the minimal path problem, and the topological sorting problem. Certain restricted forms of them fall into PsubLIN. We also consider a stronger version of "sub-linear," called "hypo-linear." Additionally, we refer to a relationship to a practical working hypothesis known as the linear space hypothesis.

Keywords: Sub-linear space · Hypo-linear space · Directed s-t-connectivity · NL search · NL optimization · Short reduction · Linear space hypothesis

1 Background and Overview

1.1 Solvability of the Directed *s-t* Connectivity Problem

Polynomial-time computation has been widely acknowledged as a natural, reasonable, theoretical model of tractable computation and all such tractable

This work was done at the University of Toronto between August 2016 and March 2017 and was supported by the Natural Sciences and Engineering Council of Canada.

M. Hague and I. Potapov (Eds.): RP 2017, LNCS 10506, pp. 176–191, 2017.
DOI: 10.1007/978-3-319-67089-8_13

decision problems are known to form a complexity class, known as P. For polynomial-time computation, we are more keen to its minimal use of memory space from theoretical and practical interest. A typical example of small memory usage may be *logarithmic-space computation* (or *log-space computation*, in short), which requires $O(\log n)$ memory space to complete its computation on each input of size n. The complexity class L is composed of all decision problems solvable in polynomial time using log space and its nondeterministic counterpart is known as NL. Unlike NP (nondeterministic polynomial time), NL is known to be closed under complementation [8,14]. Besides the well-studied P = NP question, one of the most challenging open questions is the decades-old L = NL question, which asks whether NL decision problems are all solvable using log space.

One of the most studied NL problems is probably the *directed s-t connectivity problem*[1] (DSTCON) concerning the reachability of vertices in a directed graph.

DIRECTED *s-t* CONNECTIVITY PROBLEM (DSTCON):

○ INSTANCE: a directed graph G and two designated vertices s and t.
○ QUESTION: is there any path from s to t in G?

Decades ago, Jones [9] demonstrated that DSTCON is NL-complete (under logspace many-one reductions). Even though instances are restricted to directed acyclic graphs of maximum degree at most 3 (3DSTCON), the *s-t* connectivity problem still remains NL-complete. Nonetheless, DSTCON has since then played a key role as a typical NL-complete problem in quest of determining the exact computational complexity of NL.

In order to solve DSTCON, a straightforward exhaustive search algorithm requires simultaneously $O(m + n)$ time and $O(n \log n)$ space for any directed graph of n vertices and m edges. A more sophisticated deterministic algorithm of Barnes et al. [4] solves it in polynomial time using at most $n/2^{c\sqrt{\log n}}$ space for a certain constant $c > 0$. This space bound is only slightly below a linear function. For restricted graphs such as planar directed graphs, on the contrary, Asano et al. [3] gave a polynomial-time, $\sqrt{n}\,\ell(n)$-space algorithm for DSTCON, where ℓ refers to a certain suitable polylogarithmic function. Moreover, Kannan et al. [10] designed an $n^{\varepsilon}\ell(n)$-space algorithm for so-called directed unique-path graphs, where ε is a constant in $(0, 1)$. In particular, when directed graphs are regular, DSTCON is solvable using $O(\log n)$ space [12]. For single-source planar directed acyclic graphs, there is an $O(\log n)$-space algorithm to determine their *s-t* connectivity [1]. The *s-t* connectivity problem for undirected graphs (USTCON) can be solved using only $O(\log n)$ space [11]. In contrast, if we allow super-polynomial (i.e., $\Theta(n^{\log n})$) execution time, then there is a known deterministic algorithm solving DSTCON using $O(\log^2 n)$ space [13].

Despite decades of vigorous studies, it is still unknown whether DSTCON or its search version can be solved in polynomial time using "significantly less" memory space than any linear function.

---

[1] This is also known as the graph accessibility problem and the graph reachability problem in the literature.

A search version of the DSTCON, denoted by Search-DSTCON, is to find a (not necessary simple) path in a given directed graph between two specified vertices if any (otherwise, it outputs a designated symbol "$\perp$"). Such a path can be easily found using log space with an adaptive queries to oracles in NL. Search-BFT, for example, is an NL search problem of constructing from a given directed graph a breadth-first tree rooted at a given starting vertex and a typical approach to solve DSTCON is to construct such breadth-first trees. In a similar fashion, many NL decision problems can be turned into *NL search problems* and *NL optimization problems* (or NLO problems, in short) [15, 16].

1.2   Size Parameters and Parameterized Problems

We are more concerned with problems, which are parameterized by certain "size parameters," where size parameters in practice play important roles in measuring the precise computational complexity of the problems. All the space-complexity bounds stated in Sect. 1.1 concern with DSTCON parameterized by two particular size parameters, one of which is the total number $m_{ver}(x)$ of vertices and the other is the number $m_{edg}(x)$ of edges of a graph in a graph-related instance x. Generally, the choice of different size parameters tends to lead to different complexities. To certain restricted variants of DSTCON and Search-DSTCON, however, m_{ver} and m_{edg} endow the same complexity.

1.3   Sub-Linear and Hypo-Linear Space

For a further discussion and exposition, it is imperative to clarify our terminology of the "sub-linearity." Even though slightly unusual but for our convenience, we informally use two different terms to describe a space bound below any linear function. The informal term "sub linear" indicates functions of the form $m(x)^{\varepsilon}\ell(|x|)$ on instances x for a *certain* constant $\varepsilon \in (0, 1)$ and a suitable polylogarithmic function ℓ [17], whereas the term "hypo linear" (or possibly "far sub-linear") means functions upper-bounded by $m(x)^{\varepsilon}\ell(|x|)$ on instances x for an *arbitrary* choice of $\varepsilon \in (0, 1)$. The multiplicative factor ℓ may become redundant when $m(x)$ is relatively large (e.g., $m(x) \geq (\log |x|)^c$ for any constant $c \geq 1$). Corresponding to the above terms, we express as PsubLIN the class of all (parameterized) decision/search problems solvable in polynomial time using sub-linear space [17]. Similarly, PhypoLIN is defined using hypo-linear space.

1.4   Short Reductions

The notion of reducibility has served as an effective tool in comparing the computational complexity of problems.

As noted earlier, it is unknown whether DSTCON is in PsubLIN. To solve this open question, it is imperative to understand the structure of the class PsubLIN (as well as PhypoLIN). For our purpose, we will investigate the relative complexity of DSTCON and its natural variants based on appropriately chosen "reducibilities," in particular, space-bounded many-one and Turing reducibilities, which are technical tools in measuring the relative complexity of two given problems. Since we are concerned with sub-linear and hypo-linear space computations, for our study, we particularly need a quite restricted form of reducibility, which are known as "short" reducibility [17].

Polynomial-time sub-linear-space computability makes quite different effects on various NL-complete problems. Notably, even if DSTCON is polynomial-time, sub-linear-space solvable, many other NL-complete problems may not be solved in polynomial time using sub-linear space. Let us recall 3DSTCON. The problem BDSTCON is to ask whether an s-t path of length at most k exists in a directed graph. These problems 3DSTCON and BDSTCON are NL-complete but they are not known to have the same complexity as DSTCON does from a viewpoint of polynomial-time sub-linear-space computability.

This circumstance no longer makes a standard log-space reduction suitable for our study on PsubLIN. For this very reason, we intend to use *short reducibility*, in which an outcome of a reduction must be *linear* in the size parameter of each instance. This linear-size requirement is sufficient to guarantee the closure property of PsubLIN under those short reductions.

Here, we consider three types of short reducibilities $\leq_m^{sL}$, $\leq_T^{sL}$, and $\leq_T^{sSLRF}$, whose precise definitions will be given in Sect. 3.2. These short reducibilities help us classify various NL decision, search, and optimization problems from the viewpoint of polynomial-time sub-linear-space computability.

1.5   Major Contributions

A main motivation of this work is to determine the polynomial-time sub-linear-space solvability/insolvability of DSTCON. We hope that this work will pave a way to determining the minimum space usage necessary for all NL-complete problems, which may lead us to an answer to the NL $\subseteq$?PsubLIN problem or even the decades-old L $=$?NL problem. In this preliminary report, we will provide a number of results for DSTCON and other graph-related problems, aiming at the better understandings of the *relative complexity* of DSTCON and its variants parameterized by size parameters. The use of short reductions help us obtain a classification of the computational complexity of those parameterized problems. This classification result is summarized in Fig. 1, in which a lower problem is $\leq_T^{sSLRF}$-reducible to an upper problem, both of which are parameterized by m_{ver}. In what follows, we will give a brief explanation of the problems cited in the figure.

One of the important properties of directed graphs is *acyclicity*, where a graph is *acyclic* if there is no cycle (including self-loops) in it. We write ADSTCON for the *acyclic directed s-t connectivity problem*, in which we determine the existence of an s-t path in each given directed acyclic graph. Technically speaking, this problem is a so-called "promise problem" because the acyclic property of a graph G is guaranteed *a priori* when instances (G, s, t) of ADSTCON are given. In contrast, the problem DCYCLE asks whether there is a cycle in a given directed graph.

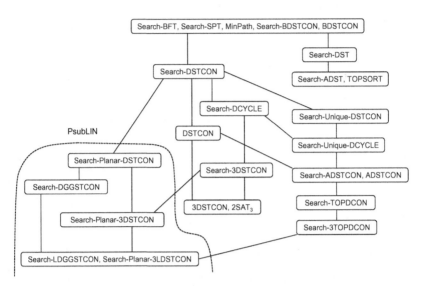

Fig. 1. $\leq_T^{\mathrm{sSLRF}}$-reducibility relationships among decision/search problems parameterized by m_{ver}. Problems below the dotted curved line are shown to be in PsubLIN.

It is useful to deal with an instance graph, which has *at most one s-t path*. This restriction gives rise to another problem, called the *unique directed s-t connectivity problem* (UniqueDSTCON). Similarly, we consider the *unique directed cycle problem* (UniqueDCYCLE) by requiring "at most one cycle."

Planarity is another important property, where a graph is *planar* if it can be drawn on a plane in a way that no two edges intersect with each other except for their endpoints. Such a drawing is called a *planar combinatorial embedding*, which is a permutation of the edges adjacent to each vertex. We write PlanarDSTCON for DSTCON whose inputs are planar graphs. Similarly, we define Planar3DSTCON from 3DSTCON.

A directed graph $G = (V, E)$ is said to be *layered* if the vertex set V is partitioned into $L_1, L_2, \ldots, L_k$ with $k \in \mathbb{N}^+$ such that, for every $i \in [k-1]$, all edges from L_i are directed to certain vertices in L_{i+1}. We write 3LDSTCON for 3DSTCON limited to inputs of layered graphs.

As a special case of planar graphs, a *grid graph* is a graph $G = (V, E)$ in which $V \subseteq \mathbb{N} \times \mathbb{N}$ and all edges are of the form either $((i, j), (i + b, j))$ or $((i, j), (i, j + b))$ for a certain $b \in \{\pm 1\}$. We consider the *directed grid graph s-t connectivity problem* (DGGSTCON). A directed grid graph is called *layered* if it contains only edges directed to east and south (i.e., rightward and downward edges). The layered version of DGGSTCON is denoted by LDGGSTCON.

All the aforementioned problems are decision problems. To refer to their associated search version, we use a simple notation of Search-P for each decision problem P. For example, a search version of DSTCON is Search-DSTCON, which is to find an *s-t* path in a given directed graph G.

The *minimum path problem*, Min-Path, is an optimization problem of finding a minimal *s-t* path in a directed graph G from each instance of the form (G, s, t).

The detailed explanations of the following graph-related concepts will be given in Sect. 4.2. The notation Search-DST denotes the problem of finding a *(directed) spanning tree* of any given directed graph G, rooted at a specified vertex r in G. When instance graphs to Search-DST are promised to be directed acyclic graphs, we write Search-ADST instead of Search-DST. We denote by Search-SPT the problem of finding from each instance (G, r) a *shortest-path tree* rooted at r. Search-BFT is the problem of finding a *breadth-first tree* of a given directed graph rooted at a given vertex (with the left vertex condition).

In many application of DSTCON, certain features of instance graphs are often used to simplify NL-completeness proofs. One such feature is *topological ordering* of vertices of a given graph. Here, a topologically-ordered version of DSTCON (resp., 3DSTCON) is denoted by TOPDCON (resp., 3TOPDCON). In contrast, TOPSORT is a search problem whose task is to produce a topological ordering of a given directed acyclic graph starting at a given vertex.

A sophisticated algorithm of Barnes et al. [4] together with the equivalence in complexity among parameterized problems (Search-BFT, m_{ver}), (Search-SPT, m_{ver}), and (Min-Path, m_{ver}) (see Proposition 9(2)) leads to the following solvability result of them.

Theorem 1. (Search-BFT, m_{ver}), (Search-SPT, m_{ver}), *and* (Min-Path, m_{ver}) *are solved in polynomial time using at most* $n/2^{c\sqrt{\log n}}$ *space for an absolute constant* $c > 0$.

Lately, the *linear space hypothesis* or *LSH*—a practical working hypothesis—was introduced in [17] in connection to polynomial-time sub-linear-space computability. The hypothesis LSH for $2SAT_3$ asserts that no polynomial-time sub-linear-space deterministic algorithm solves $2SAT_3$, which is the satisfiability problem restricted to 2CNF formulas, each variable of which appears at most 3 times as literals. It was shown in [17] that LSH for $2SAT_3$ implies that 3DSTCON does not fall into PsubLIN. What follows in the next theorem is a simple application of LSH for $2SAT_3$ to the computational complexity of (TOPSORT, m_{ver}). An argument similar to [17, Sect. 6] proves the insolvability of (TOPSORT, m_{ver}).

Theorem 2. *Assuming LSH for* $2SAT_3$, *no deterministic Turing machine solves* (TOPSORT, m_{ver}) *in polynomial time using* $O(m_{ver}(x)^{\varepsilon/2})$ *space on instances* x *to TOPSORT for any fixed constant* $\varepsilon \in [0, 1)$.

2 Basic Notions and Notation

2.1 Numbers and Graphs

Let $\mathbb{N}$ be the set of *natural numbers* (i.e., nonnegative integers) and set $\mathbb{N}^+ = \mathbb{N} - \{0\}$. Two notations $\mathbb{R}$ and $\mathbb{R}^{\geq 0}$ denote respectively the set of all *real numbers* and that of all *nonnegative real numbers*. For two integers m and n with $m \leq n$, an *integer interval* $[m, n]_{\mathbb{Z}}$ is the set $\{m, m + 1, m + 2, \ldots, n\}$. When $n \geq 1$, we conventionally write $[n]$ in place of $[1, n]_{\mathbb{Z}}$.

All *polynomials* have nonnegative integer coefficients and all *logarithms* are to base 2, provided that "$\log 0$" is conveniently set to be 0. A *polylogarithmic (or polylog) function* ℓ is a function mapping $\mathbb{N}$ to $\mathbb{R}^{\geq 0}$ for which there exists a polynomial p satisfying $\ell(n) = p(\log n)$ for all $n \in \mathbb{N}$.

A *directed graph* G is expressed as (V, E) with a set V of vertices and a set E of edges. We explicitly express edges as pairs of vertices and this convention eliminates multi-edges. In a given graph G, a *path* from s to t is a series $(x_1, x_2, \ldots, x_n)$ of vertices in G with $n \geq 2$ such that $x_1 = s$, $x_n = t$, and (x_i, x_{i+1}) is an edge in G for every index $i \in [n-1]$. A path is called *simple* if no internal vertex is repeated (i.e., there is no cycle or self-loop in it). An *s-t path* is a path from vertex s to vertex t and is expressed as $s \rightsquigarrow t$. The *length* of a path from v to u is the number of edges in the path. and the notation $dis(u, v)$ denotes the *distance* from u to v, which is the minimal length of any path from u to v. A directed graph G is *(weakly) connected* if its underlying undirected graph is connected. For each vertex $v \in V$, let $in(v) = \{u \in V \mid (u, v) \in E\}$ and $out(v) = \{u \in V \mid (v, u) \in E\}$. Each vertex v has *indegree* $|in(v)|$ and *outdegree* $|out(v)|$. We simply call $|in(v) \cup out(v)|$ the *degree* of vertex v. A *source* is a vertex of indegree 0 and a *sink* is that of outdegree 0.

Let $G = (V, E)$ be any directed graph. Given a subset S of V, we write $G \setminus S$ for the graph obtained from G by removing all vertices in S and all edges incident on them. A subset S of V in G is called a *planarizing set* if $G \setminus S$ is a planar graph. A subset S of V is said to be *separating* if $G \setminus S$ is disconnected, and *nonseparating* otherwise.

2.2 Machine Models, Parameterized Problems, and Size Parameters

Our basic model of computation is a multi-tape Turing machine of the following form. Our *Turing machine* consists of a read-only input tape, (possibly) a write-only output tape, and a constant number of read/write work tapes. A tape head on the output tape moves only to the right if it writes a non-blank symbol, and it stays still otherwise. All other tape heads move in both directions (to the right and to the left) unless it stays still. An *oracle Turing machine* is further equipped with a *query tape*—a special output tape—on which the machine produces query strings (or query words) to transmit to the oracle for its answer. Given an oracle P, the notation $M^P(x)$ indicates an outcome of M on input x by making queries to the oracle P.

We will study the computational complexity of problems based on a suitable choice of "size parameters" in place of a standard size parameter, which is the total length $|x|$ of the binary representation of an input instance x. To emphasize the choice of m, we often write (P, m) in place of P (when we use the standard "length" of instances, we omit "m" and write P instead of (P, m)). A *(log-space) size parameter* $m(x)$ for a problem P is formally a function mapping Σ^* to $\mathbb{N}$

such that (i) $m(x)$ must be computed using $O(\log|x|)$ space and (2) there exists a polynomial p satisfying $m(x) \leq p(|x|)$ for all instances x of P.

For any graph-related problem P, let $m_{edg}(x)$ and $m_{ver}(x)$ denote respectively the total number of edges and that of vertices of a graph given as a part of instance x of P. We say that a Turing machine M uses *logarithmic space* (or *log space*, in short) with respect to size parameter m if there exist two absolute constants $c, d \geq 0$ such that, on each input x, each of the work tapes (not including input and output tapes) used by M on x are upper-bounded by $c \log m(x) + d$.

Associated with log-space computability, L and NL are respectively the classes of all decision problems solvable on deterministic and nondeterministic Turing machines using log space. It is known that the additional requirement of "polynomial runtime" does not change these classes. The notation FL stands for a class of polynomially-bounded functions that can be computed using space at most $O(\log|x|)$.

An *NL search problem* P parameterized by a (log-space) size parameter $m(x)$ is a pair (P, m) with $P = (I, SOL)$ satisfying $I \in$ L and $I \circ SOL \in$ auxFL, where I consists of (admissible) instances and SOL is a function from I to a set of strings such that, for any (x, y), $y \in SOL(x)$ implies $|y| \leq m(x)$, where $I \circ SOL$ for the set $\{(x, y) \mid x \in I, y \in SOL(x)\}$ [15,16]. In addition, for each fixed constant $k > 0$, the notation $(I \circ SOL)_m^\exists$ denotes the set $\{x \in I \mid \exists y \in SOL(x) \, [|y| \leq km(x)+k \wedge (x, y) \in I \circ SOL\,]\}$. We say that a deterministic Turing machine M *solves* (P, m) with $P = (I, SOL)$ if, for any instance $x \in I$, M takes x as input and produces a solution in $SOL(x)$ if $SOL(x) \neq \emptyset$, and produces a designated symbol, $\perp$, otherwise. We denote by Search-NL a collection of all NL search problems. For convenience, its polynomial-time counterpart is denoted by Search-NP. It follows that Search-NL $\subseteq$ Search-NP. Search-PsubLIN denotes a search version of PsubLIN.

3   Sub-Linear/Hypo-Linear Space and Short Reductions

3.1   Sub-Linear and Hypo-Linear Space Computation

Our target is search and optimization problems parameterized by suitable size parameters $m(x)$ for instances x. Throughout this paper, we informally use the term "sub-linear" to mean a function of the form $m(x)^\varepsilon \ell(|x|)$ on input instances x for a certain constant $\varepsilon \in (0,1)$ and a certain polylog function $\ell(n)$. In contrast, "hypo linear" (or possibly "far sub linear") refers to functions upper-bounded by the function $m(x)^\varepsilon \ell(|x|)$ on instances x for an arbitrary choice of constant $\varepsilon \in (0,1)$ and for a certain polylog function $\ell(n)$.

A (parameterized) search problem (P, m) with $P = (I, SOL)$ is said to be *solvable in polynomial time using sub-linear space* (resp., *using hypo-linear space*) if, for a certain choice of constant $\varepsilon \in (0,1)$ (resp., for an arbitrary choice of $\varepsilon \in (0,1)$), there exist a deterministic Turing machine M_ε, a polynomial p_ε, and a polylog function ℓ_ε for which M finds a valid solution in $SOL(x)$ in at most $p_\varepsilon(|x|)$ steps using at most $m(x)^\varepsilon \ell_\varepsilon(|x|)$ tape cells for all admissible instances x in I. We use PsubLIN (resp., PhypoLIN) to denote the collection of all decision problems (P, m) that are solvable in polynomial time using sub-linear space (resp., hypo-linear space), where the suffix "P" refers to "polynomial time."

Moreover, we introduce the notation PTIME,SPACE($s(n)$) to denote a class composed of all (parameterized) decision problems (P, m) solvable deterministically in polynomial time (in $|x|$) using space at most $s(m(x))$ on any instance x to P. It thus follows that L $\subseteq$ PhypoLIN $\subseteq$ PsubLIN $\subseteq$ P. Note that L $=$ P implies L $=$ PhypoLIN $=$ PsubLIN $=$ P.

3.2 Short Reductions Among Decision and Search Problems

Let us first extend the existing notion of short reducibilities, which was first discussed in [17] for (parameterized) decision problems, to search problems.

We start with standard L-m-reducibility. For any two (parameterized) search problems (P_1, m_1) and (P_2, m_2) with $P_1 = (I_1, SOL_1)$ and $P_2 = (I_2, SOL_2)$, we say that (P_1, m_1) is *L-m-reducible to* (P_2, m_2), denoted by $(P_1, m_1) \leq_m^L (P_2, m_2)$, if there are two functions $(f, \|), (g, \|) \in$ FL (where $\|$ refers to the bit length) and two constants $k_1, k_2 > 0$ such that, for any x and y, (i) $x \in I_1$ implies $f(x) \in I_2$, (ii) $x \in I_1$ and $y \in SOL_2(f(x))$ imply $g(x, y) \in SOL_1(x)$, and (iii) $m_2(f(x)) \leq m_1(x)^{k_1} + k_1$, and (iv) $m_1(g(x, y)) \leq m_2(y)^{k_2} + k_2$. As for decision problems, we simply drop Condition (iv). Notice that all functions in FL are, by their definition, polynomially bounded.

To discuss the sub-linear-space solvability, however, we need to restrict the L-m-reducibility, which we call the *short L-m-reducibility* (or sL-m-reducibility, in short), obtained by replacing two equalities $m_2(f(x)) \leq m_1(x)^{k_1} + k_1$ and $m_1(g(x, y)) \leq m_2(y)^{k_2} + k_2$ in the above definition of $\leq_m^L$ with $m_2(f(x)) \leq k_1 m_1(x) + k_1$ and $m_1(g(x, y)) \leq k_2 m_2(y) + k_2$, respectively. To express this new reducibility, we use another notation of $\leq_m^{sL}$. Obviously, every $\leq_m^{sL}$-reduction is an $\leq_m^L$-reduction but the converse does not hold in general [17].

We say that (P_1, m_1) is *SLRF-T-reducible to* (P_2, m_2), denoted by $(P_1, m_1) \leq_T^{SLRF} (P_2, m_2)$, if, for every fixed value $\varepsilon > 0$, there exist an oracle Turing machine M_ε, a polynomial p_ε, a polylog function ℓ_ε, and three constants $k_1, k_2, k_3 \geq 1$ such that, (1) $M_\varepsilon^{P_2}(x)$ runs in at most $p_\varepsilon(|x|)$ time using at most $m_1(x)^\varepsilon \ell_\varepsilon(|x|)$ space for all instances x of P_1, provided that its query tape is not subject to a space bound, (2) when $M_\varepsilon^{P_2}(x)$ queries to P_2 with query word z written on a write-only query tape, $m_2(z) \leq m_1(x)^{k_1} + k_1$ and $|z| \leq |x|^{k_3} + k_3$ hold for all instances x to P_1, (3) for any oracle answer y, $m_1(M_\varepsilon^{P_2}(x)) \leq m_2(y)^{k_2} + k_2$, and (4) in response to the same word queries at any moment, the oracle P_2 always returns the same answer, which is a valid solution to P_2. Any oracle answer must be written on a *read-once answer tape*, in which its tape head moves from the left to the right whenever it reads a non-blank symbol. After M_ε makes a query, in a single step, it erases its query tape, it returns its tape head back to the initial cell, and an oracle writes its answer directly onto the answer tape.

We also define *short SLRF-T-reducibility* (or sSLRF-T-reducibility) by replacing the above inequalities $m_2(z) \leq m_1(x)^{k_1} + k_1$ and $m_1(M_\varepsilon^{P_2}(x)) \leq m_2(y)^{k_2} + k_2$ with $m_2(z) \leq k_1 m_1(x) + k_1$ and $m_1(M_\varepsilon^{P_2}(x)) \leq k_2 m_2(y) + k_2$,

respectively. We tend to use the notation $\leq_T^{\text{sSLRF}}$ to denote this new reducibility. Every $\leq_T^{\text{sSLRF}}$-reduction is obviously an $\leq_T^{\text{SLRF}}$-reduction. In the case where
M_ε is limited to log-space usage, we use a new notation $\leq_T^{\text{sL}}$. Note that any
$\leq_T^{\text{sSLRF}}$-reduction is an $\leq_T^{\text{SLRF}}$-reduction but the converse is not true because
there is a pair of problems reducible by $\leq_T^{\text{SLRF}}$-reductions but not by $\leq_T^{\text{sSLRF}}$-
reductions [17].

We list several fundamental properties of short reductions [17].

Lemma 3. [17]

1. $(P_1, m_1) \leq_m^L (P_2, m_2)$ *implies* $(P_1, m_1) \leq_T^L (P_2, m_2)$, *which further implies
   that* $(P_1, m_1) \leq_T^{\text{SLRF}} (P_2, m_2)$. *The same statement holds also for* $\leq_m^{\text{sL}}$, $\leq_T^{\text{sL}}$,
   and $\leq_T^{\text{sSLRF}}$.
2. *The reducibilities* $\leq_T^{\text{SLRF}}$ *and* $\leq_T^{\text{sSLRF}}$ *are reflexive and transitive.*
3. PhypoLIN *is closed under* $\leq_T^{\text{SLRF}}$*-reductions and* PsubLIN *is closed under*
   $\leq_T^{\text{sSLRF}}$*-reductions.*

Given any reduction, say, $\leq_r$, we say that A is $\leq_r$-*equivalent to* B, denoted
by $A \equiv_r B$, if both $A \leq_r B$ and $B \leq_r A$ hold.

4   Relative Complexity of Search-DSTCON and Variants

The short reductions given in Sect. 3.2 are quite useful in determining the relative
complexity of various decision, search, and optimization problems in connection
to the polynomial-time sub-linear-space solvability. Figure 1 has shown numerous
reducibility relationships among those problems in terms of $\leq_T^{\text{sSLRF}}$-reducibility.
In what follows, we will verify each of the relationships in the figure.

4.1   Connectivity of Acyclic, Planar, and Grid Graphs

We begin with DSTCON, ADSTCON, and DCYCLE and their search versions. It is important to note that a decision problem and its search version
are not necessarily equivalent in complexity. For acyclic graphs, however, their
associated decision and search problems are actually $\leq_T^{\text{sL}}$-equivalent; namely,
(Search-ADSTCON, m) $\equiv_T^{\text{sL}}$ (ADSTCON, m) for any $m \in \{m_{ver}, m_{edg}\}$. This
property is not yet observed for general graphs. For instance, we do not know
whether (DSTCON, m) $\equiv_m^{\text{sL}}$ (Search-DSTCON, m).

The uniqueness condition makes (Search-UniqueDSTCON, m)
and (Search-UniqueDCYCLE, m) $\leq_m^{\text{sL}}$-reducible to (Search-DSTCON, m) and
(Search-DCYCLE, m), respectively, for each size parameter $m \in \{m_{ver}, m_{edg}\}$.
In addition, the following relationships hold.

Lemma 4. *Let* $m \in \{m_{ver}, m_{edg}\}$.

1. (Search-DCYCLE, m) $\leq_T^{\text{sL}}$ (Search-DSTCON, m).
2. (Search-UniqueDCYCLE, m) $\leq_T^{\text{sL}}$ (Search-UniqueDSTCON, m).
3. (Search-ADSTCON, m) $\leq_T^{\text{sL}}$ (Search-UniqueDCYCLE, m).

Proof. (1) The desired $\leq_T^{\mathrm{sL}}$-reduction works as follows. Let $G = (V, E)$ be given as an instance to Search-DCYCLE. Recursively, we choose one edge (s, t) in G. We then define another graph $G' = (V', E')$ with $V' = V$ and $E' = E - \{(s, t)\}$ and make a query of the form (G', s, t) to Search-DSTCON, used as an oracle. If the s-t path exists in G', then G must have a cycle passing through s and t. Otherwise, we choose another edge in the above recursion.

(2) This is essentially the same as (1).

(3) Given $x = (G, s, t)$ with $G = (V, E)$ as an instance to Search-ADSTCON, we define another graph $G' = (V', E')$ by setting $V' = V$ and $E' = E \cup \{(t, s)\}$. Since G is guaranteed to be acyclic, G' has a cycle (passing through s and t) iff there is an s-t path in G. Note that such a cycle is unique if it actually exists. Since $|V'| = |V|$ and $|E'| = |E| + 2$, it follows that (Search-ADSTCON, m) $\leq_T^{\mathrm{sL}}$ (Search-UniqueDCYCLE, m). □

Concerning the planarity property, the problem PlanarDSTCON belongs to UL [5], where UL is a natural variant of NL. Note that testing whether a given graph G is planar can be done in log space because such testing is reducible to USTCON [2], where USTCON is known to belong to L [11]. Moreover, a planar combinatorial embedding can be computed in log space [2].

At this point, we need to discuss the difference between two size parameters m_{ver} and m_{edg}. In certain restricted cases, the choice of those size parameters does not affect the computational complexity of graph-related problems.

Proposition 5. *1.* (Search-DSTCON, m_{edg}) $\leq_m^{\mathrm{sL}}$ (Search-DSTCON, m_{ver}).
2. (Search-3DSTCON, m_{ver}) $\equiv_m^{\mathrm{sL}}$ (Search-3DSTCON, m_{edg}).
3. (Search-PlanarDSTCON, m_{ver}) $\equiv_m^{\mathrm{sL}}$ (Search-PlanarDSTCON, m_{edg}).

It is not known at present that the opposite direction of Proposition 5(1) holds; namely, (Search-DSTCON, m_{ver}) $\leq_m^{\mathrm{sL}}$ (Search-DSTCON, m_{edg}).

Proof of Proposition 5. (1) Consider the following reduction function f. Given a graph $G = (V, E)$, if either s or t is an isolated vertex, then f immediately outputs a graph consisting of $\{s, t\}$ with no edges. Assuming otherwise, f transforms G into another graph $G' = (V', E)$ by removing all isolated vertices from G. Since $|E| \geq \frac{1}{2}|V'|$, it follows that $m_{ver}(G', s, t) \leq 2m_{edg}(G, s, t)$.

(2) An argument similar to (1) works for Search-3DSTCON, and we then obtain (Search-3DSTCON, m_{ver}) $\leq_m^{\mathrm{sL}}$ (Search-3DSTCON, m_{edg}). Conversely, let $x = (G, s, t)$ with $G = (V, E)$ be any instance to Search-3DSTCON. Assume, without loss of generality, that s is a source, t is a sink, and no isolated vertex exists in G. Since G has maximum indegree 2 and maximum outdegree 2, it follows that $|E| \leq 4|V|$. This implies that (Search-3DSTCON, m_{edg}) $\leq_m^{\mathrm{sL}}$ (Search-3DSTCON, m_{ver}).

(3) This comes from the fact that, for any planar graph $G = (V, E)$, if $|V| \geq 3$, then $|E| \leq 3|V| - 6$ holds. □

The problem LDGGSTCON is shown to be in UL ∩ co-UL [1] (stated as a comment after Theorem 20 in [1]). Note that Allender et al. [1] proved that (DGGSTCON, m_{ver}) $\equiv_m^{\mathrm{L}}$ (PlanarDSTCON, m_{ver}), but their L-m-reduction from PlanarDSTCON to DGGSTCON is *not* a short reduction.

Proposition 6. *Let* $m \in \{m_{ver}, m_{edg}\}$.

1. (Search-DGGSTCON, m) $\leq^{sL}_m$ (Search-Planar3DSTCON, m).
2. (Search-LDGGSTCON, m) $\equiv^{sL}_T$ (Search-Planar3LDSTCON, m).

A (k, ℓ)-*graph* is a graph in which every vertex has indegree at most k and outdegree at most ℓ. When instance graphs are limited to (k, ℓ)-graphs, we write, for example, (k, ℓ)DSTCON in place of DSTCON.

Proof Sketch. In this proof, we will show only (2). We first claim that (Search-Planar$(2, 2)$LDSTCON, m) $\equiv^{sL}_m$ (Search-Planar3LDSTCON, m). Next, we claim that (Search-Planar$(2, 2)$LDSTCON, m) $\equiv^{sL}_m$ (Search-LDGGSTCON, m). The reduction (Search-LDGGSTCON, m) $\leq^{sL}_m$ (Search-Planar$(2, 2)$ LDSTCON, m) is obvious. For the other direction, we use an argument of Allender et al. [1], who demonstrated that PlanarDSTCON is $\leq^L_m$-reducible to DGGSTCON. Note that their L-m-reduction is not a short reduction, and thus we need a slight modification of their reduction using the fact that our instance graphs are layered.

One way to extend the notion of planarity is to consider embedding onto orientable surfaces of genus more than 1, where the *genus* of a closed orientable surface is roughly the number of "handles" added to a sphere. Given a constant $k \in \mathbb{N}^+$, EOS(k) denotes a set of all directed/undirected graphs whose underlying undirected graphs can be embedded on orientable surfaces of genus g. For a function $g : \mathbb{N} \to \mathbb{N}$, EOSDCON($g$) is DSTCON whose instance graphs $G = (V, E)$ are restricted to EOS($g(|V|)$). In particular, EOSDCON(0) coincides with PlanarDSTCON.

Theorem 7. *Let* $m \in \{m_{ver}, m_{edg}\}$.

1. (Search-PlanarDSTCON, m) $\in$ PsubLIN.
2. *For any constant* $\varepsilon \in (0, 1)$, (Search-EOSDCON(n^ε), m) $\in$ PsubLIN.
3. (Search-LDGGSTCON, m) $\in$ PhypoLIN.

Proof Sketch. (1)–(2) follow directly from [3,6].

(3) Let ε be any constant in $[0, 1)$. It suffices to show that (Search-LDGGSTCON, m_{ver}) belongs to PTIME,SPACE($n^\varepsilon \cdot polylog(n)$). Let $x = (G, s, t)$ be any instance to Search-LDGGSTCON. Let $G = (V, E)$ and assume that $V = [n] \times [n]$ for simplicity. Let $\varepsilon \in (0, 1)$. For the value n^ε, we set $S = \{(a, b) \in [n] \times [n] \mid a + b = n^\varepsilon + 1\}$, $V_1 = \{(a, b) \in [n] \times [n] \mid a + b < n^\varepsilon + 1\}$, and $V_2 = \{(a, b) \in [n] \times [n] \mid a + b > n^\varepsilon + 1\}$. Note that $|S| \leq n^\varepsilon$ and $|V_1| \leq \sum_{i=1}^{n^\varepsilon - 1} i = \frac{(n^\varepsilon - 1)n^\varepsilon}{2}$. Pick $(a, b) \in S$. Consider a restricted grid graph with source (a, b) and sink (n, n). Let $V_{a,b} = \{(i, j) \mid a \leq i \leq n, b \leq j \leq n\}$. Note that $|V_{a,b}| = (n - a + 1)(n - b + 1)$. Recursively, we split this graph and then compute a path.

The optimization problem Min-Path is known to be complete for NLO∩PBO (i.e., a class of nondeterministic log-space optimization problems whose solutions are polynomially bounded) under approximation-preserving AC^0-reductions [15,16] but it is not known to be complete for NLO. In contrast, the problem Max-Path of finding the maximum simple paths of directed graphs is shown to be NPO-complete.

Given a function $f : \mathbb{N} \to \mathbb{N}$, we further define (Min-BPath($f(n)$), m) as a parameterized problem of finding a minimum s-t path of length at most $f(m(x))$ on every instance x to Min-Path. Here, we claim that (Min-Path, m) can be reduced to its restricted form (Min-BPath(n^ε), m) for each constant $\varepsilon \in (0,1)$.

Theorem 8. *For any* $m \in \{m_{ver}, m_{edg}\}$ *and* $\varepsilon \in (0,1)$, (BDSTCON, m) $\equiv_T^{sL}$ (Min-Path, m) $\equiv_T^{sSLRF}$ (Min-BPath(n^ε), m).

Proof. Let $m \in \{m_{ver}, m_{edg}\}$ and $\varepsilon \in (0,1)$. To show (Min-Path, m) $\leq_T^{sL}$ (BDSTCON, m), we start with $x = (G, s, t)$, obtain the minimal length, say, ℓ of any s-t path by making queries to BDSTCON, and construct a path by setting $v_1 = s$ and by finding recursively v_{i+1} from $(v_1, v_2, \ldots, v_i)$ so that G has a v_i-t path of length $\ell - i + 1$. The converse (BDSTCON, m) $\leq_m^{sL}$ (Min-Path, m) is obvious.

It is easy to see that (Min-BPath(n^ε), m) $\leq_m^{sL}$ (Min-Path, m). For the converse, it suffices to show that (BDSTCON, m) $\leq_T^{sSLRF}$ (Min-BPath(n^ε), m). Let $x = (G, s, t, k)$ with $G = (V, E)$ be any instance to BDSTCON. We want to design an algorithm that determines whether the distance between s and t is at most k.

Let $|V| = n$ and $\tilde{n} = \lceil n^\varepsilon \rceil$. At stage $i \geq 1$, compute $D_0^{(i)} = \{u \in V \mid dis(s, u) = i\}$ by making queries of the form (G, s, u) to Min-BPath(n^ε). If $|D_0^{(i)}| > n^{1-\varepsilon}$, then move to the next stage $i + 1$. Assume otherwise. Starting with $j = 1$, recursively compute $D_j^{(i)} = \{u \in V \mid \exists w \in D_{j-1}^{(i)}[dis(w, u) = \tilde{n}]\}$. If $|D_j^{(i)}| > n^{1-\varepsilon}$, then move to stage $i + 1$. Otherwise, increment j by one and continue until j reaches $\lfloor (k - i)/n^\varepsilon \rfloor + 1$. We then decide whether $dis(w, t) \leq \tilde{n}$ for a certain $w \in D_j^{(i)}$. This establishes the reducibility relation (BDSTCON, m) $\leq_T^{sSLRF}$ (Min-BPath(n^ε), m). $\qquad\square$

4.2 Breadth-First Search and Topological Sorting

We have discussed in Sect. 1.5 a number of search and optimization problems without giving the meaning of technical terminology used to describe these problems. First of all, we will explain such technical terminology to clarify the definitions of Search-DST, Search-ADST, Search-SPT, Search-BFT, Search-TOPDCON, and TOPSORT, and we will verify the reducibility relationships, presented in Fig. 1, among these problems. See [7] for more information on the terminology.

Let us explain a general notion of spanning trees used for Search-DST. A *(directed) spanning tree* for a given directed graph G from vertex r is a directed tree T rooted at r for which T is a subgraph of G and all vertices reachable in G from r are also in T.

An *ordered tree* is a rooted tree in which the children of each internal vertex are linearly-ordered (in the left-to-right order among those children). Here, we assume a fixed linear ordering of vertices. For two vertices, u and v, u is *to the left of* v in G if either (i) u and v are children of a common parent and u is smaller than v or (ii) a certain ancestor of u is to the left of a certain ancestor of v. Similarly, we can define the notion of "to the right of".

In Search-SPT, a *shortest-path tree* from vertex r in a directed graph G is a directed tree T rooted at r that contains all vertices v reachable in G from r in such a way that any path in T from r to v must be a shortest path in G. All shortest-path trees are obviously spanning trees. Hence, it follows that (Search-DST, m) $\leq_m^{sL}$ (Search-SPT, m).

Breadth-first trees used in Search-BFT are a special case of ordered, shortest-path trees. A *breadth-first tree* of a directed graph G from a vertex r is an ordered, shortest-path tree T of G, rooted at r, satisfying the following *left vertex condition*: for any vertices u and v in G, (u, v) is incident to v in T iff u is to the left of every vertex w in G and (w, v) is incident to v. Search-BFT is closely related to an NL optimization problem of finding the shortest s-t paths in given directed graphs. Concerning the complexity of Search-BFT, we obtain (Search-DSTCON, m) $\leq_m^{sL}$ (Search-BFT, m) for each size parameter $m \in \{m_{ver}, m_{edg}\}$. Barnes et al. [4] demonstrated in essence that (Search-BFT, m_{ver}) $\in$ PTIME,SPACE($n/2^{\ell\sqrt{\log n}}$) for a certain constant $\ell > 0$.

Known polynomial-time algorithms solving DSTCON require more or less a (partial) construction of either breadth-first or depth-first trees from a given directed graph. Thus, we immediately obtain (Search-DSTCON, m) $\leq_m^{sL}$ (Search-BFT, m) for any size parameter $m \in \{m_{ver}, m_{edg}\}$. Therefore, it is important to investigate the space complexity of the breadth-first (and depth-first) tree search problems.

Theorem 9. *For any size parameter* $m \in \{m_{ver}, m_{edg}\}$, *(Search-BFT, m)* $\equiv_T^{sL}$ *(Search-SPT, m)* $\equiv_T^{sL}$ *(Min-Path, m).*

Proof. Since (Search-SPT, m) $\leq_m^{sL}$ (Search-BFT, m), it suffices to show that (a) (Min-Path, m) $\leq_m^{sL}$ (Search-SPT, m) and (b) (Search-BFT, m) $\leq_T^{sL}$ (Min-Path, m).

(a) Given an instance $x = (G, s, t)$ to Min-Path, we make a query of the form (G, s) to Search-SPT, which returns a breadth-first tree rooted at s if it exists. We then output a unique s-t path in this tree. By the definition of breadth-first trees, this s-t path must be the shortest in G.

(b) Let $x = (G, r)$ with $G = (V, E)$ be any instance to Search-BFT. For each vertex $v \in V$, we make a query of the form (G, r, v) and calculate the minimum path length, $dis(r, v)$, between r and v from its oracle answer. Let L_i be a set of all vertices v satisfying $dis(r, v) = i$. Note that we can enumerate all elements in L_i according to a fixed linear ordering for G. We define a new graph $G' = (V', E')$ by setting $V' = V$ and $(u, v) \in E'$ whenever there exists an index $i \geq 1$ such that (i) $u \in L_i$, $v \in L_{i+1}$, and $(u, v) \in E$ and (ii) for any $w \in L_i$ with $w < u$, $(w, v) \notin E$. Clearly, G' is a breadth-first tree of G. $\square$

A topological sort (topological order or topological numbering) used for the search problem TOPSORT serves as a key ingredient to the development of many elementary graph algorithms. Given a directed acyclic graph $G = (V, E)$, a *topological sort* of G from source s is a linear ordering of all its vertices starting at s satisfying that, for any edge $(u, v) \in E$, $u < v$ holds, where "$<$" is a logarithmic-space computable linear order. We express such a linear ordering as $(v_1, v_2, \ldots, v_n)$, where $n = |V|$. In Search-TOPDCON, however, we are given a directed graph $G = (V, E)$ such that (1) all vertices of G are numbered between 0 and n and (2) for any pair $i, j \in [n]$, if $(i, j) \in E$, then $i < j$ holds. The task of this problem is to find a path in G from vertex 0 to vertex n.

Lemma 10. *Let $m \in \{m_{ver}, m_{edg}\}$.*

1. (Search-TOPDCON, m) $\leq_m^{sL}$ (Search-ADSTCON, m).
2. (Search-LDGGSTCON, m) $\leq_m^{sL}$ (Search-3TOPDCON, m).

Proof. We will prove only (2). Let $x = (G, s, t)$ be any instance to Search-LDGGSTCON with $G = (V, E)$. Without loss of generality, we assume that $V = [n]$, $s = (1, 1)$, and $t = (n, n)$. We define a linear ordering $<$ over all vertices as follows: $(1, 1) < (1, 2) < (2, 1) < \cdots < (1, i) < (2, i - 1) < \cdots < (i, 1) < \cdots < (n, n)$. Since G has only edges of the form $((i, j), (i, j + 1))$ and $((i, j), (i + 1, j))$, the above ordering satisfies that $(u, v) \in E$ implies $u < v$. This is clearly an instance to Search-(2, 2)TOPDCON.

Next, we transform Search-(2, 2)TOPDCON to Search-3TOPDCON. For each vertex v, we can compute the degree $deg(v)$ of v. Given each vertex v, we remove all of its outgoing edges and, instead, add an extra vertex v' and an edge set $\{(v, v'), (v', w) \mid (v, w) \in E\}$. Finally, we define a new linear order $<^*$ as follows: (1) if $u, w \in V$, then $u <^* w$ iff $u < w$, (2) $v <^* v'$, and (3) if $u = v'$, then $v' <^* w$ iff $v < w$.   □

Proposition 11. *For every size parameter m taken from $\{m_{ver}, m_{edg}\}$, (TOPSORT, m) $\equiv_T^{sL}$ (Search-ADST, m) $\leq_m^{sL}$ (Search-DST, m).*

Proof. Let $m \in \{m_{ver}, m_{edg}\}$. It is obvious that (Search-ADST, m) $\leq_m^{sL}$ (Search-DST, m). Hereafter, we want to show the $\leq_m^{sL}$-equivalence between TOPSORT and Search-ADST. Let $x = (G, s)$ with $G = (V, E)$ be any instance to TOPSORT. Assume that all vertices in G are linearly ordered. Note that G is a directed acyclic graph. Let T be a depth-first tree of G from r, which is obtained by making a query (G, r) to Search-ADST.

Let $n = |V|$. Recursively, we define L_i for $i \in [n]$. Initially, we set $L_0 = \{r\}$. For each index $i \geq 1$, from T, we determine the set L_i of all vertices in T of distance i from r. We sort L_i's according to the value i and then sort all vertices in L_i by a given linear order. Since T is a spanning tree, this process enumerates all vertices in G connected from r. This establishes (TOPSORT, m) $\leq_T^{sL}$ (Search-ADST, m).

Conversely, given an instance (G, s) to Search-ADST, we make a query to TOPSORT and obtain a topological sorting $(x_1, x_2, \ldots, x_n)$ of G starting at s.

Choose $i = n$ and consider the set $in(x_n)$. Choose the smallest index i for which x_i belongs to $in(x_n)$, keep the edge (x_i, x_n), and discard all the other edges (x_j, x_n) with $x_j \in in(x_n)$. Change i to $i - 1$ and repeat this process until $i < 0$. It is not difficult to show that the resulted graph is a spanning tree of G.   □

References

1. Allender, E., Barrington, D.A.M., Chakraborty, T., Datta, S., Roy, S.: Planar and grid graph reachability problems. Theory Comput. Syst. **45**, 675–723 (2009)
2. Allender, E., Mahajan, M.: The complexity of planarity testing. Inf. Comput. **189**, 117–134 (2004)
3. Asano, T., Kirkpatrick, D., Nakagawa, K., Watanabe, O.: $\tilde{O}(\sqrt{n})$-space and polynomial-time algorithm for planar directed graph reachability. In: Csuhaj-Varjú, E., Dietzfelbinger, M., Ésik, Z. (eds.) MFCS 2014. LNCS, vol. 8635, pp. 45–56. Springer, Heidelberg (2014). doi:10.1007/978-3-662-44465-8_5
4. Barnes, G., Buss, J.F., Ruzzo, W.L., Schieber, B.: A sublinear space, polynomial time algorithm for directed s-t connectivity. SIAM J. Comput. **27**, 1273–1282 (1998)
5. Bourke, C., Tewari, R., Vinodchandran, N.V.: Directed planar reachability is in unambiguous logspace. In: Proceedings CCC 2007, 217–221 (2007)
6. Chakraborty, D., Pavan, A., Tewari, R., Vinodchandran, N.V., Yang, L.F.: New time-space upperbounds for directed reachability in high-genus and H-minor-free graphs. In: The Proceedings of FSTTCS 2014, Leibniz International Proceedings in Informatics, pp. 585–595 (2014)
7. Gross, J.L., Yellen, J., Zhang, P.: Handbook of Graph Theory. CRC Press, Boca Raton (2014)
8. Immerman, N.: Nondeterministic space is closed under complement. SIAM J. Comput. **17**, 935–938 (1988)
9. Jones, N.D.: Space-bounded reducibility among combinatorial problems. J. Comput. Syst. Sci. **11**, 68–75 (1975)
10. Kannan, S., Khanna, S., Roy, S.: STCON in directed unique-path graphs. In: Proceedings of FSTTCS 2008, UPIcs 2, pp. 256–267 (2008)
11. Reingold, O.: Undirected connectivity in log-space. J. ACM **55**, 1–24 (2008)
12. Reingold, O., Trevisan, L., Vadhan, S.P.: Pseudorandom walks on regular digraphs and the RL vs. L problem. In: The Proceedings of STOC 2006, pp. 457–466 (2006)
13. Savitch, W.J.: Relationships between nondeterministic and deterministic tape complexities. J. Comput. Syst. Sci. **4**, 177–192 (1970)
14. Szelepcsényi, R.: The method of forced enumeration for nondeterministic automata. Acta Inf. **26**, 279–284 (1988)
15. Tantau, T.: Logspace optimization problems and their approximation properties. Theory Comput. Syst. **41**, 327–350 (2007)
16. Yamakami, T.: Uniform-circuit and logarithmic-space approximations of refined combinatorial optimization problems. In: Widmayer, P., Xu, Y., Zhu, B. (eds.) COCOA 2013. LNCS, vol. 8287, pp. 318–329. Springer, Cham (2013). doi:10.1007/978-3-319-03780-6_28. A complete version is available at arXiv:1601.01118v1
17. Yamakami, T.: The 2CNF Boolean formula satisfiability problem and the linear space hypothesis. In: The Proceedings of MFCS 2017, 7–11 August 2017. Leibniz International Proceedings in Informatics (2017, to appear)

Author Index

Printed in the United States
By Bookmasters